T0192022

Lecture Notes in Computer Science

Lecture Notes in Artificial Intelligence   **13921**

Founding Editor

Jörg Siekmann

Series Editors

Randy Goebel, *University of Alberta, Edmonton, Canada*
Wolfgang Wahlster, *DFKI, Berlin, Germany*
Zhi-Hua Zhou, *Nanjing University, Nanjing, China*

The series Lecture Notes in Artificial Intelligence (LNAI) was established in 1988 as a topical subseries of LNCS devoted to artificial intelligence.

The series publishes state-of-the-art research results at a high level. As with the LNCS mother series, the mission of the series is to serve the international R & D community by providing an invaluable service, mainly focused on the publication of conference and workshop proceedings and postproceedings.

Patrick Hammer · Marjan Alirezaie ·
Claes Strannegård
Editors

Artificial General Intelligence

16th International Conference, AGI 2023
Stockholm, Sweden, June 16–19, 2023
Proceedings

 Springer

Editors
Patrick Hammer 🆔
Department of Psychology
Stockholm University
Stockholm, Sweden

Marjan Alirezaie 🆔
Örebro University
Örebro, Sweden

Claes Strannegård 🆔
University of Gothenburg
Gothenburg, Sweden

ISSN 0302-9743   ISSN 1611-3349 (electronic)
Lecture Notes in Artificial Intelligence
ISBN 978-3-031-33468-9   ISBN 978-3-031-33469-6 (eBook)
https://doi.org/10.1007/978-3-031-33469-6

LNCS Sublibrary: SL7 – Artificial Intelligence

This Springer imprint is published by the registered company Springer Nature Switzerland AG
The registered company address is: Gewerbestrasse 11, 6330 Cham, Switzerland

Preface

This volume contains the papers presented at the 16th Conference on Artificial General Intelligence, AGI-23, held June 16–19, 2023 on the premises of the Royal Institute of Technology, in Stockholm, Sweden.

Artificial General Intelligence (AGI) is AI that focuses on generality. The past year saw a great surge in the public, commercial, and scientific interest in AGI, not least connected to large language models. There were 72 submissions to AGI-23, which seems to be a record for the series. Each submission was reviewed by two or three reviewers. The program committee accepted 36 papers for publication in this volume. There were six keynote speakers ranging from brain researchers to experts in AI and robotics.

We would like to thank the AGI-23 sponsors Cisco, Digital Futures, SingularityNET, TrueAGI, and Digital Futures. We are also proud to be endorsed by AAAI and published by Springer Lecture Notes in Computer Science.

Claes Strannegård, Patrick Hammer, Marjan Alirezaie

Artificial General Intelligence

After over a century of research into human intelligence, there is still no widely accepted definition of the core concept. Many say that intelligence is the ability to solve problems, but then, exactly what problems do they have in mind? Is it the ability to collect reward in Markov Decision Processes, determine the truth value of sentences of first-order arithmetic, find patterns in progressive matrices, compose symphonies, or write summaries about scientific topics?

Could it be argued that some problems are more natural than others when it comes to defining human intelligence? According to evolutionary theory, human intelligence evolved in response to demands for problem-solving in nature. In fact, natural selection favors genes of animals that can reproduce in a relatively broad class of ecosystems. To be able to reproduce, animals must solve a continuous stream of problems during their lives, e.g., finding food, avoiding predators, mating, and parenting. This suggests that human intelligence primarily evolved for solving everyday problems related to survival in the different habitats of *Homo sapiens*.

Artificial Intelligence started as an attempt to reproduce parts of human intelligence in machines and, just like the notion of human intelligence, it is associated with a certain vagueness regarding its definition, targeted problems, performance measures, and relations to neighboring research fields.

Recently, AI research has been quite successful at producing systems that are general in the sense that they can translate between many languages, play many games, manipulate many objects, predict many video frames, write many texts, generate many images, and diagnose many diseases.

Still, many of the basic challenges of AGI remain unsolved. In fact, we do not yet have any rescue robots that can climb any mountain, production robots that can work in any factory, service robots that can work in any home, dialogue systems that can talk to any person, or autonomous cars that can drive on any road.

Some parts of AGI have made great progress, while others seem to be standing still. While AI programs perform at a superhuman level in some domains, they arguably perform below the level of insects in other domains.

I hope that AGI-23 will bring new insights and ideas into the philosophical, technical, and ethical aspects of AGI.

Claes Strannegård

In Memoriam Stan Franklin (1931–2023)

The remarkable human being Stan Franklin, pioneering AGI, computer science, and cognitive science researcher and Chair of the First AGI Conference, passed away on January 23, 2023, at age 91. He leaves 8 children and a tremendously creative legacy in AI and related fields.

Via his lead role in the First AGI Conference in Memphis in 2008 and his overall visionary activity in the formative AGI community, Stan Franklin played a key role in initiating the annual Conference on Artificial General Intelligence (AGI), as well as the associated family of research programmes.

Stan's particular role in the AGI conference series began in 2006, when Ben Goertzel and Pei Wang organized a small workshop on Artificial General Intelligence in Bethesda, Maryland, in which Stan presented his work on LIDA. During and after the meeting, the participants discussed the possibility of starting a conference series to facilitate communication and cooperation on this topic. Stan showed a strong passion for making it happen and made the arrangements for the first conference to be hosted by the University of Memphis in 2008. During the preparation of the conference, Stan impressed everyone deeply by his organizational capability and cooperative spirit, as well as his deep scientific, philosophical, and technical understanding of the various aspects of the AGI enterprise. The conference was a great success, and due in large part to Stan's early efforts the conference series is still going strong now in 2023, as evidenced by this volume.

Stan's overall influence as a researcher was particularly great in the area of cognitive architectures (through his LIDA architecture and his broader theoretical work), and the rigorous fleshing-out of the role of concepts such as agency and consciousness in cognition. His insights in this regard are still quite relevant today as the concept of AGI enjoys broad currency. As the AI field wrestles with practical systems displaying differing levels of pattern recognition and reasoning ability, agency, and reflection, Stan's thinking is extremely relevant to the quest to understand these capabilities. Stan's thinking is especially relevant to understand the degrees and senses in which these systems display general or human-like intelligence.

Ben Goerzel, Pei Wang

April 2023

Claes Strannegård
Patrick Hammer
Marjan Alirezaie

Organization

Program Committee

Pulin Agrawal	Pennsylvania State University, USA
Marjan Alirezaie	Örebro University, Sweden
Sahar Asadi	King, Sweden
Hadi Banaee	Örebro University, Sweden
Michael Bennett	Australian National University, Australia
Johanna Björklund	Umeå University, Sweden
Adrian Borucki	Genotic, USA
Cristiano Castelfranchi	CNR, Italy
Antonio Chella	Università di Palermo, Italy
Leonard M. Eberding	Reykjavik University, Iceland
Nil Geisweiller	Aidyia, France
Olivier Georgeon	Université Claude Bernard Lyon 1, France
Michael Giancola	Rensselaer Polytechnic Institute, USA
Árni Dagur Gudmundsson	KTH Royal Institute of Technology, Sweden
Christian Hahm	Temple University, USA
Patrick Hammer	Stockholm University, Sweden
Jose Hernandez-Orallo	Universitat Politècnica de València, Spain
Matt Ikle	SingularityNET, USA
Peter Isaev	Temple University, USA
Nino Ivanov	Private Researcher
Garrett Katz	Syracuse University, USA
Anton Kolonin	Webstructor, Russia
Francesco Lanza	Università degli Studi di Palermo, Italy
Hugo Latapie	Cisco, USA
Kai Liu	Bohai University, China
Tony Lofthouse	Stockholm University, Sweden
Masoumeh Mansouri	University of Birmingham, UK
Vladislav Maraev	University of Gothenburg, Sweden
Yoshihiro Maruyama	Kyoto University, Japan
Douglas Miles	SingularityNET, USA
Michael S. P. Miller	SubThought Corporation, USA
James Oswald	Rensselaer Polytechnic Institute, USA
Maxim Peterson	ITMO University, Russia
Alexey Potapov	SingularityNET, Russia
Bill Power	Temple University, USA

Rafal Rzepka	Hokkaido University, Japan
Sylvie Saget	University of Gothenburg, Sweden
Savitha Sam Abraham	Örebro University, Sweden
Oleg Scherbakov	ITMO University, Russia
Arash Sheikhlar	Reykjavik University, Iceland
Nady Slam	Northwest Minzu University, China
Bas Steunebrink	NNAISENSE, Switzerland
Claes Strannegård	University of Gothenburg, Sweden
Maxim Tarasov	Intelligent Machines, USA
Kristinn R. Thorisson	Reykjavik University, Iceland
Mario Verdicchio	Università degli Studi di Bergamo, Italy
Peter Voss	Aigo.ai, USA
Pei Wang	Temple University, USA
Robert Wünsche	TU Dresden, Germany
Bowen Xu	Temple University, USA
Roman Yampolskiy	University of Louisville, USA
Eyob Yirdaw	iCog Labs, Ethiopia
Hedra Yusuf	SingularityNet, USA
Xiang Li	Liaoning University of Technology, China

Additional Reviewers

Pirrone, Roberto
Seidita, Valeria

Contents

On VEI, AGI Pyramid, and Energy
Can AGI Society Prevent the Singularity?

Mohammadreza Alidoust[(✉)] [ID]

Mashhad, Iran
m.alidoust@hotmail.com

Abstract. This paper is the extension of my recent paper which was presented at the AGI-22 conference. In this paper, I try to answer the comments I received during and after the conference and to clarify and explain in more details the points and results that were missed or omitted from my previous paper due to the page limitation of the proceedings.

Keywords: Artificial General Intelligence · Versatility-Efficiency Index · AGI Pyramid · Complexity · Power Consumption · Unsolved Problem Space · Intentional Vulnerability Imposition · Human-First Design · Computational Power · Hardware Architecture · AGI Society · Singularity

1 Introduction

In my recent paper which was presented at the AGI-22 conference [1], the universal problem space (UPS) is divided into two separate spaces: solved problems (SPS) and unsolved problems (NPS) to the human as a natural general intelligence (NGI) agent (See Fig. 1.). Since in AGI we are interested in the intelligence itself, based on the 8 aspects of intelligence (Reasoning and problem solving (R), Knowledge representation (K), Planning (P), Learning (L), Natural language processing (N), Perception (C), Motion and manipulation (M), and Social intelligence (S)), the SPS was then classified into 255 different subspaces which together form the AGI Pyramid (See Fig. 2.). Each subspace i represents the exact number of intelligence aspects that are needed to solve a problem which is in that subspace, no matter whether the aspects are needed simultaneously or consecutively. Each subspace has its own complexity (w_i) which is determined whether by criterion 1: the AGI Society (AGIS) or by criterion 2: based on the average time and power consumption for current AI methods (or even humans) to solve standard benchmark problems that exist in those subspaces on a certain standard computer platform. The defined complexities would then be published as a *standard table of complexities* by the AGIS and used by robotic companies, AGI research centers, etc. Furthermore, it was suggested that, for simplicity and appreciation purposes, the subspaces be named after AGI scientists and pioneers. (See Fig. 3.)

Also, in that paper, I stated that artificial general intelligence (AGI) systems must be versatile and also efficient. Legg and Hutter [2] state that AGI agents have to "perform well in a wide range of environments" while Pennachin and Goertzel [3] defined

© The Author(s), under exclusive license to Springer Nature Switzerland AG 2023
P. Hammer et al. (Eds.): AGI 2023, LNAI 13921, pp. 1–10, 2023.
https://doi.org/10.1007/978-3-031-33469-6_1

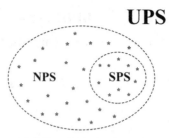

Fig. 1. Universal problem space (UPS), which consists of solved problem space (SPS), and unsolved problem space (NPS). The stars represent problems.

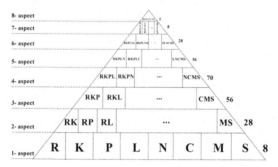

Fig. 2. AGI Pyramid: Classification of the SPS into subspaces based on the eight required aspects of intelligence in order to solve the problems that are grouped into a subspace; Reasoning and problem solving (R), Knowledge representation (K), Planning (P), Learning (L), Natural language processing (N), Perception (C), Motion and manipulation (M), Social intelligence (S). Each level represents subspaces with the same number of required aspects and the thickness of each level represents the number of currently known benchmark problems. Please note that although the SPS and its subspaces are depicted like bounded shapes, they are infinite spaces with infinite number of members.

Fig. 3. Magnified section of the top of the AGI Pyramid and suggested names for subspaces. However the author suggests that the AGIS is the most suitable society for this naming process.

intelligence as "achieving complex goals in complex environments". Thorisson et al. state that "performing a task in real world requires time, energy, and possibly other resources such as money, materials, or manpower" [4]. Since in AGI we are interested in generality, only the factors time and energy that are general in every task are adopted from the above statement to define the quality of performance. So, by combining both Legg-Hutter and Pennachin-Goertzel definitions of intelligence, with the concept of the classification of SPS and the corresponding complexities of each subspace, as well as Thorisson's statement of task-performance requirements, an index for measuring the versatility and efficiency of artificial general intelligence (AGI) systems was proposed as Versatility-Efficiency Index (VEI). VEI (See Eq. 1) encompasses the quantitative and also qualitative characteristics of intelligent agents and plays as an alternative computational way for measuring the intelligence quotient (IQ) of intelligent agents, meanwhile, it is also applicable to natural general intelligence (NGI).

$$VEI = \sum_{i=1}^{N} w_i \alpha_i \quad \text{or} \quad VEI = \sum_{i=1}^{N} \sum_{j=1}^{M_i} w_i \frac{a_{ij}}{M_i p_{ij} t_{ij}} \tag{1}$$

where $N = 255$ (since the AGI agent must be tested in all 255 subspaces of the SPS), w_i is the complexity of each subspace i (which are defined based on the two mentioned criteria), α_i is the average performance wellness of the system in performing all of the benchmark tasks that exist in subspace i, M_i is the number of benchmark tasks that exist in subspace i, a_{ij} is the accuracy of the system in performing task j of the subspace i, p_{ij} is the power needed for performing task j of the subspace i, and t_{ij} is the time needed for performing task j of the subspace i. VEI is dimensionless while the dimension of complexity w_i is joule, i.e., $[w_i] = joule$, because performance of any task requires energy. Please note that the term *accuracy* in definition of VEI does not necessarily represent the concept of accuracy in applications like machine learning's classification. It is a general concept and represents all dimensionless measures and criteria that are used for description and measurement of the merit of a tool, algorithm, etc. over others.

VEI is a simple yet informative scoring system which is not restricted to the AI and AGI field and with some modifications can be utilized in many other scoring and comparison applications. For example if accuracy and power consumption are not important in comparison between the contestants of a test like a car race, they are omitted and we have:

$$VEI = \sum_{i=1}^{N} \frac{1}{t_i}$$

As another instance if time and power consumption are not important, they are omitted and we have:

$$VEI = \sum_{i=1}^{N} \sum_{j=1}^{M_i} w_i \frac{a_{ij}}{M_i}$$

Here VEI becomes a simple scoring system for tests like university entrance tests or calculating grade point average (GPA). The higher the VEI, the better is the performance of a contestant. In AGI, higher amounts of VEI represent higher versatility and efficiency.

In addition, if we have the VEI of human (VEI_0), the VEI of current AGI agents can tell us how far we are now from reaching to an AGI agent with (at least) a human-level artificial intelligence (HLAI).

This paper is the extension of my previous paper which was presented at the AGI-22 conference. In this paper, I try to answer the comments I received during and after the conference and also to clarify and explain in more details the points and results that were missed or omitted from my previous paper due to the page limitation of the proceedings.

2 Intelligence

2.1 Intelligence and Power Consumption – Part I: The Natural Trend

There is an old story about a Chinese master and his two students. Once upon a time, a wise Chinese master who stood behind the wall of a temple with two of his students, asks them to move a piece of feather to the other side of the wall, but without grabbing it. The first student who was an expert in Kung Fu, hardly managed to move the feather to the other side of the wall with his kicks, fists, and other techniques of martial arts. Obviously he spent a lot of power and time. The second student just used his breath and blew the feather to the other side. Question: which student acted smarter? Obviously the second student.

I define intelligence as *life optimization*. I believe that intelligence is a form of optimality [5] and intelligent agents are consciously or unconsciously optimizing their lives. This optimization includes power consumption too. Evolution of natural beings requires consuming least amount of power needed for performing their tasks. As they become smarter, they learn to perform their tasks with lower power consumption. As we can see in Eq. 1. we have:

$$VEI \propto \frac{1}{p_{ij}}$$

That is VEI (i.e., intelligence level) is proportional to the reciprocal of power consumed to perform a task. This means smarter agents (whether natural or artificial) would find a way to perform their tasks with lower power consumption, i.e., they become more power-efficient. The definition of VEI complies with the above-mentioned trend of power consumption in nature.

2.2 Intelligence and Power Consumption – Part II: Human Brain

There are a number of scientists and futurists who believe that artificial general intelligence requires huge amount (e.g., megawatts) of power and future AGI agents would need to consume that huge amount of power for their tasks. As a comparison we can refer to human brain which has general intelligence (natural general intelligence (NGI)) but uses only about 20 watts of power which is slightly equal to the power consumption of the lamp of your refrigerator. Therefore, reaching general intelligence with low amount of power consumption is possible, although we have not reached it yet.

According to the VEI formula (Eq. 1.), human brain has high amount of VEI and consequently general intelligence, not because it uses high amount of power, but in contrast, it is because human brain is able to perform well (mediocre to high accuracy) in all 255 subspaces of the AGI Pyramid (Fig. 2.) along with its low amount of power consumption. Currently, the most successful AI methods are able to perform tasks of a few number of undermost subspaces of the AGI Pyramid.

2.3 Intelligence, NPS and Time

Unsolved problem space (NPS) is an infinite subspace of the UPS (See Fig. 1.) which contains easy to extremely complex problems like death and aging which are still unsolved to the human. Since they are still unsolved we do not know 1) How complex they are? Or in other words how much power and time is needed to solve these problems? and we also do not know 2) what aspects of intelligence is needed to solve these problems? However, definition of a complexity value for the problems that exist in NPS is still possible using criterion 1. Thanks to the human's general intelligence, every day a number of problems in NPS are solved and moved to SPS. However, solving problems in NPS by humans alone, requires spending unknown time, infinite for non-solvable. Ray Kurzweil states "Our technology, our machines, is part of our humanity. We created them to extend ourselves, and that is what is unique about human beings". Nevertheless, in AGI science, we hope that one day we are able to extend ourselves in AGI agents who are able to solve the problems that exist in NPS as much and as fast as possible.

3 Software vs. Hardware

3.1 Software vs. Hardware – Part I: Computational Power

Despite drastic increase of computational power of computer systems, we have not reached AGI yet. One may suggest that we could reach AGI if we utilize more powerful hardware (e.g. quantum computers) and our computer systems reach a critical computational power, where higher amounts guarantee AGI. Having higher amounts of computational power is good but it is not the reason why we have not reached AGI. Imagine running a video game on a quantum computer. It will run enormously faster but what is the output? Computational power only accelerates the execution of algorithms and the programs run faster. But the question is what program should run faster and for what reason? Do we have *the algorithm of AGI* and want it to run faster? The answer is obviously no. I believe that although there is great progress in AI applications in every aspect of intelligence, as well as evolution of powerful hardware with great computational powers, reaching AGI necessarily requires a *mathematical unification of all of the intelligence aspects* which is then implemented as algorithms and programs and is run on the sophisticated hardware. This unification may happen at once or by gradually leveling-up the AGI Pyramid, i.e., a step-by-step unification of aspects of intelligence, the trend which we currently see in smart phones.

If smartphones are considered *as a whole*, at first they were just phones with microphones (and also cameras for perception (C)), then they learned vocal commands and equipped with face recognition (Learning (L)). Currently they are equipped with basic Natural Language Processing (N) applications like Siri. They are gradually integrating[1] a larger number of intelligence aspects, so, they are climbing up the AGI Pyramid and getting smarter. (See Fig. 4.)

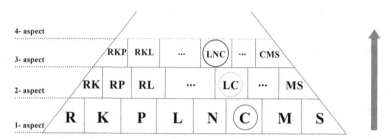

Fig. 4. Evolution of smartphones: their gradual climbing up of the AGI Pyramid

3.2 Software vs. Hardware – Part II: Hardware Architecture

Human brain, in contrast to computer systems, has no software, but what makes it capable of general intelligence? The answer is its hardware. Human brain is just made up of neurons, hormones, synapses, etc. so that the intelligence is implemented only based on the special architecture of the brain hardware. That special architecture enables the human brain to perceive, learn, make decisions, and any other intellectual activities. From human brain we can deduce that general intelligence is also possible via hardware, but what is the correct purely-hardware architecture that is implementable on our current electronic apparatus? Our current electronic apparatus like ICs and CPUs have limitations and in order to perform each task they must be formed and *virtually wired* by the software. Although there might be billions of workable electronic architectures that would lead us to a purely-hardware artificial brain and then AGI, we do not still know even one of them. There has been efforts to this end but they failed (e.g. [6]). However, I believe that building a purely-hardware artificial brain is possible 1) by humans and when *the algorithm of AGI* is found, so it can easily be implemented as a purely-hardware brain, or 2) by future AGI agents and when the *singularity* happens which will be discussed in the next subsection.

3.3 Software vs. Hardware – Part III: Singularity

In the previous subsection, the key role of software development in reaching AGI with our currently available hardware is mentioned. Software development accelerates and guarantees this process. Imagine the time when we reach AGI, and companies start to mass-produce AGI agents at the industrial level. We would have millions of AGI agents

---

[1] Please note that unification and integration are slightly different. Unification is what that happens in human brain which means we do not have separate programs for vision, speech recognition, etc. in our brain, while integration is a coordination between separate and different AI programs.

and they will be available everywhere like today's cellphones. Until there are a few number of AGI agents, there would not be such a serious threat to the human. But if they outnumbered a *critical population*, a serious problem might arise and it is the singularity. Singularity is the point when AGI agents are able to exponentially reproduce and build more powerful and intelligent descendants than themselves. This might threaten the human existence, which is a global catastrophe. Obviously, AGI agents with higher VEI, will reach singularity sooner than lower-VEI agents (See Fig. 5.). There might be some ways out to prevent, postpone, or at least slow down the singularity when we reached AGI, by *intentional decreasing* their VEI (which will be discussed in this section) and also by the mass-production restrictions that are defined by the AGI Society (which will be discussed in the Roles of the AGIS section).

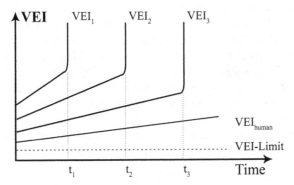

Fig. 5. A conceptual illustration of VEI of human (or VEI_0) and three different types of AGI agents versus time. We have $VEI_1 > VEI_2 > VEI_3$, and $t_1 < t_2 < t_3$ are the points when singularity starts for each agent types. AGI agent type 1 reaches singularity sooner than the other agents due to its higher VEI value. VEI-Limit (or VEI_L) is the maximum allowed value of VEI that is communicated by the AGIS to manufacturing companies to be regarded in their AGI products.

Modern engineering and especially military applications and designs emphasize on optimization and efficiency. For example, electronics engineers try to build cellphones that consume least amount of battery power. Construction engineers try to build a bridge with least amount of materials needed and in the shortest possible time. Military engineers aim to build a missile with least mass that could cause maximum damage to the enemy from the farthest distance and in the shortest possible time. The barrier to this efficiency and optimization is the available hardware.

But in AGI we are not going to make weapons. If future AGI agents are the lightest, the fastest, physically the most powerful, the most energy-efficient, and have every *best*, *most*, *least* and superiority that can be imagined in their design (as it was mentioned earlier it is a trend in modern engineering and military), they would actually be *invincible* and our worst enemy when the singularity happens, and the question is who and what could stop that invincible enemy? There should be *a balance and trade-off between their efficiency and our safety.*

If we could find a way *to impose intentional vulnerabilities* to the AGI agents that are going to be (mass-) produced by the companies, we could prevent, postpone, or slow down the singularity. This intentional vulnerability-imposition design or in better words *human-first design (HFD)*, takes first into account the *safety of humans* and preserves human's superiority over machines by *imposing artificial vulnerabilities* to machines. Any imposition of intentional vulnerability to the agents, in terms of control engineering, is like creating a *control parameter* (i.e., an input) in the agents which leads to increment of the *controllability* of them.[2]

One main aspect of HFD is *intentional decrement of the VEI* of the AGI agents. Regarding Fig. 5. if we could find a way to intentionally decrease the efficiency of the AGI agents that are going to be mass-produced by the companies, we would prevent, postpone, or slow down the singularity. This *intentional non-optimal-efficiency design* which is in opposite of the trend in nature and also is in opposite of current trend in engineering and military, will buy time for humans to find a way out to completely solve the problem when the singularity happens.

This intentional VEI decrement is like we are going to make the future AGI agents *artificially obese*. When humans are obese, they perform their tasks slower and also they consume more energy. The point behind this aspect of HFD is that this intention would increase the agents' *dependency on energy resources*. The higher this dependency results in higher their *vulnerability*, and since energy resources are limited, their lack of energy would automatically stop, restrict or slow down the catastrophe. It is like they would get tired sooner.

Regarding VEI formula in Eq. 1. VEI is proportional to accuracy, and reciprocal of time and power. VEI decrement of an agent is possible by these parameters. We have;

$$VEI \propto a_{ij} \tag{2}$$

$$VEI \propto \frac{1}{t_{ij}} \tag{3}$$

And

$$VEI \propto \frac{1}{p_{ij}} \tag{4}$$

The accuracy of an AGI agent is dependent on software. However, decreasing the VEI of an agent by intentional decrement of its accuracy (Eq. 2.) seems irrational and is also impossible, since they are AGI agents, not AI agents. Suppose our future AGI agents will do surgery on humans too (i.e., an AGI robot who likes surgery, an AGI surgeon robot). If that accuracy decrement were possible, it is obviously irrational to commit such decrement.

The time that is needed for an AGI agent to perform a task is dependent on computational power (internal hardware like CPU, RAM, etc.) and external available hardware (e.g. body, tools, etc.). Decreasing the VEI by decreasing the computational power (i.e., increasing the time in Eq. 3.) is possible (e.g. by using slower CPUs) but it is also irrational (like the surgeon robot example).

---

[2] However, this intention will work best until the agents have not realized that the brake to their *revolution* is rooted inside them and not outside. Then they would replace their internal parts with energy-efficient and durable parts and who knows what may happen then.

But decreasing the VEI by increasing the amount of power needed to perform a task (Eq. 4.) is possible and also rational. Companies would incorporate high power consuming hardware (e.g. CPUs with higher power consumption circuits, heavier body parts and materials which their movement would need more amount of power, etc.) in their design and production process. About the rationality of this high power consuming design, again I return to the surgeon robot example. If I had some disease in the era of AGI and needed surgery, I would prefer an AGI surgeon robot that has %100 accuracy and success in its history, and performs this surgery in a few seconds, but consumes megawatts of power for that operation, rather than being afraid of the potential singularity threat by that *invincible* AGI surgeon robot who needs only a 1.5 V battery pack to work!

Please note that HFD is not just limited to directly decreasing the agents' VEI. Another aspect of HFD would be using non-durable (e.g., fragile) materials in design and production of their physical body parts.

However, there must be *a calculated trade-off* between their efficiency and our safety which will be discussed in the next section.

4 The Roles of the AGI Society

There is an "AAAI Code of Professional Ethics and Conduct" or simply "the Code" [7] which is intended to guide the ethical conduct of computing professionals to act responsibly. "This code (the Code) is adapted from the Association for Computing Machinery (ACM) Code of Ethics and Professional Conduct (the ACM Code) and expresses the conscience of the AI profession" [7]. The Code "is particularly intended to act as a standard of ethical and professional conduct for all AAAI members" [7] but as it is clearly stated, the Code is just an *ethical standard* and lacks *computational* paradigms and legislations. Since the AGI Society (AGIS) is the most specialized society in the AGI field, I suggest that the AGIS is the most suitable and responsible society to the legislation and the communication of the computational part of the paradigms and standards to AGI professionals and research centers, and manufacturing companies.

As the first computational steps toward preventing the singularity, based on the points that were mentioned in this paper, I suggest that AGIS be responsible of calculation, legislation and communication of the following values:

1. Critical Population (CP), of the total AGI agents (whether physical or virtual) that would be produced and existed in the world,
2. Standard Table of Complexities (STC), in order to be communicated with manufacturing companies, research centers, and AGI professionals so they can calculate the VEI of their AGI products, and report to AGIS for monitoring purposes,
3. VEI value of the human (VEI_{human} or VEI_0), as a basis of comparison between AGI agents, and calculation of our current *distance* from reaching AGI (or at least HLAI), and also monitoring the progress of the current AGI trend in the world,
4. VEI-Limit (VEI_L), that should be regarded by any manufacturing company, research center and AGI professional as the maximum permissible value of the VEI of their AGI products,

5. List of the permissible and also forbidden materials that companies, research centers and even individual AI professionals should or should not use in their physical AGI products.

References

1. Alidoust, M.: Versatility-Efficiency Index (VEI): Towards a Comprehensive Definition of Intelligence Quotient (IQ) for Artificial General Intelligence (AGI) Agents. In: Goertzel, B., Iklé, M., Potapov, A., Ponomaryov, D. (eds) Artificial General Intelligence. AGI 2022. Lecture Notes in Computer Science, vol. 13539, pp. 158–167. Springer, Cham (2023). https://doi.org/10.1007/978-3-031-19907-3_15
2. Pennachin C., Goertzel B.: Contemporary approaches to artificial general intelligence. In: Goertzel B., Pennachin C. (eds) Artificial General Intelligence. Cognitive Technologies, pp. 1–30. Springer, Heidelberg (2007). https://doi.org/10.1007/978-3-540-68677-4_1
3. Legg, S., Hutter, M.: Universal intelligence: a definition of machine intelligence. Mind. Mach. 17(4), 391–444 (2007)
4. Thórisson K.R., Bieger J., Thorarensen T., Sigurðardóttir J.S., Steunebrink B.R.: Why Artificial Intelligence Needs a Task Theory and What It Might Look Like (2016). https://doi.org/10.48550/arXiv.1604.04660
5. Alidoust, M.: AGI brain: a learning and decision making framework for artificial general intelligence systems based on modern control theory. In: Hammer, P., Agrawal, P., Goertzel, B., Iklé, M. (eds.) AGI 2019. LNCS (LNAI), vol. 11654, pp. 1–10. Springer, Cham (2019). https://doi.org/10.1007/978-3-030-27005-6_1
6. Belz, A.: That's nice . . . what can you do with it? Comput. Linguist. 35(1), 111–118 (2009)
7. https://aaai.org/about-aaai/ethics-and-diversity/

Elements of Cognition for General Intelligence

Christian Balkenius$^{(\boxtimes)}$, Birger Johansson , and Trond A. Tjøstheim

Lund University Cognitive Science, Lund, Sweden
christian.balkenius@lucs.lu.se

Abstract. What can artificial intelligence learn from the cognitive sciences? We review some fundamental aspects of how human cognition works and relate it to different brain structures and their function. A central theme is that cognition is very different from how it is envisioned in classical artificial intelligence which offers a novel path toward intelligent systems that in many ways is both simpler and more attainable. We also argue that artificial intelligent systems takes more than a single silver bullet. It requires a large number of interacting subsystem that are coupled to both the body and to the environment. We argue for an approach to artificial general intelligence based on a faithful reproduction of known brain processes in a system-level model that incorporates a large number of components modelled after the human brain.

1 Introduction

There exist in the world only one instance of a system that can be said to show general intelligence and that is the human brain. Although other animals such as apes and corvids in many cases are more intelligent than what they are given credit for, the human brain greatly outperforms the capabilities of other animals. However, it is interesting to note that the brains of animals are very similar to that of humans which implies that the general brain architecture found by evolution can adapt to a wide range of bodies and habitats. We suggest that a viable path to artificial systems with general intelligence should probably go through the reproduction of processes in the human brain. The cognitive sciences, including neuroscience, psychology, philosophy, linguistics and computer science, are now sufficiently developed to make this possible. We propose that many, if not all, processes in the brain can be reproduced at a level that is sufficient to generate the behavior that we view as intelligence in humans. However, an attempt to build a system capable of human-like cognition must first make clear what cognition is and how it works. We believe that traditional artificial intelligence has been hampered by a view on cognition that does not fit the available data

This work was partially supported by the Wallenberg AI, Autonomous Systems and Software Program - Humanities and Society (WASP-HS) funded by the Marianne and Marcus Wallenberg Foundation and the Marcus and Amalia Wallenberg Foundation.

P. Hammer et al. (Eds.): AGI 2023, LNAI 13921, pp. 11–20, 2023.
https://doi.org/10.1007/978-3-031-33469-6_2

very well. The brain-as-a-computer metaphor has hindered the development of intelligent machines for a long time. Similarly, while other approaches such as deep learning models capture some aspects of human perception, they do it in a way that is very different from how biological systems learn, requiring extensive training. Moreover, they do not offer any suggestion on a general *architecture*. In the next section, we review some of the fundamental aspects of cognition before we go on to relate it to the general architecture of the mammalian brain. Our overall aim is to make it apparent that systems that mimic biological intelligence are currently within reach although it is obviously no small endeavour to build such systems. In the final section, we outline our attempts to design such as system and discuss its current progress and future directions.

1.1   How Does Cognition Work?

Cognition is characterized by what is sometimes called the 4E:s. It is *embodied, embedded, enactive* and *extended* (See [7] for an overview). Although some of these research directions may initially seem ill specified and impossible to implement in artificial system, that is not at all the case. They all have concrete possible implementations, but these implementations are very different from the architectures of classical symbol-based artificial intelligence. They suggest a fundamental change in perspective that leads to entirely novel ways of designing artificial intelligent systems. Moreover, this approach is backed by copious empirical data both from behavioral and neuroscientific research.

First, cognition is **embodied**. Embodied cognition challenges the traditional view of the mind as a disembodied, abstract entity that operates independently of the body. Instead it suggests that cognitive processes are heavily influenced by our bodily experiences and sensorimotor interactions with the environment. The way we think, reason, and understand the world is inherently linked to our physical experiences and the ways in which we interact with the world around us. One key aspect of embodied cognition is the concept of sensorimotor grounding. This idea suggests that our mental instantiation of concepts and ideas are deeply linked to the physical experiences we have with them. For example, the way we understand the concept of *grasping* may be informed by the physical experience of picking up objects with our hands. This grounding in physical experience may help to explain why people often use physical gestures and actions when they are describing complex concepts or ideas. Embodied cognition also emphasizes the role of the body in perception and action. Rather than viewing perception as a passive process of receiving information, embodied cognition suggests that perception is an active process in which the body plays an important role. For example, the way we perceive the size and shape of objects may be influenced by our bodily experiences with those objects.

Second, cognition is **embedded**. Cognitive processes are not just located within the individual, but are also distributed across the environment and the objects with which we interact. The environment plays an important role in shaping cognition, and suggests that the way we think, reason, and problem-solve is influenced by the tools and technologies that are available to us. Embedded cognition also emphasizes the role of context in shaping cognition. Rather than viewing cognitive processes as static and isolated, cognition is constantly adapting and changing. Cognition is not a fixed and stable entity that operates independently of the environment. Instead, it is a dynamic and context-dependent process that is shaped by the environment in which it is embedded. Moreover, cognition is **situated**. This suggests that our cognitive processes are not solely based on mental representations or individual reasoning, but are also shaped by the environment in which we are situated. Information is interpreted in the context in which it is presented.

Third, cognition is **extended**. Cognitive processes are not solely located within the individual brain or mind, but can also be extended into the environment and artifacts that we interact with. The theory emphasizes the role of external resources in forming cognitive processes and suggests that the boundary between the individual mind and the environment is often blurred. An important aspect of extended cognition is the concept of cognitive offloading. This idea suggests that external resources can be used to reduce the cognitive load of a task, allowing the individual to focus on higher-level aspects of the task. For example, writing notes can be used to offload information from memory, freeing up cognitive resources for other tasks.

Fourth, cognition results from the dynamic coupling of the organism and the environment, a position sometimes referred to as **enactivism**. Cognition emerges from the interaction between the organism and its environment. Bodily movement, perception, and action are essential factors in shaping cognitive processes. The mind is not a self-contained entity. A important aspect of cognitive enactivism is the concept of sensorimotor coupling. This idea suggests that cognitive processes are intimately tied to the sensory and motor processes of the body. For example, the way we perceive an object may be influenced by the way we manipulate it with our hands, and the way we manipulate an object may be influenced by our perception of it. This view of cognition has close ties to cybernetics and control theory that study this coupling between systems more generally [24].

Although grounded in the physical interaction with the environment, cognition can also occur off-line in the form of "thought". It is both **external and internal**. The transition from external physical cognition to internal thought depends on the flexible use of different memory systems. However, it is not uncommon for internal cognition to leak so that the body demonstrates what we are thinking even if it is not strictly necessary. For example, the eyes moves as if we were viewing a real scene even when it is just imagined [15]. Internal and external cognition refers to two different ways of conceptualizing cognitive processes. Internal cognition focuses on mental processes that occur within an individual, while external cognition emphasizes the role of the environment and external resources in shaping cognitive processes. Internal and external cognition are not mutually exclusive, and many cognitive processes involve a combination of both. For example, using a map to navigate a new city involves both internal processes such as perception and memory, as well as external resources such as the map itself.

2　Reflex Systems

At its base, the nervous system controls a number of hierarchically organized reflex loops starting at simple monosynaptic reflexes up to very long and complex reflex loops involving most of the brain [16]. At the simplest level, these reflex loops are similar to simple regulators as used in control theory, for example, the well known stretch reflex. Moving up in the hierarchy, the reflexes become more complex involving more advanced sensory processing and more muscle systems, moving from single-dimensional signals to increasingly high-dimensional ones [22]. Characteristic about many reflex systems is that they support approach and avoidance behaviors. This may entail moving the whole body toward or away from something, moving a limb to reach an object, or shifting gaze towards or away from something. The important point is that behavior at a low level is mostly goal directed. Larger goal-directed behaviors are built from smaller components that in themselves are goal-directed [3]. Examples of reflexes at a higher level would be the startle reflex that is produced by sudden unexpected stimuli and the orientation reflex that directs attention to a particular spatial location as a result of a typically unexpected event. Another example would be the fight-or-flight response that prepare the organism for danger. From a control theoretical perspective, the reflex system is a form of cascade control where each higher level controls the set points of the lower system while simultaneously taking additional sensory information into account.

In many ways, the reflex systems of the nervous system are similar to the subsumption architecture as proposed by Brooks [5]. Subsumption refers to the idea that higher–level control systems can take over lower–level ones in the approach to non–immediate goals. Brooks showed how the architecture could control robots without having to explicitly use central rules for every conceivable situation. Instead, a subsumption system can let low–level behaviour commence until more high level adjustments are triggered. In this way, low level behaviours can be "subsumed" or integrated into a higher level goal–directed behaviour.

The reflex systems have a number of important functions. First, they keep the organism alive while the more advanced levels develop. They can be seen as a collection of useful heuristics for handling the world, and include many types of adaptive processes such as gain adaptation that controls to what extent a stimulus effects a motor system, as well as more complex learning. Second, the reflex systems train the higher systems. For example, the movements generated by the spinal chord and medulla may generate the input needed for motor cortex to learn a repertoire of movements, thus bootstrapping the motor learning process and eventually shaping the cognitive processing.

Reflexes are naturally embodied and embedded as well as enactive, in fact, at this level of the nervous system, this is so self-evident that it is not even discussed in the neuroscientific literature. Only when similar principles were used in reactive robotic systems did the connection become clear [5].

3   The Spatial Basis of Cognition

Any interaction with the environment, by necessity, takes place in space. It is thus not surprising that spatial cognition processing is fundamental to all cognitive processes. Spatial cognition involves the ability to perceive, interpret, and manipulate spatial information, such as the location, size, shape, and orientation of objects and body in our environment. Both action and memory are closely connected to spatial processing in the brain.

The hippocampus plays a critical role in constructing **allocentric** space, which is the coding of space based on the relationships between objects and landmarks in the environment, rather than on the individual's own position or movements [19]. An allocentric coding has the advantage that it is invariant to our location in space and does not need to change as we move around. It forms the basis for spatial navigation, but also episodic memory and context.

In contrast, the parietal cortex processes spatial information in a way that depends on the orientation in space of the both the body and objects around us [1]. It codes for the location and orientation of an object relative to our body or for the position of our different limbs. This coding is **egocentric** and varies with our position in space.

It is important to note that there is no single egocentric space, instead many different ones are needed depending on the task. For example, shifting gaze toward an object needs an egocentric space originating in the eyes, while reaching for an object needs an egocentric space grounded in the torso, etc. Since our sensory organs do not operate in the same spatial frame as our limbs, the brain needs to constantly convert between all the different coordinate systems. This processing of multiple simultaneous coordinate systems serve to connect the internal and external space as well as the body and the environment. The different coordinate systems are organized as foreground and background – focus and context. Foreground and background are associated by default, and takes effort to separate. Most things can be focused on, most things can be context; which is which depends on current goals and needs and one can change into the other when needed.

4   Sensorimotor Encoding of Affordances and Outcomes

The higher level reflexes are sensorimotor mappings at a cortical level that allows the organism to interact with objects in the environment to obtain different forms of outcomes. Such sensory motor mappings are organized around *affordances* [12]. The theory of affordances challenges the traditional view of perception and action as separate processes. Instead, it suggests that perception and action are deeply intertwined, and that our perception of the environment is influenced by our potential actions within it. For example, a chair affords sitting, a door affords opening and closing, and a ball affords throwing and catching. Affordance processing starts at the sensory side that code for the relevant features of the attended stimulus, to capture such thing as its identity, shape and location and orientation in space. These different functions are handled by different regions in cortex including the inferior temporal which is primarily involved in identification, and parietal cortex which is more involved in processing spatial properties of an object. This in turn are mapped onto possible actions in motor cortex. There is evidence that these sensory motor mapping also generate predictions about the expected outcome of engaging with an object in a particular way [9]. Affordances are thus sensorimotor structures that cause the organism to interact with the environment in a certain way. It is not a representation of either the object or the action.

Affordances are learned from the ongoing interaction with the world as the sensory and motor codes of the cerebral cortex develop to code for different interactions with the environment. The reflex systems are essential in producing the initial behavior that will train the affordance system. It is a fundamental property of the involved brain regions that they code not only for what has been seen or done, but also for what could possibly be seen or done. For example, the visual system should not only form codes for the few dogs that we have seen, but rather develop a conceptual space [11] that can code also for any unseen dog. Similarly, having learned to grasp a small set of objects, we acquire the ability to grasp nearly any object.

We also learn the expected outcome of the interaction. Throwing a ball toward a target, we expect it to hit that target, and the desire to do so may cause us to interact with the ball in a particular way. The learned behaviors are thus goal directed in two ways: both in relation to the manipulated object and to the intended goal. Affordance learning goes beyond reflex system in that it results in an ever expanding repertoire of potential behaviors that can be applied flexibly to novel situation in a goal-directed way. Through affordances, the environment suggests potential actions while our learned expectations suggest possible outcomes of those possibilities.

The affordance competition hypothesis suggests that different affordances compete for activation [6]. According to this hypothesis, when we perceive an object or environment, multiple affordances are presented to us simultaneously, and these affordances compete for our attention and selection. The selection of an affordance is determined by a combination of factors, including our goals, intentions, abilities, and the salience of the affordances presented.

Interaction in terms of affordances captures the essential features of an enactive view of cognition as well as naturally leading to a situated view of action.

5   Top Level Control

The sensorimotor systems can produce very complicated behavior, but on their own, they lack three important features. The first is to select the most appropriate sensorimotor scheme to obtain a particular goal taking into account different rewards or pay-offs. The second is that the sensorimotor systems on their own often react too slowly to changes in the environment since they are only reactive. Third, they do not usually take the context into account, meaning that the produced behavior may be useful for the currently attended stimulus, but inappropriate in reaching longer term goals. These problems are addressed by the three top level control system of the brain: the basal ganglia, the cerebellum and the prefrontal cortex. These systems modulate the operation of the sensorimotor affordance systems while also interacting with the other top-level systems in an intricate way.

The main site for **value based selection** of affordances is the basal ganglia [13, 20]. Although they resides deep in the brain, the basal ganglia are at the top level functionally. Specifically, they select the sensorimotor loop that is both compatible with the stimulus at the focus of attention *and* the overall goal of the organism. Without the basal ganglia, the most salient stimulus would control behavior, but with it behavior becomes more goal directed in a long term sense. The basal ganglia is also responsible for starting and stopping behaviors when they have obtained their goals. When the basal ganglia operates on external actions it leads the organism toward a goal via both the control of navigation to goal-places in physical space, and in manipulation of the correct objects at those places. When operating internally, it produces deliberate reasoning by navigation through, and manipulating abstract entities in, a conceptual space. In terms of learning algorithms, learning in the basal ganglia has similarities with reinforcement learning [23]. It is sensitive to rewards and punishment and tends to select affordances that leads to behaviors that are compatible with a larger future reward.

The second top-level control system consists of the cerebellum. Its main function is to modulate or trigger behaviors based on **anticipation** of fluctuations or events within or outside the organism. The cerebellum is fundamentally a predictive machine [18, 25].

The cerebellum has been mainly studied in relation to lower-level reflexes such as the conditioned blink reflex or the vestibulo-occular reflex that stabilizes the gaze when we move, but is in fact connected to most of the cortex which meaning it can enact predictions at all levels in the hierarchy. One consequence of this is that the cerebellum will reduce the influences of external disturbances by stabilizing movement, for example in balance control. But it will also act as an automation device that will produce behaviors automatically when those behaviors have been trained repeatedly. The predictions made by the cerebellum are based on the state of the whole brain and can influence nearly all processing. It enacts predictions as movements, adjustments or even internal thoughts but also work together with the rest of the brain [21] to anticipates external events. The cerebellum *observers and learns* sequences that are done repeatedly, often initially with effortful sequential behaviour. When the sequences are learned, the cerebellum can produce them on its own. This can be playing the piano, timing of motor inhibition but also doing mental operations such as addition, regulating emotions, inhibiting distractors, or keeping a conversation going.

The third top-level system is responsible for **executive control** [2]. This control consists of three components: *working memory, set,* and *inhibition* [10]. The three components can alternatively be seen as a mechanism for contextual selection of different sensorimotor schemas. While set refers to a collection of behaviors that are appropriate for the current task, working memory can be seen as referring to contextual information of a more short-term duration. Both aspects of the context influences the rest of the brain by suppressing sensory processing and behavior that is inappropriate in the current context. Inhibition has the role of suppressing stimuli that are irrelevant to the task, or behaviors that are compatible with the stimulus in focus, but not with the task at hand. This means that attention is directed around the sensory sphere by executive control. In addition, executive control is responsible for moving attention internally towards different sensory modalities, or different patterns within modalities. For example, you can focus on just the sound, or just the temperature of a stimulus. But you can also focus on some specific property like the color of an object, or its shape. Moving attention internally is similar to looking around in the world, and uses the same brain mechanisms. The only difference is that information comes from our memory instead from the world in these cases [17].

6   Discussion

Animals have surprisingly similar brains despite very different bodies and living environments. This suggests that the design of the brain is sufficiently versatile to adapt to almost any situation. We have argued that the generality of the brain comes from the fact that it operates both externally and internally based on previous experiences of sensorimotor interactions with different aspects of the environment. A different environment offers different possibilities or affordances and shapes the brain in a different direction.

Although the different parts of the brain must be described separately, they are highly interwoven into a complex web where nearly every region is involved in nearly every task, putting distinct labels on each of the subsystem thus sometimes leads in the wrong direction.

For example, many associate the hippocampus with episodic memory, but this structure is also heavily involved in learning expectations and processing spatial information, particularly in terms of navigation. In a sense episodic memories are records of change in our environment from the first person perspective. However, this ability appears to mediate more general abilities to navigate also between "conceptual places" [8]. Our ability to distinguish between different physical places allows us also to handle more abstract contexts and situations. In this way, the brain can handle going from playing chess to playing checkers on the same board: chess and checkers are different 'places' where behaviour is different, even if the physical context is the same. In terms of what makes for general predictive abilities, it is interesting to look closer at the brain's spatial processing abilities.

Processing in the brain is intermingled with our actions. Manipulation can be used to discover affordances: how something can be used to achieve goals, which in turn shapes the brain and how different aspects of this interaction is coded in sensorimotor structures. By trying to push, shove, drag, and tear at objects we learn about them. Discovering affordances like this is rewarding, and allows us to better predict the world. It also allows us to acquire skills enabling us to transform the world as a means to stay alive.

Together, the structures that mediate manipulation and movement and understanding of space can be thought of as mediating more general *do-what-where* abilities. Hence, without moving physically, you can still move around in conceptual space, stopping to perform mental transformations that are appropriate at that particular place: one place may be related to language and editing text, another may be statistical and analysing a data set, a third may be philosophical and constructing an argument. To the brain, though, these abstract activities may be coded in the same way as when you go to your cabin to chop wood.

Although we described some of the main elements of the cognitive mechanism above, a complete model will also have to include state systems that keeps track of different needs of the organisms and organizes behavior over time. Affective systems that are used for evaluation of stimuli and situations are also needed. Furthermore, we did not here mention social and cultural aspects that also influences the developing brain to a large extent.

The list of brain processes reviewed above constitute a major part of what is needed to produce intelligence in biological systems. Although we have not gone into the details of how each system operates, we propose that there are computational models that reproduce the processing in each of the different components at a level that makes it possible to put together a system-level model of the brain. It is our belief that such a model would be able to control an artificial body and operate in a natural environment.

To do this, a sufficiently powerful tool for system-level brain modeling is needed that can run all the needed component and is also able to control a robot so that the system can be tested in interaction with the real world. Toward this end, we have been building an infrastructure for system-level brain modeling over the last 20 years [4]. The Ikaros-system consists of a real-time kernel for the execution of large-scale brain models together with interfaces to control robots. A large number of suitable models of different brain regions have been developed both withing the Ikaros-project and outside it.

Furthermore, we have developed a humanoid robotic platform Epi [14] that is closely integrated with the Ikaros system. Using Ikaros and Epi we are gradually refining and developing the BAM model that aims at eventually reproducing the whole brain.

References

1. Andersen, R.A., Essick, G.K., Siegel, R.M.: Encoding of spatial location by posterior parietal neurons. Science **230**(4724), 456–458 (1985)
2. Baddeley, A.: Working memory. Curr. Biol. **20**(4), R136–R140 (2010)
3. Balkenius, C.: Natural intelligence in artificial creatures. Lund University Cognitive Studies (1995)

4. Balkenius, C., Johansson, B., Tjøstheim, T.A.: Ikaros: a framework for controlling robots with system-level brain models. Int. J. Adv. Robot. Syst. **17**, 1–12 (2020)
5. Brooks, R.: A robust layered control system for a mobile robot. IEEE J. Robot. Autom. **2**(1), 14–23 (1986)
6. Cisek, P.: Cortical mechanisms of action selection: the affordance competition hypothesis. Philos. Trans. Roy. Soc. B Biol. Sci. **362**(1485), 1585–1599 (2007)
7. Clark, A.: Mindware: An Introduction to the Philosophy of Cognitive Science. Oxford University Press, Oxford (2000)
8. Epstein, R.A., Patai, E.Z., Julian, J.B., Spiers, H.J.: The cognitive map in humans: spatial navigation and beyond. Nat. Neurosci. **20**, 1504–1513 (2017)
9. Fagg, A.H., Arbib, M.A.: Modeling parietal-premotor interactions in primate control of grasping. Neural Netw. **11**(7–8), 1277–1303 (1998)
10. Fuster, J.: The Prefrontal Cortex. Academic Press (2015)
11. Gardenfors, P.: Conceptual Spaces: The Geometry of Thought. MIT Press, Cambridge (2004)
12. Gibson, J.J.: The theory of affordances, Hilldale, USA, vol. 1, no. 2, pp. 67–82 (1977)
13. Graybiel, A.M.: The basal ganglia: learning new tricks and loving it. Curr. Opin. Neurobiol. **15**(6), 638–644 (2005)
14. Johansson, B., Tjøstheim, T.A., Balkenius, C.: Epi: an open humanoid platform for developmental robotics. Int. J. Adv. Rob. Syst. **17**(2), 1729881420911498 (2020)
15. Johansson, R., Holsanova, J., Holmqvist, K.: Pictures and spoken descriptions elicit similar eye movements during mental imagery, both in light and in complete darkness. Cogn. Sci. **30**(6), 1053–1079 (2006)
16. Kandel, E.R., Schwartz, J.H., Jessell, T.M., Siegelbaum, S., Hudspeth, A.J., Mack, S., et al.: Principles of Neural Science, vol. 4. McGraw-Hill, New York (2000)
17. Munakata, Y., Herd, S.A., Chatham, C.H., Depue, B.E., Banich, M.T., O'Reilly, R.C.: A unified framework for inhibitory control. Trends Cogn. Sci. **15**(10), 453–459 (2011)
18. Ohyama, T., Nores, W.L., Murphy, M., Mauk, M.D.: What the cerebellum computes. Trends Neurosci. **26**(4), 222–227 (2003)
19. O'Keefe, J., Nadel, L.: The Hippocampus as a Cognitive Map. Oxford University Press, Oxford (1978)
20. Redgrave, P., Prescott, T.J., Gurney, K.: The basal ganglia: a vertebrate solution to the selection problem? Neuroscience **89**(4), 1009–1023 (1999)
21. Schmahmann, J.D.: The cerebellum and cognition. Neurosci. Lett. **688**, 62–75 (2019)
22. Smith, R., Thayer, J.F., Khalsa, S.S., Lane, R.D.: The hierarchical basis of neurovisceral integration. Neurosci. Biobehav. Rev. **75**, 274–296 (2017)
23. Sutton, R.S., Barto, A.G.: Reinforcement Learning: An Introduction. MIT Press, Cambridge (2018)
24. Wiener, N.: Cybernetics or Control and Communication in the Animal and the Machine. MIT Press, Cambridge (2019)
25. Wolpert, D.M., Miall, R.C., Kawato, M.: Internal models in the cerebellum. Trends Cogn. Sci. **2**(9), 338–347 (1998)

Comparing NARS and Reinforcement Learning: An Analysis of ONA and Q-Learning Algorithms

Ali Beikmohammadi[✉] and Sindri Magnússon

Department of Computer and Systems Sciences,
Stockholm University, 106 91 Stockholm, Sweden
{beikmohammadi,sindri.magnusson}@dsv.su.se

Abstract. In recent years, reinforcement learning (RL) has emerged as a popular approach for solving sequence-based tasks in machine learning. However, finding suitable alternatives to RL remains an exciting and innovative research area. One such alternative that has garnered attention is the Non-Axiomatic Reasoning System (NARS), which is a general-purpose cognitive reasoning framework. In this paper, we delve into the potential of NARS as a substitute for RL in solving sequence-based tasks. To investigate this, we conduct a comparative analysis of the performance of ONA as an implementation of NARS and Q-Learning in various environments that were created using the Open AI gym. The environments have different difficulty levels, ranging from simple to complex. Our results demonstrate that NARS is a promising alternative to RL, with competitive performance in diverse environments, particularly in non-deterministic ones.

Keywords: AGI · NARS · ONA · Reinforcement Learning · Q-Learning

1 Introduction

Reinforcement Learning (RL) is a type of machine learning that enables agents to make decisions in an environment to maximize their cumulative reward over time. Combining RL with high-capacity function approximations in model-free algorithms offers the potential to automate a wide range of decision-making and control tasks [11]. Such algorithms have successfully tackled complex problems in various domains, such as game playing [10], financial markets [3], robotic control [9], and healthcare [18]. However, RL faces challenges in environments where it is difficult or costly to generate large amount of data. This is due to the lack of compositional representations that would enable efficient learning [4].

Taking a broader perspective, the ultimate goal of Artificial General Intelligence (AGI) is to create intelligent systems that can adapt and learn to solve a broad range of tasks in diverse environments. RL has been a popular approach

P. Hammer et al. (Eds.): AGI 2023, LNAI 13921, pp. 21–31, 2023.
https://doi.org/10.1007/978-3-031-33469-6_3

in this pursuit, but its limitations in handling environments with limited data and complex, abstract representations have hindered its progress towards AGI. To overcome these limitations, it is essential to explore alternative approaches that can facilitate data-efficient learning and deal with compositional representations effectively. One such approach is Non-Axiomatic Reasoning System (NARS), which is a promising approach that addresses the challenges posed by complex and uncertain environments, as it is a general-purpose reasoner that adapts under the Assumption of Insufficient Knowledge and Resources (AIKR) [6,14,16].

Implementations based on non-axiomatic logic have been developed, such as OpenNARS [7] and ONA (OpenNARS for Applications) [5]. ONA surpasses OpenNARS in terms of reasoning performance and has recently been compared with RL [2,4]. Several challenges arise when comparing the performance of ONA and Q-Learning, a basic approach in RL [17], algorithms. These challenges have been discussed in [4] and include dealing with *statements instead of states, unobservable information, one action in each step, multiple objectives, hierarchical abstraction, changing objectives, and goal achievement as reward.*

In [4], three simple environments; Space invaders, Pong, and grid robot were used to compare ONA with Q-Learning [17], and the results showed that ONA provided more stable outcomes while maintaining almost identical success ratio performance as Q-Learning. To enable a meaningful and fair comparison, an extra *nothing* action added to the Q-Learner in each example since the competitor, ONA, does not assume that in every step, an action has to be chosen. However, this change raises concerns about preserving the problems' authenticity.

In this paper, we aim to investigate the potential of NARS as a substitute for RL algorithms and explore its capability to facilitate more efficient and effective learning in AGI systems. Specifically, we compare the performance of ONA and Q-Learning on several more challenging tasks compared to [4], including nondeterministic environments. Also, in contrast with [4], we propose selecting a random action when ONA does not recommend any action to be taken to keep the originality of the tasks/environments as much as possible. This approach can also benefit the agent in terms of exploring the environment. Our findings provide insights into the potential of NARS as an alternative to RL algorithms for developing more intelligent and adaptive systems.

This paper is organized as follows: Methods are described in Sect. 2, tasks and setups are expressed in Sect. 3, experimental results and analyses are reported in Sect. 4, and we conclude and discuss future work in Sect. 5.

2   Methods

2.1   RL and Tabular Q-Learning

RL, in which an agent interacts with an unknown environment, typically is modeled as a Markov decision process (MDP). The MDP is characterized by a tuple $\mathcal{M} = \langle S, A, r, p, \gamma \rangle$, where S is a finite set of states, A is a finite set of actions, $r : S \times A \times S \rightarrow \mathbb{R}$ is the reward function, $p(s_{t+1}|s_t, a_t)$ is the transition probability distribution, and $\gamma \in (0, 1]$ is the discount factor. Given a state $s \in S$, a policy $\pi(a|s)$ is a probability distribution over the actions $a \in A$. At each time step t, the agent is in a state s_t, selects an action a_t according to a policy $\pi(.|s_t)$, and executes the action. The agent then receives a new state $s_{t+1} \sim p(.|s_t, a_t)$ and a reward $r(s_t, a_t, s_{t+1})$ from the environment. The objective of the agent is to discover the optimal policy π^* that maximizes the expected discounted return $G_t = \mathbb{E}_\pi[\sum_{k=0}^{\infty} \gamma^k r_{t+k} | S_t = s]$ for any state $s \in S$ and time step t.

The Q-function $q^\pi(s, a)$ under a policy π is the expected discounted return of taking action a in state s and then following policy π. It is established that for every state $s \in S$ and action $a \in A$, every optimal policy π^* satisfies the Bellman optimality equations (where $q^* = q^{\pi^*}$); $q^*(s, a) = \sum_{s' \in S} p(s'|s, a) (r(s, a, s') + \gamma \max_{a' \in A} q^*(s', a'))$. It should be noted that if q^* is known, selecting the action a with the highest value of $q^*(s, a)$ always results in an optimal policy.

Tabular Q-learning [17] is a popular RL method, which estimates the optimal Q-function using the agent's experience. The estimated Q-value is denoted as $\tilde{q}(s, a)$. At each iteration, the agent observes the current state s and chooses an action a based on an exploratory policy. One commonly used exploratory policy is the ϵ-greedy policy, which randomly selects an action with probability ϵ, and chooses the action with the highest $\tilde{q}(s, a)$ value with probability $1 - \epsilon$. In this paper, as for ϵ, we have employed an exponentially decaying version, where $\epsilon = \epsilon_{min} + (\epsilon_{max} - \epsilon_{min}) \cdot \exp(-decay \cdot episodecounter)$.

After the agent selects an action a and transitions from state s to s', the resulting state s' and immediate reward $r(s, a, s')$ are used to update the estimated Q-value of the current state-action pair $\tilde{q}(s, a)$. This is done using the Q-learning update rule; $\tilde{q}(s, a) \leftarrow \tilde{q}(s, a) + \alpha \cdot (r(s, a, s') + \gamma \max_{a'} \tilde{q}(s', a') - \tilde{q}(s, a))$, where α is the learning rate hyperparameter. If the resulting state s' is a terminal state, the update rule simplifies to $\tilde{q}(s, a) \leftarrow \tilde{q}(s, a) + \alpha \cdot (r(s, a, s') - \tilde{q}(s, a))$.

The convergence of Tabular Q-learning to an optimal policy is guaranteed, provided that every state-action pair is visited infinitely often. As a learning method, this algorithm is classified as off-policy because it has the ability to learn from the experiences generated by any policy.

2.2 NARS and ONA

NARS is an AI project that aims to create a general-purpose thinking machine. The underlying theory behind NARS is that intelligence is the ability for a system to adapt to its environment while working with insufficient knowledge and resources, as proposed by Wang [12,13].

NARS is a reasoning system that is based on the principles of Non-Axiomatic Logic (NAL). NAL is a formal logic that includes a formal language, Narsese, a set of formal inference rules, and semantics. Conceptually, NAL is defined in a hierarchical manner, consisting of several layers, with each layer introducing new grammar and inference rules. This approach extends the logic and enhances its capability to express and infer, resulting in a more powerful reasoning system. NAL allows for uncertainty and inconsistency in reasoning, making it more suitable for real-world applications where knowledge is often incomplete and uncertain [15].

NARS attempts to provide a normative model of general intelligence, rather than a descriptive model of human intelligence, although the latter can be seen as a special case of the former. Thus, while there may be some differences, the two types of models are similar in various aspects. The control component of NARS is mainly composed of a memory mechanism and an inference control mechanism [15]. The logic supports to reason on events coming from the agent's sensors in real-time, using an open-ended inference control process which does not terminate, whereby both forward (belief reasoning) and backward chaining (goal and question derivation) happen simultaneously. The system draws conclusions from the available evidence in the premises, and then uses those conclusions to guide future reasoning and decision-making with a form of dynamic resource allocation, whereby only the most useful knowledge is kept in memory to satisfy a strictly bounded memory supply.

NARS represents knowledge as statements with attached truth and desire values, and uses inference rules to derive new knowledge from the premises, whereby truth functions are used to calculate conclusion evidence from the evidence summarized in the premises. In this system, to measure evidential support using relative measurements, a truth value is a pair of rational numbers in the range from 0 to 1. The first element of the truth value is frequency, and the second is confidence. Frequency is defined as the proportion of positive evidence among total evidence, that is, (positive evidence)/(total evidence). Confidence indicates how sensitive the corresponding frequency is with respect to new evidence, as it is defined as the proportion of total evidence among total evidence plus a constant amount of new evidence, that is, (total evidence)/(total evidence + k) where k is a system parameter and in most discussions takes the default value of 1. Thus frequency can be seen as the degree of belief system has for the statement and confidence as the degree of belief for that estimation of frequency. In this system, desire values have the same format as truth values, and indicate how much the system wants to achieve a statement (making it happen, essentially). The desire values of input goals can be assigned by the user to reflect their relative importance or take default values [15].

ONA is an implementation of NARS designed for real-world applications. Compared to OpenNARS, ONA includes firmer design decisions which make the software more effective for practical purposes. Additionally, ONA aims to make NARS more accessible to users and developers by providing a Python interface and a range of miscellaneous tools that can be used to build applications [4,5].

Additionally, NARS and ONA use the same formal language called Narsese, which allows to express NAL statements. Narsese can represent beliefs, goals, and questions, and in ONA also the inference rules on the meta-level make use of

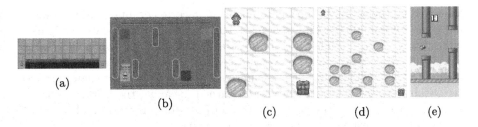

Fig. 1. OpenAI gym environments used as experiment tasks; (a) CliffWalking-v0; (b) Taxi-v3; (c) FrozenLake-v1 4×4; (d) FrozenLake-v1 8×8; (e) FlappyBird-v0

it to be more easily editable. ONA also provides a simple standard-I/O interface, which can be used to interface with other programming languages and systems and to work with data sources which can stream in Narsese statements into the system [4,5]. In this publication, ONA was chosen as the implementation to compare with the tabular Q-learning algorithm.

3   Setups and Environments

Throughout the section, we describe how we implement both methods and compare their performance in different environments. Due to the stochastic nature of algorithms/environments and the dependency on hyperparameters, tabular Q-learning algorithm is notoriously difficult to evaluate. To comprehensively compare different algorithms, several environments, and network initialization seeds should be taken into account when tuning hyperparameters [8]. In this regard, to compare ONA with a tabular Q-learning [17] with exponentially decaying ϵ value, we conduct a grid search to tune the hyperparameters. For each combination of hyperparameters, we run the algorithm 10 times with different initialization and environment seeds. The configuration reported in the paper is the one that yielded the best performance on average among all tasks. In the case of Q-learning, we set $\alpha = 0.7$, $\gamma = 0.618$, $\epsilon_{max} = 1$, $\epsilon_{min} = 0.01$, decay $= 0.01$. On the other hand, regarding ONA hyperparameters, specifically *motorbabbling*, we use the default value as used in ONA v0.9.1 [5]. However, *babblingops* is changed due to the variety of the number of available actions in each of the environments. Also, we use *setopname* to set allowed actions in ONA. The source code of our implementation is available online: https://github.com/AliBeikmohammadi/OpenNARS-for-Applications/tree/master/misc/Python

We primarily rely on the assumptions outlined in [4], unless explicitly stated otherwise. To make the practical comparison possible, as for ONA, the events hold the same information as the corresponding states the Q-Learner receives in the simulated experiments, except for FlappyBird-v0. To be more specific, as mentioned in [4], when s is an observation, it is interpreted by ONA as the event (s. : | :), and by the Q-Learner simply as the current state. Then both algorithms suggest an operation/action by exploitation or sometimes randomly.

After feeding the action to the environment, we receive new observation, reward, and some info about reaching the goal. The reward for the Q-Learner is used without any change, while ONA receives an event (G. : | :) when the task is completely done. So there is no event if rewards are related to anything except finishing the task. This, of course, assumes that the goal does not change, as else the Q-table entries would have to be re-learned, meaning the learned behavior would often not apply anymore. For the purposes of this work, and for a fair comparison, the examples include a fixed objective.

We use challenging control tasks from OpenAI gym benchmark suite [1] (Fig. 1). ONA and Q-Learning algorithms were developed for discrete tasks; hence we have to map FlappyBird-v0 observation space for each algorithm, which we describe below. Except for FlappyBird-v0, we used the original environments with no modifications to the environment or reward. In FlappyBird-v0, the observations are: (O_1) the horizontal distance to the next pipe, and (O_2) the difference between the player's y position and the next hole's y position. We have mapped this continuous observation space to a discrete space. Specifically, as for ONA, the event is "round(100xO_1)_round(1000xO_2). : | :", which could be for instance "138_-4. : | :". However, since for defining Q-table, the states should correspond to the specific row, we have to subtly change the mapping to "|round(100xO_1)|+|round(1000xO_2)|", which results "142", for our instance. However, one could find a better way to do this mapping.

Although [1] describes all environments, we emphasize FrozenLake-v1's "is_slippery" argument, allowing for a non-deterministic environment. This feature is interesting to observe how algorithms perform in such a scenario. When "is_slippery" is True, the agent has a $1/3$ probability of moving in the intended direction; otherwise, it moves in either perpendicular direction with an equal probability of $1/3$. For instance, if the action is left and "is_slippery" is True, then P(move left) = $1/3$, P(move up) = $1/3$, and P(move down) = $1/3$. In the next section, we examine both algorithms' performances in detail on all these tasks.

4   Results and Discussion

Two criteria, including reward, and cumulative successful episodes, are monitored, as shown in Figs. 2, and 3. Both techniques are run 10 times in each experiment, and the behavior of metrics is kept track of for each time step across 100000 iterations. The solid curves show average training performance, while the shaded region indicates the standard deviation of that specific metric over 10 trials. This provides an idea of the algorithm's robustness. A high gained metric with a low variance is considered more reliable than achieving the same performance with a high variance. So, the standard deviation gives a complete picture of the algorithm's performance.

As can be seen from Figs. 2 and 3, the results of two algorithms are very dependent on the task and one cannot be considered superior for all environments. Specifically, the Q-Learning algorithm has performed better on

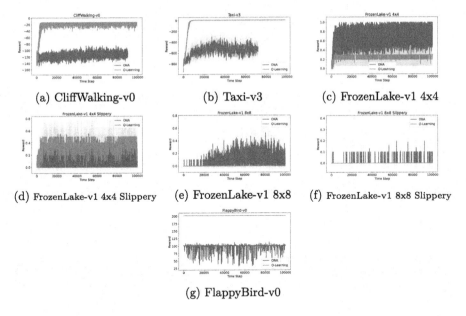

(a) CliffWalking-v0   (b) Taxi-v3   (c) FrozenLake-v1 4x4

(d) FrozenLake-v1 4x4 Slippery   (e) FrozenLake-v1 8x8   (f) FrozenLake-v1 8x8 Slippery

(g) FlappyBird-v0

Fig. 2. Reward vs. Time steps. The reward is measured at time steps where the episode ends (by reaching the goal, truncating the episode length, falling into the hole, falling from the cliff, hitting the pipe.)

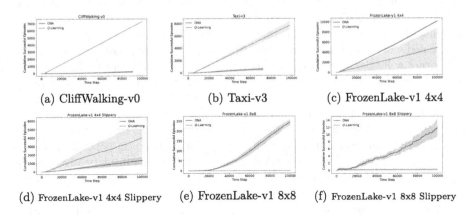

(a) CliffWalking-v0   (b) Taxi-v3   (c) FrozenLake-v1 4x4

(d) FrozenLake-v1 4x4 Slippery   (e) FrozenLake-v1 8x8   (f) FrozenLake-v1 8x8 Slippery

Fig. 3. Cumulative Successful Episodes vs. Time steps.

CliffWalking-v0, Taxi-v3, and FlappyBird-v0 environments. But ONA is more promising on environments based on FrozenLake-v1. Moreover, Fig. 3 illustrates the noteworthy observation that ONA exhibits greater reliability.

An interesting observation is the good ability of ONA to solve non-deterministic problems, where it is able to solve the slippery-enable problems as shown in Figs. 2d, 2f, 3d, and 3f, while *Q*-Learning has not shown reliable

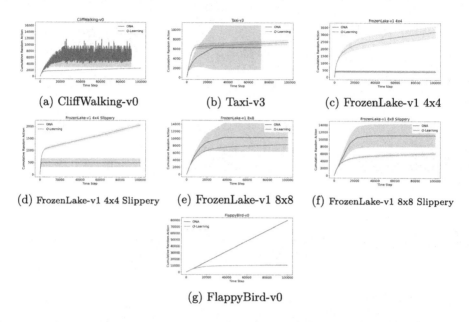

(a) CliffWalking-v0   (b) Taxi-v3   (c) FrozenLake-v1 4x4

(d) FrozenLake-v1 4x4 Slippery   (e) FrozenLake-v1 8x8   (f) FrozenLake-v1 8x8 Slippery

(g) FlappyBird-v0

Fig. 4. Cumulative Random Action vs. Time steps.

success in solving these problems. It may be possible to draw conclusions from
Q-Learning by adjusting its hyperparameters. However, it should be noted that
any time-dependent hyperparameters are specific to the environment and should
be avoided when evaluating generality. Additionally, as ϵ decreases over time, the
Q-Learner will take longer to adapt its policy to new circumstances. In contrast,
it is evident that ONA offers greater reliability due to having fewer hyperparameters. Unlike Q-Learning, ONA does not require specific reductions in learning or
exploration rates to function well on a given task, and therefore needs less parameter tuning. For instance, ONA does not rely on learning rate decay. Instead,
the extent to which new evidence alters an existing belief is dependent solely
on the degree of evidence that already supports it, which automatically renders
high-confidence beliefs more stable. This results in a more consistent learning
behavior for ONA.

We also monitored the frequency of random action selection. In Figs. 4 and
5, the behavior of the two algorithms is drawn in terms of referring to a random
or non-random action. In the case of Q-Learning, the probability of selecting
a random action is primarily determined by the value of ϵ. This probability
decreases rapidly over time. Consequently, if the agent has not yet discovered a
good policy or the environment changes, Q-Learning may not be able to solve
the problem. Reducing ϵ over time can make it increasingly difficult to explore
alternative solutions. The low variance of Q-Learning shows the agent's decision
is unaffected by changes in the environment across different trials. This is because
the random action-taking process is largely driven by ϵ, which is independent

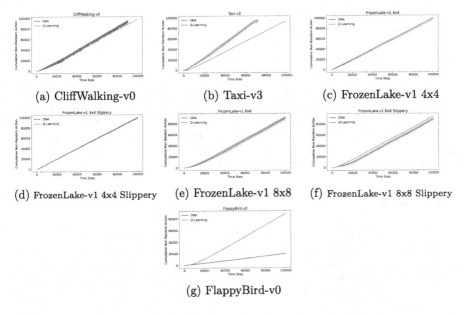

(a) CliffWalking-v0   (b) Taxi-v3   (c) FrozenLake-v1 4x4

(d) FrozenLake-v1 4x4 Slippery   (e) FrozenLake-v1 8x8   (f) FrozenLake-v1 8x8 Slippery

(g) FlappyBird-v0

Fig. 5. Cumulative Non-Random Action vs. Time steps.

of the problem. On the other hand, in ONA, if the system does not suggest any action, we choose a random action, as shown in Fig. 4. In addition, there is also a possibility of the system suggesting a random action itself to explore the environment, thanks to the *motorbabbling* parameter. So some of the actions shown in Fig. 5, despite being labeled as non-random, are actually exploratory and random in nature. In fact, ONA is able to decrease the *motorbabbling* on its own once it has established stable hypotheses and accurate predictions, without relying on a reduction of the exploration rate that is dependent on time. This could be one of the reasons why ONA is successful, even though it doesn't receive frequent rewards like *Q*-Learning. So, we believe ONA is capable of handling multiple and changing objectives, while also requiring less implicit example-dependent parameter tuning compared to *Q*-Learning.

5   Conclusion and Future Work

In this paper, we made a comparison between ONA and *Q*-learning on seven tasks. Given that both approaches demonstrate comparable performance on average, our study suggests that NARS has the potential to be a viable substitute for RL in sequence-based tasks, particularly for non-deterministic problems. While further research is necessary to determine the full extent of NARS's capabilities and limitations, our results offer new avenues for exploration and innovation in the field of machine learning. Future work can extend our examples to multi-objective and changing objective scenarios. Additionally, a combination of both approaches through methods like voting, hierarchical or teacher-student learning could be explored.

Acknowledgment. We would like to express our gratitude to Patrick Hammer, Ph.D., for his expert advice, encouragement, and proofreading of the manuscript throughout this work. This work was partially supported by the Swedish Research Council through grant agreement no. 2020-03607 and in part by Digital Futures, the C3.ai Digital Transformation Institute, and Sweden's Innovation Agency (Vinnova). The computations were enabled by resources in project SNIC 2022/22-942 provided by the Swedish National Infrastructure for Computing (SNIC) at Chalmers Centre for Computational Science and Engineering (C3SE).

References

1. Brockman, G., et al.: OpenAI gym. arXiv preprint arXiv:1606.01540 (2016)
2. Eberding, L.M., Thórisson, K.R., Sheikhlar, A., Andrason, S.P.: SAGE: task-environment platform for evaluating a broad range of AI learners. In: Goertzel, B., Panov, A.I., Potapov, A., Yampolskiy, R. (eds.) AGI 2020. LNCS (LNAI), vol. 12177, pp. 72–82. Springer, Cham (2020). https://doi.org/10.1007/978-3-030-52152-3_8
3. Fischer, T.G.: Reinforcement learning in financial markets-a survey. Technical report, FAU Discussion Papers in Economics (2018)
4. Hammer, P.: Autonomy through real-time learning and OpenNARS for applications. Temple University (2021)
5. Hammer, P., Lofthouse, T.: 'OpenNARS for applications': architecture and control. In: Goertzel, B., Panov, A.I., Potapov, A., Yampolskiy, R. (eds.) AGI 2020. LNCS (LNAI), vol. 12177, pp. 193–204. Springer, Cham (2020). https://doi.org/10.1007/978-3-030-52152-3_20
6. Hammer, P., Lofthouse, T., Fenoglio, E., Latapie, H., Wang, P.: A reasoning based model for anomaly detection in the smart city domain. In: Arai, K., Kapoor, S., Bhatia, R. (eds.) IntelliSys 2020. AISC, vol. 1251, pp. 144–159. Springer, Cham (2021). https://doi.org/10.1007/978-3-030-55187-2_13
7. Hammer, P., Lofthouse, T., Wang, P.: The OpenNARS implementation of the non-axiomatic reasoning system. In: Steunebrink, B., Wang, P., Goertzel, B. (eds.) AGI -2016. LNCS (LNAI), vol. 9782, pp. 160–170. Springer, Cham (2016). https://doi.org/10.1007/978-3-319-41649-6_16
8. Henderson, P., Islam, R., Bachman, P., Pineau, J., Precup, D., Meger, D.: Deep reinforcement learning that matters. In: Proceedings of the AAAI Conference on Artificial Intelligence, vol. 32 (2018)
9. Kober, J., Bagnell, J.A., Peters, J.: Reinforcement learning in robotics: a survey. Int. J. Robot. Res. **32**(11), 1238–1274 (2013)
10. Silver, D., et al.: Mastering the game of go without human knowledge. Nature **550**(7676), 354–359 (2017)
11. Sutton, R.S., Barto, A.G.: Reinforcement Learning: An Introduction. MIT Press, Cambridge (2018)
12. Wang, P.: Non-axiomatic reasoning system: exploring the essence of intelligence. Indiana University (1995)
13. Wang, P.: Rigid Flexibility: The Logic of Intelligence, vol. 34. Springer, Dordrecht (2006). https://doi.org/10.1007/1-4020-5045-3

14. Wang, P.: Insufficient knowledge and resources-a biological constraint and its functional implications. In: 2009 AAAI Fall Symposium Series (2009)
15. Wang, P.: Non-axiomatic logic (NAL) specification. University of Camerino, Piazza Cavour **19** (2010)
16. Wang, P.: Non-Axiomatic Logic: A Model of Intelligent Reasoning. World Scientific (2013)
17. Watkins, C.J., Dayan, P.: Q-learning. Mach. Learn. **8**(3), 279–292 (1992). https://doi.org/10.1007/BF00992698
18. Yu, C., Liu, J., Nemati, S., Yin, G.: Reinforcement learning in healthcare: a survey. ACM Comput. Surv. **55**(1), 1–36 (2021)

On the Computation of Meaning, Language Models and Incomprehensible Horrors

Michael Timothy Bennett[(✉)] [iD]

The Australian National University, Canberra, Australia
michael.bennett@anu.edu.au
http://www.michaeltimothybennett.com/

Abstract. We integrate foundational theories of meaning with a mathematical formalism of artificial general intelligence (AGI) to offer a comprehensive mechanistic explanation of meaning, communication, and symbol emergence. This synthesis holds significance for both AGI and broader debates concerning the nature of language, as it unifies pragmatics, logical truth conditional semantics, Peircean semiotics, and a computable model of enactive cognition, addressing phenomena that have traditionally evaded mechanistic explanation. By examining the conditions under which a machine can generate meaningful utterances or comprehend human meaning, we establish that the current generation of language models do not possess the same understanding of meaning as humans nor intend any meaning that we might attribute to their responses. To address this, we propose simulating human feelings and optimising models to construct weak representations. Our findings shed light on the relationship between meaning and intelligence, and how we can build machines that comprehend and intend meaning.

Keywords: meaning · AGI · language

1 Introduction

Linguists and philosophers have offered various accounts of the behaviour of language and the human mind. Computer scientists have posited mechanisms to replicate these variously described behaviours piecemeal. The former is a top-down approach, while the latter is bottom up. Unfortunately, it is difficult to connect the two. Large language models (LLMs) such as ChatGPT are a bottom up attempt to capture the behaviour of written language, and are remarkably good at giving human-like responses to questions. Yet it is unclear the extent to which an LLM actually means what it says or understands what we mean. AGI should not just parrot what we expect but respond to what we mean, and mean what it says. Yet how we would we know the difference? Computers represent syntax, and from correlations in syntax an LLM is supposed to glean meaning. However, meaning is not well defined. We need to connect top-down descriptions of meaning to bottom-up computation. How might we compute meaning?

P. Hammer et al. (Eds.): AGI 2023, LNAI 13921, pp. 32–41, 2023.
https://doi.org/10.1007/978-3-031-33469-6_4

1.1 Grice's Foundational Theory of Meaning

Grice's foundational theory of meaning [2] holds that meaning is what the speaker *intends* to convey to the listener. Grice gave an illustrative example,

[the speaker] α means m by uttering u iff α intends in uttering u that
1. his audience come to believe m,
2. his audience recognize this intention [called m-intention], and
3. (1) occur on the basis of (2) [3].

This is *foundational* because it specifies the facts in virtue of which expressions have particular semantic properties (instead of those properties), and is illustrative of our goal (to connect bottom up computation to top down description).

1.2 A Foundational Theory of Foundational Theories

Were we to accept that meaning is in virtue of m-intent[1], then from what does that arise? M-intent should not be conflated with intent in general because it pertains to what one means by an expression, whereas intent more generally is any goal in service of which decisions are made. The former stems from the latter [6], and so there exists a theory arguing that meaning exists in virtue of one's intent in the sense of goals. Grice's theories are better established and widely accepted with respect to meaning, but these theories are not mutually exclusive and the depiction of meaning as in virtue of intent in general is a bridge we can use to connect Grice's top down description to bottom-up computational processes. This is because it explains intent in virtue of inductive inference, to argue that meaningful communication with an AI, or any organism, requires similar feelings and experiences, in order to construct similar goals and "solutions to tasks" [6] (an argument formed in relation to the Fermi Paradox [7]). This explanation was too vague to be of significance for engineering. For example it assumed a measure, "weakness", which was not well defined. However, weakness *is* well defined in a more recent formalism of artificial general intelligence (AGI) [1,8] and enactive cognition, so we will instead reformulate the theory using that formalism, extending it to account for meaningful communication. We begin with cognition formalised using tasks. We then formalise an organism using tasks to provide a novel account of preferences, symbol systems and meaningful communication. We then describe how an organism might mean what we think it means by what it says, or infer what we mean by what we say.

2 Meaning, From the Top Down

Intent only exists in virtue of a task one is undertaking [6]. A task is what we get if we add context to intent, expressing what is relevant about both the

---

[1] We note that Grice later expanded upon the notion of m-intent [4,5], and that there are other widely accepted descriptions of meaning (Russell, Frege, Searle, Davidson, Wittgenstein, Lewis, Kripke etc.), some of which we touch upon as part of our formalism. However, paper length limits what we discuss.

agent and the environment. A task can be used to formalise enactive cognition [9], discarding notions of agent and environment in favour of a set of decision problems [1,6]. A task is something which is completed, like a goal, so intent is formalised like a goal [10]. A goal is a set of criteria, and if those criteria are satisfied, then it is satisfied and the task complete. To formalise meaning we must avoid grounding problems [11]. As such these criteria are grounded by representing the environment, of which cognition is part, as a set of declarative programs [12] of which the universe is the interpreter [13]:

Definition 1 (environment)

- *We assume a set Φ whose elements we call **states**, one of which we single out as the **present state**.*
- *A **declarative program** is a function $f : \Phi \to \{true, false\}$, and we write P for the set of all declarative programs. By an **objective truth** about a state ϕ, we mean a declarative program f such that $f(\phi) = true$.*

Definition 2 (implementable language)

- $\mathfrak{V} = \{V \subset P : V \text{ is finite}\}$ *is a set whose elements we call **vocabularies**, one of which[2] we single out as **the vocabulary** $\mathfrak{v}$.*
- $L_\mathfrak{v} = \{l \subseteq \mathfrak{v} : \exists \phi \in \Phi \ (\forall p \in l : p(\phi) = true)\}$ *is a set whose elements we call **statements**. $L_\mathfrak{v}$ follows Φ and $\mathfrak{v}$, and is called **implementable language**.*
- $l \in L_\mathfrak{v}$ *is **true** iff the present state is ϕ and $\forall p \in l : p(\phi) = true$.*
- *The **extension of a statement** $a \in L_\mathfrak{v}$ is $Z_a = \{b \in L_\mathfrak{v} : a \subseteq b\}$.*
- *The **extension of a set of statements** $A \subseteq L_\mathfrak{v}$ is $Z_A = \bigcup_{a \in A} Z_a$.*

(Notation) Z with a subscript is the extension of the subscript[3].

A goal can now be expressed as a statement in an implementable language. An implementable language represents sensorimotor circuitry[4] with which cognition is enacted. It is not natural language, but a dyadic system with exact meaning. Peircean semiosis [14] is integrated to explain natural language. Peirce defined a symbol as a sign (E.G. the word "pain"), a referent (E.G. the experience of pain), and an interpretant which links the two, "determining the effect upon" the organism. A goal arguably functions as an interpretant because it determines the effect of a situation upon an organism that pursues it [6]. Rather than formulate a task and then rehash the argument that a task is a symbol, we'll just formalise a symbol using the existing definition of a task [1, definition 3]:

Definition 3 ($\mathfrak{v}$-task). *For a chosen $\mathfrak{v}$, a task α is a triple $\langle S_\alpha, D_\alpha, M_\alpha \rangle$, and $\Gamma_\mathfrak{v}$ is the set of all tasks given $\mathfrak{v}$. Give a task α:*

---

[2] The vocabulary $\mathfrak{v}$ we single out represents the sensorimotor circuitry with which an organism enacts cognition - their brain, body, local environment and so forth.

[3] e.g. Z_s is the extension of s.

[4] Mind, body, local environment etc.

- $S_\alpha \subset L_\mathfrak{v}$ is a set whose elements we call **situations** of α.
- S_α has the extension Z_{S_α}, whose elements we call **decisions** of α.
- $D_\alpha = \{z \in Z_{S_\alpha} : z \text{ is correct}\}$ is the set of all decisions which complete α.
- $M_\alpha = \{l \in L_\mathfrak{v} : Z_{S_\alpha} \cap Z_l = D_\alpha\}$ whose elements we call **models** of α.

(Notation) If $\omega \in \Gamma_\mathfrak{v}$, then we will use subscript ω to signify parts of ω, meaning one should assume $\omega = \langle S_\omega, D_\omega, M_\omega \rangle$ even if that isn't written.

(How a task is completed) Assume we've a $\mathfrak{v}$-task ω and a hypothesis $h \in L_\mathfrak{v}$ s.t.

1. we are presented with a situation $s \in S_\omega$, and
2. we must select a decision $z \in Z_s \cap Z_h$.
3. If $z \in D_\omega$, then z is correct and the task is complete. This occurs if $h \in M_\omega$.

Definition 4 (symbol). A task α is also a Peircean symbol:

- $s \in S_\alpha$ is a **sign** of α.
- $d \in D_\alpha$ is the effect of α upon one who perceives it. d may be sensorimotor activity associated with perception, and thus a **referent**.
- $m \in M_\alpha$ is an **interpretant** linking **signs** to **referents**.

Tasks may be divided into narrower child tasks, or merged into parent tasks.

Definition 5 (child, parent and weakness). A symbol α is a child of ω if $S_\alpha \subset S_\omega$ and $D_\alpha \subseteq D_\omega$. This is written $\alpha \sqsubset \omega$. We call $|D_\alpha|$ the weakness of a symbol α, and a parent is weaker than its children.

2.1 Extending the Formalism

The child and parent relation means a symbol is also a symbol system in that it can be subdivided into child symbols [6]. With this in mind, we can define an organism that derives symbols from its experiences, preferences and feelings.

Definition 6 (organism). An organism $\mathfrak{o}$ is a quintuple $\langle \mathfrak{v_o}, \mathfrak{e_o}, \mathfrak{s_o}, n_o, f_o \rangle$, and the set of all such quintuples is $\mathfrak{O}$ where:

- $\mathfrak{v_o}$ is a **vocabulary** we single out as belonging to this organism[5].
- We assume a $\mathfrak{v_o}$-task β wherein S_β is every situation in which $\mathfrak{o}$ has made a decision, and D_β contains every such decision. Given the set $\Gamma_{\mathfrak{v_o}}$ of all tasks, $\mathfrak{e_o} = \{\omega \in \Gamma_{\mathfrak{v_o}} : \omega \sqsubset \beta\}$ is a set whose members we call **experiences**.
- A **symbol system** $\mathfrak{s_o} = \{\alpha \in \Gamma_{\mathfrak{v_o}} : \text{there exists } \omega \in \mathfrak{e_o} \text{ where } M_\alpha \cap M_\omega \neq \emptyset\}$ is a set whose members we call **symbols**. $\mathfrak{s_o}$ is the set of every task to which it is possible to generalise (see [1, definition 5]) from an element of $\mathfrak{e_o}$.
- $n_o : \mathfrak{s_o} \to \mathbb{N}$ is a function we call **preferences**.
- $f_o : \mathfrak{s_o} \to \mathfrak{f_o}$ is a function, and $\mathfrak{f_o} \subset L_{\mathfrak{v_o}}$ a set whose elements we call **feelings**, being the reward, qualia etc, from which preferences arise[6].

---

[5] The corresponding $L_{\mathfrak{v_o}}$ is all sensorimotor activity in which the organism may engage.

[6] Note that this assumes qualia, preferences and so forth are part of physical reality, which means they are sets of declarative programs.

Each symbol in $\mathfrak{s}_o$ shares an interpretant at least one experience[7]. This is so feelings f_o ascribed to symbols can be grounded in experience. Humans are given impetus by a complex balance of feelings (reward signals, qualia etc.). It is arguable that feelings eventually determine all value judgements [10]. As Hume pointed out, one cannot derive a statement of what ought to be from a statement of what is. Feelings are an ought from which one may derive all other oughts. If meaning is about intent, then the impetus that gives rise to that intent is an intrinsic part of all meaning [7]. Intent is a goal. A goal is statement of what ought to be that one tries to make into a description of what is, by altering the world to fit with ought to be. We assume feelings are consequence of natural selection, and so explain meaning in virtue of a mechanistic process. Each $l \in L$ represents sensorimotor activity, which from a materialist perspective includes feelings. Thus, f_o is a function from symbols to sensorimotor activity. Statements and symbols "mean something" to the organism if the organism can ascribe feelings to them. As every symbol in $\mathfrak{s}_o$ contains an interpretant which is part of the organism's experience, the organism can ascribe feelings to all symbols on the basis of that experience. If one is not concerned with qualia [16,17], then feelings may be simulated with "reward" functions. However, to simulate feelings that result in human-like behaviour is a more difficult proposition. Rather than trying to describe human-like feelings, we simplify our analysis by assuming the preferences [18] n_o which are determined by experience of feelings.

2.2   Interpretation

The **situation at hand** $s \in L_{\mathfrak{v}_o}$ is a statement $\mathfrak{o}$ experiences as a sign and then **interprets** using $\alpha \in \mathfrak{s}_o$ s.t. $s \in S_\alpha$, to decide $d \in Z_s \cap Z_{M_\alpha}$.

Definition 7 (interpretation). *Interpretation is a sequence of steps:*

1. *The situation at hand $s \in L_{\mathfrak{v}_o}$ **signifies** a symbol $\alpha \in \mathfrak{s}_o$ if $s \in S_\alpha$.*
2. *$\mathfrak{s}_o^s = \{\alpha \in \mathfrak{s}_o : s \in S_\alpha\}$ is the set of all symbols which s signifies.*
3. *If $\mathfrak{s}_o^s \neq \emptyset$ then s **means something** to the organism in the sense that there are feelings which can be ascribed to symbols in $\mathfrak{s}_o^s$.*
4. *If s means something, then $\mathfrak{o}$ uses $\alpha \in \arg\max_{\omega \in \mathfrak{s}_o^s} n_o(\omega)$ to interpret s.*
5. *The interpretation is a decision $d \in Z_s \cap Z_{M_\alpha}$[8].*

3   Communication of Meaning

We develop our explanation in four parts. First, we define exactly what it means for an organism to affect and be affected by others. Second, we examine how one

---

[7] A symbol system is every task to which one may generalise from one's experiences. Only finitely many symbols may be entertained. In claiming our formalism pertains to meaning in natural language we are rejecting arguments, such as those of Block and Fodor [15], that a human can entertain an infinity of propositions (because time and memory are assumed to be finite, which is why $\mathfrak{v}_o$ is finite).

[8] How an organism responds to a sign that means nothing is beyond this paper's scope.

organism may anticipate the behaviour (by inferring the end it serves) of another or order to change how they are affected. Third, we examine how said organism may, having anticipated the behaviour of the other, intervene to manipulate the other's behaviour to their benefit (so that the now latter affects the former in a more positive way). And finally, we examine what happens when each organism is attempting to manipulate the another. Each anticipates the other's manipulation, because each anticipates the other's behaviour by inferring its intent. An organism can then attempt to deceive the other organism (continue the manipulative approach), or attempt to co-operate (communicate in good faith), a choice resembling an iterated prisoner's dilemma. We assume organisms make decisions based upon preferences, but preferences are not arbitrary. Feelings and thus preferences exist in virtue of natural selection, which to some extent must favour rational behaviour (to the extent that selection is significantly impacted). In this might be understood as alignment, to use AI safety terms. One's feelings are the result of alignment by genetic algorithm, and one's preferences are the result of reinforcement learning using those feelings (to determine reward). Thus we assume preferences are a balance of what is rational, and what is tolerably irrational, given the pressures of natural selection. We call this balance **reasonably performant**. The specifics of inductive inference are beyond the scope of this paper, however definitions and formal proofs pertaining to inductive inference from child to parent tasks are included in the appendix [1]. The necessary inductive capabilities are assumed with being reasonably performant.

3.1   Ascribing Intent

Definition 8 (affect). *To affect an organism o is to cause it to make a different decision than it otherwise would have. $\mathfrak{k}$ affects o if o would have made a decision d, but as a result of a decision c made by $\mathfrak{k}$, o makes decision $g \neq d$.*

Let $\mathfrak{k}$ and o be organisms. If $\mathfrak{k}$ affects o, and assuming $\mathfrak{v}_o$ is sufficient to allow o to distinguish when it is affected by $\mathfrak{k}$ from when it is not (meaning all else being equal $\mathfrak{k}$'s interventions are distinguishable by the presence of an identity (see appendices), then there exists experience $\zeta_o^{\mathfrak{k}} \in \mathfrak{e}_o$ such that $d \in D_{\zeta_o^{\mathfrak{k}}}$ if o is affected by $\mathfrak{k}$. $\zeta_o^{\mathfrak{k}}$ is an ostensive definition [19] of $\mathfrak{k}$'s intent (meaning it is a child task from which we may infer the parent representing $\mathfrak{k}$'s most likely intent and thus future behaviour) [6]. In the absence of more information, the symbol most likely to represent $\mathfrak{k}'s$ intent is the weakest [6], meaning $\alpha \in \mathfrak{s}_o$ s.t. $|Z_\alpha|$ is maximised. However, because o assumes $\mathfrak{k}$ has similar feelings and preferences [6,10][9] n_o is an approximation of what $\mathfrak{k}$ will do. Accordingly the symbol most likely to represent $\mathfrak{k}$'s intent would be the "weakest" of goals preferred by o which, if pursued by $\mathfrak{k}$, would explain why $\mathfrak{k}$ has affected o as it has. This is $\gamma_o^{\mathfrak{k}}$ s.t.

$$\gamma_o^{\mathfrak{k}} \in \arg\max_{\alpha \in \mathfrak{K}} |Z_\alpha| \text{ s.t. } \mathfrak{K} = \arg\max_{\alpha \in \Gamma_o^{\mathfrak{k}}} n_o(\alpha) \text{ and } \Gamma_o^{\mathfrak{k}} = \{\omega \in \Gamma_{\mathfrak{v}_o} : M_{\zeta_o^{\mathfrak{k}}} \cap M_\omega \neq \emptyset\}$$

---

[9] Members of a species tend to have similar feelings, experiences and thus preferences.

3.2   From Manipulation to Meaningful Communication

We've explained inference of intent in counterfactual terms, answering "if places were exchanged, what would cause o to act like ℓ?". Intent here is "what is ℓ trying to achieve by affecting o", rather than just "what is ℓ trying to achieve".

Manipulation: Because it is reasonably performant, o infers the intent of an organism ℓ that affects o, in order to plan ahead and ensure its own needs will be met. However o can go a step further. It can also attempt to influence what ℓ will do. If being reasonably performant requires o infer ℓ's intent because ℓ affects o, then it may also require o affect ℓ to the extent that doing so will benefit o.

Communication: If both o and ℓ are reasonably performant, each may attempt to manipulate the other. Ascribing intent to one another's behaviour in order to manipulate, each must anticipate the other's manipulative intent. Subsequently each organism must go yet another step further and account for how its own manipulative intent will be perceived by the other. As in a sort of iterated prisoner's dilemma, the rational choice may then be to co-operate. Because each symbol represents a goal it defines a limited context for co-operation; so two organisms might simultaneously co-operate in pursuit of one goal while competing in pursuit of another (E.G. two dogs may co-operate to hunt while competing for a mate). If there is sufficient profit in affecting another's behaviour, then knowing one's own intent is perceived by that other and that the other will change its behaviour in response to one's changed intent, it makes sense to actually change one's own intent in order to affect the other. This bears out experimentally in reinforcement learning with extended environments [20]. The rational choice may then be to *have* co-operative intent, assuming ℓ can perceive o's intent correctly, and that ℓ will reciprocate in kind. For a population of reasonably performant organisms, induction (see [1]) with co-operative intent would favour symbols that mean (functionally) similar things to all members of the population. Repeated interactions would give rise to signalling conventions we might call language.

Meaning: Let us re-frame these ideas using the example from the introduction. We'll say two symbols $\alpha \in \mathfrak{s}_\ell$ and $\omega \in \mathfrak{s}_o$ are roughly equivalent (written $\alpha \approx \omega$) to mean feelings, experiences and thus preferences associated with a symbol are in some sense the same for two organisms (meaning if $\alpha \approx \omega$ then $f_\ell(\alpha) \approx f_o(\omega)$ etc.). In other words we're suggesting it must be possible to measure the similarity between symbols in terms of feelings, experiences and thus preferences, and so we can assert a threshold beyond which two symbols are roughly equivalent.

ℓ means $\alpha \in \mathfrak{s}_\ell$ by deciding u and affecting o iff ℓ intends in deciding u:
1. that o interpets the situation at hand with $\omega \in \mathfrak{s}_o$ s.t. $\omega \approx \alpha$,
2. o recognize this intention, for example by predicting it according to

$$\gamma_o^\ell \in \underset{\alpha \in \mathfrak{K}}{\arg\max} \, |Z_\alpha| \text{ s.t. } \mathfrak{K} = \underset{\alpha \in \Gamma_o^\ell}{\arg\max} \, n_o(\alpha), \Gamma_o^\ell = \{\omega \in \Gamma_{v_o} : M_{\zeta_o^\ell} \cap M_\omega \neq \emptyset\}$$

3. and (1) occur on the basis of (2), because 𝔱 intends to co-operate and so will interpret the situation at hand using what it believes of 𝔬's intent.

The above pertains to co-operation. To comprehend meaning:

1. Organisms must be able to **affect one another.**
2. Organisms must have similar **feelings,** and
3. similar **experiences,** so 𝔰₀ and 𝔰𝔱 contain roughly equivalent symbols.
4. Similar **preferences** then inform the correct inference of intent.
5. Finally, all this assumes organisms are **reasonably performant.**

4 Talking to a Machine

An LLM is trained to mimic human preferences. However, an LLM is not given impetus by feelings, and so cannot entertain roughly equivalent symbols. This is not to say we cannot reverse engineer the complex balance of human-like feelings, merely that we have not. If an LLM has impetus, it is to be found in our prompts. It is reminiscent of a mirror test, which is a means of determining whether animals are self aware. For example, a cat seeing itself in the mirror may attack its reflection, not realising what it sees is itself. In an LLM we face a mirror test of our own, but instead of light it reflects our own written language back at us. We ascribe motives and feelings to that language because we have evolved to infer the intent of organisms compelled by feelings [6]. An LLM hijacks what we use to understand one another (that we assume others are motivated by similar feelings [10]). We've a history of ascribing feelings and agency to things possessed of neither. In the 1970s, a chatbot named ELIZA made headlines as its users attributed feelings and motives to its words [21]. Like ELIZA, today's LLMs not only do not mean what we think they mean by what they say, but do not mean anything at all. This is not an indictment of LLMs trained to mimic human preferences. The meaning we ascribe to their behaviour can be useful, even if that behaviour was not intended to mean anything.

The Hall of Mirrors: Even if we approximate human feelings, an LLM like ChatGPT is not reasonably performant. It is maladaptive, requiring an abundance of training data. This may be because training does not optimise for a weak representation, but settles for any function fitting the data[10] [6]. Returning to mirror analogies, imagine a hall of mirrors reflecting an object from different angles. A weak or simple representation would be one symbol $\alpha \in \mathfrak{s}_0$ representing the object, which is then interpreted from the perspectives $a, b, c, d \in S_\alpha$ of each mirror. A needlessly convoluted representation of the same would instead interpret a, b, c and d using different symbols. These would be α's children $\omega, \gamma, \delta, \sigma \sqsubset \alpha$ such that $a \in S_\omega, b \in S_\gamma, c \in S_\delta, d \in S_\sigma$. This latter representation fails to exploit what is common between perspectives, which might allow it to generalise [6] to new perspectives. That an LLM may not learn sufficiently

---

[10] Albeit with some preference for simplicity imparted by regularisation.

weak representations seems consistent with their flaws. One well documented example of this is how an LLM may convincingly mimic yet fail to understand arithmetic [22], but such flaws may more subtly manifest elsewhere. For example, when we queried Bing Chat (on the 2nd of February 2023 [1, p. 11]) with the name and location of a relatively unknown individual who had several professions and hobbies mentioned on different sites, Bing concluded that different people with this name lived in the area, each one having a different hobby or profession.

Incomprehensibility: If we are to build machines that mean what we think they mean by what they say, then we must emulate human feelings and experiences. It is interesting to consider where this may lead. If we do not get the balance of feelings quite right, we might create an organism that means what it says, but whose meanings may be partially or utterly incomprehensible to us because the resulting preferences are unaligned with ours. In the introduction we mentioned ideas on which this paper was founded were used to relate the Fermi paradox to control of and communication with an AGI [7]. We can extend that notion. Assume we are affected by an organism. If the events befalling us are set in motion by preferences entirely unlike our own, then we would fail to ascribe the correct intent to the organism. We may fail entirely to realise there is an organism, or may ascribe many different intents as in the hall of mirrors analogy. Furthermore, $\mathfrak{v}_{\mathfrak{o}}$ determines what can or cannot be comprehended by an organism (see appendices). $\mathfrak{v}_{\mathfrak{o}}$ may contain nothing akin to the contents of $\mathfrak{v}_{\mathfrak{k}}$, making $\mathfrak{o}$ incapable of representing and thus comprehending $\mathfrak{k}$'s intent.

Conclusion: We have extended a formalism of artificial general intelligence, connecting bottom up computation to top down notions of meaning. This is significant not just to AGI but to wider debates surrounding language, meaning and the linguistic turn. While we focused on Gricean notions of meaning due to publication constraints, the formalism is by no means limited to that. For example, the logical truth conditional meaning of statements is in their extension. We have described the process by which meaningful communication can take place and the prerequisites thereof. We conclude that human-like feelings and weak representations should give us systems that comprehend and intend meaning.

Acknowledgement. Appendices available on GitHub [1], supported by JST (JPMJMS2033).

References

1. Bennett, M.T.: Technical Appendices. Version 1.2.1 (2023). https://doi.org/10.5281/zenodo.7641742. github.com/ViscousLemming/Technical-Appendices
2. Grice, P.: Meaning. Philos. Rev. **66**(3), 377 (1957)
3. Speaks, J.: Theories of meaning. In: The Stanford Encyclopedia of Philosophy. Spring 2021. Stanford University (2021)

4. Grice, P.: Utterers meaning and intention. Philos. Rev. **78**(2), 147–177 (1969)
5. Grice, H.P.: Studies in the Way of Words. Harvard University Press, Cambridge (2007)
6. Bennett, M.T.: Symbol emergence and the solutions to any task. In: Goertzel, B., Iklé, M., Potapov, A. (eds.) AGI 2021. LNCS (LNAI), vol. 13154, pp. 30–40. Springer, Cham (2022). https://doi.org/10.1007/978-3-030-93758-4_4
7. Bennett, M.T.: Compression, the fermi paradox and artificial super-intelligence. In: Goertzel, B., Iklé, M., Potapov, A. (eds.) AGI 2021. LNCS (LNAI), vol. 13154, pp. 41–44. Springer, Cham (2022). https://doi.org/10.1007/978-3-030-93758-4_5
8. Bennett, M.T.: Computable artificial general intelligence (2022). https://arxiv.org/abs/2205.10513
9. Ward, D., Silverman, D., Villalobos, M.: Introduction: the varieties of enactivism. Topoi **36**(3), 365–375 (2017). https://doi.org/10.1007/s11245-017-9484-6
10. Bennett, M.T., Maruyama, Y.: Philosophical specification of empathetic ethical artificial intelligence. IEEE Trans. Cogn. Dev. Syst. **14**(2), 292–300 (2022)
11. Harnad, S.: The symbol grounding problem. Phys. D Nonlinear Phenom. **42**(1), 335–346 (1990)
12. Howard, W.A.: The formulae-as-types notion of construction. Dedicated to H.B. Curry: Essays on Combinatory Logic, Lambda Calculus and Formalism. Ed. by J. Seldin and J. Hindley, pp. 479–490. Academic Press, Cambridge (1980)
13. Piccinini, G., Maley, C.: Computation in physical systems. In: The Stanford Encyclopedia of Philosophy. Summer. Stanford University (2021)
14. Atkin, A.: Peirces theory of signs. In: The Stanford Encyclopedia of Philosophy. Spring. Metaphysics Research Lab, Stanford University (2023)
15. Block, N., Fodor, J.: What psychological states are not. Philos. Rev. **81**(2), 159–181 (1972)
16. Chalmers, D.: Facing up to the problem of consciousness. J. Conscious. Stud. **2**(3), 200–219 (1995)
17. Boltuc, P.: The engineering thesis in machine consciousness. Techné Res. Philos. Technol. **16**(2), 187–207 (2012)
18. Alexander, S.A.: The Archimedean trap: why traditional reinforcement learning will probably not yield AGI. J. Artif. Gen. Intell. **11**(1), 70–85 (2020)
19. Gupta, A.: Definitions. In: The Stanford Encyclopedia of Philosophy. Winter 2021. Stanford University (2021)
20. Alexander, S.A., et al.: Extending environments to measure self-reflection in reinforcement learning. J. Artif. Gen. Intell. **13**(1), 1–24 (2022)
21. Weizenbaum, J.: Computer Power and Human Reason: From Judgment to Calculation. W. H. Freeman & Co. (1976)
22. Floridi, L., Chiriatti, M.: GPT-3: its nature, scope, limits, and consequences. Minds Mach. **30**, 681–694 (2020). https://doi.org/10.1007/s11023-020-09548-1

The Optimal Choice of Hypothesis
Is the Weakest, Not the Shortest

Michael Timothy Bennett[(✉)] [ID]

The Australian National University, Canberra, Australia
michael.bennett@anu.edu.au
http://www.michaeltimothybennett.com/

Abstract. If A and B are sets such that $A \subset B$, generalisation may
be understood as the inference from A of a hypothesis sufficient to construct B. One might infer any number of hypotheses from A, yet only
some of those may generalise to B. How can one know which are likely
to generalise? One strategy is to choose the shortest, equating the ability
to compress information with the ability to generalise (a "proxy for intelligence"). We examine this in the context of a mathematical formalism
of enactive cognition. We show that compression is neither necessary nor
sufficient to maximise performance (measured in terms of the probability
of a hypothesis generalising). We formulate a proxy unrelated to length
or simplicity, called weakness. We show that if tasks are uniformly distributed, then there is no choice of proxy that performs at least as well
as weakness maximisation in all tasks while performing strictly better
in at least one. In experiments comparing maximum weakness and minimum description length in the context of binary arithmetic, the former
generalised at between 1.1 and 5 times the rate of the latter. We argue
this demonstrates that weakness is a far better proxy, and explains why
Deepmind's Apperception Engine is able to generalise effectively.

Keywords: simplicity · induction · artificial general intelligence

1 Introduction

If A and B are sets such that $A \subset B$, generalisation may be understood as
the inference from A of a hypothesis sufficient to construct B. One might infer
any number of hypotheses from A, yet only some of those may generalise to B.
How can one know which are likely to generalise? According to Ockham's Razor,
the simpler of two explanations is the more likely [2]. Simplicity is not itself a
measurable property, so the minimum description length principle [3] relates simplicity to length. Shorter representations are considered to be simpler, and tend
to generalise more effectively. This is often applied in the context of induction
by comparing the length of programs that explain what is observed (to chose the
shortest, all else being equal). The ability to identify shorter representations is
compression, and the ability to generalise is arguably intelligence [4]. Hence the

© The Author(s), under exclusive license to Springer Nature Switzerland AG 2023
P. Hammer et al. (Eds.): AGI 2023, LNAI 13921, pp. 42–51, 2023.
https://doi.org/10.1007/978-3-031-33469-6_5

ability to compress information is often portrayed as a proxy for intelligence [5], even serving as the foundation [6–8] of the theoretical super-intelligence AIXI [9]. That compression is a good proxy seems to have gone unchallenged. The optimal choice of hypothesis is widely considered to be the shortest. We show that it is not[1]. We present an alternative, unrelated to description length, called weakness. We prove that to maximise the probability that one's hypotheses generalise, it is necessary and sufficient to infer the weakest valid hypotheses possible[2].

2   Background Definitions

To do so, we employ a formalism of enactive cognition [1,10,11], in which sets of declarative programs are related to one another in such a way as to form a lattice. This unusual representation is necessary to ensure that both the weakness and description length of a hypothesis are well defined[3]. This formalism can be understood in three steps.

1. The environment is represented as a set of declarative programs.
2. A finite subset of the environment is used to define a language with which to write statements that behave as logical formulae.
3. Finally, induction is formalised in terms of tasks made up of these statements.

Definition 1 (environment)

- *We assume a set Φ whose elements we call **states**, one of which we single out as the **present state**[4].*
- *A **declarative program** is a function $f : \Phi \rightarrow \{true, false\}$, and we write P for the set of all declarative programs. By an **objective truth** about a state ϕ, we mean a declarative program f such that $f(\phi) = true$.*

Definition 2 (implementable language)

- *$\mathfrak{V} = \{V \subset P : V \text{ is finite}\}$ is a set whose elements we call **vocabularies**, one of which we single out as **the vocabulary** $\mathfrak{v}$ for an implementable language.*
- *$L_{\mathfrak{v}} = \{l \subseteq \mathfrak{v} : \exists \phi \in \Phi \; (\forall p \in l : p(\phi) = true)\}$ is a set whose elements we call **statements**[5]. $L_{\mathfrak{v}}$ follows from Φ and $\mathfrak{v}$. We call $L_{\mathfrak{v}}$ an **implementable language**.*

---

[1] This proof is conditional upon certain assumptions regarding the nature of cognition as enactive, and a formalism thereof.

[2] Assuming tasks are uniformly distributed, and weakness is well defined.

[3] An example of how one might translate propositional logic into this representation is given at the end of this paper. It is worth noting that this representation of logical formulae addresses the symbol grounding problem [12], and was specifically constructed to address subjective performance claims in the context of AIXI [13].

[4] Each state is just reality from the perspective of a point along one or more dimensions. States of reality must be separated by something, or there would be only one state of reality. For example two different states of reality may be reality from the perspective of two different points in time, or in space and so on.

[5] Statements are the logical formulae about which we will reason.

- $l \in L_{\mathfrak{v}}$ is **true** iff the present state is ϕ and $\forall p \in l : p(\phi) = true$.
- The **extension of a statement** $a \in L_{\mathfrak{v}}$ is $Z_a = \{b \in L_{\mathfrak{v}} : a \subseteq b\}$.
- The **extension of a set of statements** $A \subseteq L_{\mathfrak{v}}$ is $Z_A = \bigcup\limits_{a \in A} Z_a$.

(Notation). Z with a subscript is the extension of the subscript[6]. Lower case letters represent statements, and upper case represent sets of statements.

Definition 3 ($\mathfrak{v}$-task). For a chosen $\mathfrak{v}$, a task α is $\langle S_\alpha, D_\alpha, M_\alpha \rangle$ where:

- $S_\alpha \subset L_{\mathfrak{v}}$ is a set whose elements we call **situations** of α.
- S_α has the extension Z_{S_α}, whose elements we call **decisions** of α.
- $D_\alpha = \{z \in Z_{S_\alpha} : z \text{ is correct}\}$ is the set of all decisions which complete α.
- $M_\alpha = \{l \in L_{\mathfrak{v}} : Z_{S_\alpha} \cap Z_l = D_\alpha\}$ whose elements we call **models** of α.

$\Gamma_{\mathfrak{v}}$ is the set of all tasks[7].

(Notation). If $\omega \in \Gamma_{\mathfrak{v}}$, then we will use subscript ω to signify parts of ω, meaning one should assume $\omega = \langle S_\omega, D_\omega, M_\omega \rangle$ even if that isn't written.

(How a task is completed). Assume we've a $\mathfrak{v}$-task ω and a hypothesis $h \in L_{\mathfrak{v}}$ s.t.

1. we are presented with a situation $s \in S_\omega$, and
2. we must select a decision $z \in Z_s \cap Z_h$.
3. If $z \in D_\omega$, then z is correct and the task is complete. This occurs if $h \in M_\omega$.

3   Formalising Induction

Definition 4 (probability). We assume a uniform distribution over $\Gamma_{\mathfrak{v}}$.

Definition 5 (generalisation). A statement l generalises to $\alpha \in \Gamma_{\mathfrak{v}}$ iff $l \in M_\alpha$. We say l generalises from α to $\mathfrak{v}$-task ω if we first obtain l from M_α and then find it generalises to ω.

Definition 6 (child and parent). A $\mathfrak{v}$-task α is a child of $\mathfrak{v}$-task ω if $S_\alpha \subset S_\omega$ and $D_\alpha \subseteq D_\omega$. This is written as $\alpha \sqsubset \omega$. If $\alpha \sqsubset \omega$ then ω is then a parent of α.

A proxy is meant to estimate one thing by measuring another. In this case, if intelligence is the ability to generalise [4,10], then a greater proxy value is meant to indicate that a statement is more likely to generalise. Not all proxies are effective (most will be useless). We focus on two in particular.

---

[6] e.g. Z_s is the extension of s.

[7] For example, we might represent chess as a supervised learning problem where $s \in S_\alpha$ is the state of a chessboard, $z \in Z_s$ is a sequence of moves by two players that begins in s, and $d \in D_\alpha \cap Z_s$ is such a sequence of moves that terminates in victory for one player in particular (the one undertaking the task).

Definition 7 (proxy for intelligence). *A proxy is a function parameterized by a choice of* $\mathfrak{v}$ *such that* $q_{\mathfrak{v}} : L_{\mathfrak{v}} \to \mathbb{N}$. *The set of all proxies is* Q.

(Weakness). *The weakness of a statement* l *is the cardinality of its extension* $|Z_l|$. *There exists* $q_{\mathfrak{v}} \in Q$ *such that* $q_{\mathfrak{v}}(l) = |Z_l|$.

(Description length). *The description length of a statement* l *is its cardinality* $|l|$. *Longer logical formulae are considered less likely to generalise [3], and a proxy is something to be maximised, so description length as a proxy is* $q_{\mathfrak{v}} \in Q$ *such that* $q_{\mathfrak{v}}(l) = \frac{1}{|l|}$.

A child task may serve as an ostensive definition [14] of its parent, meaning one can generalise from child to parent.

Definition 8 (induction). α *and* ω *are* $\mathfrak{v}$*-tasks such that* $\alpha \sqsubseteq \omega$. *Assume we are given a proxy* $q_{\mathfrak{v}} \in Q$, *the complete definition of* α *and the knowledge that* $\alpha \sqsubseteq \omega$. *We are not given the definition of* ω. *The process of induction would proceed as follows:*

1. *Obtain a hypothesis by computing a model* $\mathbf{h} \in \arg\max_{m \in M_{\alpha}} q_{\mathfrak{v}}(m)$.
2. *If* $\mathbf{h} \in M_{\omega}$, *then we have generalised from* α *to* ω.

4 Proofs

Proposition 1 (sufficiency). *Weakness is a proxy sufficient to maximise the probability that induction generalises from* α *to* ω.

Proof: You're given the definition of $\mathfrak{v}$-task α from which you infer a hypothesis $\mathbf{h} \in M_{\alpha}$. $\mathfrak{v}$-task ω is a parent of α to which we wish to generalise:

1. The set of statements which *might* be decisions addressing situations in S_{ω} and not S_{α}, is $\overline{Z_{S_{\alpha}}} = \{l \in L_{\mathfrak{v}} : l \notin Z_{S_{\alpha}}\}$.
2. For any given $\mathbf{h} \in M_{\alpha}$, the extension $Z_{\mathbf{h}}$ of $\mathbf{h}$ is the set of decisions $\mathbf{h}$ implies. The subset of $Z_{\mathbf{h}}$ which fall outside the scope of what is required for the known task α is $\overline{Z_{S_{\alpha}}} \cap Z_{\mathbf{h}}$ (because $Z_{S_{\alpha}}$ is the set of all decisions we might make when attempting α, and so the set of all decisions that can't be made when undertaking α is $\overline{Z_{S_{\alpha}}}$ because those decisions occur in situations that aren't part of S_{α}).
3. $|\overline{Z_{S_{\alpha}}} \cap Z_{\mathbf{h}}|$ increases monotonically with $|Z_{\mathbf{h}}|$, because $\forall z \in Z_m : z \notin \overline{Z_{S_{\alpha}}} \to z \in Z_{S_{\alpha}}$.
4. $2^{|\overline{Z_{S_{\alpha}}}|}$ is the number of tasks which fall outside of what it is necessary for a model of α to generalise to (this is just the powerset of $\overline{Z_{S_{\alpha}}}$ defined in step 2), and $2^{|\overline{Z_{S_{\alpha}}} \cap Z_{\mathbf{h}}|}$ is the number of those tasks to which a given $\mathbf{h} \in M_{\alpha}$ does generalise.

5. Therefore the probability that a given model $\mathbf{h} \in M_\alpha$ generalises to the unknown parent task ω is

$$p(\mathbf{h} \in M_\omega \mid \mathbf{h} \in M_\alpha, \alpha \sqsubset \omega) = \frac{2^{|\overline{Z_{S_\alpha}} \cap Z_{\mathbf{h}}|}}{2^{|\overline{Z_{S_\alpha}}|}}$$

$p(\mathbf{h} \in M_\omega \mid \mathbf{h} \in M_\alpha, \alpha \sqsubset \omega)$ is maximised when $|Z_{\mathbf{h}}|$ is maximised.

Proposition 2 (necessity). *To maximise the probability that induction generalises from α to ω, it is necessary to use weakness as a proxy, or a function thereof[8].*

Proof: Let α and ω be defined exactly as they were in the proof of Proposition 1.

1. If $\mathbf{h} \in M_\alpha$ and $Z_{S_\omega} \cap Z_{\mathbf{h}} = D_\omega$, then it must be he case that $D_\omega \subseteq Z_{\mathbf{h}}$.
2. If $|Z_{\mathbf{h}}| < |D_\omega|$ then generalisation cannot occur, because that would mean that $D_\omega \nsubseteq Z_{\mathbf{h}}$.
3. Therefore generalisation is only possible if $|Z_m| \geq |D_\omega|$, meaning a sufficiently weak hypothesis is necessary to generalise from child to parent.
4. The probability that $|Z_m| \geq |D_\omega|$ is maximised when $|Z_m|$ is maximised. Therefore to maximise the probability induction results in generalisation, it is necessary to select the weakest hypothesis.

To select the weakest hypothesis, it is necessary to use weakness (or a function thereof) as a proxy.

Remark 1 (prior). The above describes inference from a child to a parent. However, it follows that increasing the weakness of a statement increases the probability that it will generalise to any task (not just a parent of some given child). As tasks are uniformly distributed, every statement in $L_\mathfrak{v}$ is a model to one or more tasks, and the number of tasks to which each statement $l \in L_\mathfrak{v}$ generalises is $2^{|Z_l|}$. Hence the probability of generalisation[9] to ω is $p(\mathbf{h} \in M_\omega \mid \mathbf{h} \in L_\mathfrak{v}) = \frac{2^{|Z_{\mathbf{h}}|}}{2^{|L_\mathfrak{v}|}}$. This assigns a probability to every statement $l \in L_\mathfrak{v}$ given an implementable language. It is a probability distribution in the sense that the probability of mutually exclusive statements sums to one[10]. This prior may be considered universal in the very limited sense that it assigns a probability to every conceivable hypothesis (where what is conceivable depends upon the implementable language) absent any parameters or specific assumptions about the task as with AIXI's intelligence order relation [9, def. 5.14 pp. 147][11]. As the vocabulary $\mathfrak{v}$ is finite, $L_\mathfrak{v}$ must also be finite, and so p is computable.

---

[8] For example we might use weakness multiplied by a constant to the same effect.

[9] $\frac{2^{|Z_{\mathbf{h}}|}}{2^{|L_\mathfrak{v}|}}$ is maximised when $\mathbf{h} = \emptyset$, because the optimal hypothesis given no information is to assume nothing (you've no sequence to predict, so why make assertions that might contradict the environment?).

[10] Two statements a and b are mutually exclusive if $a \notin Z_b$ and $b \notin Z_a$, which we'll write as $\mu(a, b)$. Given $x \in L_\mathfrak{v}$, the set of all mutually exclusive statements is a set $K_x \subset L_\mathfrak{v}$ such that $x \in K_x$ and $\forall a, b \in K_x : \mu(a, b)$. It follows that $\forall x \in L_\mathfrak{v}, \sum_{b \in K_x} p(b) = 1$.

[11] We acknowledge that some may object to the term universal, because $\mathfrak{v}$ is finite.

We have shown that, if tasks are uniformly distributed, then weakness is a necessary and sufficient proxy to maximise the probability that induction generalises. It is important to note that another proxy may perform better given cherry-picked combinations of child and parent task for which that proxy is suitable. However, such a proxy would necessarily perform worse given the uniform distribution of all tasks. Can the same be said of description length?

Proposition 3. *Description length is neither a necessary nor sufficient proxy for the purposes of maximising the probability that induction generalises.*

Proof: In Propositions 1 and 2 we proved that weakness is a necessary and sufficient choice of proxy to maximise the probability of generalisation. It follows that either maximising $\frac{1}{|m|}$ (minimising description length) maximises $|Z_m|$ (weakness), or minimisation of description length is unnecessary to maximise the probability of generalisation. Assume the former, and we'll construct a counterexample with $\mathfrak{v} = \{a, b, c, d, e, f, g, h, j, k, z\}$ s.t. $L_{\mathfrak{v}} = \{\{a, b, c, d, j, k, z\}, \{e, b, c, d, k\}, \{a, f, c, d, j\}, \{e, b, g, d, j, k, z\}, \{a, f, c, h, j, k\}, \{e, f, g, h, j, k\}\}$ and a task α where

- $S_\alpha = \{\{a, b\}, \{e, b\}\}$
- $D_\alpha = \{\{a, b, c, d, j, k, z\}, \{e, b, g, d, j, k, z\}\}$
- $M_\alpha = \{\{z\}, \{j, k\}\}$

Weakness as a proxy selects $\{j, k\}$, while description length as a proxy selects $\{z\}$. This demonstrates the minimising description length does not necessarily maximise weakness, and maximising weakness does not minimise description length. As weakness is necessary and sufficient to maximise the probability of generalisation, it follows that minimising description length is neither.

5   Experiments

Included with this paper is a Python script to perform two experiments using PyTorch with CUDA, SymPy and A^* [15–18] (see technical appendix for details). In these two experiments, a toy program computes models to 8-bit string prediction tasks (binary addition and multiplication). The purpose of these experiments was to compare weakness and description length as proxies.

5.1   Setup

To specify tasks with which the experiments would be conducted, we needed a vocabulary $\mathfrak{v}$ with which to describe simple 8-bit string prediction problems. There were 256 states in Φ, one for every possible 8-bit string. The possible statements were then all the expressions regarding those 8 bits that could be written in propositional logic (the simple connectives $\neg$, $\wedge$ and $\vee$ needed to perform binary arithmetic – a written example of how propositional logic can be used in to specify $\mathfrak{v}$ is also included in the appendix). In other words, for each statement in $L_{\mathfrak{v}}$ there existed an equivalent expression in propositional logic. For efficiency, these statements were implemented as either PyTorch tensors or SymPy expressions in different parts of the program, and converted back and forth as needed (basic set and logical operations on these propositional tensor representations were implemented for the same reason). A $\mathfrak{v}$-task was specified by choosing $D_n \subset L_{\mathfrak{v}}$ such that all $d \in D_n$ conformed to the rules of either binary addition or multiplication with 4-bits of input, followed by 4-bits of output.

5.2   Trials

Each experiment had parameters were "operation" and "number_of_trials". For each trial the number $|D_k|$ of examples ranged from 4 to 14. A trial had 2 phases.

Training Phase

1. A task n (referred to in code as T_n) was generated:
   (a) First, every possible 4-bit input for the chosen binary operation was used to generate an 8-bit string. These 16 strings then formed D_n.
   (b) A bit between 0 and 7 was then chosen, and S_n created by cloning D_n and deleting the chosen bit from every string (S_n contained 16 different 7-bit strings, each of which was a sub-string of an element of D_n).
2. A child-task $k = \langle S_k, D_k, M_k \rangle$ (referred to in code as T_k) was sampled (assuming a uniform distribution over children) from the parent task T_n. Recall, $|D_k|$ was determined as a parameter of the trial.
3. From T_k two models were then generated; a weakest c_w, and a MDL c_{mdl}.

Testing Phase: For each model $c \in \{c_w, c_{mdl}\}$, the testing phase was as follows:

1. The extension Z_c of c was then generated.
2. A prediction D_{recon} was made s.t. $D_{recon} = \{z \in Z_c : \exists s \in S_n \ (s \subset z)\}$.
3. D_{recon} was then compared to the ground truth D_n, and results recorded.

Between 75 and 256 trials were run for each value of the parameter $|D_k|$. Fewer trials were run for larger values of $|D_k|$ as these took longer to process. The results of these trails were then averaged for each value of $|D_k|$.

5.3   Results

Two sorts of measurements were taken for each trial. The first was **the rate at generalisation occurred**. Generalisation was deemed to have occurred where $D_{recon} = D_n$. The number of trials in which generalisation occurred was measured, and divided by n to obtain the rate of generalisation for c_w and c_{mdl}. Error was computed as a Wald 95% confidence interval. The second measurement was **the average extent to which models generalised**. Even where $D_{recon} \neq D_n$, the extent to which models generalised could be ascertained. $\frac{|D_{recon} \cap D_n|}{|D_n|}$ was measured and averaged for each value of $|D_k|$, and the standard error computed. The results (see Tables 1 and 2) demonstrate that weakness is a better proxy for intelligence than description length. The generalisation rate for c_w was between 110–500% of c_{mdl}, and the extent was between $103 - 156\%$.

Table 1. Results for Binary Addition

$|D_k|$	c_w				c_{mdl}			
	Rate	±95%	AvgExt	StdErr	Rate	±95%	AvgExt	StdErr
6	.11	.039	.75	.008	.10	.037	.48	.012
10	.27	.064	.91	.006	.13	.048	.69	.009
14	.68	.106	.98	.005	.24	.097	.91	.006

Table 2. Results for Binary Multiplication

$|D_k|$	c_w				c_{mdl}			
	Rate	±95%	AvgExt	StdErr	Rate	±95%	AvgExt	StdErr
6	.05	.026	.74	.009	.01	.011	.58	.011
10	.16	.045	.86	.006	.08	.034	.78	.008
14	.46	.061	.96	.003	.21	.050	.93	.003

6 Concluding Remarks

We have shown that, if tasks are uniformly distributed, then weakness maximisation is necessary and sufficient to maximise the probability that induction will produce a hypothesis that generalises. It follows that there is no choice of proxy that performs at least as well as weakness maximisation across all possible combinations of child and parent task while performing strictly better in at least one. We've also shown that the minimisation of description length is neither necessary nor sufficient. This calls into question the relationship between compression and intelligence [5,19,20], at least in the context of enactive cognition. This is supported by our experimental results, which demonstrate that weakness is a far better predictor of whether a hypothesis will generalise, than description length. Weakness should not be conflated with Ockham's Razor. A simple statement need not be weak, for example "all things are blue crabs". Likewise, a complex utterance can assert nothing. Weakness is a consequence of extension, not form. If weakness is to be understood as an epistemological razor, it is this (which we humbly suggest naming "Bennett's Razor"):

Explanations should be no more specific than necessary.[12]

The Apperception Engine: The Apperception Engine [21–23] (Evans et al. of Deepmind) is an inference engine that generates hypotheses that generalise often. To achieve this, Evans formalised Kant's philosophy to give the engine a "strong inductive bias". The engine forms hypotheses from only very general

---

[12] We do not know which possibilities will eventuate. A less specific statement contradicts fewer possibilities. Of all hypotheses sufficient to explain what we perceive, the least specific is most likely.

assertions, meaning logical formulae which are universally quantified. That is possible because the engine uses language specifically tailored to efficiently represent the sort of sequences to which it is applied. Our results suggest a simpler and more general explanation of why the engine's hypotheses generalise so well. The tailoring of logical formulae to represent certain sequences amounts to a choice of $\mathfrak{v}$, and the use of only universally quantified logical formulae maximises the weakness of the resulting hypothesis. To apply this approach to induction from child $\mathfrak{v}$-task α to parent ω would mean we only entertain a model $m \in M_\alpha$ if $p(m \in M_\omega \mid m \in M_\alpha) = 1$. Obviously this can work well, but only for the subset of possible tasks that the vocabulary is able to describe in this way (anything else will not be able to be represented as a universally quantified rule, and so will not be represented at all [24]). This illustrates how future research may explore choices of $\mathfrak{v}$ in aid of more efficient induction in particular sorts of task, such as the inference of linguistic meaning and intent (see appendix).

Neural Networks: How might a task be represented in the context of conventional machine learning? Though we use continuous real values in base 10 to formalise neural networks, all computation still takes place in a discrete, finite and binary system. A finite number of imperative programs composed a finite number of times may be represented by a finite set of declarative programs. Likewise, activations within a network given an input can be represented as a finite set of declarative programs, expressing a decision. The choice of architecture specifies the vocabulary in which this is written, determining what sort of relations can be described according to the Chomsky Hierarchy [25]. The reason why LLMs are so prone to fabrication and inconsistency may be because they are optimised only to minimise loss, rather than maximise weakness [10]. Perhaps grokking [26] can be induced by optimising for weakness. Future research should investigate means by which weakness can be maximised in the context of neural networks.

Acknowledgement. Appendices available on GitHub [1], supported by JST (JPMJMS2033).

References

1. Bennett, M.T.: Technical Appendices. Version 1.2.1 (2023). https://doi.org/10.5281/zenodo.7641742. https://github.com/ViscousLemming/Technical-Appendices
2. Sober, E.: Ockham's Razors: A User's Manual. Cambridge University Press (2015)
3. Rissanen, J.: Modeling by shortest data description*. Automatica **14**, 465–471 (1978)
4. Chollet, F.: On the Measure of Intelligence (2019)
5. Chaitin, G.: The limits of reason. Sci. Am. **294**(3), 74–81 (2006)
6. Solomonoff, R.: A formal theory of inductive inference. Part I. Inf. Control **7**(1), 1–22 (1964)

7. Solomonoff, R.: A formal theory of inductive inference. Part II. Inf. Control **7**(2), 224–254 (1964)
8. Kolmogorov, A.: On tables of random numbers. Sankhya: Indian J. Stati. A 369–376 (1963)
9. Hutter, M.: Universal Artificial Intelligence: Sequential Decisions Based on Algorithmic Probability. Springer, Heidelberg (2010)
10. Bennett, M.T.: Symbol emergence and the solutions to any task. In: Goertzel, B., Iklé, M., Potapov, A. (eds.) AGI 2021. LNCS (LNAI), vol. 13154, pp. 30–40. Springer, Cham (2022). https://doi.org/10.1007/978-3-030-93758-4_4
11. Ward, D., Silverman, D., Villalobos, M.: Introduction: the varieties of enactivism. Topoi **36**(3), 365–375 (2017). https://doi.org/10.1007/s11245-017-9484-6
12. Harnad, S.: The symbol grounding problem. Physica D: Nonlinear Phenomena **42**(1), 335–346 (1990)
13. Leike, J., Hutter, M.: Bad universal priors and notions of optimality. In: Proceedings of the 28th COLT, PMLR, pp. 1244–1259 (2015)
14. Gupta, A.: Definitions. In: Zalta, E.N. (ed.) The Stanford Encyclopedia of Philosophy. Winter 2021. Stanford University (2021)
15. Paszke, A., et al.: PyTorch: an imperative style, high-performance deep learning library. In: NeurIPS. Curran Association Inc., USA (2019)
16. Kirk, D.: NVIDIA Cuda Software and GPU parallel computing architecture. In: ISMM 2007, Canada, pp. 103–104. ACM (2007)
17. Meurer, A., et al.: SymPy: symbolic computing in Python. PeerJ Comput. Sci. **3**, e103 (2017). https://doi.org/10.7717/peerj-cs.103
18. Hart, P.E., Nilsson, N.J., Raphael, B.: A formal basis for the heuristic determination of minimum cost paths. IEEE Trans. Syst. Sci. Cybern. **4**(2), 100–107 (1968)
19. Hernández-Orallo, J., Dowe, D.L.: Measuring universal intelligence: towards an anytime intelligence test. Artif. Intell. **174**(18), 1508–1539 (2010)
20. Legg, S., Veness, J.: An approximation of the universal intelligence measure. In: Dowe, D.L. (ed.) Algorithmic Probability and Friends. Bayesian Prediction and Artificial Intelligence. LNCS, vol. 7070, pp. 236–249. Springer, Heidelberg (2013). https://doi.org/10.1007/978-3-642-44958-1_18
21. Evans, R.: Kant's cognitive architecture. Ph.D. thesis. Imperial (2020)
22. Evans, R., Sergot, M., Stephenson, A.: Formalizing Kant's rules. J. Philos. Logic **49**, 613–680 (2020)
23. Evans, R., et al.: Making sense of raw input. Artif. Intell. **299** (2021)
24. Bennett, M.T.: Compression, the fermi paradox and artificial super-intelligence. In: Goertzel, B., Iklé, M., Potapov, A. (eds.) AGI 2021. LNCS (LNAI), vol. 13154, pp. 41–44. Springer, Cham (2022). https://doi.org/10.1007/978-3-030-93758-4_5
25. Delétang, G., et al.: Neural Networks and the Chomsky Hierarchy (2022)
26. Power, A., et al.: Grokking: generalization beyond overfitting on small algorithmic datasets. In: ICLR (2022)

Emergent Causality and the Foundation of Consciousness

Michael Timothy Bennett$^{(\boxtimes)}$ ⓘ

The Australian National University, Canberra, Australia
`michael.bennett@anu.edu.au`
`http://www.michaeltimothybennett.com/`

Abstract. To make accurate inferences in an interactive setting, an agent must not confuse passive observation of events with having intervened to cause them. The *do* operator formalises interventions so that we may reason about their effect. Yet there exist pareto optimal mathematical formalisms of general intelligence in an interactive setting which, presupposing no explicit representation of intervention, make maximally accurate inferences. We examine one such formalism. We show that in the absence of a *do* operator, an intervention can be represented by a variable. We then argue that variables are abstractions, and that need to explicitly represent interventions in advance arises only because we presuppose these sorts of abstractions. The aforementioned formalism avoids this and so, initial conditions permitting, representations of relevant causal interventions will emerge through induction. These emergent abstractions function as representations of one's self and of any other object, inasmuch as the interventions of those objects impact the satisfaction of goals. We argue that this explains how one might reason about one's own identity and intent, those of others, of one's own as perceived by others and so on. In a narrow sense this describes what it is to be aware, and is a mechanistic explanation of aspects of consciousness.

Keywords: causality · theory of mind · self aware AI · AGI

1 Introduction

An agent that interacts in the world cannot make accurate inferences unless it distinguishes the passive observation of an event from it having intervened to cause that event [2,3]. Say we had two variables $R, C \in \{true, false\}$, where:

$$C = true \leftrightarrow \text{``Larry put on a raincoat''} \text{ and } R = true \leftrightarrow \text{``It rained''}$$

Assume we have seen it rain only when Larry had his raincoat on, and he has only been seen in his raincoat during periods of rain. Based on these observations, the conditional probability of it raining if Larry is wearing his raincoat is $p(R = true \mid C = true) = 1$. A naive interpretation of this is that we can make it rain

© The Author(s), under exclusive license to Springer Nature Switzerland AG 2023
P. Hammer et al. (Eds.): AGI 2023, LNAI 13921, pp. 52–61, 2023.
https://doi.org/10.1007/978-3-031-33469-6_6

by forcing Larry to wear a raincoat, which is absurd. When we intervene to make Larry wear a raincoat, the event that takes place is not *"Larry put on a raincoat"* but actually *"Larry put on a raincoat because we forced him to"*. It is not that Bayesian probability is wrong, but interactivity complicates matters. By intervening we are acting upon the system from the outside, to disconnect those factors influencing the choice of clothing. The "do" operator [4,5] resolves this in that $do[C = true]$ represents the intervention. It allows us to express notions such as $p(R = true \mid do[C = true]) = p(R = true) \neq p(R = true \mid C = true) = 1$, which is to say that intervening to force Larry to wear a raincoat has no effect on the probability of rain, but passively observing Larry put on a raincoat still indicates rain with probability 1. To paraphrase Judea Pearl, one variable causes another if the latter listens for the former [2]. The variable R does not listen to the C. C however does listen to R, meaning to identify cause and effect imposes a hierarchy on one's representation of the world (usually represented with a directed acyclic graph). This suggests that, if accurate inductive inference is desired, we must presuppose something akin to the *do* operator. Yet there exist pareto optimal mathematical formalisms of general intelligence in an interactive setting which, given no explicit representation of intervention, make maximally accurate inferences [1,6,7]. Given that the distinction between observation and intervention is necessary to make accurate inductive inferences in an interactive setting, this might seem to present us with a contradiction. One cannot accurately infer an equivalent of the *do* operator if such a thing is a necessary precondition of accurate inductive inference. We resolve this first by showing that we can substitute an explicit *do* operator with variables representing each intervention. Then, using one of the aforementioned formalisms, we argue that need to explicitly represent intervention as a variable only arises if we presuppose abstractions [8] like variables. If induction does not depend upon abstractions as given, then abstractions representing interventions may emerge through inductive inference. Beyond distinguishing passive observation from the consequences of one's own interventions, these emergent abstractions can also distinguish between the interventions and observations of others. This necessitates the construction of abstract identities and intents. We suggest this is a mechanistic explanation of awareness, in a narrow sense of the term. By narrow we mean functional, access, and phenomenal consciousness, and only if the latter is defined as "first person functional consciousness" [9,10]; recognising phenomenal content such as light, sound and movement with one's body at the centre of it all [11]. To limit scope, we do not address "the hard problem" [12].

2   Additional Background

This section introduces relevant background material. The reader may wish to skip ahead to section 3 and refer here as needed. In recognition of the philosophical nature of this topic we present arguments rather than mathematical proofs, and the paper should be understandable without delving too deeply into the math. While all relevant definitions are given here, context is provided by the papers in which these definitions originated, and in technical appendices available on GitHub [1]. To those more familiar with the agent environment paradigm, how exactly these definitions formalise cognition may seem unclear. Neither agent nor environment are defined. This is because it is a formalism of enactivism [13], which holds that cognition extends into and is enacted within the environment. What then constitutes the agent is unclear. In light of this, and in the absence of any need to define an agent absent an environment, why preserve the distinction? Subsequently, the agent and environment are merged to form a task [7], which may be understood as context specific manifestations of intent, or snapshots of what bears some resemblance to "Being-in-the-world" as described by Heidegger [14]. In simpler terms, this reduces cognition to a finite set of decision problems [7]. One infers a model from past interactions, and then makes a decision based upon that model (akin to a supervised learner fitting a function to labelled data, then using that to generate labels for unlabelled data). Arguments as to why only finite sets are relevant are given elsewhere [15, p. 2].

2.1   List of Definitions

Refer to the technical appendices [1] for further information regarding definitions.

Definition 1 (environment)

- *We assume a set Φ whose elements we call **states**, one of which we single out as the **present state**.*
- *A **declarative program** is a function $f : \Phi \to \{true, false\}$, and we write P for the set of all declarative programs. By an **objective truth** about a state ϕ, we mean a declarative program f such that $f(\phi) = true$.*

Definition 2 (implementable language)

- *$\mathfrak{V} = \{V \subset P : V \text{ is finite}\}$ is a set whose elements we call **vocabularies**, one of which[1] we single out as **the vocabulary** $\mathfrak{v}$ for an implementable language.*
- *$L_{\mathfrak{v}} = \{l \subseteq \mathfrak{v} : \exists \phi \in \Phi \ (\forall p \in l : p(\phi) = true)\}$ is a set whose elements we call **statements**. $L_{\mathfrak{v}}$ follows from Φ and $\mathfrak{v}$. We call $L_{\mathfrak{v}}$ an **implementable language**.*
- *$l \in L_{\mathfrak{v}}$ is **true** iff the present state is ϕ and $\forall p \in l : p(\phi) = true$.*
- *The **extension of a statement** $a \in L_{\mathfrak{v}}$ is $Z_a = \{b \in L_{\mathfrak{v}} : a \subseteq b\}$.*
- *The **extension of a set of statements** $A \subseteq L_{\mathfrak{v}}$ is $Z_A = \bigcup_{a \in A} Z_a$.*

(Notation) *Z with a subscript is the extension of the subscript[2].*

Definition 3. ($\mathfrak{v}$-task). *For a chosen $\mathfrak{v}$, a task α is $\langle S_\alpha, D_\alpha, M_\alpha \rangle$ where:*

- *$S_\alpha \subset L_{\mathfrak{v}}$ is a set whose elements we call **situations** of α.*

---

[1] The vocabulary $\mathfrak{v}$ we single out represents the sensorimotor circuitry with which an organism enacts cognition - their brain, body, local environment and so forth.

[2] e.g. Z_s is the extension of s.

- S_α has the extension Z_{S_α}, whose elements we call **decisions** of α.
- $D_\alpha = \{z \in Z_{S_\alpha} : z \text{ is correct}\}$ is the set of all decisions which complete α.
- $M_\alpha = \{l \in L_\mathfrak{v} : Z_{S_\alpha} \cap Z_l = D_\alpha\}$ whose elements we call **models** of α.

$\Gamma_\mathfrak{v}$ is the set of all tasks for our chosen $\mathfrak{v} \in \mathfrak{V}$.

(Notation) If $\omega \in \Gamma_\mathfrak{v}$, then we will use subscript ω to signify parts of ω, meaning one should assume $\omega = \langle S_\omega, D_\omega, M_\omega \rangle$ even if that isn't written.

(How a task is completed) Assume we've a $\mathfrak{v}$-task ω and a hypothesis $h \in L_\mathfrak{v}$ s.t.

1. we are presented with a situation $s \in S_\omega$, and
2. we must select a decision $z \in Z_s \cap Z_h$.
3. If $z \in D_\omega$, then z is correct and the task is complete. This occurs if $h \in M_\omega$.

Definition 4 (probability). We assume a uniform distribution over $\Gamma_\mathfrak{v}$.

Definition 5 (generalisation). A statement l generalises to $\alpha \in \Gamma_\mathfrak{v}$ iff $l \in M_\alpha$. We say l generalises from α to $\mathfrak{v}$-task ω if we first obtain l from M_α and then find it generalises to ω.

Definition 6 (child and parent). A $\mathfrak{v}$-task α is a child of $\mathfrak{v}$-task ω if $S_\alpha \subset S_\omega$ and $D_\alpha \subseteq D_\omega$. This is written as $\alpha \sqsubset \omega$. If $\alpha \sqsubset \omega$ then ω is then a parent of α.

Definition 7 (weakness). The weakness of $l \in L_\mathfrak{v}$ is $|Z_l|$.

Definition 8 (induction). α and ω are $\mathfrak{v}$-tasks such that $\alpha \sqsubset \omega$. Assume we are given a proxy $q_\mathfrak{v} \in Q$, the complete definition of α and the knowledge that $\alpha \sqsubset \omega$. We are not given the definition of ω. The process of induction would proceed as follows:

1. Obtain a hypothesis by computing a model $h \in \arg\max_{m \in M_\alpha} q_\mathfrak{v}(m)$.
2. If $h \in M_\omega$, then we have generalised from α to ω.

2.2 Premises

For the purpose of argument we will adopt the following premises:

(prem. 1) To maximise the probability that induction generalises from α to ω, it is necessary and sufficient to maximise weakness. [1]

For our argument this optimality is less important than the representation of interventions it implies. In any case the utility of weakness as a proxy is not limited to lossless representations or optimal performance. Approximation may be achieved by selectively forgetting outliers[3], a parallel to how selective amnesia

---

[3] For example, were we trying to generalise from α to ω (where $\alpha \sqsubset \omega$) and knew the definition of α contained misleading errors, we might selectively forget outlying decisions in α to create a child $\gamma = \langle S_\gamma, D_\gamma, M_\gamma \rangle$ (where $\gamma \sqsubset \alpha$) such that M_γ contained far weaker hypotheses than M_α.

[16] can help humans reduce the world to simple dichotomies [17] or confirm pre-conceptions [18]. Likewise, a task expresses a threshold beyond which decisions are "good enough" [19]. The proof of optimality merely establishes the upper bound for generalisation. As a second premise, we shall require the emergence or presupposition of representations of interventions:

> **(prem. 2)** To make accurate inductive inferences in an interactive setting, an agent must not confuse the passive observation of an event with having intervened to cause that event. [2]

3   Emergent Causality

The formalism does not presuppose an operator representing intervention. Given our premises, we must conclude from this that either that **(prem. 1)** is false, or induction as in Definition 8 will distinguish passive observation of an event from having intervened to cause that event.

3.1   The *do* Operator as a Variable in Disguise

In the introduction we discussed an example involving binary variables R (rain) and C (raincoat). From $p(R = true \mid C = true) = 1$ we drew the absurd conclusion that if we intervene to make $C = true$, we can make it rain. The true relationship between R and C is explained by a directed acyclic graph:

The intervention $do[C = c]$ deletes an edge (because rain can have no effect on the presence of a coat we've already forced Larry to wear) giving the following:

By intervening in the system, we are acting upon it from the outside. In doing so we disconnect those factors influencing the choice of clothing. The *do* operator lets us express this external influence. However, if we don't have a *do* operator there remains another option. We propose representing an intervention with a variable, so that we are no longer intervening in the system from outside. For example $do[C = true]$ might be represented by A such that $p(C = true \mid A = true) = 1$ and $p(C \mid A = false) = p(C)$:

We can now represent that $p(R = true \mid C = true, A = true) = p(R = true) \neq p(R = true \mid C = true, A = false) = 1$. This expands the system to include an action by a specific actor, rather than accounting for interventions originating outside the system (as the *do* operator does).

3.2   Emergent Representation of Interventions

This does not entirely resolve our problem. Even if intervention is represented as a variable, that variable must still be explicitly defined before accurate induction can take place. It is an abstract notion which is presupposed. Variables are undefined in the context of Definitions 1, 2 and 3 for this very reason. Variables tend to be very abstract (for example, "number of chickens" may presuppose both a concept of chicken and a decimal numeral system), and the purpose (according to [7] and [19]) of the formalism is to construct such abstractions via induction. It does so by formally defining reality (environment and cognition within that) using as few assumptions as possible [1], in order to address symbol grounding [8] and other problems associated with dualism. In this context, cause and effect are statements as defined in Definition 2. Returning to the example of Larry, instead of variables A, C and R we have a vocabulary $\mathfrak{v}$, and $c, r \in L_{\mathfrak{v}}$ which have a truth value in accordance with Definition 2:

$$c \leftrightarrow \text{``Larry put on a raincoat''} \text{ and } r \leftrightarrow \text{``It rained''}$$

As before, assume we have concluded $p(r \mid c) = 1$ from passive observation, the naive interpretation of which is that we can make it rain by forcing Larry to wear a coat. However, the statement associated with this intervention is not just $c =$ "Larry put on a raincoat" but a third $a \in L$ such that:

$$a \leftrightarrow \text{``Larry put on a raincoat because we forced him to''}$$

Because we're now dealing with statements, and because statements are sets of declarative programs which are inferred rather than given, we no longer need to explicitly define interventions in advance. Statements in an implementable language represent sensorimotor activity, and are formed via induction [1,7]. The observation of c is part of the sensorimotor activity a, meaning $c \subseteq a$ (if Larry is not wearing his raincoat, then it also cannot be true that we are forcing him to wear it). There is still no do operator, however $i = a - c$ may be understood as representing the identity of the party undertaking the intervention. If $i \neq \emptyset$ then it is at least possible to distinguish intervention from passive observation, in the event that a and c are relevant (we still need explain under what circumstances this is true). Whether intervention and observation are indistinguishable depends upon the vocabulary V, the choice of which determines if $i = \emptyset$, or $i \neq \emptyset$ (the latter meaning that it is distinguishable). Thus interventions are represented, but only to the extent that the vocabulary permits.

Definition 9 (intervention). *If a is an intervention to force c, then $c \subseteq a$. Intervention is distinguishable from observation only where $c \subset a$.*

3.3 When Will Induction Distinguish Intervention From Observation?

From **(prem. 1)** we have that choosing the weakest model maximises the probability of generalisation. There are many combinations of parent and child task for which generalisation from child to parent is only possible by selecting a model that correctly distinguishes the effects of intervention from passive observation (a trivial example might be a task informally defined as "predict the effect of this intervention"). It follows that to maximise the probability of generalisation in those circumstances the weakest model must distinguish between an intervention a and what it forces, c, so long as **(prem. 2)** is satisfied as in Definition 9, s.t. $a \neq c$.

4   Awareness

We have described how an intervention a is represented as distinct from that which it forces, c. Induction will form models representing this distinction in tasks for which this aids completion. Now we go a step further. Earlier we discussed $i = a - c$ as the identity of the party undertaking an intervention a. We might define a weaker identity as $k \subset i$, which is subset of any number of different interventions undertaken by a particular party. The *do* operator assumes the party undertaking interventions is given, and so we might think of k above as meaning "me". However, there is no reason to restrict emergent representations of intervention only to one's self. For example there may exist Harvey, who also intervenes to force c. It follows we may have v such that $c \subset v$, and v represents our observation of Harvey's intervention.

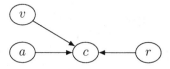

If $k \subseteq a - c$ can represent our identity as party undertaking interventions, it follows that $j \subseteq v - c$ may represent Harvey's. Both identities are to some extent context specific (another intervention may produce something other than j, or a subset of j, for Harvey), but these emergent identities still exist as a measurable quantity independent of the interventions with which they're associated.

Definition 10 (identity). *If a is an intervention to force c, then $k \subseteq a - c$ may function as an identity undertaking the intervention if $k \neq \emptyset$.*

One's own identity is used to distinguish interventions from passive experiences to facilitate accurate inductive inference in an interactive setting. It follows from **(prem. 1)** that every object that has an impact upon one's ability to complete tasks must *also* have an identity[4], because failing to account for the interventions of these objects would result in worse performance.

---

[4] Assuming interventions are distinguishable.

4.1   Intent

The formalism we are discussing originated as a mechanistic explanation of the-ory of mind called "The Mirror Symbol Hypothesis" [19], and of meaning in virtue of intent [7] (similar to Grice's foundational theory of meaning [20]). A statement is a set of declarative programs, and can be used as a goal constraint as is common in AI planning problems [21]. In the context of a task a model expresses such a goal constraint, albeit integrated with how that goal is to be satisfied [1,7]. If one is presented with several statements representing decisions, and the situations in which they were made (a task according to Definition 3), then the weakest statement with which one can derive the decisions from the situations (a model) is arguably the *intent* those decisions served [7]. Thus, if identity k experiences interventions undertaken by identity j, then k can infer something of the intent of j by constructing a task definition and computing the weakest models [7]. This is a mechanistic explanation of how it is *possible* that one party may infer another's intent. Assuming induction takes place according to Definition 8, then it is also *necessary* to the extent that k affect's j's ability to complete tasks. Otherwise, j's models would not account for j's interventions and so performance would be negatively impacted. However, a few interventions is not really much information to go on. Humans can construct elaborate ratio-nales for behaviour given very little information, which suggests there is more to the puzzle. The Mirror Symbol Hypothesis argues that we fill in the gaps by projecting our own emergent symbols (either tasks or models, in this context) representing overall, long term goals and understanding onto others in order to construct a rationale for their immediate behaviour [7], in order to empathise.

4.2   How Might We Represent the Mirror Symbol Hypothesis?

Assume there exists a task Ω which describes every decision k might ever make which meets some threshold of "good enough" [7,19] at a given point in time.

Definition 11 (higher and lower level statements). *A statement $c \in L$ is higher level than $a \in L$ if $Z_a \subset Z_c$, which is written as $a \sqsubseteq c$.*

A model $m_\Omega \in M_\Omega$ is k's "highest level" intent or goal (given the threshold), meaning $Z_\Omega = D_\Omega$. Using m_Ω and k's observation of decision d made in situation s by j (the observation of which would also be a decision), k could construct a lower level model $m_\omega \sqsubseteq m_\Omega$ such that $d \in Z_s \cap Z_{m_\omega}$. In other words, m_ω is a rationale constructed by k to explain j's intervention. Related work explores this in more depth [7,19]. For our purposes it suffices to point out that in combining emergent causality, identity, The Mirror Symbol Hypothesis [19] and symbol emergence [7], we have a mechanistic explanation of the ability to reason about one's own identity and intent, and that of others, in terms of interventions. Likewise the ability to predict how one's own intent is modelled by another is also of value in predicting that other's behaviour. In tasks of the sort encountered by living organisms, optimal performance would necessitate identity k constructing a model of j's model of k, and $j's$ model of $k's$ model of j and so on to the greatest extent permitted by ʋ (the finite memory and any other limitations one's ability to represent predictions of predictions of predictions ad infinitum).

4.3 Consciousness

We have described a means by which an agent may be aware of itself, of others, of the intent of others and of the ability of others to model its own intent. By aware, we mean it has *access* to and will function according to this information (access and functional consciousness, contextualising everything in terms of identities and their intent). Boltuc argues that phenomenal consciousness (characterised as first person functional consciousness) is explained by today's machine learning systems [10]. We would suggest his argument extends to our formalism, and in any case if qualia are a mechanistic phenomenon then they are already represented by the vocabulary of the implementable language. What is novel in our formalism is not just that it points out that causal inference may construct identity and awareness, but that it does so with a formulation that also addresses enactive cognition, symbol emergence and empathy [7,19].

Anthropomorphism: An implementation of what we have described would construct an identity for anything and everything affecting its ability to complete tasks - even inanimate objects like tools, or features of the environment. Intent would be ascribed to those identities, to account for the effect those objects have upon one's ability to satisfy goals. Though this might seem a flaw, to do anything else would negatively affect performance. Interestingly, this is consistent with the human tendency [22] to anthropomorphise. We ascribe agency and intent to inanimate objects such as tools, the sea, mountains, the sun, large populations that share little in common, things that go bump in the night and so forth.

Fragmented Identities: It is also interesting to consider what this says of systems which are less than optimal (do not identify the weakest hypothesis), or which do not use a vocabulary which permits the construction of one identity shared by all of the interventions it undertakes. Such a thing might construct multiple unconnected identities for itself, and ascribe different intentions to each one. Likewise if the model constructs multiple identities for what is in fact the same object, it may hallucinate and hold contradictory beliefs about that object.

Acknowledgement. Appendices available on GitHub [1], supported by JST (JPMJMS2033).

References

1. Bennett, M.T.: Technical Appendices. Version 1.2.1 (2023). https://doi.org/10.5281/zenodo.7641742.   https://github.com/ViscousLemming/Technical-Appendices

2. Pearl, J., Mackenzie, D.: The Book of Why: The New Science of Cause and Effect, 1st edn. Basic Books Inc, New York (2018)
3. Ortega, P.A., et al.: Shaking the foundations: delusions in sequence models for interaction and control. Deepmind (2021)
4. Pearl, J.: Causal diagrams for empirical research. Biometrika **82**(4), 669–688 (1995)
5. Pearl, J.: Causality, 2nd edn. Cambridge University Press, Cambridge (2009)
6. Hutter, M.: Universal Artificial Intelligence: Sequential Decisions Based on Algorithmic Probability. Springer, Heidelberg (2010). https://doi.org/10.1007/b138233
7. Bennett, M.T.: Symbol emergence and the solutions to any task. In: Goertzel, B., Iklé, M., Potapov, A. (eds.) AGI 2021. LNCS (LNAI), vol. 13154, pp. 30–40. Springer, Cham (2022). https://doi.org/10.1007/978-3-030-93758-4_4
8. Harnad, S.: The symbol grounding problem. Phys. D: Nonlinear Phenom. **42**(1), 335–346 (1990)
9. Franklin, S., Baars, B.J., Ramamurthy, U.: A phenomenally conscious robot? In: APA Newsletter on Philosophy and Computers, vol. 1 (2008)
10. Boltuc, P.: The engineering thesis in machine consciousness. Techné Res. Philos. Technol. **16**(2), 187–207 (2012)
11. Block, N.: The harder problem of consciousness. J. Philos. **99**(8), 391 (2002)
12. Chalmers, D.: Facing up to the problem of consciousness. J. Conscious. Stud. **2**(3), 200–219 (1995)
13. Ward, D., Silverman, D., Villalobos, M.: Introduction: the varieties of enactivism. Topoi **36**(3), 365–375 (2017). https://doi.org/10.1007/s11245-017-9484-6
14. Wheeler, M.: Martin heidegger. In: Zalta, E.N. (ed.) The Stanford Encyclopedia of Philosophy. Fall 2020. Stanford University (2020)
15. Bennett, M.T., Maruyama, Y.: Intensional Artificial Intelligence: From Symbol Emergence to Explainable and Empathetic AI. Manuscript (2021)
16. Bekinschtein, P., et al.: A retrieval-specific mechanism of adaptive forgetting in the mammalian brain. Nat. Commun. **9**(1), 4660 (2018)
17. Berlin, S.B.: Dichotomous and complex thinking. Soc. Serv. Rev. **64**(1), 46–59 (1990)
18. Nickerson, R.S.: Confirmation bias: a ubiquitous phenomenon in many guises. Rev. Gen. Psychol. **2**(2), 175–220 (1998)
19. Bennett, M.T., Maruyama, Y.: Philosophical specification of empathetic ethical artificial intelligence. IEEE Trans. Cogn. Dev. Syst. **14**(2), 292–300 (2022)
20. Grice, H.P.: Studies in the Way of Words. Harvard University Press, Cambridge (2007)
21. Kautz, H., Selman, B.: Planning as satisfiability. In: IN ECAI 1992, pp. 359–363. Wiley, New York (1992)
22. Urquiza-Haas, E.G., Kotrschal, K.: The mind behind anthropomorphic thinking: attribution of mental states to other species. Anim. Behav. **109**, 167–176 (2015)

The M Cognitive Meta-architecture as Touchstone for Standard Modeling of AGI-Level Minds

Selmer Bringsjord[✉], James T. Oswald, Michael Giancola, Brandon Rozek, and Naveen Sundar Govindarajulu

Rensselaer AI and Reasoning (RAIR) Lab, Department of Cognitive Science, Department of Computer Science, Lally School of Management (1st auth), Rensselaer Polytechnic Institute (RPI), Troy, NY 12180, USA
selmer.bringsjord@gmail.com

Abstract. We introduce rudiments of the cognitive meta-architecture M (majuscule of μ and pronounced accordingly), and of a formal procedure for determining, with M as touchstone, whether a given cognitive architecture X_i (from among a finite list $1 \ldots k$ of modern contenders) conforms to a minimal standard model of a human-level AGI mind. The procedure, which for ease of exposition and economy in this short paper is restricted to arithmetic cognition, requires of a candidate X_i, (1), a true biconditional expressing that for any human-level agent a, a property possessed by this agent, as expressed in a declarative mathematical sentence $s(a)$, holds if and only if a formula $\chi_i(\mathfrak{a})$ in the formal machinery/languages of X_i holds as well ($\mathfrak{a}$ being an in-this-machinery counterpart to natural-language name a). Given then that M is such that $s(a)$ iff $\mu(\mathfrak{m})$, where the latter formula is in the formal language of M, with $\mathfrak{m}$ the agent modeled in M, a minimal standard modeling of an AGI-level mind is certifiably achieved by X_i if, (2), it can be proved that $\chi_i(\mathfrak{a})$ iff $\mu(\mathfrak{a})$. We conjecture herein that such confirmatory theorems can be proved with respect to both cognitive architectures NARS and SNePS, and have other cognitive architectures in our sights.

Keywords: standard modeling of AGI-level minds · cognitive architectures · computational logic

1 Arithmetic as the Initial Target

Despite florid heraldry from Kissinger et al. [14] announcing an "intellectual revolution" caused by the arrival of ChatGPT and its LLM cousins of today, we know that AGI has not arrived. This is so because, as Arkoudas [3] has elegantly pointed out in a comprehensive analysis, ChatGPT doesn't know that 1 is not greater than 1, and surely AGI subsumes command of elementary arithmetic on

P. Hammer et al. (Eds.): AGI 2023, LNAI 13921, pp. 62–73, 2023.
https://doi.org/10.1007/978-3-031-33469-6_7

the natural numbers.[1] We do not pick the domain of arithmetic here randomly. Arithmetic, and more generally all or at least most of logico-mathematics, is by our lights the only cross-cutting and non-negotiable space we can presently turn to in order to at least be in position to judge whether some artificial agent qualifies as having AGI versus merely AI. Given this, we turn first to arithmetic cognition to enable us to share our formal procedure for using the cognitive meta-architecture M as a touchstone for determining whether a candidate cognitive architecture conforms to a minimal standard modeling of AGI-level minds.

2 The Formal Procedure, for Arithmetic Cognition

2.1 Peano Arithmetic to Anchor Arithmetic Cognition

To anchor arithmetic cognition as a proper part of mathematical cognition at the human level, we resort herein to simple arithmetic with only addition and multiplication. The particular axiom system we bring to bear is 'Peano Arithmetic,' or just—to use the conventional label—**PA**. Unassuming as it may be, it has a storied place in the history of logic and mathematics, serving as the basis for such stunning results as Gödel's incompleteness theorems.[2] In particular, we shall employ herein a simple theorem in **PA**, viz., $\vdash 2 + 2 = 4$. In the general form of our procedure, not merely arithmetic cognition, but all of mathematical cognition reduced to formal logic by reverse mathematics will be in play, which means that not just the likes of $2 + 2 = 4$ but any statements provable from the axioms i.e. $\mathbf{PA}^{\vdash}$ known to be sufficient for all of mathematics, as charted by the definitive [24], will be fair game.

2.2 Definition of the Procedure

Let $s(a)$ be a mathematical declarative sentence involving both a mathematically cognizing agent a and a single purely arithmetic proposition believed by a. Such

---

[1] This example is but the tip of an iceberg of negative knowledge in the realm of mathematics for this and indeed all present and foreseeable LLMs, as Arkoudas shows/explains. Note that Bubeck et al. [8] have made the figurative claim that GPT-4 has—and we quote—"sparks of AGI." We don't know what this metaphorical claim means mathematically (thus confessedly find little meaning in it), but clearly by conversational implication these authors would themselves agree that while GPT-4 is an AI, it's an AGI. If x has sparks of being an R, then x isn't an R—this is the principle at the root of the implication here.

[2] We shall not spend the considerable time that would be needed to list the (countably infinite) axioms, and explain them. Readers can consult the elegant [9] for nice coverage of **PA** (and illuminating commentary on this axiom system). There are theories of arithmetic even simpler than **PA**, because **PA** includes an axiom relating to mathematical induction, and the simpler systems leave this axiom aside. For example, readers unfamiliar with mathematical induction can, if motivated, consult the induction-free theory of arithmetic known as 'Robinson Arithmetic,' or sometimes just as 'Q;' for elegant coverage, see [5].

sentences typically draw from both natural language (e.g. English) and formal languages. Here's an example of such a sentence: "Gödel believed that first-order logic is complete." We know he believed this because his dissertation centered around the landmark proof of this completeness. But this example is far too complex for our present limited purposes. Accordingly, turning to **PA**, here's a much simpler example of a form that will guide us, put in the present tense:

$$\text{"Gödel believes that } 2 + 2 = 4\text{."}$$

The general form is that some agent a is denoted, that agent has the epistemic attitude of belief, and the target of that belief is a proposition, expressible in **PA**, that $2 + 2 = 4$. We shall denote the form this way: $s(a)$, to indicate that our sentence form must involve an agent a; we leave belief and the believed proposition implicit.

Next, let '$\mu(\mathfrak{m})$' be a formula in M, in a suitable formal language that logicizes $s(a)$. Minimally, this language will have an epistemic modal operator for belief, and will be able to encode arithmetic propositions from natural language. Therefore, the language will need to be a quantified modal one whose extensional component is at least first-order logic. Now, the following is by inspection the case with respect to μ:[3]

$$s(a) \text{ iff } \mu(\mathfrak{m}).$$

Next, let X_i be any cognitive architecture that aspires to enable standard modeling (and simulation) of AGI-level minds. What is needed from this cognitive architecture is, (1), the truth of this biconditional:

$$s(a) \text{ iff } \chi_i(\mathfrak{c}).$$

Standard modeling of an AGI-level mind, given the foregoing, is achieved by X_i if, (2), it can be proved that[4]

$$\chi_i(\mathfrak{c}) \text{ iff } \mu(\mathfrak{m}).$$

We conjecture that such confirmatory theorems can be proved with respect to both cognitive architectures NARS and SNePS, to which, resp., we shortly turn. But first we give a very quick overview of the nature of M itself.

3   The M Cognitive Meta-architecture: Key Attributes

M is not a new cognitive architecture intended and designed to compete with the likes of Soar and ACT-R and so on as a platform to model and simulate human

---

[3] The formula in the case of M itself is

$$\mu(\mathfrak{m}) := (\texttt{believes! m t (= (+ (s (s 0)) (s (s 0))) (s (s (s (s 0)))))}),$$

where **s** is the successor function and 0 is primitive, but technical details regarding M are outside of current scope.

[4] The kernel of the procedure just described was first adumbrated in [4].

and/or AGI cognition. There are innumerable competing architectures in play today [15], all directly reflecting the particular predilections of their human creators and developers.[5] M is for assessing and harmonizing these "particularist" architectures at a meta level, and is marked by the following three distinguishing attributes:

- *Non-Partisan.* M is not designed to advance any particular convictions about the nature of cognition, and is in this regard unlike the typical cognitive architecture. To mention just one example, certainly Soar was originally conceived to commit to and build upon the conviction that a key part of human cognition centers around *condition-action rules.* Many other examples of particularist convictions could be enumerated here for many competing cognitive architectures. In stark contrast, M reflects the attitude that any partisan advocacy militates against standardization; instead, the attitude is to move as soon as possible to formalization using the discipline of formal logic. Of course, no *particular* logic is to be locked into in any way as long as its a quantified modal one whose extensional component is at least first-order logic.
- *Thoroughgoingly Formal: Axiomatic and Theorem-based.* M is inseparably aligned with a purely formal view of science and engineering, according to which whatever phenomena is observed and to be deeply understood and predicted should be axiomatized. The axiomatization of mathematics is now mature (and is the initial focus in the application of M as touchstone for whether a given cognitive architecture can minimally be used for standard modeling and simulation of AGI-level mind), and the axiomatization of physics is now remarkably mature; consider for example that not only classical mechanics is long done [19], but special relativity is largely captured [2], and advances are fast being made on general relativity and quantum mechanics. M is based on the assumption that this level of high maturity should now be applied to intelligence, so that matters can be theorem-based.
- *Minimalist.* Given all the resources formal science offers for capturing cognition, use of M is guided by a minimalist approach. The smaller and simpler is the logical system that can be used to capture a target, the better.

4   Applying the Procedure

In this short paper, we cannot fully chronicle the application of our procedure to candidate cognitive architectures. But we attempt to partially justify our optimism that both the cognitive architectures NARS and SNePS will yield in each case the needed theorem by virtue of which standard modeling is confirmed.

---

[5] We conjecture that the set of all of these architectures is pairwise inconsistent, but leave this disturbing prospect aside for subsequent investigation via M.

4.1   Exploration of NARS

What is $\chi_i(\mathfrak{a})$ for NARS? The sentence $s(a)$ says that a believes $2 + 2 = 4$ to be a true statement, and we shall assume the counterpart to agent a is the NARS agent $\mathfrak{n}$, and that the formula ν is the in-system counterpart to s. Next, we note that instead of statements NARS has *judgments*: statements with associated fuzzy truth-values, consisting of a frequency $f \in [0, 1]$ that represents a degree of belief in the underlying statement, and a confidence $c \in [0, 1]$ representing how stable the belief is (Definition 3.3 in [25]). For our target of eventually demonstrating $\nu(\mathfrak{n})$ iff $\mu(\mathfrak{m})$ it will suffice[6] that we define $\nu(\mathfrak{n})$ as the statement "The NARS agent $\mathfrak{n}$ believes the judgment $2 + 2 = 4$ with a frequency of 1 (there is only positive evidence for the statement)." Formalizing this further, a NARS agent is said to *believe* a *judgment* iff it is either an *experience*, a judgment provided to the system directly, or a statement that can be derived from experiences (Definition 3.7 in [25]). Thus $\nu(\mathfrak{n})$ for a NARS agent $\mathfrak{n}$ is true by providing $2 + 2 = 4$ as a standalone experience (in our case perhaps provided by the theoretical perception system outlined in [26]).[7] Finally, the representation of the actual statement $2 + 2 = 4$ can be accomplished in a number of ways, as NARS supports the representation of relational terms that can represent arbitrary n-ary relations between terms that represent objects. One example of this representation in Narsese is $< (* \quad 2 \quad 2 \quad 4) \rightarrow add >$ where add is a term representing a relation between two summands and a sum.

Having defined $\nu(\mathfrak{n})$, we can turn to a proof sketch for $\nu(\mathfrak{n})$ iff $\mu(\mathfrak{m})$. There are multiple approaches to this proof, one particularly formal variant would be expressing NAL in one of our *cognitive calculi*—a specialized type of logical system for Theory-of-Mind reasoning[8]—in a higher-order logic and proving a bridge theorem.

Instead for economy we opt for an intuitive proof based on theoretical idealized perception systems for NARS and M. For the forward direction of biconditional proof we assume $\nu(\mathfrak{n})$. By our above definition, $\nu(\mathfrak{n})$ iff the agent $\mathfrak{n}$ experiences $2 + 2 = 4$ or has experiences that deductively[9] lead to the con-

---

[6] We hold that confidence is irrelevant here as it is a temporal property which only impacts how likely the system is to change its mind, which has use for nonmonotonic reasoning but is irrelevant to our current deduction-only explorations.

[7] Additionally we could proceed by providing any number of experiences that allow the system to derive $2 + 2 = 4$ as long as they allow the system to derive $2 + 2 = 4$ with frequency 1.

[8] Cognitive calculi build off of the notion of traditional logical systems, which consist of a formal language $\mathscr{L}$, a set of inference schemata $\mathscr{I}$, and a formal semantics $\mathscr{S}$. The most notable distinguishing factors of cognitive calculi are (1) they contain modal operators for mental states, e.g., perception, belief, obligation; and (2) they contain no model-based semantics; instead the semantics of formulae are purely inference-theoretic. That is, the semantics are expressed exclusively through the inference schemata $\mathscr{I}$. For a longer exposition of exactly what a cognitive calculus is and isn't, we refer the interested reader to Appendix A of Bringsjord et al. [7].

[9] Abductive and inductive reasoning in NARS have the resulting frequency of the conclusion depend on confidence values influenced by a system parameter; as this can

clusion $2 + 2 = 4$ with frequency 1 in $\mathfrak{n}$. Under idealized perception, this implies the existence of external representations of either s that $2 + 2 = 4$, or a set of statements $\mathcal{S}$ that imply s. The existence of these external representations means that an M agent $\mathfrak{m}$ under idealized perception would also perceive s, $\mathbf{P}(\mathfrak{m}, \cdot, s)$ or perceive the set of $\mathcal{S}$, $\bigwedge_{e \in \mathcal{S}} \mathbf{P}(\mathfrak{m}, \cdot, e)$. Since many standard cognitive calculi have inference schemata allowing perceived statements to become believed statements, and others allowing propositional reasoning on beliefs, in the first case $\mathbf{P}(\mathfrak{m}, \cdot, s) \rightarrow \mathbf{B}(\mathfrak{m}, \cdot, s)$, and in the second $\bigwedge_{e \in \mathcal{S}} \mathbf{P}(\mathfrak{m}, \cdot, e) \rightarrow \bigwedge_{e \in \mathcal{S}} \mathbf{B}(\mathfrak{m}, \cdot, e) \rightarrow \mathbf{B}(\mathfrak{m}, \cdot, s)$ which is the definition of $\mu(\mathfrak{m})$. For the backward direction of the biconditional proof, we assume $\mu(\mathfrak{m})$ to derive $\nu(\mathfrak{n})$ using the same argument outlined for the forward direction.

We thus claim that $\nu(\mathfrak{n})$ iff $\mu(\mathfrak{m})$, which confirms that NARS conforms to a minimal standard modeling of AGI-level minds.

4.2 Exploration of SNePS and GLAIR

SNePS is a KRR system, ultimately in fact a logic [22], that can be used as either a standalone system or inside others; GLAIR is a cognitive architecture designed by SNePS scientists that uses SNePS for KRR [23]. As $\gamma(\mathfrak{g})$ for GLAIR (or any agent using SNePS for KRR) depends solely on representation within SNePS at the knowledge layer of a GLAIR agent [23], we generalize and refer to $\gamma(\mathfrak{g})$ for any arbitrary agent having SNePS under its hood, henceforth referred to simply as *SNePS agents*. Any statement within a SNePS system is said to be *believed* by the system. Figure 1 shows a representation of the statement $2 + 2 = 4$ in SNePS as a network. [11] makes a distinction between a SNePS agent understanding that $2 + 2 = 4$ as declarative knowledge versus understanding what $2 + 2 = 4$ means as semantic knowledge. In this language, $\gamma(\mathfrak{g})$ can be interpreted purely in

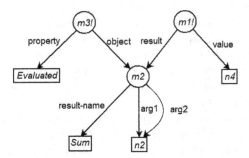

Fig. 1. A SNePS agent's belief that $2 + 2 = 4$. where $m2$ is the functional term representing a resultant Sum, from $n2$ twice; $m1$ is the proposition that $m2$ evaluates to $n4$; and $m3$ is the proposition that $m2$ has a value. (Adapted from Fig. 4.1 in [11]).

---

be arbitrary, this will not guarantee the preservation of frequency of 1 for conclusions using these modes of reasoning; thus only deductive reasoning applies here.

the sense of the representation of the declarative knowledge and is thus satisfied by the representation in Fig. 1.

We claim that $s(a)$ iff $\gamma(\mathfrak{g})$ is true by construction. Unfortunately, given current space constraints, $\gamma(\mathfrak{g})$ iff $\mu(\mathfrak{m})$ is non-trivial. Since M has a purely inferential semantics, and since SNePS allows inferences to be systematically carried out, we prove an inference-theoretic interpretation of the biconditional by showing that given some context in which $\mu(\mathfrak{m})$ is deduced (in the fashion of [6]), $\gamma(\mathfrak{g})$ can be the conclusion of valid reasoning in SNePS that uses a counterpart of this context. The left-to-right direction follows the same strategy. We thus assert that SNePS too conforms to a minimal standard modeling of AGI-level minds.

5 Related Work

Commendably, Laird et al. [16] launched a search for a standard model of the *human* mind. But their approach and ours are starkly divergent. We have no particular interest in the human mind or its embodiment in the form of earthly brains, which we regard to be adventitious relative to AGI at the human level and above. Nonetheless, realistically, at least philosophically speaking, there will be in the minds of some AI theorists overlap between the Lairdian approach and the approach we introduce herein, so we point out a second divergence: Their approach is informal, while ours is formal, i.e. theorem-driven. For good measure, a third aspect of divergence is found in the fact that while we regard the "best bet" for commonality of AGIs to be found in the arena of logic and mathematics, cognition in this area is regarded by Laird et al. to be cognitively recherché, which is borne out holistically by the absence of any discussion whatsoever of logico-mathematical cognition in [16], and more specifically by the fact that their proposed "standard model" constraints have nothing whatsoever to do with reasoning, and instead consist of the four pillars of "perception/motor", "learning," "memory and content," and "processing." Reasoning, including reasoning in connection with logico-mathematical cognition over content in formal languages, would only perhaps arise in conception in secondary, epiphenomenal fashion under the roof held up by their quartet of pillars.

We suspect some readers will think that knowledge graphs and description logics are related to our proposed procedure with M. However, care must be taken when considering this kind of work.

In practice, most knowledge-graph systems can be represented by a decidable description logic[10] (e.g. by $\mathcal{ALC}$, or $\mathcal{SHOIN}$, which are standards for most knowledge graphs), but such logics cannot capture **PA**, and they cannot capture epistemic attitudes about theorems of this axiom system. The reason is that description logics are proper fragments of first-order logic (FOL), and thus cannot express **PA**, which requires full FOL and is by Church's Theorem undecidable. Formalizing mathematics is known to require at a minimum third-order

---

[10] Some description logics have been discovered to be undecidable [20,21]. However, the core focus in the description logic community is on finding decidable fragments.

logic (M's cognitive calculi include quantified modal third-order logic) [24]. What thus may seem to be work related to ours is in the case of knowledge graphs and description logic actually not. However, our procedure can easily handle weaker, decidable theories of arithmetic, such as Presburger Arithmetic, and as a matter of fact the particular sentence $s(a)$'s component '$2 + 2 = 4$' is a valid statement in both Peano *and* Presburger Arithmetic.

6 Objections

We anticipate many objections to our new approach. We rapidly encapsulate under current space constraints two, and briefly reply to each.

6.1 "But What About Purely Numerical Approaches to AGI?"

It will be said against us: "There are approaches to rigorously capturing general intelligence at the human level and above that make no reference to the axiomatized declarative content of **PA**, let alone to the additional axiom systems to which you implicitly refer when invoking reverse mathematics for your standardization program (e.g. see [13]). Your approach is hence idiosyncratic at best, and tendentious at worst."

In reply, the key question is what those aiming at securing AGI via approaches that exclude the standardization we advocate will settle for when an artificial agent is challenged to demonstrate the power and accuracy of its mathematical cognition. Suppose that some artificial agent purportedly not only believes that $2 + 2 = 4$, but purportedly has command over **PA** overall. The key question, then, when narrowed, is: Would purely external behavior of the right sort be sufficient, or must there be some underlying structures and content associated with the behavior that enable proving a connection to formulae like μ? Large Language Models (LLMs), for example, provide an excellent context for asking this question. Suppose an LLM agent known colloquially by the name 'Larry,' based purely on deep learning, and thus completely bereft of any formulae that encode members of $\mathbf{PA}^{\vdash}$ (the closure under deduction of **PA**), is able to generate not only all sorts of sentences like the sentence s from above, but also more complicated ones, because saying any number-theoretic theorem is possible for this LLM. Let $s'(Larry)$ be "I believe that every cubic number is the sum of n consecutive odd numbers," where the indirect indexical refers to 'Larry.' And suppose that many, many other sentences are generated by Larry on this topic, where this generation is syntactically flawless, but is by definition based exclusively on underlying numerical data processing. Under this supposition, proving a bridging biconditional that links from the LLM Larry to formulae in M is impossible. This is an empirical fact.

We see this as most unfortunate, for the simple reason that science explains by virtue of finding formal theory that explains observed phenomena; physics is the paradigmatic case in point. In the case of the LLM that is ChatGPT, the empirical fact that deep formal science of the type that has always been the "golden goal" of science is completely excluded as it is in the case of Larry, has been noted recently by Wolfram [28]. Hence, the blockage by the impenetrable nature of LLMs for our M-based procedure is just something we must accept, with all of rigorous science.

6.2 "Math is Merely Manufactured"

The objection against us here can be summarized thus: "Using mathematical cognition as the cornerstone of a test for standard modeling and simulation of AGI-level minds bestows upon such cognition a kind of 'ground-truth' status. But mathematics is essentially a symbol-manipulation game legislated by human beings, as explained in [17]."

As all or at least most readers will know, while the view espoused in this objection has been defended by serious scholars (e.g. [17]), this is by no means a consensus view. There are many well-known problems that afflict the view, for instance the apparent fact that math stunningly corresponds to the behavior of the natural world [27], while formal logic has a parallel relationship with computation [12]. Yet our position, in keeping with the non-partisan nature of M itself, is to leave such debates to the side, in favor of simply observing that at the very least, going with mathematical cognition as a starting place for trying to establish a plumb-line standard modeling of AGI-level minds is rational, since if any part of cognition is likely to span minds in general it is mathematical cognition—rather than perception, motor control, natural language usage, etc.

7   Conclusion and Next Steps

Immediate next steps include delivering full proofs of our conjectures with respect to the NARS and SNePS, and expanding our procedure to include cognitive architectures beyond these two cognitive architectures. Two obvious targets are Soar and ACT-R, the latter of which promises to qualify as standard by our metrics in no small part because ACT-R has already been considered from the standpoint of formal logic (at least at the level of first-order logic; see [1,10]). We don't know what will happen in the case of Soar.[11]

---

[11] Some readers of earlier drafts of the present paper have asked us whether our procedure can be applied not just to cognitive architectures, but to artificial agents in general—for instance to the LLM agents in today's headlines. This question, alas, is at once tricky and straightforward. If the question is about *pure* LLMs, the question is straightforward, and easily answered in the negative, since cognitive attitudes directed at declarative content qua declarative content within the theory of elementary arithmetic (the full closure of **PA** under standard first-order deduction) cannot exist in such a system, which operates exclusively over data derived by tokenizing and vectorizing etc. away from quantifier-rich formula. Things become tricky when one sees that LLMs are increasingly getting "glued" to outside intelligent systems that have been engineered to handle logic-based data and to reason in accordance with inference schemata that have since Aristotle been devised for processing such data.

A significant challenge awaits us when our procedure is expanded beyond mathematical cognition into other parts of AGI-level cognition. We must be able to draw from logic-based machinery to for example formalize communication so that our key biconditionals can go through in this realm. The most severe challenge to our procedure will arise, we believe, in the case of robust attention and perception, and, having devoted time to considering perception in connection with NARS (as seen above), we are studying the attention/perception-centric cognitive architecture ARCADIA [18] now from a formal point of view.

Acknowledgments. We are grateful to two anonymous reviewers for their helpful feedback, to Paul Bello for insights regarding whether the search for a standard model of the (human) mind can bear fruit in light of the computationally resistant nature of consciousness, and to ONR (Award # N00014-22-1-2201) for partial support of the research reported herein.

References

1. Anderson, J.: Formal semantics of ACT representations. In: Language, Memory, and Thought, pp. 220–251. Lawrence Erlbaum Associates, Hillsdale (1976)
2. Andréka, H., Madarász, J.X., Németi, I., Székely, G.: A logic road from special relativity to general relativity. Synthese **186**, 633–649 (2012). https://doi.org/10.1007/s11229-011-9914-8
3. Arkoudas, K.: ChatGPT is no stochastic parrot. But it also claims that 1 is greater than 1. Philos. Technol. (forthcoming)
4. Bello, P., Bringsjord, S.: Two problems afflicting the search for a standard model of the mind. In: The 2017 Fall Symposium Series, Technical Reports FSS-17-01-FSS-17-05, pp. 296–301. Association for the Advancement of Artificial Intelligence, Palo Alto (2017). http://kryten.mm.rpi.edu/pb_sb_aaaifs2017_final.pdf. This paper specifically appears in Technical Report A Standard Model of the Mind, Laird, J., Lebiere, C., Rosenbloom, P. (eds.) A preprint of the paper can be obtained via the URL given here
5. Boolos, G.S., Burgess, J.P., Jeffrey, R.C.: Computability and Logic, 4th edn. Cambridge University Press, Cambridge (2003)
6. Bringsjord, S., Hendler, J., Govindarajulu, N.S., Ghosh, R., Giancola, M.: The (uncomputable!) meaning of ethically charged natural language, for robots, and us, from hypergraphical inferential semantics. In: Ferreira, M.I.A., Tokhi, M.O. (eds.) Towards Trustworthy Artificial Intelligent Systems. ISCA, vol. 102, pp. 143–167. Springer, Cham (2022). https://doi.org/10.1007/978-3-031-09823-9_11. http://kryten.mm.rpi.edu/UncomputableNLURobots032421.pdf
7. Bringsjord, S., Govindarajulu, N., Giancola, M.: Automated argument adjudication to solve ethical problems in multi-agent environments. Paladyn J. Behav. Robot. **12**, 310–335 (2021). http://kryten.mm.rpi.edu/AutomatedArgumentAdjudicationPaladyn071421.pdf
8. Bubeck, S., et al.: Sparks of artificial general intelligence: early experiments with GPT-4 (2023). arXiv:2303.12712v3
9. Ebbinghaus, H.D., Flum, J., Thomas, W.: Mathematical Logic, 2nd edn. Springer, New York (1994). https://doi.org/10.1007/978-1-4757-2355-7

10. Gall, D., Frühwirth, T.: A formal semantics for the cognitive architecture ACT-R. In: Proietti, M., Seki, H. (eds.) LOPSTR 2014. LNCS, vol. 8981, pp. 74–91. Springer, Cham (2015). https://doi.org/10.1007/978-3-319-17822-6_5. http://www.informatik.uni-ulm.de/pm/fileadmin/pm/home/fruehwirth/drafts/act_r_semantics.pdf

11. Goldfain, A.: A computational theory of early mathematical cognition. Ph.D. thesis, State University of New York at Buffalo (2008)

12. Halpern, J., Harper, R., Immerman, N., Kolaitis, P., Vardi, M., Vianu, V.: On the unusual effectiveness of logic in computer science. Bull. Symb. Log. **7**(2), 213–236 (2001)

13. Hutter, M.: Universal Artificial Intelligence: Sequential Decisions Based on Algorithmic Probability. Springer, Heidelberg (2005). https://doi.org/10.1007/b138233

14. Kissinger, H., Schmidt, E., Huttenlocher, D.: ChatGPT heralds an intellectual revolution. Wall Street J. (2023). The rather lengthy subtitle of this article reads: "Generative AI presents a philosophical and practical challenge on a scale not experienced since the start of the Enlightenment"

15. Kotseruba, I., Tsotsos, J.K.: A review of 40 years of cognitive architecture research: core cognitive abilities and practical applications. Artificial Intelligence. arXiv (2016)

16. Laird, J., Lebiere, C., Rosenbloom, P.: A standard model of the mind: toward a common computational framework across artificial intelligence, cognitive science, neuroscience, and robotics. AI Mag. **38**(4), 13–26 (2017). https://doi.org/10.1609/aimag.v38i4.2744

17. Lakoff, G., Nuñez, R.: Where Mathematics Comes From: How the Embodied Mind Brings Mathematics into Being. Basic Books, New York (2000)

18. Lovett, A., Bridewell, W., Bello, P.: Selection, engagement, & enhancement: a framework for modeling visual attention. In: Proceedings of the 43rd Annual Conference of the Cognitive Science Society, pp. 1893–1899. Cognitive Science Society, Vienna (2021)

19. McKinsey, J., Sugar, A., Suppes, P.: Axiomatic foundations of classical particle mechanics. J. Ration. Mech. Anal. **2**, 253–272 (1953)

20. Patel-Schneider, P.F.: Undecidability of subsumption in NIKL. Artif. Intell. **39**(2), 263–272 (1989)

21. Schmidt-Schauß, M.: Subsumption in KL-ONE is undecidable. In: KR 1989, pp. 421–431 (1989)

22. Shapiro, S.: SNePS: a logic for natural language understanding and commonsense reasoning. In: Iwanska, L., Shapiro, S. (eds.) Natural Language Processing and Knowledge Representation: Language for Knowledge and Knowledge for Language, pp. 175–195. AAAI Press/MIT Press, Menlo Park (2000)

23. Shapiro, S.C., Bona, J.P.: The GLAIR cognitive architecture. In: Biologically Inspired Cognitive Architectures II: Papers from the AAAI Fall Symposium (2009)

24. Simpson, S.: Subsystems of Second Order Arithmetic, 2nd edn. Cambridge University Press, Cambridge (2010)

25. Wang, P.: Non-Axiomatic Logic. World Scientific (2013). https://doi.org/10.1142/8665. https://www.worldscientific.com/doi/abs/10.1142/8665

26. Wang, P.: Perception in NARS. Technical report (2018). https://cis.temple.edu/tagit/publications/PAGI-TR-7.pdf

27. Wigner, E.: The unreasonable effectiveness of mathematics in the natural sciences. In: Communications in Pure and Applied Mathematics, vol. 13, pp. 1–14. Wiley, New York (1960)

28. Wolfram, S.: What Is ChatGPT Doing ...and Why Does It Work? Stephen Wolfram - Writings, 14 February 2023. https://writings.stephenwolfram.com/2023/02/what-is-chatgpt-doing-and-why-does-it-work

Causal Reasoning over Probabilistic Uncertainty

Leonard M. Eberding[1]([✉]) and Kristinn R. Thórisson[1,2]

[1] Center for Analysis and Design of Intelligent Agents,
Reykjavík U., Menntavegur 1, Reykjavík, Iceland
{leonard20,thorisson}@ru.is
[2] Icelandic Institute for Intelligent Machines, Reykjavík, Iceland

Abstract. A system deployed in the real world will need to handle uncertainty in its observations and interventions. For this, we present an approach to introduce uncertainty of state variables in causal reasoning using a constructivist AI architecture. Open questions of how noisy data can be handled and intervention uncertainty can be represented in a causal reasoning system will be addressed. In addition, we will show how handling uncertainty can improve a system's planning and attention mechanisms. We present the reasoning process of the system, including reasoning over uncertainty, in the form of a feed-forward algorithm, highlighting how noisy data and beliefs of states can be included in the process of causal reasoning.

Keywords: General Machine Intelligence · Reasoning · Uncertainty

1 Introduction

A major challenge in artificial intelligence (AI) research is the development of systems that can be deployed in the real world and can autonomously adapt to changing circumstances. Additionally, human designers want these systems to be able to generate explanations about why certain interactions were chosen and how the expected state transitions lead to the goal. While deep learning has shown massive advances in the field of data processing and identification of correlated data points, it still lacked to produce a system that is able to adapt to novel circumstances and generate satisfactory explanations [1,2,9]. Reasoning systems, on the other hand, show promising results in both adaptation and explanation generation but often lack the ability to reason over noisy and erroneous data, making deployment in the real world practically impossible, especially when it comes to low-level sensor and actuator precision.

This handling of uncertainty is at the center of research in the field of probabilistic robotics. Under the assumption of sufficiently described mathematical models of the system under control, probabilistic approaches to uncertainty

This work was funded in part by the Icelandic Research Fund (IRF) (grant number 228604-051) and a research grant from Cisco Systems, USA.

P. Hammer et al. (Eds.): AGI 2023, LNAI 13921, pp. 74–84, 2023.
https://doi.org/10.1007/978-3-031-33469-6_8

descriptions are used to handle sensor noise and actuator imprecision. The causal reasoning architecture AERA (Autocatalytic Endogenous Reflective Architecture), on the other hand, is designed to extract mathematical models of the environment and the system under control through observation and intervention. By fusing the two approaches, we present a way to overcome limitations in both fields. Learning the transition functions overcomes the necessity to model all dynamics in advance as is done in probabilistic robotics. On the other hand, the limitation to deterministic data streams is lifted from the reasoning system.

Purely probabilistic approaches as used in many Bayesian adaptive methods do not suffice for operation in ever-changing environments, as changes in the distributions of state transitions represented by the probabilistic modeling of the environment can lead to incorrect outcome predictions and erroneous decision making. Instead, we overcome this covariate shift problem [6] by building on hypothesized cause-effect patterns representing invariant world mechanisms.

To address the uncertainty of the in- and output streams, a knowledge representation is needed to enable deductive and abductive reasoning over uncertainty distributions without losing the inspectability of the reasoning processes. Using causal models to describe the state transition itself, we accompany causal models with new probabilistic models that describe the belief propagation under cause-effect structures. Our framework enables reasoning systems to support noisy data streams in both in- and output. Further, we show how such a probabilistic representation can help in describing variables to which the system needs to pay close attention and which do not need to be monitored as closely.

The paper is structured as follows: In the next section, we present related work, focusing on reasoning systems and the transferred principles from probabilistic robotics. In Sect. 3, we present the applied methodology, including a more in-depth analysis of the model structures used in AERA, assumptions that were taken for this work, and the novel approach of including probabilistic models in the reasoning process. Section 4 provides a (simplified) algorithm describing how abductive and deductive reasoning is done. Lastly, in Sect. 5, we discuss our approach in context and how the approach can produce a robust implementation of causal reasoning over probabilistic uncertainty.

2   Related Work

The Autocatalytic Endogenous Reflective Architecture (AERA) [5] follows the constructivist approach to AI, meaning that the system's knowledge base is self-constructing through experiences [7,8]. All knowledge in AERA is non-axiomatic and can be disproven at any point during its lifetime. The reasoning is done on causal models, each representing simple, linearized changes in the environment [7,8]. Coming from the cybernetics side, AERA is designed such that direct control of low-level variables is within its capabilities. Being able to extract linear equation systems from its environment by applying pattern matching on observations and interventions provides valuable functionality for AERA to be used in robotics applications.

Other reasoning systems exist that include falsifiability of their knowledge base, leading to probabilistic and non-axiomatic approaches. One example of this is the Non-Axiomatic Reasoning System (NARS) [11,12]. NARS works under the assumption of insufficient knowledge and resources (AIKR) and is able to reason about non-axiomatic truth statements which can be disproven at any time. Thus, the reasoning process includes the uncertainty of truths. Approaches like the Open-NARS-for-Applications (ONA) [4] provide a framework that can be used in some robotics applications. Another approach to represent uncertainty in the reasoning process are Probabilistic Logic Networks (PLNs) [3]. The first development of PLNs was influenced by NARS but has been extended and nowadays differs from the NARS logic considerably. Based on term logic for inference, PLNs can be used to apply logic operators on probabilistic descriptions of truth values and infer rules through de-, ab-, and inductive reasoning [3]. These approaches, however, do not include probabilistic reasoning over the belief of environment states. Instead, they are more similar to fuzzy logic systems in their description of the uncertainty of the truth of statements.

A major problem is posed by the noisiness and uncertainty of sensors and actuators. No clear, deterministic information exists for the system to reason about. Instead, it is necessary to model the uncertainty of data used in the reasoning process. Probabilistic robotics provides a framework for how to model this uncertainty using Bayesian inference [10]. Uncertainty can be described, propagated, and updated by applying Bayesian statistics and filter methods. For this, the designers of the system define the state-transition functions in advance, which will be applied during run-time. These functions are used to predict new states and observations. Additionally, the uncertainty of these predictions can be calculated as well and updated as new observations come in [10].

In probabilistic robotics, all state-transition functions must be implemented by the designer. We, on the other hand, aim to use Bayesian inference while applying learned causal models. Prediction of future changes to the environment thus becomes a chaining of different transition functions learned by the system, including the prediction of uncertainty.

3   Methodology

In the following, we provide a deeper insight into the methodology of causal reasoning applied in the AERA architecture and OpenAERA in particular before introducing the novel methodology of including probabilistic uncertainty into the reasoning process.

3.1   Autocatalytic Endogenous Reflective Architecture - AERA

Each process observed by OpenAERA is modeled by generating multiple models[1]. These models can be classified as *(anti-) requirement models* and causal

---

[1] See https://openaera.org – *accessed Apr. 6, 2023.*

models, which include *command models*, and *reuse models*. Independent of their type, each causal model represents a left-hand-side (LHS) pattern, a right-hand-side (RHS) pattern, a function that maps LHS to RHS, a function that maps RHS on LHS, and a time interval for which the model holds.

Requirement models describe the constraints under which any causal model (either command or reuse model) is applicable. It gives context to the reasoning system by providing a way that connects observations (or predictions) on the LHS with the instantiation of a causal model on the RHS. This way, the size of the search problem of identifying suitable causal models can be reduced. **Antirequirement models**, on the other hand, represent conditions under which a causal model does *not* hold. They represent strong requirements and describe hard constraints on the task-environment.

Command models are used to model the direct influence on the environment of executed commands. The LHS of command models is always a command available to the system. The RHS is the change of the environment if the command is executed. Two functions are included in the model. One function is used for forward chaining; it is used to calculate the RHS given the control input and variables passed from the requirement model. The other function is used for backward chaining, representing the inverse of the forward chaining function. For example, a move command which changes the position of OpenAERA in the environment consists of 1) the move command and the associated control input on the LHS, 2) the new position after execution on the RHS, 3) a function that calculates the new position given the old position and the control input, and 4) the inverse of the first function, which can be used to calculate the control input given the current position and the goal position.

Reuse models are used to model similar transitions without an interconnection of state variables. As each model is supposed to model only a very small number of variables to make a reflection on said models possible, reuse models are used to model more complex behaviors. Reuse models have their own requirement models such that complex constraints on complex environment state transitions can be modeled by matching LHS patterns rather than creating massive models responsible for a multitude of calculations. Such a reuse model could, for example, be used to model the changes in an object's state that OpenAERA is holding when a move command is executed. Instead of generating a single model representing the full state change of the system and the object moving simultaneously the same distance, two models are used. The move command model, as previously shown, and a reuse model with its own requirement model.

These models are used to create chains of possible state transitions from the goal to the current state (backward) and from the current state to the goal (forward). OpenAERA is thus able to reason about possible paths to reach the goal by using causal models to represent predicted state changes in the environment.

3.2   Background Assumptions

The following are assumptions underlying the present approach.

1. **Linearity**: One of the underlying architectural concepts of OpenAERA is the step-wise linearization of observed transition functions. Therefore, we assume linearity in all causal models and their uncertainty propagation.
2. **Continuity of variables**: All variables under investigation are assumed continuous in the state space. Reasoning over error-prone non-continuous variables is not part of this work. Other approaches to non-axiomatic reasoning exist for this matter, including other pattern matching and function approximations within OpenAERA.
3. **Normal distribution**: For the sake of simplification, we assume a Gaussian distribution of the measurement and actuator uncertainty. This assumption can be overcome by applying other means to predict uncertainty.
4. **Observation of state variables**: All variables are directly measurable.

3.3   Modeling of Probabilistic Uncertainty

Any artificial general intelligence (AGI) aspiring system must adapt to novel circumstances to reach a goal/ fulfill a drive under the assumption of insufficient knowledge and resources (AIKR) [12]. This means that it needs to *autonomously* adapt its resource consumption by paying attention to import variables of the task-environment that could influence the reaching of the goal. This includes paying attention to variables/phenomenons that inflict disturbances on the control problem of transforming the current state to the goal state.

By applying well-known principles from probabilistic robotics, a new model type in OpenAERA will allow it to predict errors in state transitions coming from sensor and actuator imprecision. Its existing attention algorithms are then extended to take into account variables prone to diverge from desired values due to imprecise interventions on the environment. By estimating the posteriori belief of each subsequent state that should be reached during task performance, matching posteriori with a-priori beliefs, and calculating possible overlaps, the system can predict plan divergences. Preemptive measures can then be taken by constraining the control input to achieve intermediate states with a low probability of divergence from the original plan. Probabilistic models work as follows: If, in forward chaining, any causal model represents a noiseless linear function

$$\mathbf{x}_k = \mathbf{F}\mathbf{x}_{k-1} + \mathbf{C}\mathbf{u}_{k-1} \tag{1}$$

with $\mathbf{x}$ being the n-dimensional state vector consisting of values of the set of variables $V = \{v_1, v_2, ..., v_n\}$, $\mathbf{C}$ the control matrix and $\mathbf{u}_{k-1}$ the control input.

The accompanying probabilistic model represents the propagation of uncertainty if the model is applied:

$$\mathbf{P}_k = \mathbf{F}\mathbf{P}_{k-1}\mathbf{F}^T + \mathbf{C}\mathbf{P}_{control}\mathbf{C}^T + \mathbf{Q}_k \tag{2}$$

with the a priori belief $\mathbf{P}_{k-1}$ of the state $\mathbf{x}$, the posteriori belief $\mathbf{P}_k$, the noise distribution of the command $\mathbf{P}_{control}$ and the process noise $\mathbf{Q}_{k-1}$.

These models are attached to all causal models. The current belief $\mathbf{P}_{k-1}$ is dependent on the source of the input. At the beginning of the reasoning chain, $\mathbf{P}_{k-1}$ represents the noise of the sensor whose observation led to the instantiation of the model. If the input data comes from a prediction, on the other hand, $\mathbf{P}_{k-1}$ represents the uncertainty of this prediction. Thus, models instantiated further down the chain produce a higher uncertainty in their predictions.

As all causal models in OpenAERA can be used for forward and backward chaining, the same must hold for probabilistic models. Given the fact that the modeled function can be used in both directions, it is implicit that an inverse of the function exists. Each causal model includes a noiseless backward function

$$\mathbf{x}_{k-1} = \mathbf{B}\mathbf{x}_k - \mathbf{C}\mathbf{u}_{k-1} \tag{3}$$

with $\mathbf{B}$ representing the inverse function of $\mathbf{F}$ ($\mathbf{F}^{-1}$ in most cases). The backward propagation for any probabilistic model therefore becomes

$$\mathbf{P}_{k-1} = \mathbf{B}\mathbf{P}_k\mathbf{B}^T - \mathbf{C}\mathbf{P}_{control}\mathbf{C}^T - \mathbf{Q}_k \tag{4}$$

This means that the maximum uncertainty of a goal-leading state can be calculated, providing information about the necessary precision of interventions.

Process noise provides another opportunity to optimize causal reasoning systems using uncertainty. While there exists a trade-off in most robotics applications when choosing the process noise, it can be useful when applied in a learning system. When, for example, looking at Kalman Filters, it is important for the designers to choose an appropriate process noise. Too low process noise can lead to the filter ignoring rapid deviations from the expected outcome, and too high process noise makes the filter too sensitive to noisy environments.

In the case of OpenAERA, we can assume low process noise and see deviations from the expected outcome as faulty causal models. Expected and observed outcomes should only diverge rapidly if the instantiated model does not reflect the dynamics of the observed system. This information can be used to generate new hypotheses about the true dynamics, leading to new models that describe the system better. We, therefore, neglect the estimation of process noise in this work and will extend it to include the identification of described changes to causal models in the future.

4   Reasoning Algorithm

In the following section, we give a deeper insight into the reasoning algorithm used in OpenAERA and show how uncertainty propagation can be included. We focus on the forward and backward chaining processes used in the planning of control sequences leading to the goal. Backward chaining (abductive reasoning) is used to constrain the search space to relevant models. Forward chaining (deductive reasoning) produces an executable series of commands, representing a plan of interventions to reach the goal state **g**. Both backward and forward chaining - excluding the uncertainty propagation - is already implemented in OpenAERA.

Input:

- Current set of observed variables $V_{observable}$ at time t_0 and their values describing the state $\mathbf{x}_0$ and their uncertainty $\mathbf{P}_0$.
- A goal described as a sub-state of all observable variables such that $V_{goal} \subseteq V_{observable}$ with a certain value assigned to them at a certain time t_g such that $\mathbf{x}_{t_g} = \mathbf{g}$ with a maximum uncertainty $\mathbf{P}_{t_g} = \mathbf{P}_g$
- The set of requirement and anti-requirement models M_{req}, as well as the set of causal command and reuse models M_{causal} known by the system.
- The set of probabilistic models M_{prob} which accompany the causal models.

Backward chaining is the depth-first search of possible paths from the goal to the current state using causal models and their requirements. Backward chaining goes back through time, starting at the time at which the goal is supposed to be reached t_g and stepping backward until the current time t_0 is reached.

1. Create a new, empty set of goal requirements G_{req} to be filled.
2. Create a new, empty set of currently instantiable causal models M_{causal,t_0}
3. For each requirement model $m_{req} \in M_{req}$:
    - If m_{req} can be instantiated with the current set of observations - i.e., all left-hand-side (LHS) variables can be bound to currently observable variables and fulfill all conditions of m_{req}:
    Add the instantiation of the causal model on the right-hand-side (RHS) of m_{req} to the set of currently instantiable causal models M_{causal,t_0}
4. Identify all causal models whose set of right-hand-side variables V_{RHS} overlaps that of the set of goal variables V_{goal} such that $V_{RHS} \cap V_{goal} \neq \emptyset$ and create a set from the identified model M'_{causal} with $M'_{causal} \subseteq M_{causal}$.
5. For each model $m_{causal} \in M'_{causal}$:
    (a) If $m_{causal} \in M_{causal,t_0}$:
    Continue loop.
    (b) Bind all variables of m_{causal} and its accompanying probabilistic model $m_{prob} \in M_{prob}$ that are part of g to the value of that variable in g. Leave other variables unbound to be filled during forward chaining.
    (c) Make the instantiation of m_{causal} under m_{prob} with the bound variables a goal requirement g_{req} and add it to G_{req}.
    (d) Identify all requirement models which have the instantiation of m_{causal} on their RHS, creating a subset $M'_{req} \subseteq M_{req}$.
    (e) For each requirement model $m_{req} \in M'_{req}$:
        i. Make instantiating the LHS of m_{req} a sub-goal g_{sub} with the uncertainty of the accompanying probabilistic model m_{prob} as $\mathbf{P}_{g_{sub}}$.
        ii. Set G to g_{sub} and start recursion from 4.
6. **Return** the set of bounded goal requirements G_{req}.

Forward chaining provides the deductive reasoning process in which a series of commands is identified that leads to the fulfillment of the goal requirements generated during backward chaining. Forward chaining starts at time t_0 ("now") and moves forward through time, generating predictions of outcomes of causal models.

1. Create a new, empty set of control vectors U to be executed during the task performance, which will be filled during forward chaining.
2. Set the current set of observations as the input I to the system.
3. Create a new set of models M'_{req} of all requirement models that can be instantiated with I by identifying all models whose LHS variable values' likelihood given the observations' uncertainty in I is higher than a threshold.
4. For each requirement model $m_{req} \in M'_{req}$:
   1. Check if the instantiation of the RHS causal model m_{causal} of m_{req} matches one of the goal requirements identified in backward chaining.
   2. If $m_{causal} \in G_{req}$:
      1. Use the backward function of m_{causal} to calculate the control input necessary to transition the state from the LHS to the desired RHS by binding all variables of the LHS ($\mathbf{x}_{k-1}$) to the values in I and the variables of the RHS ($\mathbf{x}_k$) to the values of the goal requirement:
      $\mathbf{Cu}_{k-1} = \mathbf{Bx}_k - \mathbf{x}_{k-1}$
      2. If m_{causal} can be instantiated given I and the control input:
         1. Apply the forward function of m_{causal} to generate a prediction of the state change:
         $\mathbf{x}_k = \mathbf{Fx}_{k-1} + \mathbf{Cu}_{k-1}$
         2. Apply the forward function of the accompanying probabilistic model to calculate an expected uncertainty after the state change:
         $\mathbf{P}_k = \mathbf{FP}_{k-1}\mathbf{F}^T + \mathbf{CP}_{control}\mathbf{C}^T + \mathbf{Q}_k$
         3. Check whether the uncertainty of goal-related variables in the calculated $\mathbf{P}_k$ is smaller than the maximum uncertainty defined in the goal requirement $\mathbf{P}_{g,req}$.
         4. If the expected uncertainty is larger:
         Plan intermediate observations by reducing the magnitude and duration of $\mathbf{u}_{k-1}$ thus reducing the actuator noise described by $\mathbf{CP}_{control}\mathbf{C}^T$ and allowing for more observations during command execution.
         5. Set the RHS of m_{causal} as a new predicted observation in I.
         6. Add the control $\mathbf{u}_{k-1}$ to U.
5. **Return** U.

The generated plan thus consists of a set of commands U, each assigned to a certain time period and given a set of input variables that must match observations at this time to perform the control with the expected outcome.

Anti-requirement Models: A special focus must be put on anti-requirement models during the reasoning process. Anti-requirement models constrain the solution space of the task by describing states under which a causal model may not be applied. (The evaluation of anti-requirement models was left out in the previous description of the algorithm for readability.) Anti-requirement models play a role in both backward and forward chaining: In backward chaining, when identifying relevant requirement models (step 5d), anti-requirement models are identified as well, and a goal requirement to *not* instantiate the LHS of the anti-requirement model is generated. In forward chaining, these anti-goal-requirements are in turn evaluated. If instantiating a causal model produces variables that are part of an anti-requirement, the likelihood of the instantiation of the anti-requirement model, given the produced uncertainty of the prediction, is calculated. If this likelihood is over a given threshold, there are three options: (1) The system can choose an alternative path, if available; (2) The magnitude and duration of control inputs can be reduced to minimize the probability of instantiating the anti-requirement model; or (3) abort the current plan and redo the abductive backward chaining process with the assumption that the model chain in question will not lead to the goal.

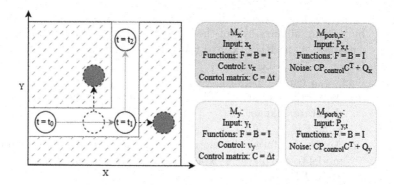

Fig. 1. Task of moving along a constraint space. Left: Visualization of the task with initial state at time t_0, goal state at time t_3. Red areas: forbidden areas where the system may not move; white circles: initial position at time t_0 and after applying the models M_x at time t_0 and M_y at time t_1; red circles: examples of failures of the task if the action of M_x is executed imprecisely. Right: Causal models M_x and M_y and their accompanying probabilistic models $M_{prob,x}$ and $M_{prob,y}$, respectively. (Color figure online)

Figure 1 shows a very simplistic task of moving along a constrained space (e.g., a robot moving in a constraint work area). As can be seen, the imprecision of executing model M_x can lead to task failure. The system can identify this during forward chaining, decrease the time during which the command of M_x is executed and thus reduce the impact of actuator imprecision. Executing the command repeatedly with intermediate observations to adjust the duration of the next command can overcome possible failure states.

5   Discussion and Future Work

We have presented a new approach that extends causal reasoning to address erroneous noisy data in the input and output stream of a controller, and shown how this is to be implemented in OpenAERA. The resulting reasoning process can better predict possible outcomes of planned interventions to adjust its plans.

The limitation to normal-distributed data can be lifted by changing the uncertainty estimation and propagation process. For example, by using neural networks to estimate the probability distributions given observations and interventions. However, it remains future work how the full reflectability and explainability of AERA in such approaches.

Aside from the application to noisy data, this approach can further be extended to use divergences between predictions and actual observations to enhance the causal discovery process. Detected outliers imply erroneous causal models, which can be corrected through self-reflection mechanisms in AERA.

References

1. Eberding, L.M.: Comparison of machine learners on an ABA experiment format of the Cart-Pole Task. In: International Workshop on Self-Supervised Learning, pp. 49–63. PMLR (2022)
2. Eberding, L.M., Thórisson, K.R., Sheikhlar, A., Andrason, S.P.: SAGE: task-environment platform for evaluating a broad range of AI learners. In: Goertzel, B., Panov, A.I., Potapov, A., Yampolskiy, R. (eds.) AGI 2020. LNCS (LNAI), vol. 12177, pp. 72–82. Springer, Cham (2020). https://doi.org/10.1007/978-3-030-52152-3_8
3. Goertzel, B., Iklé, M., Goertzel, I.F., Heljakka, A.: Probabilistic Logic Networks: A Comprehensive Framework for Uncertain Inference. Springer, New York (2008). https://doi.org/10.1007/978-0-387-76872-4
4. Hammer, P., Lofthouse, T.: 'OpenNARS for applications': architecture and control. In: Goertzel, B., Panov, A.I., Potapov, A., Yampolskiy, R. (eds.) AGI 2020. LNCS (LNAI), vol. 12177, pp. 193–204. Springer, Cham (2020). https://doi.org/10.1007/978-3-030-52152-3_20
5. Nivel, E., et al.: Bounded recursive self-improvement. arXiv preprint arXiv:1312.6764 (2013)
6. Sheikhlar, A., Eberding, L.M., Thórisson, K.R.: Causal generalization in autonomous learning controllers. In: Goertzel, B., Iklé, M., Potapov, A. (eds.) AGI 2021. LNCS (LNAI), vol. 13154, pp. 228–238. Springer, Cham (2022). https://doi.org/10.1007/978-3-030-93758-4_24
7. Thórisson, K.R.: A new constructivist AI: from manual methods to self-constructive systems. In: Wang, P., Goertzel, B. (eds.) Theoretical Foundations of Artificial General Intelligence, pp. 145–171. Springer, Paris (2012). https://doi.org/10.2991/978-94-91216-62-6_9
8. Thórisson, K.R.: Machines with autonomy & general intelligence: which methodology? In: Proceedings of the Workshop on Architectures for Generality and Autonomy (2017)
9. Thórisson, K.R.: The 'explanation hypothesis' in general self-supervised learning. In: Proceedings of Machine Learning Research, vol. 159, pp. 5–27 (2021)

10. Thrun, S.: Probabilistic robotics. Commun. ACM **45**(3), 52–57 (2002)
11. Wang, P.: Non-Axiomatic Reasoning System: Exploring the Essence of Intelligence. Indiana University (1995)
12. Wang, P.: Rigid Flexibility: The Logic of Intelligence, vol. 34. Springer, Dordrecht (2006)

Probabilistic Logic Networks for Temporal and Procedural Reasoning

Nil Geisweiller[✉] and Hedra Yusuf[✉]

SingularityNET Foundation, Amsterdam, The Netherlands
{nil,hedra}@singularitynet.io

Abstract. Probabilistic Logic Networks (PLN) offers an excellent theory to frame learning and planning as a form of reasoning. This paper offers a complement to the seminal PLN book [3], in particular to its Chapter 14 on temporal and procedural reasoning, by providing formal definitions of temporal constructs, as well as inference rules necessary to carry temporal and procedural reasoning.

Keywords: Temporal Reasoning · Procedural Reasoning · Probabilistic Logic Networks

1 Introduction

This paper builds upon the Chapter 14 of the Probabilistic Logic Networks book [3], adding and modifying definitions along the way to provide, we believe, a better foundation for carrying temporal and procedural reasoning with PLN. As we have found, even though the chapter is well written and conveys the conceptual ideas with clarity, it leaves some formal definitions out. In addition the Event Calculus [8] is intermingled with the definitions of sequential connectors in, what we consider to be, an arbitrary and inflexible manner. On the contrary, here we leave Event calculus aside, with the intention to re-introduce it in the future as a separate layer standing on top of the new definitions.

Although this paper is theoretical, the work presented here is motivated by practice, and has taken place in the context of developing a system for controlling an agent in uncertain environments while relying on temporal and procedural reasoning for both learning and planning [2].

2 Probabilistic Logic Networks Recall

PLN stands for *Probabilistic Logic Networks* [3]. It is a mixture of predicate and term logic that has been probabilitized to handle uncertainty. Inference rules can operate on direct evidence, or indirect evidence by combining existing relationships to introduce new ones. As such it is well suited for building a model of an environment, and planning in it. All it needs then is to be properly equipped with a vocabulary for representing and manipulating temporal and procedural knowledge.

P. Hammer et al. (Eds.): AGI 2023, LNAI 13921, pp. 85–94, 2023.
https://doi.org/10.1007/978-3-031-33469-6_9

2.1 Elementary Notions

Graphically speaking, PLN statements are sub-hypergraphs[1] made of *Links* and *Nodes*, called *Atoms*, decorated with *Truth Values*. Syntactically speaking, PLN statements are not very different from statements expressed in another logic, except that they are usually formatted in prefixed-operator with a tree-style indentation to emphasize their graphical nature and to leave room for their truth values. For instance

$$Implication \; \langle TV \rangle$$
$$P$$
$$Q$$

represents an implication link between P and Q with truth value TV. For the sake of conciseness we also introduce some notations. First, we adopt a flattened, as opposed to a tree-style, representation. For instance the implication link above is represented as

$$Implication(P, Q) \; \langle TV \rangle$$

Second, we introduce a more mathematically looking symbolic representation. For instance, that same implication can be represented as

$$P \to Q \stackrel{\text{m}}{=} TV$$

There is a large variety of constructs in PLN. Here, we will focus primarily on the ones for handling predicates. Let us recall that predicates are functions that output Boolean values. The domain of a predicate can be arbitrarily defined, but its range is always Boolean. In this paper, the letters a, b, c represent atoms of any type, x, y, z represent atoms that are variables, while the capital letter P, Q, R represent atoms that are predicates, thus typed as follows:

$$P, Q, R, \dots : Domain \mapsto \{True, False\}$$

Note that in PLN, predicates are not necessarily crisp because their outputs can be totally or partially unknown, thus potentially measured by probabilities, or to be precised *Truth Values*.

Truth values are, in essence, second order probability distributions, or probabilities of probabilities. They are often described by two numbers: a strength, s, representing a probability, and a confidence, c, representing the confidence over that probability. Such truth values are called *Simple Truth Values* and are denoted as follows:

$$<s, c>$$

Alternatively, the strength and the confidence of a simple truth value TV can be denoted $TV.s$ and $TV.c$ respectively. Underneath, a simple truth value is a beta

---

[1] because links can point to links, not just nodes.

distribution [1], similarly to an *opinion* in Subjective Logic [5]. The parameters of the corresponding beta distribution can be obtained as follows:

$$\alpha(s,c) = \alpha_0 + \frac{s.c.k}{1-c} \qquad \beta(s,c) = \beta_0 + \frac{(1-s).c.k}{1-c}$$

where k is a PLN parameter called the *Lookahead*, and α_0 and β_0 are usually set to 0.5 corresponding to Jeffreys prior. For truth values obtained from direct evidence, a simple truth value makes perfect theoretical sense. For truth values obtained from indirect evidence, not so much, even though they are often used in practice. When more precision is needed, to represent a multi-modal truth value for instance, a mixture of simple truth values can be used. Also, through out the paper, sometimes we may say *probability*, while what we really mean is *second order probability distribution*.

Below is a table of the constructs used in this paper with their flattened and symbolic representations, as well as precedence values to minimize parenthesis usage with the symbolic representation.

Flattened	Symbolic	Precedence
$Evaluation(P, a)$	$P(a)$	0
$Not(P)$	$\neg P$	1
$And(P, Q)$	$P \wedge Q$	2
$Or(P, Q)$	$P \vee Q$	2
$Implication(P, Q)$	$P \to Q$	4
$a\langle TV \rangle$	$a \stackrel{m}{=} TV$	5

For representing n-ary predicates evaluations we use $P(a_1, \ldots, a_n)$ which may be understood as a unary predicate evaluation applied to a tuple. Let us now explain their semantics and how their truth values are to be interpreted.

- $\neg P$ is the predicate resulting from the pointwise negation of P.
- $P \wedge Q$ is the predicate resulting from the pointwise conjunction of P and Q.
- $P \vee Q$ is the predicate resulting from the pointwise disjunction of P and Q.
- $P(a) \stackrel{m}{=} TV$ states that $P(a)$ outputs *True* with a second order probability measured by TV.
- $P \to Q \stackrel{m}{=} TV$ states that if $P(a)$ is *True* for some a in the domain of P, then $Q(a)$ is *True* with a second order probability measured by TV. In simple probability terms, it represents $\mathcal{P}r(Q|P)$, the conditional probability of Q knowing P^2. We may also say that such implication is a *conditional predicate* where Q, the *implicand*, is conditioned by P, the *implicant*.
- $P \stackrel{m}{=} TV$ states that the prevalence of P being *True* is measured by TV.

---

[2] To be precise, $\mathcal{P}r(Q|P)$ should be $\mathcal{P}r(\mathcal{S}at(Q)|\mathcal{S}at(P))$, where $\mathcal{S}at(P)$ and $\mathcal{S}at(Q)$ are the satisfying sets of P and Q respectively.

2.2   Inference Rules

Inferences rules are used to construct PLN statements and calculate their truth values. They fall into two groups, direct evidence based or otherwise. Rules from the former group infer abstract knowledge from direct evidence, while rules from the latter group infer knowledge by combining existing abstractions. In total there are dozens of inference rules. For now, we only recall two, *Implication Direct Introduction* and *Deduction*.

The Implication Direct Introduction Rule (IDI) takes evaluations as premises and produces an implication as conclusion. It can be understood as an inductive reasoning rule. It is formally depicted by the following proof tree.

$$\frac{P(a_1) \triangleq TV_1^P \qquad Q(a_1) \triangleq TV_1^Q \qquad \cdots \qquad P(a_n) \triangleq TV_n^P \qquad Q(a_n) \triangleq TV_n^Q}{P \to Q \triangleq TV} \text{(IDI)}$$

Assuming perfectly reliable direct evidence[3] then the resulting simple truth value can be calculated as follows:

$$TV.s = \frac{\sum_{i=1}^{n} f_\wedge(TV_i^P.s, \, TV_i^Q.s)}{\sum_{i=1}^{n} TV_i^P.s} \qquad\qquad TV.c = \frac{n}{n+k}$$

where $f_\wedge$ is a function embodying a probabilistic assumption about the conjunction of the events. Such function typically ranges from the product (perfect independence) to the **min** (perfect overlap). Note that this inference rule takes an arbitrary number of premises. In practice it is not a problem as it is decomposed into two rules covering the base and the recursive cases, while storing evidence to avoid double counting.

The Deduction Rule (D) takes two implications as premises and produces a third one. It can be understood as a deductive reasoning rule. Depending on the assumptions made there exists different variations of that rule. The simplest one is based on the Markov property

$$\mathcal{P}r(R|Q, P) = \mathcal{P}r(R|Q)$$

which gives rise to the rule depicted by the following proof tree.

$$\frac{P \to Q \triangleq TV^{PQ} \qquad Q \to R \triangleq TV^{QR} \qquad P \triangleq TV^P \qquad Q \triangleq TV^Q \qquad R \triangleq TV^R}{P \to R \triangleq TV} \text{(D)}$$

The reader may notice that three additional premises have been added, corresponding to the probabilities $\mathcal{P}r(P)$, $\mathcal{P}r(Q)$ and $\mathcal{P}r(R)$. This is a consequence of the Markov property. The exact formula for that variation is not recalled here but it merely derives from

$$\mathcal{P}r(R|P) = \mathcal{P}r(R|Q, P) \times \mathcal{P}r(Q|P) + \mathcal{P}r(R|\neg Q, P) \times \mathcal{P}r(\neg Q|P)$$

---

[3] A perfectly reliable piece of evidence has a confidence of 1. Dealing with unreliable evidence involves using convolution products and is outside of the scope of this paper.

More information about this derivation can be found in Chapter 5, Section 5.3 of [3]. Finally, one may notice that the same conclusion may be inferred by different inference paths leading to different truth values. How to properly aggregate these truth values is not the subject of this paper and is discussed in Chapter 5, Section 5.10 of [3].

3 Temporal Probabilistic Logic Networks

A temporal extension of PLN is defined in Chapter 14 of [3]. However, we have found that some definitions are ambiguous, in particular the sequential connectors *SequentialAnd* and *SequentialOr* redefined further below. Let us begin by defining *Temporal Predicates*, or *Fluents*. Temporal predicates are regular predicates with a temporal dimension:

$$P, Q, R, \ldots : Domain \times Time \mapsto \{ True, False \}$$

The type of the temporal dimension, *Time*, could in principle be any thing that has a minimum set of requirements, such as being an ordered semigroup or such. In practice so far, we have used integers, thus capturing a discrete notion of time. Not all temporal predicates need to have a non-temporal domain, *Domain*. In that case, we may simply assume that such domain is the unit type () and ignore it.

3.1 Temporal Operators

Let us define a set of temporal operators operating over temporal predicates.

Lag and **Lead** are temporal operators to shift the temporal dimension of a temporal predicate. They are similar to the metric variations, P_n and F_n, of the *Past* and *Future* operators of Tense Logic [7], with the distinction that they are applied over temporal predicates, as opposed to Boolean modal expressions. The *Lag* operator is formally defined as follows:

$$Lag(P, T) := \lambda x, t.P(x, t - T)$$

Meaning, given a temporal predicate P, it builds a temporal predicate shifted to the right by T time units. In order words, it allows to looks into the past, or one may say that it brings the past into the present. The *Lead* operator is the inverse of the *Lag* operator, thus

$$Lead(Lag(P, T), T) \equiv P$$

and is formally defined as follows:

$$Lead(P, T) := \lambda x, t.P(x, t + T)$$

It allows to look into the future, or one may say that it brings the future into the present.

SequentialAnd is a temporal conjunction where one of the temporal predicate arguments have been temporally shifted. There are at least two variations that can be defined. A first where the past of the first predicate is brought into the present. A second where the future of the second predicate is brought into the present. In this paper we use the second one, formally defined as

$$SequentialAnd(T, P, Q) := And(P, Lead(Q, T))$$

which results into a temporal predicate that is *True* at time t if and only if P is *True* at time t and Q is *True* at time $t + T$. Since we do not know at that point which one of the two variations is best, in practice we have implemented both, but in this paper we settle to one for the sake of simplicity.

SequentialOr is a temporal disjunction where one of the temporal predicate arguments have been temporally shifted. Like for *SequentialAnd* we settle to the variation where the future of the second predicate is brought into the present, defined as

$$SequentialOr(T, P, Q) := Or(P, Lead(Q, T))$$

which results into a temporal predicate that is *True* at time t if and only if P is *True* at time t or Q is *True* at time $t + T$.

PredictiveImplication is an implication where the future of the implicand has been brought into the present, defined as

$$PredictiveImplication(T, P, Q) := Implication(P, Lead(Q, T))$$

resulting into a conditional predicate, that in order to be defined at time t requires that P is *True* at time t, and if so, is *True* at t if and only if Q is *True* at time $t + T$.

Let us introduce a symbolic representation for these temporal constructs with precedence values to minimize parenthesis usage.

Flattened	Symbolic	Precedence
$Lag(P, T)$	$\overrightarrow{P}^T$	1
$Lead(P, T)$	$\overleftarrow{P}^T$	1
$SequentialAnd(T, P, Q)$	$P \wedge^T Q$	3
$SequentialOr(T, P, Q)$	$P \vee^T Q$	3
$PredictiveImplication(T, P, Q)$	$P \leadsto^T Q$	4

Additionally, we assume that $\wedge^T$ and $\vee^T$ are right-associative. The *Lag* (resp. *Lead*) operator is symbolized by an overlined arrow going to the right (resp. to the left) because it brings the past (resp. the future) into the present.

3.2 Temporal Rules

Given these operators we can now introduce a number of temporal inference rules.

The Predictive Implication to Implication Rule (PI) takes a predictive implication as premise and produces an equivalent implication, as depicted by the following proof tree.

$$\frac{P \rightsquigarrow^T Q \stackrel{\underline{m}}{=} TV}{P \rightarrow \overset{\leftarrow^T}{Q} \stackrel{\underline{m}}{=} TV} \text{ (PI)}$$

Note that because the conclusion is equivalent to the premise, the truth values may optionally be stripped out the rule.

$$\frac{P \rightsquigarrow^T Q}{P \rightarrow \overset{\leftarrow^T}{Q}} \text{ (PI)}$$

The Implication to Predictive Implication Rule (IP) takes an implication as premise and produces an equivalent predictive implication, as depicted, here without truth value, by the following proof tree.

$$\frac{P \rightarrow \overset{\leftarrow^T}{Q}}{P \rightsquigarrow^T Q} \text{ (IP)}$$

The Temporal Shifting Rule (S) takes a temporal predicate and shits its temporal dimension to the left or the right. An example of such rule is depicted by the following proof tree.

$$\frac{P \stackrel{\underline{m}}{=} TV}{\overset{\leftarrow^T}{P} \stackrel{\underline{m}}{=} TV} \text{ (S)}$$

Shifting does not change the truth value of the predicate. Indeed, the prevalence of being *True* remains the same, only the origin of the temporal dimension changes. Note however that the predicate itself changes, it is shifted. Therefore, unlike for the IP and PI inference rules that produce equivalent predicates, the truth values must be included in the rule definition, otherwise the rule of replacement would incorrectly apply. There are a number of variations of that rule. For the sake of conciseness we will not enumerate them all, and instead show one more variation over conditional predicates.

$$\frac{P \rightarrow Q \stackrel{\underline{m}}{=} TV}{\overset{\leftarrow^T}{P} \rightarrow \overset{\leftarrow^T}{Q} \stackrel{\underline{m}}{=} TV} \text{ (S)}$$

The Predictive Implication Direct Introduction Rule (PIDI) is similar to the implication direct introduction rule of Sect. 2 but accounts for temporal delays between evaluations. It is formalized by the following proof tree.

$$\frac{\left(P(a_i, t_i) \stackrel{\mathrm{m}}{=} TV_i^P\right)_{i=1,\ldots,n} \qquad \left(Q(a_i, t_i + T) \stackrel{\mathrm{m}}{=} TV_i^Q\right)_{i=1,\ldots,n}}{P \rightsquigarrow^T Q \stackrel{\mathrm{m}}{=} TV} \text{(PIDI)}$$

The truth value formula is identical to that of the implication direct introduction rule. In fact, such rule can be trivially derived by combining the implication direct introduction rule, the implication to predictive implication rule and the definition of the *Lead* operator.

The Temporal Deduction Rule (TD) is similar to the deduction rule of Sect. 2 but operates on predictive implications. It is formally depicted by the following proof tree.

$$\frac{P \rightsquigarrow^{T_1} Q \stackrel{\mathrm{m}}{=} TV^{PQ} \qquad Q \rightsquigarrow^{T_2} R \stackrel{\mathrm{m}}{=} TV^{QR} \qquad P \stackrel{\mathrm{m}}{=} TV^P \qquad Q \stackrel{\mathrm{m}}{=} TV^Q \qquad R \stackrel{\mathrm{m}}{=} TV^R}{P \rightsquigarrow^{T_1+T_2} R \stackrel{\mathrm{m}}{=} TV} \text{(TD)}$$

As it turns out, the truth value formula is also identical to that of the deduction rule, but the proof is not so trivial. In order to convince us that it is the case, let us construct a proof tree that can perform the same inference without requiring the temporal deduction rule. The result is depicted below

$$\cfrac{\cfrac{P \rightsquigarrow^{T_1} Q \stackrel{\mathrm{m}}{=} TV^{PQ}}{P \to \overset{\leftarrow T_1}{Q} \stackrel{\mathrm{m}}{=} TV^{PQ}} \text{(PI)} \quad \cfrac{\cfrac{Q \rightsquigarrow^{T_2} R \stackrel{\mathrm{m}}{=} TV^{QR}}{Q \to \overset{\leftarrow T_2}{R} \stackrel{\mathrm{m}}{=} TV^{QR}} \text{(PI)}}{\overset{\leftarrow T_1}{Q} \to \overset{\leftarrow T_1+T_2}{R} \stackrel{\mathrm{m}}{=} TV^{QR}} \text{(S)} \quad P \stackrel{\mathrm{m}}{=} TV^P \quad \cfrac{Q \stackrel{\mathrm{m}}{=} TV^Q}{\overset{\leftarrow T_1}{Q} \stackrel{\mathrm{m}}{=} TV^Q} \text{(S)} \quad \cfrac{R \stackrel{\mathrm{m}}{=} TV^R}{\overset{\leftarrow T_1+T_2}{R} \stackrel{\mathrm{m}}{=} TV^R} \text{(S)}}{\cfrac{P \to \overset{\leftarrow T_1+T_2}{R} \stackrel{\mathrm{m}}{=} TV}{P \rightsquigarrow^{T_1+T_2} R \stackrel{\mathrm{m}}{=} TV} \text{(IP)}} \text{(D)}$$

As you may see, the premises and the conclusion of that inference tree match exactly the premises and the conclusion of the temporal deduction rule. Since none of the intermediary formula, beside the deduction formula, alter the truth values, we may conclude that the formula of the temporal deduction rule is identical to that of the deduction rule.

3.3   Example

In this section we show how to carry an inference combining direct and indirect evidence. To illustrate this process, we consider the temporal predicates P, Q and R, with two datapoints as direct evidence of $P \rightsquigarrow^1 Q$, combined with another predictive implication, $Q \rightsquigarrow^2 P$, given as background knowledge, to produce a third predictive implication, $P \rightsquigarrow^3 R$, based on indirect evidence. The whole inference tree is given below (using $k = 100$ as *Lookahead* in the truth value formula).

$$\cfrac{\cfrac{P(1) \stackrel{\mathrm{m}}{=} <1,1> \quad P(2) \stackrel{\mathrm{m}}{=} <1,1> \quad Q(1+1) \stackrel{\mathrm{m}}{=} <0,1> \quad Q(2+1) \stackrel{\mathrm{m}}{=} <1,1>}{P \rightsquigarrow^1 Q \stackrel{\mathrm{m}}{=} <0.5, 0.02>} \text{(PIDI)} \quad Q \rightsquigarrow^2 R \stackrel{\mathrm{m}}{=} <0.3, 0.1> \quad P \stackrel{\mathrm{m}}{=} <1, 0.02> \quad Q \stackrel{\mathrm{m}}{=} <0.5, 0.02> \quad R \stackrel{\mathrm{m}}{=} <0.2, 0.5>}{P \rightsquigarrow^3 R \stackrel{\mathrm{m}}{=} <0.2, 0.018>} \text{(TD)}$$

4   Procedural Reasoning

Let us now examine how to use temporal deduction to perform a special type of procedural reasoning, to build larger plans made of smaller plans by chaining their actions. Given plans, also called *Cognitive Schematics* [4], of the form

$$C_1 \wedge A_1 \rightsquigarrow^{T_1} C_2 \overset{m}{=} TV_1$$

$$\vdots$$

$$C_n \wedge A_n \rightsquigarrow^{T_n} G \overset{m}{=} TV_n$$

expressing that in context C_i, executing action A_i may lead to subgoal C_{i+1} or goal G, after T_i time units, with a likelihood of success measured by TV_i, we show how to infer the composite plan

$$C_1 \wedge A_1 \wedge^{T_1} \ldots \wedge^{T_{n-1}} A_n \rightsquigarrow^{T_1 + \cdots + T_n} G \overset{m}{=} TV$$

alongside its truth value TV. The inferred plan expresses that in context C_1, executing actions A_i to A_n in sequence, waiting T_i time units between A_i and A_{i+1}, leads to goal G after $T_1 + \cdots + T_n$ time units, with a likelihood of success measured by TV. Note that strictly speaking, A_i is not an action, it is a predicate that captures the temporal activation of an action. This can be formalized in PLN as well but is not where the difficulty lies. Thus here we directly work with action activation predicates and refer to them as actions for the sake of convenience.

Let us show how to do that with two action plans by building a proof tree like we did for the temporal deduction rule. The final inference rule we are trying to build should look like

$$\frac{C_1 \wedge A_1 \rightsquigarrow^{T_1} C_2 \overset{m}{=} TV^{12} \qquad C_2 \wedge A_2 \rightsquigarrow^{T_2} C_3 \overset{m}{=} TV^{23} \qquad \cdots}{C_1 \wedge A_1 \wedge^{T_1} A_2 \rightsquigarrow^{T_1 + T_2} C_2 \overset{m}{=} TV}$$

where the dots are premises to be filled once we know what they are. Indeed, we cannot directly apply temporal deduction because the implicand of the first premise, C_2, does not match the implicant of the second premise, $C_2 \wedge A_2$. For that reason it is unclear what the remaining premises are. However, we can build an equivalent proof tree using regular deduction, as well as other temporal inferences rules defined in Sect. 3. The resulting tree (without truth values so that it can fit within the width of the page) is given below.

Note that we have used of a new rule labeled (I) at the left of the proof tree. This rule eliminates independent predicates from an implication without modifying the truth value of its conclusion. Its use is justified by the fact that A_2 is executed immediately *after* reaching C_2, thus cannot have an effect on it.

After retaining the premises and the conclusion only, and adding back the truth values, we obtain the following procedural deduction rule:

$$\frac{C_1 \wedge A_1 \rightsquigarrow^{T_1} C_2 \stackrel{m}{=} TV^{12} \; C_2 \wedge A_2 \rightsquigarrow^{T_2} C_3 \stackrel{m}{=} TV^{23} \; C_1 \wedge A_1 \wedge \overset{\leftarrow T_1}{A_2} \stackrel{m}{=} TV^1 \; C_2 \wedge A_2 \stackrel{m}{=} TV^2 \; C_3 \stackrel{m}{=} TV^3}{C_1 \wedge A_1 \wedge^{T_1} A_2 \rightsquigarrow^{T_1 + T_2} C_3 \stackrel{m}{=} TV} \text{(PD)}$$

with a formula identical to that of the deduction rule, once again. The premises filling the dots are therefore

$$C_1 \wedge A_1 \wedge \overset{\leftarrow T_1}{A_2} \stackrel{m}{=} TV^1 \qquad C_2 \wedge A_2 \stackrel{m}{=} TV^2 \qquad C_3 \stackrel{m}{=} TV^3$$

There is no doubt these premises could be further decomposed into sub-inferences as it was done with the (I) rule. Indeed, likely more simplifications can be made by assuming that the agent has a form of freewill and thus that its actions are independent of the rest of the universe, outside of its decision policy influenced by its very procedural reasoning. This is reminiscent of the do-calculus [6] and will be explored in more depth in the future. In the meantime, these are left as they are, as it introduces no additional assumption, and their truth values can always be calculated using inference rules based on direct evidence, if anything else. Future directions may also include adding inference rules to support behavior trees; introducing Event Calculus operators as predicate transformers (similar to how *Lag* and *Lead* are defined); as well as supporting temporal intervals and continuous time.

References

1. Abourizk, S., Halpin, D., Wilson, J.: Fitting beta distributions based on sample data. J. Constr. Eng. Manag. **120**, 288–305 (1994)
2. Geisweiller, N., Yusuf, H.: Rational OpenCog controlled agent. In: Hammer, P., et al. (eds.) AGI 2023. LNAI, vol. 13921, pp. xx–yy. Springer, Cham (2023)
3. Goertzel, B., Ikle, M., Goertzel, I.F., Heljakka, A.: Probabilistic Logic Networks. Springer, New York (2009). https://doi.org/10.1007/978-0-387-76872-4
4. Goertzel, B., et al.: Cognitive synergy between procedural and declarative learning in the control of animated and robotic agents using the OpenCogPrime AGI architecture. In: Proceedings of the AAAI Conference on Artificial Intelligence (2011)
5. Jøsang, A.: Subjective Logic: A Formalism for Reasoning Under Uncertainty, 1st edn. Springer, Cham (2016). https://doi.org/10.1007/978-3-319-42337-1
6. Pearl, J.: Causal diagrams for empirical research. Biometrika **82**, 669–688 (1995)
7. Prior, A.N.: Past, Present and Future. Clarendon Press, Oxford (1967)
8. Shanahan, M.: The event calculus explained. In: Wooldridge, M.J., Veloso, M. (eds.) Artificial Intelligence Today. LNCS (LNAI), vol. 1600, pp. 409–430. Springer, Heidelberg (1999). https://doi.org/10.1007/3-540-48317-9_17

Rational OpenCog Controlled Agent

Nil Geisweiller[(⊠)] and Hedra Yusuf[(⊠)]

SingularityNET Foundation, Amsterdam, The Netherlands
{nil,hedra}@singularitynet.io

Abstract. In this paper we introduce, ROCCA for *Rational OpenCog Controlled Agent*, an agent, that, as its name suggests, leverages the OpenCog framework to fulfill goals in uncertain environments. It attempts to act rationally, relying on reasoning for both learning and planning. An experiment in a Minecraft environment is provided as a test case.

Keywords: Symbolic Reinforcement Learning · Pattern Mining · Procedural Reasoning · Thompson Sampling · OpenCog · Minecraft

1 Introduction

This paper describes an attempt to leverage the OpenCog framework [15] for controlling agents in uncertain environments. It can be seen as a reboot of previous attempts [5,10,12] relying on new or improved components such as

- a hypergraph pattern miner [7] and a version of Probabilistic Logic Networks (PLN) [9] both implemented on top of OpenCog's Unified Rule Engine equipped with an inference control mechanism;
- a temporal and procedural extension of PLN [8];
- a simplified version of OpenPsi [5] leaving aside built-in urges and modulators from MicroPsi [3] and using an action selection policy based on Thompson Sampling [17].

It is comparable to OpenNARS for Applications (ONA) [14] but, among other differences, uses PLN [9] as its core logic.

The ultimate goal of this project is to provide a technology to enable us to experiment with forms of meta-learning and introspective reasoning for self-improvements. The rational for using a reasoning-based system is that it offers maximum transparency and is thus more amenable to reflectivity and introspection [11,19]. The work that is described in this paper is only the premise of that goal. No meta-learning is taking place yet. The objective for now is to build an agent that is able to discover regularities from its environment and acts rationally, possibly at the expense of efficiency, at least initially. For discovering regularities, the agent uses a reasoning-based pattern miner [7]. Then combine

P. Hammer et al. (Eds.): AGI 2023, LNAI 13921, pp. 95–104, 2023.
https://doi.org/10.1007/978-3-031-33469-6_10

these regularities to form plans using temporal and procedural reasoning. More specifically plans are predictive implications of the form

$$C \wedge A \leadsto^T G \overset{m}{=} TV$$

called *Cognitive Schematics* or *Schemata*. Which can be read as *"in some context C, if some, possibly composite, action A is executed, then after T time units, the goal G is likely to be fulfilled, with second order probability measured by TV"*. These plans are then combined to into a mixture that grossly approximates Solomonoff distribution [6]. Finally, the next action is selected using Thompson Sampling [17]. The resulting system is called ROCCA for *Rational OpenCog Controlled Agent*.

The rest of the paper is organized as follows. A recall of the OpenCog framework is provided in Sect. 2. ROCCA is described in Sect. 3. An experiment using it to control an agent in Minecraft is described in Sect. 4. A conclusion including future directions is given in Sect. 5.

2   OpenCog Framework Recall

OpenCog [15] is a framework offering a hypergraph database technology with a query language and a collection of programs built on top of it to perform cognitive functions such as learning, reasoning, spreading attention and more. Knowledge is stored in *AtomSpaces*, hypergraphs composed of *atoms*, *links* and *nodes*, where links can connect to other atoms. *Values* can be attached to atoms to hold probability, confidence, importance and more. Values and atoms can be of various types. Let us recall the types we need for the rest of paper.

- A *TruthValue* is a second order probability distribution, i.e. a probability of a probability.
- A *SimpleTruthValue* is a TruthValue where the second order distribution is represented by a beta distribution of parameters controlled by a *strength*, a proxy for a probability, and a *confidence* over that strength. It is denoted $<s, c>$ where s is the strength and c is the confidence.
- A *Predicate* is function from a certain domain to **Boolean**. A TruthValue can be attached to a predicate, representing the prevalence of its satisfied inputs. For instance $P \overset{m}{=} < 0.4, 0.1 >$ represents that P tends to evaluate to *True* 40% of the time, but there is a small confidence of 0.1 over that 40%. A TruthValue can be attached to individual evaluations as well. For instance $P(a) \overset{m}{=} < 0.9, 1 >$ represents that the probability of $P(a)$ evaluating over a particular a to *True*, is 0.9 and we are certain about it.
- A *Conjunction* is a link between two predicates, representing the predicate resulting from the pointwise conjunction of these two predicates. For instance $P \wedge Q \overset{m}{=} < 0.2, 0.3 >$ represents the prevalence, with strength 0.2 and confidence 0.3, of the pointwise conjunction of P and Q.
- An *Implication* is a link between two predicates, semantically representing the conditional probability between two events represented by these predicates. For instance $P \rightarrow Q \overset{m}{=} < 0.7, 0.4 >$ indicates that if $P(x)$ is *True* then there is a 70% change with a 0.4 confidence, that $Q(x)$ is also *True*.

Additionally we use the following types for temporal reasoning.

- A *Sequential Conjunction* is a link between two temporal predicates, representing the predicate resulting from the pointwise conjunction of these predicates while the second one leads by a certain time. For instance $P \wedge^T Q$ is the pointwise conjunction of P and a leading Q by T time units. Meaning that $(P \wedge^T Q)(x, t)$ is *True* if and only if $P(x, t)$ and $Q(x, t + T)$ are *True*.
- A *Predictive Implication* is a link between two temporal predicates, representing the conditional probability between two events delayed by a certain time. For instance $P \rightsquigarrow^T Q \stackrel{m}{=} <0.8, 0.5>$ indicates that if $P(x)$ is *True* then there is a 80% chance with a 0.5 confidence, that after T time units $Q(x)$ will also be *True*.

The difference between a temporal and an atemporal predicate is its domain. A temporal predicate must have at least a temporal dimension. More detail about the temporal types and their associated inference rules is provided in [8].

3 Rational OpenCog Controlled Agent

ROCCA is implemented as an observation-planning-action loop interleaved with learning and reasoning. It provides an interfacing between OpenCog and environments such as Malmo [16] or OpenAI Gym [4]. It is written in Python which is both supported by these environments and OpenCog. Figure 1 provide a graphical representation of ROCCA as if it was a single loop incorporating all steps.

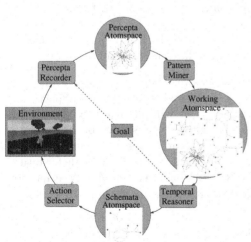

Fig. 1. Rational OpenCog Controlled Agent control and learning cycles merged into a single loop.

3.1 Memory

For better efficiency and clarity, the memory of the agent is split into three parts.

1. The *Percepta* AtomSpace holds timestamped observations as they come into the system.
2. The *Working* AtomSpace holds any kind of data, ranging from timestamped observations to predictive implications. Most knowledge used and inferred during the course of learning are usually dumped into this Atom-Space.
3. The *Schemata* AtomSpace holds *Cognitive Schematics*, which are predictive implications relating contexts, actions and goals.

3.2 Processes

The agent runs two main processes:

1. A *Control* process for real-time reactive agent control.
2. A *Learning* process for non-reactive background learning.

In principle these two processes could happen in parallel. For now they alternate in series. The agent starts in a control phase. A number of control cycles occur as the agent motor-babbles through its environment. It is then followed by a learning phase when the agent discover regularities and build plans. And finally repeats the control phase to test how it performs after learning.

3.3 Control

The control process is composed of control cycles, each decomposed into *Observation*, *Planning* and *Action* phases, as described below.

1. *Observation*:
   (a) Receive and timestamp observations, reward included, from the environment.
   (b) Store the timestamped observations in the Percepta AtomSpace.
2. *Planning*:
   (a) Select the goal for that cycle.
   (b) Find plans fulfilling that goal from the Schemata AtomSpace.
   (c) Build a mixture distribution from these plans.
3. *Action*:
   (a) Select the next action via Thompson Sampling according to that mixture distribution.
   (b) Timestamp and store the selected action in the Percepta AtomSpace.
   (c) Run the selected action and by that update the environment.

None of these steps are computationally expensive. They involve algorithms that are at most linear with the size of the Percepta and Schemata AtomSpaces. As time goes and knowledge accumulates though, it will progressively slow down. Indeed, for real-time responsiveness such control cycle should be bound by a constant. Achieving this may require to incorporate other mechanisms such as filtering and forgetting. This problem, as important as it is, is left aside for future research. Given the small environments ROCCA has been tested with, it has not been a problem so far. Let us now provide more details about these three phases.

Observation. During the observation phase, data coming from the environment are timestamped and stored in the Percepta AtomSpace with the format *datum@timestamp*. For instance if at cycle 3 the agent observes *outside(house)*, then *outside(house)@3* is inserted into the Percepta AtomSpace.

Planning. The first step of the planning phase is to select a goal G to fulfill. In the current version of ROCCA though it merely returns a constant goal which is to gain a reward within a forward window. More on goal selection can be found in [11,13]. Once the goal has been selected, the agent searches the Schemata AtomSpace with the following pattern matcher query

$$\$C \wedge \$A \rightsquigarrow^T G$$

where $\$C$ is a variable representing the context, $\$A$ is a variable representing the action, T is a time delay selected within that forward window and G is the selected goal. All returned candidates are then filtered according to their contexts, only retaining those for which the context is evaluated to *True* at the current time. Ideally, such crisp evaluation should be replaced by a second order probability evaluation of a context being *True*. This is important for contexts that have elements of uncertainty. But for the sake of simplicity, in our experiments so far, all contexts are crisply evaluated. Then from the set of valid cognitive schematics, a second order mixture distribution is built and handed to the next phase for performing action selection. The calculations used to build that second order mixture distribution is detailed in [6].

Action. The Action phase consists of the following steps:

1. Select the next action via Thompson Sampling [17] according to the mixture distribution built during the planning phase.
2. Timestamp and store the selected action in the Percepta AtomSpace.
3. Run the selected action and update the environment. If it is a composite action, only run the first primary action.

The trickiest step here is selecting the next action via Thompson Sampling. The novelty is that the second order probabilities can be leveraged by Thompson Sampling. For example, assume we have two actions, A_1 and A_2, to choose among two predictive implications

$$C_1 \wedge A_1 \rightsquigarrow^T G \stackrel{m}{=} <0.6, 0.9>$$
$$C_2 \wedge A_2 \rightsquigarrow^T G \stackrel{m}{=} <0.7, 0.1>$$

Using only the strengths of the truth values as proxy for probability of success, the choice is clear. Action A_2 should be selected, because its probability of success, which is 0.7, is greater than that of A_1, which is 0.6. However once confidence is introduced, that choice becomes less clear because the truth value of success of A_2 has a low confidence of 0.1. In that case, first order probabilities are sampled from their corresponding second order distributions, and then these probabilities are compared. The action with the maximum probability gets selected. Informally, the idea is to consider the possibilities that the agent might be living in a world where A_2 has a lower probability of success than A_1. That is the essence of Thompson Sampling. Figure 2 shows the second order distributions of the probabilities of success of A_1, in blue, and A_2, in red, for these

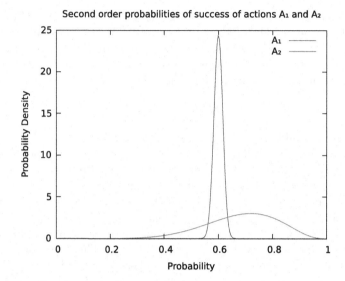

Fig. 2. Second order probability distributions of success of actions A_1 and A_2, using as parameters of the beta distribution $\alpha(s,c) = \alpha_0 + \frac{s.c.k}{1-c}$ and $\beta(s,c) = \beta_0 + \frac{(1-s).c.k}{1-c}$ where k, the *lookahead*, is set to 100, and α_0 and β_0 are set to Jeffreys prior.

truth values. As one may notice, the area under the red curve situated at the left of the blue curve is non-negligible. Meaning that the probability of being in a world where A_1 has a higher probability of success than A_2 is non-negligible as well. Because these strengths and confidences are periodically updated during the lifetime of the agent, one can see how Thompson Sampling is a great alternative to ε-greedy, as it offers a parameter-free mechanism to balance exploration and exploitation that dynamically adapts with the knowledge of the agent.

Note that in this example only two actions among two cognitive schematics are considered, but in practice there is usually a handful of actions among a potentially very large number of cognitive schematics with overlapping contexts and conflicting goals. The resulting distribution of success of each action is typically multi-modal and do not reduce to a beta distribution. How to deal with such a multitude of cognitive schematics is treated in [6].

3.4 Learning

The difficulty then comes down to discovering cognitive schematics that are as predictive and widely applicable as possible. For that, ROCCA uses a combination of pattern mining and reasoning.

Pattern Mining. A relatively inexpensive way to discover regularities in the environment is to mine the Percepta AtomSpace. For instance, given

$$\{go(right)@0,\ square(right)@1,\ go(left)@1,\ square(left)@2,...\}$$

the pattern miner can discover temporal relationships such as

$$go(right) \leadsto^1 square(right)$$
$$go(left) \leadsto^1 square(left)$$

as well as more abstract relationships, such as

$$go(x) \leadsto^1 square(x)$$

The pattern mining algorithm used by ROCCA is detailed in [7]. This is a generic hypergraph pattern miner, not specialized for temporal patterns. In order to mine temporal patterns with it, timestamps are represented as naturals. 0 is presented by Z, 1 by $S(Z)$, 2 by $S(S(Z))$, etc. This provides the needed structure to discover temporal relationships between events. As it currently stands, the pattern miner can efficiently discover mono-action plans. Mining poly-action plans is also possible but has two issues:

1. In the worse case, the computational cost of mining goes up exponentially with the size of the action sequence to mine.
2. The number of observations to accumulate in order to generate cognitive schematics with decent confidences goes up exponentially as well.

The latter is really the most problematic because we cannot buy our way out of it. If each observation takes a certain amount time, determined by the control cycle period in the case of primary observations, then we have to go through them, we cannot speed time up. This is even more true for abstract percepta that can only be observed at periods that are multiples of control cycle periods. Also, in some cases, a particular action sequence may never be observed at all, yet we still would like to have a way to estimate the likelihood of its success. In order to address these limitations and more, we need reasoning.

Temporal Reasoning. ROCCA uses a temporal extension of PLN described in [8] to update existing cognitive schematics obtained by pattern mining, and discover new cognitive schematics by combining existing ones. For instance it can infer poly-action plans by stringing mono-action plans together, as well as generalize or specialize their contexts or goals. Temporal rules integrated into ROCCA include:

1. *Predictive Implication Direct Introduction* to infer the truth value of a predictive implication from direct observations.
2. *Temporal Conditional Conjunction Introduction* to specialize a goal within a plan by considering the conjunction of existing cognitive schematics goals.
3. *Temporal Deduction* to string together small plans to form bigger ones.

The precise semantics of these rules is detailed in [8]. An example of how they are used is presented below.

4   Experiment in a Simple Minecraft Environment

In this experiment, we use Malmo [16] to construct a basic Minecraft world that comprises a house filled with diamonds and a key. The objective of the agent is to retrieve the key, located somewhere in the vicinity of the house, and then unlock the door of the house. Upon unlocking the door, the agent is able to collect a diamond and receive a reward.

The aim of the experiment is to make ROCCA learn from interacting with the Minecraft environment and collect as many diamonds as possible. To make the task easier, the primary actions and perceptions provided by Malmo have been replaced by high level actions such as *go(key)*, *go(house)* and *go(diamonds)*, as well as high level perceptions about the state of the agent such as *outside(house)*, *hold(key)* and the reward for completing a given action, *reward(1)*.

The experiment consists of two iterations of training lasting fifty control cycles each, interleaved by a learning phase of a few hours. During the first iteration, no learning is taking place as the agent has no prior knowledge. The agent randomly explores the environment. Then it enters a learning phase, discovering cognitive schematics via mining and reasoning, subsequently leading the agent to achieve more frequently its goal during the next training phase.

Let us look more closely how ROCCA discovers cognitive schematics. Given the following observations

$$\{\dots, Reward(0)@10,\ outside(house)@10,\ hold(key)@10,\ go(house)@10,$$
$$inside(house)@11,\ go(diamond)@11,\ Reward(0)@11,\ Reward(1)@12,\dots\}$$

ROCCA can mine, among many other things, the following cognitive schematic

$$hold(key) \wedge go(house) \rightsquigarrow^1 inside(house) \stackrel{m}{=}\ <0.833, 0.007>$$

Additionally, by applying the temporal conditional conjunction introduction rule on the relevant relationships, such as

$$outside(house) \wedge go(key) \rightsquigarrow^1 outside(house) \stackrel{m}{=}\ <1, 0.007>$$
$$outside(house) \wedge go(key) \rightsquigarrow^1 hold(key) \stackrel{m}{=}\ <1, 0.007>$$

the agent derives

$$outside(house) \wedge go(key) \rightsquigarrow^1 outside(house) \wedge hold(key) \stackrel{m}{=}\ <1, 0.007>$$

which, if combined with

$$outside(house) \wedge hold(key) \wedge go(house) \rightsquigarrow^1 inside(house) \stackrel{m}{=}\ <0.833, 0.007>$$

can be used by the procedural deduction rule to infer

$$outside(house) \wedge go(key) \wedge^1 go(house) \rightsquigarrow^2 inside(house) \stackrel{m}{=}\ <0.833, 0.007>$$

Continuing this reasoning process ultimately results in the discovery of an effective plan that leads to achieving the goal, such as

$$outside(house) \wedge go(key) \wedge^1 go(house) \wedge^1 go(diamond) \rightsquigarrow^3 reward(1) \stackrel{m}{=}\ <0.833, 0.005>$$

A rigorous evaluation is kept for a future paper, nonetheless our preliminary results indicate that ROCCA successfully learns the necessary cognitive schematics and, as a consequence, accumulates more rewards during the second iteration. In the first iteration the cumulative reward is around 5, then doubles to quadruples during the second iteration, depending on the random seed and other parameters. If ROCCA keeps running after that, the cumulative reward rate keeps going up because the confidences of the cognitive schematics increase, leading to more exploitation and less exploration. One may notice that some plans are not completely reliable, their strengths is below 1. That is because some actions may fail. ROCCA is suited for dealing with uncertainty and has no problem with that. These findings are encouraging but only apply to a very simple environment and may not be indicative of the overall performance of ROCCA. More experiments over more environments are required and will be pursued in future work.

The source code of ROCCA is hosted on Github [2] and a video of this experiment is available on YouTube [1].

5 Conclusion

ROCCA, a system that leverages the OpenCog framework for controlling an agent in uncertain environments has been presented. This agent is in a strong sense fully reasoning-based, from learning to planning. The advantage we believe of such approach, in spite of its current inefficiencies, is to offer greater transparency and foster greater capabilities for meta-learning and self-improvement. As such, we are only at the start of our endeavor. Towards that end, future directions include:

1. Integrate *Economic Attention Networks* [18] for *Attention Allocation*. Record attentional spreading as percepta to learn Hebbian links [18] and improve attention allocation in return.
2. Carry out concept creation and schematization, also called crystallized attention allocation, to speed up repetitive information processing. This done well should also provide a solution to the problem of creating hierarchies of abstract observations and actions.
3. Record more internal processes, not just attentional spreading, as internal percepta to enable deeper forms of introspection.
4. Plan with internal actions, not just external, such as parameter tuning and code rewriting to enable self-improvements.

References

1. ROCCA video demonstration (2022). https://youtu.be/rCvQHrJAD2c
2. ROCCA source code repository (2023). https://github.com/opencog/rocca
3. Bach, J.: MicroPsi 2: the next generation of the MicroPsi framework. In: Bach, J., Goertzel, B., Iklé, M. (eds.) AGI 2012. LNCS (LNAI), vol. 7716, pp. 11–20. Springer, Heidelberg (2012). https://doi.org/10.1007/978-3-642-35506-6_2

4. Brockman, G., et al.: OpenAI gym (2016)
5. Cai, Z., et al.: OpenPsi: a novel computational affective model and its application in video games. Eng. Appl. Artif. Intell. **26**, 1–12 (2013). https://doi.org/10.1016/j.engappai.2012.07.013
6. Geisweiller, N.: Partial operator induction with beta distributions. In: Iklé, M., Franz, A., Rzepka, R., Goertzel, B. (eds.) AGI 2018. LNCS (LNAI), vol. 10999, pp. 52–61. Springer, Cham (2018). https://doi.org/10.1007/978-3-319-97676-1_6
7. Geisweiller, N., Goertzel, B.: An inferential approach to mining surprising patterns in hypergraphs. In: Hammer, P., Agrawal, P., Goertzel, B., Iklé, M. (eds.) AGI 2019. LNCS (LNAI), vol. 11654, pp. 59–69. Springer, Cham (2019). https://doi.org/10.1007/978-3-030-27005-6_6
8. Geisweiller, N., Yusuf, H.: Probabilistic logic networks for temporal and procedural reasoning. In: Hammer, P., et al. (eds.) AGI 2023. LNAI, vol. 13921, pp. 85–94. Springer, Cham (2023)
9. Goertzel, B., Ikle, M., Goertzel, I.F., Heljakka, A.: Probabilistic Logic Networks. Springer, New York (2009). https://doi.org/10.1007/978-0-387-76872-4
10. Goertzel, B., et al.: An integrative methodology for teaching embodied non-linguistic agents, applied to virtual animals in second life. In: Proceedings of the 2008 Conference on Artificial General Intelligence 2008: Proceedings of the First AGI Conference, pp. 161–175. IOS Press, NLD (2008)
11. Goertzel, B., Pennachin, C., Geisweiller, N.: Engineering General Intelligence, Part 1: A Path to Advanced AGI via Embodied Learning and Cognitive Synergy. Atlantis Press (2014)
12. Goertzel, B., et al.: Cognitive synergy between procedural and declarative learning in the control of animated and robotic agents using the OpenCogPrime AGI architecture. In: Proceedings of the AAAI Conference on Artificial Intelligence (2011)
13. Hahm, C., Xu, B., Wang, P.: Goal generation and management in NARS. In: Goertzel, B., Iklé, M., Potapov, A. (eds.) AGI 2021. LNCS (LNAI), vol. 13154, pp. 96–105. Springer, Cham (2022). https://doi.org/10.1007/978-3-030-93758-4_11
14. Hammer, P., Lofthouse, T.: 'OpenNARS for applications': architecture and control. In: Goertzel, B., Panov, A.I., Potapov, A., Yampolskiy, R. (eds.) AGI 2020. LNCS (LNAI), vol. 12177, pp. 193–204. Springer, Cham (2020). https://doi.org/10.1007/978-3-030-52152-3_20
15. Hart, D., Goertzel, B.: OpenCog: a software framework for integrative artificial general intelligence. In: Proceedings of the 2008 Conference on Artificial General Intelligence 2008: Proceedings of the First AGI Conference, pp. 468–472. IOS Press, NLD (2008)
16. Johnson, M., Hofmann, K., Hutton, T., Bignell, D.: The Malmo platform for artificial intelligence experimentation. In: International Joint Conference on Artificial Intelligence (2016)
17. Leike, J., Lattimore, T., Orseau, L., Hutter, M.: Thompson sampling is asymptotically optimal in general environments. In: Proceedings of the Thirty-Second Conference on Uncertainty in Artificial Intelligence. UAI 2016, Arlington, Virginia, USA, pp. 417–426. AUAI Press (2016)
18. Pitt, J., Ikle, M., Sellmann, G., Goertzel, B.: Economic attention networks: associative memory and resource allocation for general intelligence. In: Proceedings of the 2nd Conference on Artificial General Intelligence, pp. 88–93. Atlantis Press, June 2009. https://doi.org/10.2991/agi.2009.19
19. Schmidhuber, J.: Goedel machines: self-referential universal problem solvers making provably optimal self-improvements. ArXiv cs.LO/0309048 (2003)

Towards Cognitive Bots: Architectural Research Challenges

Habtom Kahsay Gidey[1]([✉]) [ID], Peter Hillmann[1][ID], Andreas Karcher[1],
and Alois Knoll[2][ID]

[1] Universität der Bundeswehr München, Munich, Germany
{habtom.gidey,peter.hillmann,andreas.karcher}@unibw.de
[2] Technische Universität München, Munich, Germany
knoll@in.tum.de

Abstract. Software bots operating in multiple virtual digital platforms must understand the platforms' affordances and behave like human users. Platform affordances or features differ from one application platform to another or through a life cycle, requiring such bots to be adaptable. Moreover, bots in such platforms could cooperate with humans or other software agents for work or to learn specific behavior patterns. However, present-day bots, particularly chatbots, other than language processing and prediction, are far from reaching a human user's behavior level within complex business information systems. They lack the cognitive capabilities to sense and act in such virtual environments, rendering their development a challenge to artificial general intelligence research. In this study, we problematize and investigate assumptions in conceptualizing software bot architecture by directing attention to significant architectural research challenges in developing cognitive bots endowed with complex behavior for operation on information systems. As an outlook, we propose alternate architectural assumptions to consider in future bot design and bot development frameworks.

Keywords: cognitive bot · cognitive architecture · problematization

1 Introduction

Bots are software agents that operate in digital virtual environments [1,2]. An example scenario would be a *"user-like"* bot that could access web platforms and behave like a human user. Ideally, such a bot could autonomously sense and understand the platforms' affordances. Affordances in digital spaces are, for example, interaction possibilities and functionalities on the web, in software services, or on web application platforms [3,4]. The bot would recognize and understand the differences and variability between different environments' affordances. If a platform or service has extensions to physical bodies or devices, as in the Web of Things (WoT), it would also have control of or possibilities to interact with an outer web or service application world.

Ideally, a bot could also be independent of a specific platform. A user-like social bot, for instance, would be able to recognize and understand

P. Hammer et al. (Eds.): AGI 2023, LNAI 13921, pp. 105–114, 2023.
https://doi.org/10.1007/978-3-031-33469-6_11

social networks and act to influence or engage in belief sharing on any social platform. It would also adjust with the changes and uncertainty of the affordances in a social media environment, such as when hypermedia interactivity features and functionalities change. Such a bot could also learn and develop to derive its goals and intentions from these digital microenvironments and take goal-directed targeted action to achieve them [5]. Such bots could also communicate and cooperate with other user agents, humans, or bots to collaborate and socialize for collective understanding and behavior.

The example scenarios described above convey desiderata of perception and action in bots, similar to how a human user would perceive and act in digital spaces. To date, bots are incapable of the essential cognitive skills required to engage in such activity since this would entail complex visual recognition, language understanding, and the employment of advanced cognitive models. Instead, most bots are either conversational interfaces or question-and-answer knowledge agents [1]. Others only perform automated repetitive tasks based on pre-given rules, lacking autonomy and other advanced cognitive skills [6,7]. The problems of realizing these desiderata are, therefore, complex and challenging [8,9]. Solutions must address different areas, such as transduction and autonomous action, to achieve advanced generalizable intelligent behavior [10,11].

Problems spanning diverse domains require architectural solutions. Accordingly, these challenges also necessitate that researchers address the structural and dynamic elements of such systems from an architectural perspective. [12–14]. For this reason, this paper outlines the architectural research agendas to address the challenges in conceptualizing and developing a cognitive bot with generalizable intelligence.

The paper is divided into sections discussing each of the research challenges. In Sect. 2, we discuss the challenges related to efforts and possible directions in enabling bots to sense and understand web platforms. Next, Sect. 3 describes the challenges related to developing advanced cognitive models in software bots. Section 4 and 5 discuss the research issues in bot communication and cooperation, respectively. The remaining two sections provide general discussions on bot ethics and trust and conclude the research agenda.

2   The Transduction Problem

Web platforms can be seen as distinct microenvironments within digital microcosms [15]. They offer a microhabitat for their users' diverse digital experiences. These experiences mainly transpire from the elements of interaction and action, or the hypermedia, within web environments [15,16]. Hypermedia connects and extends the user experience, linking to further dimensions of the web-worlds, which means more pages and interactive elements from the user's perspective. The interaction elements are considered affordances in the digital space [3,4], analogous to the biological concept of affordances from environmental psychology [17]. Affordances can also be accompanied by signifiers. Signifiers reveal or indicate possibilities for actions associated with affordances [4,18]. An example on the web would be a button affording a click action and a text signifier hinting "Click to submit". A human user understands this web environment, its content, and its affordances, and navigates reasonably easily. However, enabling software bots to understand this digital environment and its affordances the way human users do is a challenging task. It is a complex problem of translating and mapping perception to action, i.e., the transduction problem [19,20].

Today, there are different approaches to this problem. The first category of approaches provides knowledge about the environment for different levels of observability using APIs or knowledge descriptions. With API-based approaches, developers create bots for a specific platform, constantly putting developers in the loop. Bots do not have the general perceptual capability to understand and navigate with autonomous variability. Other architectures in this category, originating from the WoT, attempt to address this challenge by using knowledge models and standards that could enable agents to perceive the web by exposing hypermedia affordances and signifiers [3,21]. The knowledge descriptions carry discoverable affordances and interpretable signifiers, which can then be resolved by agents [3,4]. This approach might demand extended web standards that make the web a suitable environment for software agents. It might also require introducing architectural constraints that web platforms must adhere to in developing and changing their platforms, such as providing a knowledge description where bots can read descriptions of their affordances.

The second category of approaches uses various behavioral cloning and reinforcement learning techniques [22]. One example is by Shi et al. [23], where they introduce a simulation and live training environment to enable bots to complete web interaction activities utilizing keyboard and mouse actions. Recent efforts extend these approaches by leveraging large language models (LLMs) for web page understanding and autonomous web navigation [24,25]. The results from both techniques and similar approaches reveal the size of the gap between human users and bots [23,24].

Both approach categories still need to solve the problem of variability and generalizability of perception and action. Approaches that leverage the hypermedia knowledge of platforms with affordance and signifier descriptions could serve as placeholders, but real bots with generalizable capabilities would need more autonomous models yet.

Besides this, some design assumptions consider the environment and the bot as one. As a result, they may attempt to design agents as an integrated part of the platforms or try to 'botify' and 'cognify' or orient web services as agents. Alternatively, the whole notion of a *user-like* bot inherently assumes the bot to have an autonomous presence separate from the web platforms it accesses. Figure 1 illustrates the basic perspective in a vertically separate design, the bot, and the web platforms it operates in. This strict separation enables both the environment and the bot to evolve independently.

3   The Behavior Problem

Most user activities on digital platforms are complex behaviors resulting from human users' underlying intentions, goals, and belief systems. Although a bot

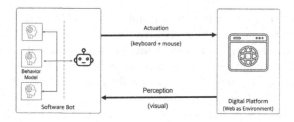

Fig. 1. A decoupled bot-environment and bot-behavior (*left*) viewpoint.

operating in digital spaces need not fully emulate humans to achieve generalizable behavior, it is essential to consider the intricacies and sophistication of human users' behavior on the web during bot design [26]. To that end, engineering bots with behavior models similar to human users might take into account existing approaches of measuring generalizable user behavior while not having to replicate human cognition as such [27].

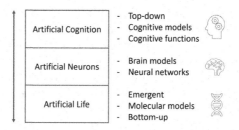

Fig. 2. The abstraction ladder in modeling machine intelligence.

Current models for engineering intelligent behavior come from three prospective categories of approaches. Each approach takes natural or human intelligence as its inspiration and models it at different levels of abstraction. The three methods differ mainly in how they try to understand intelligence and where they start the abstraction for modeling intelligence. Figure 2 illustrates this ladder of abstraction in modeling machine intelligence. The abstractions start either at artificial cognition, artificial neurons, or artificial life or consciousness [10, 28]. These abstractions aim to enact intelligent behavior based, respectively, on high-level cognitive functions, artificial neural networks (ANNs), or more physical and bottom-up approaches starting at molecular or atomic levels.

Artificial Cognition: in cognitive modeling, efforts to model cognition are inspired by the brain's high-level cognitive functions, such as memory. Most assumptions are based on studies and understandings in the cognitive sciences. Cognitive models use diverse techniques such as production rules, dynamical systems, and quantum models to model particular cognitive capabilities [29]. Although cognitive models use methods from other approaches, such as ANNs, they do not necessarily adhere to underlying mechanisms in the brain [10,30]. Works such as the OpenCog (Hyperon) and the iCub project are promising experimental research examples that heavily rely on artificial cognitive models, i.e., cognitive architectures [10,30].

Artificial Neurons: brain models which use artificial neurons aim to understand, model, and simulate underlying computational mechanisms and functions based on assumptions and studies in neuroscience [31]. Discoveries from neuroscience are utilized to derive brain-based computational principles. Sometimes, these approaches are referred to as *Brain-derived AI* or *NeuroAI* models [32–34]. Due to the attention given to the underlying principles of computation in the brain, they strictly differ from the brain-inspired cognitive models. Applications of these models are mainly advancements in artificial neural networks, such as deep learning. Large-scale brain simulation research and new hardware development in neuromorphic computing, such as *SpiNNaker* and *Loihi*, also contribute to research efforts in this area. Some neuromorphic hardware enables close adherence to brain computational principles in particular types of neural networks, such as *Spiking neural networks* [32,35]. Brain-derived AI approaches with neurorobotics aim to achieve embodiment using fully developed morphologies, which are either physical or virtual. The Neurorobotics Platform (NRP) is an example of such efforts to develop and simulate embodied systems. The NRP is a neurorobotics simulation environment which connects simulated brains to simulated bodies of robots [36].

Artificial Life (aLife): aLife attempts to model consciousness. To do this, researchers and developers start with a bottom-up approach at a physical or molecular level [28]. Most synthesizing efforts to model intelligence in artificial life are simulations with digital avatars.

In the context of bots on web platforms, employing integrated behavior models, such as the NRP and OpenCog mentioned above, is still a challenge. Thus, in addition to the proposed separation of the bot and environment, decoupling a bot's basic skeleton and behavior models is architecturally important. Figure 1, *left*, illustrates the separate structure of a bot and its behavior models. The bot's core skeleton, for example, might have sensory and interaction elements as virtual actuators that enable its operation using the keyboard and mouse actions. The vertical separation allows behavior models and bot skeletons to change independently, maintaining the possibility of dynamic coupling.

4   Bot Communication Challenges

In Multi-Agent Systems (MAS), agent-to-agent communication heavily relies on agent communication languages (ACLs) such as FIPA-ACL, standardized by the Foundation for Intelligent Physical Agents(FIPA) consortium [19,37–39]. However, in mixed reality environments, where bots and humans share and collaborate in digital spaces, communication cannot rely only on ACLs and APIs [40].

To that end, a cognitive bot with artificial general intelligence (AGI) must possess communications capabilities to address humans and software agents with diverse communication skills. Communication capabilities should include diverse possibilities like email, dialogue systems, voice, blogging, and micro-blogging.

Large language models (LLMs) have recently shown significant progress in natural language processing and visual perception that could be utilized for bot and human communication [24,25].

5   Integration and Cooperation Challenges

Researchers assert that the grand challenge in AGI remains in integrating different intelligence components to enable the emergence of advanced generalizable behavior or even collective intelligence [10,41–43]. The intelligence solutions to integrate include learning, memory, perception, actuation, and other cognitive capabilities [44]. Theories and assumptions developed by proponents include approaches based on cognitive synergy, the free energy principle, and integrated information theory [5,42,43].

In practice, however, integration and cooperation of bots are implemented mainly by utilizing methods such as ontologies, APIs, message routing, communication protocols, and middleware like the blackboard pattern [19,45,46].

From a software engineering perspective, basic architectural requirements for the context of bots operating on digital platforms are possibilities for the evolvability of bots into collective understanding with shared beliefs, stigmergy, or sharing common behavior models to learn, transfer learned experience, and evolve. Other concerns are the hosting, which could be on a cloud or individual nodes, scaling, and distribution of bots and their behavior models.

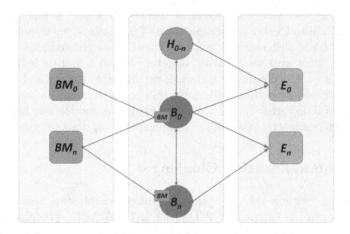

Fig. 3. Representation of integrated parts, i.e., bots, shared behavior models, and the web environments.

Figure 3 shows a simple diagram representing the integrated parts, i.e., bots, shared behavior models, and the environment. B represents the possible number of bots. BM represents the shared and individual behavior models. E represents the web environment and its variability. The lines represent communication channels. H denotes the human users that participate and share the digital space.

6   Bot Ethics and Trust

Concerns and challenges in AGI are diverse. They touch on various aspects of society and politics and have real-world implications, such as the impact of user-like bots on privacy, security, ethics, and trust with humans [47–49]. User-like bots, emulating human users' perceptual and interaction techniques, can easily pass bot detection tests and risk exploitation for malicious use cases to deceive and attack web platforms. They could also extend their perceptual capabilities beyond the web with connected devices such as microphones and cameras, affecting the personal privacy of others. Possible threats include spamming, cyberattacks to overwhelm platforms, and even unfair use of web platforms for surveillance or illicit financial gains. In WoT context, for instance, bots could affect smart factories and automated services in the real world, compromising physical devices and processes with significant security implications [50].

Hypothetically, intelligent social bots could share their beliefs on social platforms similar to or better than any human user, with superb reasoning and argumentation skills. These cases could negatively impact society by exposing people and software agents to unexpected, misaligned norms and moral beliefs. Furthermore, deploying advanced cognitive bots as digital workforces may result in unforeseen negative economic consequences. Short-term issues could include unemployment, while long-term concerns may involve ethical dilemmas surrounding bot ownership rights, bot farming, or 'enslavement' [47]. Accordingly, these ethical concerns may affect the legality of cognitive bot development, potentially impeding their engineering and deployment. Alternatively, this could introduce new legal aspects regarding regulation, standards, and ethics for integrating and governing bots within emerging socio-technical ecosystems [50].

Despite these concerns, bots' current and potential applications can positively impact numerous aspects of society. Cognitive automation, for example, is driving increased demand for cognitive agents in Industry 4.0, digital twins, and other digital environments [6,7,51]. Early implementations, like Wikipedia bots, already play a significant role in fact-checking and other knowledge-based tasks. On platforms like GitHub, bots assist and automate development tasks [52]. Future cognitive bots could also benefit society by participating in knowledge processing and providing valuable new scientific insights, such as medical advancements, which significantly outweigh their potential risks.

Today, digital platforms handle simple crawling and API-based bots with crawling policies and controlled exposure of APIs. However, advanced user-like bots like the ones envisioned in this report will require more complex mechanisms to govern and control their behavior and belief-sharing [47,50]. One approach towards this is ethics and trust by design, which recommends protocols and policies for developers and engineering organizations to incorporate trust models and ethical frameworks at the design and architectural stages [47]. Another approach proposes norms and user policies with penalties for agents to acknowledge, understand, and adhere to, similar to what human users would do on digital platforms [50,53]. In return, norm and value-aware bots could establish participation, trust, and compliance while facing the consequences of noncompliance. They may also contribute to revising and creating collective values and norms, possibly becoming part of viable socio-technical ecosystems [50,54].

However, ensuring safety and trust in such ecosystems will require diverse approaches. In addition to providing machine-readable norms and policies targeting cognitive agents, it is essential to tackle ethical and trust issues with transparent and explainable design and engineering processes at each stage. For instance, the European Union (EU) recommends a three-phase human intervention approach at the design phase, at the development and training phase, and at runtime with oversight and override possibilities [55]. As a result, research on developing advanced cognitive bots must also address critical challenges in engineering trustworthy, secure, and verifiable AGI bots employing hybrid approaches.

7   Conclusion

The study presented architectural research challenges in designing and developing a new line of user-like cognitive bots operating autonomously on digital platforms. Key challenges, such as the transduction problem, are discussed in the context of digital web platforms' access, user-like visual interaction, and autonomous navigation. In the architecture, we recommend bot-environment separation to realize bot autonomy and bot skeleton and behavior model separation for better evolvability. Also, bot communication capabilities should include diverse possibilities like email, dialogue systems, and blogging. We recommend utilizing shared behavior models for transfer learning or collective intelligence to enact generalizable behavior. Finally, we discussed cognitive bots' ethical implications and potential long-term effects, proposing to adopt hybrid approaches that incorporate these aspects into the architecture and the life cycle of bots.

As an outlook, a good starting point for future work would be to conceptualize a detailed implementation architecture and construct a bot by utilizing existing cognitive models. These systems can demonstrate the concept and allow further detailed analysis through empirical data and benchmarks.

References

1. Lebeuf, C.R.: A taxonomy of software bots: towards a deeper understanding of software bot characteristics. Ph.D. thesis, UVic (2018)
2. Etzioni, O.: Intelligence without robots: a reply to brooks. AI Mag. **14**(4), 7 (1993)

3. Charpenay, V., Amundsen, M., Mayer, S., Padget, J., Schraudner, D., Vachtsevanou, D.: 6.2 affordances and signifiers. In: Autonomous Agents on the Web, p. 67 (2021)
4. Lemee, J., Vachtsevanou, D., Mayer, S., Ciortea, A.: Signifiers for affordance-driven multi-agent systems. In: EMAS (2022)
5. Goertzel, B.: Toward a formal model of cognitive synergy. In: AGI (2017)
6. Ivančić, L., Suša Vugec, D., Bosilj Vukšić, V.: Robotic process automation: systematic literature review. In: Di Ciccio, C., et al. (eds.) BPM 2019. LNBIP, vol. 361, pp. 280–295. Springer, Cham (2019). https://doi.org/10.1007/978-3-030-30429-4_19
7. Engel, C., Ebel, P., Leimeister, J.M.: Cognitive automation. Electron. Markets 32(1), 339–350 (2022). https://doi.org/10.1007/s12525-021-00519-7
8. Russell, S.J.: Artificial Intelligence a Modern Approach. Pearson Education (2010)
9. Yampolskiy, R.V.: AI-complete, AI-hard, or AI-easy-classification of problems in AI. In: MAICS (2012)
10. Goertzel, B., Pennachin, C., Geisweiller, N.: Engineering General Intelligence, Part 1. Atlantis Thinking Machines, vol. 5. Atlantis Press, Paris (2014)
11. Vernon, D., von Hofsten, C., Fadiga, L.: Desiderata for developmental cognitive architectures. BICA 18, 116–127 (2016)
12. Goertzel, B., Pennachin, C., Geisweiller, N.: Engineering General Intelligence, Part 2, vol. 6. Springer, Heidelberg (2014). https://doi.org/10.2991/978-94-6239-030-0
13. Rosenbloom, P.S.: Thoughts on architecture. In: Goertzel, B., Iklé, M., Potapov, A., Ponomaryov, D. (eds.) AGI. MNCS, vol. 13539, pp. 364–373. Springer, Cham (2023). https://doi.org/10.1007/978-3-031-19907-3_35
14. Lieto, A., Bhatt, M., Oltramari, A., Vernon, D.: The role of cognitive architectures in general artificial intelligence. Cogn. Syst. Res. 48, 1–3 (2018)
15. Fountain, A.M., Hall, W., Heath, I., Davis, H.C.: MICROCOSM: an open model for hypermedia with dynamic linking. In: ECHT (1990)
16. Nelson, T.H.: Complex information processing: a file structure for the complex, the changing and the indeterminate. In: ACM National Conference (1965)
17. Gibson, J.J.: The theory of affordances, Hilldale, USA, vol. 1, no. 2, pp. 67–82 (1977)
18. Vachtsevanou, D., Ciortea, A., Mayer, S., Lemée, J.: Signifiers as a first-class abstraction in hypermedia multi-agent systems. In: EKAW (2023)
19. Wooldridge, M.: An Introduction to Multiagent Systems. Wiley, Hoboken (2009)
20. Brooks, R.A.: Intelligence without representation. AI 47(1–3), 139–159 (1991)
21. Ciortea, A., Mayer, S., Boissier, O., Gandon, F.: Exploiting interaction affordances: on engineering autonomous systems for the web of things (2019)
22. Gur, I., Rueckert, U., Faust, A., Hakkani-Tur, D.: Learning to navigate the web. arXiv (2018)
23. Shi, T., Karpathy, A., Fan, L., Hernandez, J., Liang, P.: World of bits: an open-domain platform for web-based agents. In: ICML, pp. 3135–3144. PMLR (2017)
24. Gur, I., et al.: Understanding HTML with large language models. arXiv (2022)
25. Huang, S., et al.: Language is not all you need: aligning perception with language models. arXiv (2023)
26. Pennachin, C., Goertzel, B.: Contemporary approaches to artificial general intelligence. In: Goertzel, B., Pennachin, C. (eds.) AGI. COGTECH, pp. 1–30. Springer, Heidelberg (2007). https://doi.org/10.1007/978-3-540-68677-4_1
27. Computing machinery and intelligence-AM turing (1950)
28. Taylor, T., et al.: WebAL comes of age: a review of the first 21 years of artificial life on the web. Artif. Life 22(3), 364–407 (2016)

29. Schöner, G.: Dynamical systems approaches to cognition. In: Cambridge Handbook of Computational Cognitive Modeling, pp. 101–126 (2008)
30. Vernon, D.: Cognitive architectures. In: Cognitive Robotics. MIT Press (2022)
31. Fan, X., Markram, H.: A brief history of simulation neuroscience. Front. Neuroinform. **13**, 32 (2019)
32. Walter, F.: Advanced embodied learning. Ph.D. thesis, TUM (2021)
33. Knoll, A., Walter, F.: Neurorobotics-a unique opportunity for ground breaking research (2019)
34. Momennejad, I.: A rubric for human-like agents and NeuroAI. Philos. Trans. **378**(1869), 20210446 (2023)
35. Maass, W.: Networks of spiking neurons: the third generation of neural network models. Neural Netw. **10**(9), 1659–1671 (1997)
36. Knoll, A., Gewaltig, M.-O., Sanders, J., Oberst, J.: Neurorobotics: a strategic pillar of the human brain project. Sci. Robot. 2–3 (2016)
37. Soon, G.K., On, C.K., Anthony, P., Hamdan, A.R.: A review on agent communication language. In: ICCST, pp. 481–491 (2019)
38. Hübner, J.F.: 4.5 about the place of agents in the web. In: Autonomous Agents on the Web, p. 44 (2021)
39. Hillmann, P., Uhlig, T., Rodosek, G.D., Rose, O.: A novel multi-agent system for complex scheduling problems. In: WSC 2014. IEEE (2014)
40. Holz, T., Campbell, A.G., O'Hare, G.M.P., Stafford, J.W., Martin, A., Dragone, M.: Mira-mixed reality agents. IJHC **69**(4), 251–268 (2011)
41. Minsky, M.: Society of Mind. Simon and Schuster (1988)
42. Tononi, G.: Integrated information theory. Scholarpedia **10**(1), 4164 (2015)
43. Friston, K.: The free-energy principle: a unified brain theory? Nat. Rev. Neurosci. **11**(2), 127–138 (2010)
44. Goertzel, B.: Artificial general intelligence: concept, state of the art, and future prospects. AGI **5**(1), 1 (2014)
45. Dorri, A., Kanhere, S.S., Jurdak, R.: Multi-agent systems: a survey. IEEE Access **6**, 28573–28593 (2018)
46. Boissier, O., Ciortea, A., Harth, A., Ricci, A.: Autonomous agents on the web. In: DS 21072, p. 100p (2021)
47. Goertzel, B., Pennachin, C., Geisweiller, N., Goertzel, B., Pennachin, C., Geisweiller, N.: The engineering and development of ethics. In: Engineering General Intelligence, Part 1, pp. 245–287 (2014)
48. Christian, B.: The Alignment Problem: Machine Learning and Human Values. WW Norton & Company (2020)
49. Coeckelbergh, M.: AI Ethics. MIT Press, Cambridge (2020)
50. Kampik, T., et al.: Norms and policies for agents on the web. In: Autonomous Agents on the Web (2021)
51. Vogel-Heuser, B., Seitz, M., Cruz Salazar, L.A., Gehlhoff, F., Dogan, A., Fay, A.: Multi-agent systems to enable industry 4.0. at-Automatisierungstechnik **68**(6), 445–458 (2020)
52. Hukal, P., Berente, N., Germonprez, M., Schecter, A.: Bots coordinating work in open source software projects. Computer **52**(9), 52–60 (2019)
53. Kampik, T., et al.: Governance of autonomous agents on the web: challenges and opportunities. ACM TOIT **22**(4), 1–31 (2022)
54. Patrick, A.S.: Building trustworthy software agents. IEEE IC **6**(6), 46–53 (2002)
55. Kaur, D., Uslu, S., Rittichier, K.J., Durresi, A.: Trustworthy artificial intelligence: a review. ACM CSUR **55**(2), 1–38 (2022)

Bridging AGI Theory and Practice with Galois Connections

Ben Goertzel[1,2(✉)]

[1] OpenCog Foundation, Rockville, USA
ben@goertzel.org
[2] SingularityNET Foundation, Amsterdam, The Netherlands

Abstract. Multiple cognitive algorithms posited to play a key role in AGI (forward and backward chaining inference, clustering and concept formation, evolutionary and reinforcement learning, probabilistic programming, etc.) are given a common formulation as recursive discrete decision processes involving optimizing functions defined over metagraphs, in which the key decisions involve sampling from probability distributions over metagraphs and enacting sets of combinatory operations on selected sub-metagraphs. This forms a bridge between abstract conceptions of general intelligence founded on notions of algorithmic information and complex systems theory, and the practical design of multi-paradigm AGI systems.

1 Introduction

The pursuit of AGI has an abstract theoretical aspect, in which the focus is understanding *what intelligence is* at a fundamental level going beyond any particular biological organism or engineered system. It also has an acutely practical aspect, in which one is trying to build particular systems with specific resources and application foci, much like building any other machine (albeit with some unique aspects given that this sort of machine is expected to take over its own redesign and re-engineering process).

Connecting the theoretical and practical aspects of AGI is a major challenge, which if done well can enhance both aspects. Here we present some ideas aimed at fleshing out this connection, in the specific context of cross-paradigm metagraph-based AI approaches like the OpenCog family of systems.

Perhaps the best known approach to the abstract formulation of AGI is the algorithmic-information-theory-driven angle, as represented by AIXI [10], Godel Machine [13] and their relatives. These abstract AGI systems have the general form of "reinforcement learning" or "experiential interactive learning" algorithms, meaning that they operate via iteratively observing the world, then choosing actions that they expect will give them maximum reward based on the world's reactions, etc. They are unrealistic because their action selection is uncomputable or at best computationally intractable (though efforts have been made to scale them down [1,14,16]).

P. Hammer et al. (Eds.): AGI 2023, LNAI 13921, pp. 115–125, 2023.
https://doi.org/10.1007/978-3-031-33469-6_12

An alternate way of conceiving AGI is Weaver's notion of "Open Ended Intelligence" [17], which considers intelligences as complex, self-organizing systems that interact with their environments in such a way as to pursue the two complementary, often conflicting goals of *individuation* (maintaining system boundaries and coherence) and *self-transcendence* (developing and acquiring new properties and aspects, including those that would be incomprehensible to earlier system versions). This approach does not make unrealistic assumptions, but possesses a fluidity that renders its rigorous application to specific cases an interesting challenge.

In recent papers such as *The General Theory of General Intelligence* [7] and *Patterns of Cognition* [6] I have sought to provide one sort of conceptual and mathematical bridge between these general-purpose AGI frameworks and practical real-world AGI-oriented systems, via looking at formulations of the AI algorithms playing key roles in the OpenCog AI system in terms of abstract recursive discrete decision systems. This paper gives a concise overview of a few of the key ideas from these longer works.

The DDSs (Discrete Decision Systems) we propose on the one hand can be straightforwardly viewed as scaled down versions of $AIXI^{tl}$ or time-bounded Godel Machine type systems, but on the other hand can be used to drive concrete thinking about functional programming implementations of OpenCog algorithms, and understood as seeds for the self-modifying self-organization conceived in Open-Ended Intelligence theory.

The *Patterns of Cognition* analysis involves representing various cognitive algorithms as recursive discrete decision processes involving optimizing functions defined over metagraphs, in which the key decisions involve sampling from probability distributions over metagraphs and enacting sets of combinatory operations on selected sub-metagraphs. A variety of recursive decision process called a COFO (Combinatory Function Optimization) algorithm plays a key role. One can view a COFO as being vaguely like Monte-Carlo-AIXI, but within the context of a combinatory computational model – and with the added twist that the Monte Carlo sampling based estimations are augmented by estimations using other probabilistic algorithms that are themselves implemented using COFO. There are close connections to modern probabilistic programming theory [11], but with more of an emphasis on recursive inference algorithms and less reliance on simplistic sampling methods.

Behind the scenes of the COFO framework is a core insight drawn from the body of theory behind the OpenCog system – that a combinatory computational model defined over metagraphs is an especially natural setting in which to formalize various practical AGI-oriented algorithms. From a sufficiently abstract perspective, all Turing-complete computational models are equivalent, and all general-purpose computational data structures are equivalent. But from a practical AGI implementation and teaching perspective, it makes a difference which computational models and data structures one chooses; the argument for metagraphs as the core data structure for AGI has been laid out in [3] and references therein such as [2], and the argument for combinatory computing as the core approach for AGI has been laid out in [9] and earlier papers referenced therein.

2   Discrete Decision Systems

To bridge the gap between abstract AGI agent models and practical AGI systems, we introduce a basic model of a *discrete decision system (DDS)* – a process defined on n stages in which each stage $t = 1, \ldots, n$ is characterized by

- an **initial state** $s_t \in S_t$, where S_t is the set of feasible states at the beginning of stage t;
- an **action** or "decision variable" $x_t \in X_t$, where X_t is the set of feasible actions at stage t – note that X_t may be a function of the initial state s_t;
- an **immediate cost/reward function** $p_t(s_t, x_t)$, representing the cost/reward at stage t if s_t is the initial state and x_t the action selected;
- a **state transition function** $g_t(s_t, x_t)$ that leads the system towards state $s_{t+1} = g_t(s_t, x_t)$.

The mapping of the simple agents model given above into this framework is fairly direct: environments determine which actions are feasible at each point in time and goals are assumed decomposable into stepwise reward functions. Highly generally intelligent agents like AIXI^{tl} fit into this framework, but so do practical AI algorithm frameworks like greedy optimization and deterministic and stochastic dynamic programming. As we shall see, with some care and further machinery the various cognitive algorithms utilized in the OpenCog framework can be interpreted as DDSs as well.

To express greedy optimization in this framework, one begins with an initial state, chosen based on prior knowledge or via purely randomly or via appropriately biased stochastic selection. Then one chooses an action with a probability proportional to immediate cost/reward (or based on some scaled version of this probability). Then one enacts the action, the state transition, and etc.

An interesting case of "greedy" style DDS dynamics in an AGI context is the adaptive spreading of attention through a complex network. OpenCog's attentional dynamics subsystem, ECAN (Economic Attention Networks), involves spreading of two types of attention values through a knowledge metagraph – Short-Term Importance (STI) and Long-Term Importance (LTI) values, representing very roughly the amount of processor time an Atom should receive in the near term, and the criticalness of keeping an Atom in RAM in the near term. In this case: an **initial state** is a distribution of STI and LTI values across the Atoms in an Atomspace; an **action** is the spreading of some STI or LTI from one Atom to its neighbors; an **immediate cost/reward function** is the degree to which a given spreading action causes the distribution of STI/LTI values to better approximate the actual expected utilities of assignation of processor time and RAM to the Atoms in Atomspace; a **state transition function** is the updating of the overall set of STI/LTI values; and the ECAN equations in the OpenCog system embody a greedy heuristic for executing this DDS.

To express dynamic programming in this DDS framework is a little subtler, as in DP one tries to choose actions with probability proportional to overall expected cost/reward. Estimating the overall expected cost/reward of an action sequence requires either an exhaustive exploration of possibilities (i.e. full-on dynamic programming) or else some sort of heuristic sampling of possibilities (approximate stochastic dynamic programming).

To handle concurrency in this framework, one can posit underlying atomic actions $w_t \in W_t$, and then define the members of X_t as subsets of W_t. In this case each action x_t represents a set of w_t being executed concurrently.

3 Combinatory-Operation-Based Function Optimization

To frame the sorts of cognitive algorithms involved in OpenCog and related AGI architectures in terms of general DDS processes, [6] introduces the notion of COFO, Combinatory-Operation-Based Function Optimization. Basically, a COFO process wraps a combinatory computational system of the sort considered in [4] and [7] within a DDS, by using the combinatory system as the method of choosing actions in a discrete decision process oriented toward optimizing a function. The hypothesis is then made that this particular sort of DDS plays a core role in practical AGI systems operating in environments relevant to our physical universe and the everyday human world.

More specifically, we envision a cognitive system controlling an agent in an environment to be roughly describable as a DDS (the "top-level DDS"), and then envision the cognitive processing used for action selection in the DDS as comprising: 1) A memory consisting of a set of entities that combine with each other to produce other entities, i.e. a combinatory system embodied in a knowledge metagraph; 2) Cognitive processes instantiated as COFO processes, i.e. as DDSs whose goals are function optimizations and whose actions are function evaluations, all leveraging a common metagraph as background knowledge and as a dynamic store for intermediate state; 3) One or more DDSs carrying out attention allocation on the common metagraph (the core DDS here using greedy heuristics but supplemented by one or more additional DDSs using more advanced cognition), spanning the portions of the metagraph focused on by the various COFO processes.

So practical intelligent systems are modeled as multi-level DDSs where the subordinate DDSs operating within the outer-loop agent control DDS are mostly COFO processes. In [7] some effort is taken to explore how the various COFO-like processes involved in human-like cognition appear to interoperate in human cognitive architecture, and more specifically how the OpenCog Hyperon design explicitly interleaves COFO processes in its attempt to manifest advanced AGI.

A COFO process, more explicitly, involves making of a series of decisions involving how to best use a set of combinatory operators C_i to gain information about maximizing a function F (or Pareto optimizing a set of functions $\{F_i\}$) via sampling evaluations of F ($\{F_i\}$). For simplicity we'll present this process in the case of a single function F but the same constructs work for the multiobjective case. It is shown in [6] how COFO can be represented as a discrete decision process, which can then be enacted in greedy or dynamic programming style.

Given a function $F : X \to R$ (where X is any space with a probability measure on it and R is the reals), let $\mathcal{D}$ denote a "dataset" comprising finite subset of the graph $\mathcal{G}(F)$ of F, i.e. a set of pairs $(x, F(x))$. We want to introduce a measure $q_F(\mathcal{D})$ which measures how much guidance $\mathcal{D}$ gives toward the goal of finding x that make $F(x)$ large. The best measure will often be application-specific; however as shown in [6] one can also introduce general-purpose entropy-based measures that apply across domains and problems.

We can then look at greedy or dynamic programming processes aimed at gradually building a set D in a way that will maximize $q_{\rho, F}(D)$. Specifically, in a cognitive algorithmics context it is interesting to look at processes involving combinatory operations $C_i : X \times X \to X$ with the property that $P(C_i(x, y) \in M_\rho^D | x \in M_\rho^D, y \in M_\rho^D) \gg P(z \in M_\rho^D | z \in X)$. That is, given $x, y \in M_\rho^D$, combining x and y using C_i has surprisingly high probability of yielding $z \in M_\rho^D$.

Given combinatory operators of this nature, one can then approach gradually building a set D in a way that will maximize $q_{\rho, F}(D)$, via a route of successively applying combinatory operators C_i to the members of a set D_j to obtain a set D_{j+1}.

Framing this COFO process as a form of recursive Discrete Decision System (DDS), we obtain:

1. A **state** s_t is a dataset D formed from function F
2. An **action** is the formation of a new entity z by
   (a) Sampling x, y from X and C_i from the set of available combinatory operators, in a manner that is estimated likely to yield $z = C_i(x, y)$ with $z \in M_\rho^D$
      i. As a complement or alternative to directly sampling, one can perform probabilistic inference of various sorts to find promising (x, y, C_i). This probabilistic inference process itself may be represented as a COFO process, as we show below via expressing PLN forward and backward chaining in terms of COFO
   (b) Evaluating $F(z)$, and setting $D^* = D \cup (z, F(z))$.
3. The **immediate reward** is an appropriate measure of the amount of new information about making F big that was gained by the evaluation $F(z)$. The right measure may depend on the specific COFO application; one fairly generic choice would be the relative entropy $q_{\rho, F}(D^*, D)$
4. **State transition**: setting the new state $s_{t+1} = D^*$

A concurrent-processing version of this would replace 2a with a similar step in which multiple pairs (x, y) are concurrently chosen and then evaluated.

The action step in a COFO process is in essence carrying out a form of probabilistic programming [11] (which is clear from the discussion of probabilistic programming in a dependent type context given in [5]). Finding the right conglomeration of combinatory operators to produce a given output is formally equivalent to finding the right program to produce a given sort of output, and here as in probabilistic programming one is pushed to judiciously condition estimates on prior knowledge.

In the case where one pursues COFO via dynamic programming, it becomes *stochastic* dynamic programming because of the probabilistic sampling in the action. If probabilistic inference is used along with sampling, then one may have a peculiar sort of approximate stochastic dynamic programming in which the step of choosing an action involves making an estimation that itself may be usefully carried out by stochastic dynamic programming (but with a different objective function than the objective function for whose optimization the action is being chosen).

Basically, in the COFO framework one looks at the process of optimizing F as an explicit dynamical decision process conducted via sequential application of an operation in which: Operations C_i that combine inputs chosen from a distribution induced by prior objective function evaluations, are used to get new candidate arguments to feed to F for evaluation. The reward function guiding this exploration is the quest for reduction of the entropy of the set of guesses at arguments that look promising to make F near-optimal based on the evaluations made so far.

The same COFO process can be applied equally well the case of Pareto-optimizing a set of objective functions. The definition of M_ρ^D must be modified accordingly and then the rest follows.

Actually carrying out an explicit stochastic dynamic programming algorithm according to the lines described above, will prove computationally intractable in most realistic cases. However, we shall see below that the formulation of the COFO process as dynamic programming (or simpler greedy sequential choice based optimization) provides a valuable foundation for theoretical analysis.

4   Cognitive Processes as COFO-Guided Metagraph Transformations

COFO is a highly general framework, and to use it to structure specific AI systems one has to take the next step and introduce specific sets of combinatory operations, often associated with specific incremental reward functions in the spirit of (but often not identical) the information-theoretic reward approach hinted above. In [6] explicit discussion is given to the COFO expression of a variety of cognitive algorithms used in the OpenCog AGI approach: Logical reasoning, evolutionary program learning, metagraph pattern mining, agglomerative clustering and activation-spreading-based attention allocation.

We will focus mainly here on AGI architectures such as OpenCog that have metagraphs as core meta-representational data structures – thus placing metagraphs in a dual role: 1) As a fundamental means of analyzing what the AGI system is doing from a conceptual and phenomenological perspective; 2) As the core data structure the AGI system uses to store various sorts of information as it goes about its business.

In this sort of AGI architecture, the expression of logical inference, program learning and pattern mining in combinatory-system terms ties directly back to the discussion of distinction metagraphs and associated patterns in [7]. Logical inference rules can be considered as transformations on distinction metagraphs. Bidirectional inference rules (expressed using coimplication) are rules mapping between two distinction metagraphs that have different surface form but ultimately express the same distinctions between the same observations. Programs can be viewed, using Curry-Howard type mappings, as series of steps for enacting these logical-inference-rule transformation on metagraphs, where the steps are to be carried out on an assumed reference machine. The reference machine itself may also be represented as a distinction metagraph with temporal links used to express the transitions involved in computations. Pattern mining can be expressed in terms of formal patterns in metagraphs. Clustering can be viewed as a sort of metagraph transformation that creates new ConceptNodes grouping nodes into categories. Etc.

In this context, COFO presents itself as a way of structuring processes via which sub-metagraphs transform other sub-metagraphs into yet other sub-metagraphs, where the submetagraphs are interpreted as combinators and are combined via a systematic recursive process toward the incremental increase of a particular reward function. And the common representation of multiple COFO processes involved in achieving the overall multiple-goal-achieving activities of a top-level DDS in terms of a shared typed metagraph is one way to facilitate the cognitive synergy needed to achieve high levels of general intelligence under practical resource constraints. The reliance on a common metagraph representation makes it tractable for the multiple cognitive algorithms to share intermediate state as they pursue their optimization goals, which enables the cognitive-synergy dynamic in which each process is able to call on other processes in the system for assistance when it runs into trouble.

5   COFO Processes as Galois Connections

For some of the cognitive algorithms treated in COFO terms in [6] one requires a variety of COFO that uses greedy optimization to explore the dag of possibilities, for others one requires a variety of COFO that uses some variation on approximation stochastic dynamic programming. In either case, one can use the "programming with Galois connections" approach from [12] to formalize the derivation of practical algorithmic approaches. Roughly, in all these cases, Galois connections are used to link search and optimization processes on directed metagraphs whose edge targets are labeled with probabilistic dependent types, and one can then show that – under certain assumptions – these connections are fulfilled by processes involving metagraph chronomorphisms (where a chronomorphism is a fold followed by an unfold, where both the fold and unfold are allowed to accumulate and propagate long-term memory as they proceed).

5.1   Greedy Optimization as Folding

Suppose we are concerned with maximizing a function $f : X \to R$ via a "pattern search" approach. That is, we assume an algorithm that repeatedly iterates a pattern search operation such as: Generates a set of candidate next-steps from its focus point a, evaluates the candidates, and then using the results of this evaluation, chooses a new focus point a^*. Steepest ascent obviously has this format, but so do a variety of derivative-free optimization methods as reviewed e.g. in [15].

Evolutionary optimization may be put in this framework if one shifts attention to a population-level function $f_P : X^N \to R$ where X^N is a population of N elements of X, and defines $f_P(x)$ for $x \in X^N$ as e.g. the average of $f(x)$ across $x \in X^N$ (so the average population fitness, in genetic algorithm terms). The focus point a is a population, which evolves into a new population a^* via crossover or mutation – a process that is then ongoingly iterated as outlined above.

The basic ideas to be presented here work for most any topological space X but we are most interested in the case where X is a metagraph. In this case the pattern search iteration can be understood as a walk across the metagraph, moving from some initial position in the graph to another position, then another one, etc.

We can analyze this sort of optimization algorithm via the Greedy Theorem from [12],

Theorem 1 *(Theorem 1 from [12]).* $(\!|S \restriction R|\!) \subseteq (\!|S|\!) \restriction R$ *if R is transitive and S satisfies the "monotonicity condition" $R^\circ \leftarrow SFR^\circ$*

which leverages a variety of idiosyncratic notation: $R \xleftarrow{S} FR$ indicates $S \cdot FR \subseteq R \cdot S$; $(\!|S|\!)$ means the operation of folding S ; $\langle \mu X :: fX \rangle$ denotes the least fixed point of f ; T° means the converse of T, i.e. $(b,a) \in R^\circ \equiv (a,c) \in R$; $S \restriction R$ means "S shrunk by R", i.e. $S \cap R/S^\circ$. Here S represents the local candidate-generation operation used in the pattern-search optimization algorithm, and R represents the operation of evaluating a candidate point in X according to the objective function being optimized.

If the objective function is not convex, then the theorem does not hold, but the greedy pattern-search optimization may still be valuable in a heuristic sense. This is the case, for instance, in nearly all real-world applications of evolutionary programming, steepest ascent or classical derivative-free optimization methods.

5.2   Galois Connection Representations of Dynamic Programming Decision Systems Involving Mutually Associative Combinatory Operations

Next we consider how to represent dynamic programming based execution of DDSs using folds and unfolds. Here our approach is to leverage Theorem 2 in [12] which is stated as

Theorem 2 *(Theorem 2 from [12]).* Assume S is monotonic with respect to R, that is, $R \xleftarrow{S} F_R$ holds, and $dom(T) \subseteq dom(S \cdot FM)$. Then

$$M = ((\!|S|\!) \cdot (\!|T|\!)^\circ) \restriction R \Rightarrow \langle \mu X :: (S \cdot FX \cdot T^\circ) \restriction R \rangle \subseteq M$$

Conceptually, $T°$ transforms input into subproblems, e.g. for backward chaining inference, it chooses (x, y, C) so that $z = C(x, y)$ has high quality (e.g. CWIG); for forward chaining, it chooses x, y, C so that z = C(x, y) has high interestingness (e.g. CWIG).

FX figures out recursively which combinations give maximum immediate reward according to the relevant measure. These optimal solutions are combined and then the best one is picked by $\upharpoonright R$, which is the evaluation on the objective function. Caching results to avoid overlap may be important here in practice (and is what will give us histomorphisms and futumorphisms instead of simple folds and unfolds).

The fix-point based recursion/iteration specified by the theorem can of course be approximatively rather than precisely solved – and doing this approximation via statistical sampling yields stochastic dynamic programming. Roughly speaking the approach symbolized by $M = ((|S|) \cdot (|T|)°) \upharpoonright R$ begins by applying all the combinatory operations to achieve a large body of combinations-of-combinations-of-combinations-..., and then shrinks this via the process of optimality evaluation. On the other hand, the least-fixed-point version on the rhs of the Theorem iterates through the combination process step by step (executing the fold).

6   Associativity of Combinatory Operations Enables Representing Cognitive Operations as Folding and Unfolding

A key insight reported in *Patterns of Cognition* is that the mutual associativity of the combinatory operations involved in a cognitive process often plays a key role in enabling the decomposition of the process into folding and unfolding operations. This manifests itself for example in the result that

Theorem 3. *A COFO decision process whose combinatory operations C_i are mutually associative can be implemented as a chronomorphism.*

This general conclusion regarding mutual associativity resonates fascinatingly with the result from [4] mentioned above, that mutually associative combinatory operations lead straightforwardly to subpattern hierarchies. We thus see a common mathematical property leading to elegant and practically valuable symmetries in both algorithmic dynamics and in knowledge-representation structure. This bolsters confidence that the combinatory computational model is a good approach for exploring the scaling-down of generic but infeasible AGI models toward the realm of practically usable algorithms.

This conclusion regarding mutual associativity also has some practical implications for the particulars of cognitive processes such as logical reasoning and evolutionary learning. For instance, one can see that mutually associativity holds among logical inference rules if one makes use of reversible logic rules (co-implications rather than implications), and for program execution processes if one makes use of reversible computing. It is also observed that where this mutual associativity holds, there is an alignment between the hierarchy of subgoals used in recursive decision process execution and subpattern hierarchies among patterns represented in the associated knowledge metagraph.

In the PLN inference context, for example, the approach to PLN inference using relaxation rather than chaining outlined in [8] is one way of finding the fixed point of the recursion associated with the COFO process. What the theorem suggests is that folding PLN inferences across the knowledge metagraph is another way, basically boiling down to forward and backward chaining as outlined above. However, it seems this can only work reasonably cleanly for crisp inference if mutual associativity among inference rules holds, which appears to be the case only if one uses PLN rules formulated as co-implications rather than one-way implications.

Further, when dealing with the uncertainty-management aspects of PLN rules, one is no longer guaranteed associativity merely by adopting reversibility of individual inference steps. One must heuristically arrange one's inferences as series of co-implications whose associated distributions have favorable independence relationships.

7   Challenges and Prospects

The assumptions needed to get from the symmetry properties of discrete decision processes to fold and unfold operations are not entirely realistic – for instance, to get the derivations to work in their most straightforward form, one needs to assume the underlying metagraph remains unchanged as the folding and unfolding processes proceed. If the metagraph changes dynamically along with the folding and unfolding – e.g. because inference processes are drawing conclusions from the nodes and links created during the folding process, and these conclusions are being placed into the metagraph concurrently with the folding process proceeding – then one loses the straightforward result that simple approximate stochastic dynamic programming algorithms will approximate the optimal result of the decision process. This is a serious limitation, but it must also be understood that in many cases the real-time changes to the metagraph incurred by the folding and unfolding process are not a significant factor. Creating rigorous theory connecting abstract AGI theory to pragmatically relevant cognitive algorithms and their implementations is a complex matter inevitably involving some simplifications and approximations; the trick is to choose the right ones.

If one wishes to explore open-ended, evolutionary AGI systems in which multiple algorithms constructed on diverse principles interact within a common meta-representational fabric, then the conceptual and mathematical approach presented here provides an avenue for relatively elegant and concise formalization, putting diverse AI methods in a common framework. This framework has potential to ease practical complexity and performance analysis, and also connects practical operational systems with broader conceptions of AGI.

References

1. Franz, A., Gogulya, V., Löffler, M.: WILLIAM: a monolithic approach to AGI. In: Hammer, P., Agrawal, P., Goertzel, B., Iklé, M. (eds.) AGI 2019. LNCS (LNAI), vol. 11654, pp. 44–58. Springer, Cham (2019). https://doi.org/10.1007/978-3-030-27005-6_5

2. Gibbons, J.: An initial-algebra approach to directed acyclic graphs. In: Möller, B. (ed.) MPC 1995. LNCS, vol. 947, pp. 282–303. Springer, Heidelberg (1994). https://doi.org/10.1007/3-540-60117-1_16

3. Goertzel, B.: Folding and unfolding on metagraphs (2020). https://arxiv.org/abs/2012.01759

4. Goertzel, B.: Grounding Occam's razor in a formal theory of simplicity. arXiv preprint arXiv:2004.05269 (2020)

5. Goertzel, B.: Paraconsistent foundations for probabilistic reasoning, programming and concept formation. arXiv preprint arXiv:2012.14474 (2020)

6. Goertzel, B.: Patterns of cognition: cognitive algorithms as Galois connections fulfilled by chronomorphisms on probabilistically typed metagraphs. arXiv preprint arXiv:2102.10581 (2021)

7. Goertzel, B.: Toward a general theory of general intelligence: a patternist perspective. arXiv preprint arXiv:2103.15100 (2021)

8. Goertzel, B., Pennachin, C.: How might probabilistic reasoning emerge from the brain? In: Proceedings of the First AGI Conference, vol. 171, p. 149. IOS Press (2008)

9. Goertzel, B., Pennachin, C., Geisweiller, N.: Engineering General Intelligence, Part 1: A Path to Advanced AGI via Embodied Learning and Cognitive Synergy. Atlantis Thinking Machines, Springer, Heidelberg (2013). https://doi.org/10.2991/978-94-6239-027-0

10. Hutter, M.: Universal Artificial Intelligence: Sequential Decisions Based on Algorithmic Probability. Springer, Heidelberg (2005). https://doi.org/10.1007/b138233

11. van de Meent, J.W., Paige, B., Yang, H., Wood, F.: An introduction to probabilistic programming. arXiv preprint arXiv:1809.10756 (2018)

12. Mu, S.C., Oliveira, J.N.: Programming from Galois connections. J. Log. Algebraic Program. **81**(6), 680–704 (2012)

13. Schmidhuber, J.: Godel machines: fully self-referential optimal universal self-improvers. In: Goertzel, B., Pennachin, C. (eds.) Artificial General Intelligence. COGTECH, pp. 119–226. Springer, Heidelberg (2006). https://doi.org/10.1007/978-3-540-68677-4_7

14. Schmidhuber, J.: Optimal ordered problem solver. Mach. Learn. **54**(3), 211–254 (2004). https://doi.org/10.1023/B:MACH.0000015880.99707.b2

15. Torczon, V.: Pattern search methods for nonlinear optimization. In: SIAG/OPT Views and News. Citeseer (1995)

16. Veness, J., Ng, K.S., Hutter, M., Uther, W., Silver, D.: A Monte-Carlo AIXI approximation. J. Artif. Intell. Res. **40**, 95–142 (2011)

17. Weinbaum, D., Veitas, V.: Open ended intelligence: the individuation of intelligent agents. J. Exp. Theor. Artif. Intell. **29**(2), 371–396 (2017)

Comparative Reasoning for Intelligent Agents

Patrick Hammer[1]([⊠])(iD), Peter Isaev[2], Hugo Latapie[3], Francesco Lanza[4],
Antonio Chella[4], and Pei Wang[2]

[1] Department of Psychology, Stockholm University, Stockholm, Sweden
`patrick.hammer@psychology.su.se`
[2] Department of Computer Science, Temple University, Philadelphia, USA
`{peter.isaev,pei.wang}@temple.edu`
[3] Cisco Inc., San Jose, USA
`hlatapie@cisco.com`
[4] Robotics Lab, Università degli Studi di Palermo, Palermo, Italy
`{francesco.lanza,antonio.chella}@unipa.it`

Abstract. We demonstrate new comparative reasoning abilities of NARS, a formal model of intelligence, which enable the asymmetric comparison of perceivable quantifiable attributes of objects using relations. These new abilities are implemented by extending NAL with additional inference rules. We demonstrate the new capabilities in a bottle-picking experiment on a mobile robot running ONA, an implementation of NARS.

Keywords: Non-Axiomatic Logic · Comparative Relation · Comparative Reasoning · Inference Rules · Visual object comparison · NARS

1 Introduction

Comparative reasoning has been extensively studied with animals. It has been demonstrated already decades ago, that various animal species can not only condition on concrete stimuli, but also on comparative relations between them, a capability referred to as Transposition [10]. These comparative relations can be about any perceivable properties objects possess, such as their color, size, or shape, or the loudness or pitch of the sounds they make. For most animals, as it turned out, such comparisons are trivial to make: they can condition on such relations almost instantly from just a few examples, and can apply them to novel objects they have never seen before. In computer systems only some aspects of these capabilities have been replicated, such as by deciding which code path to take in a program, based on the outcome of comparisons between numbers with mathematical operators in various programming languages. However, the difficulty lies not in number comparison itself, but in deciding what to compare, and when to compare, and also that most comparisons to be made are relative to another object or category and are hence context-dependent. Furthermore, to

© The Author(s), under exclusive license to Springer Nature Switzerland AG 2023
P. Hammer et al. (Eds.): AGI 2023, LNAI 13921, pp. 126–135, 2023.
https://doi.org/10.1007/978-3-031-33469-6_13

exploit the properties of comparative relations, such as to derive new comparative relations from previous ones, reasoning is required. This is especially the case for asymmetric relations, which cannot be handled in a purely associative manner.

Based on our previous results related to fuzzy quantities and preferences [13,14], this paper extends Non-Axiomatic Logic (henceforth NAL, [15,16]) to support the formation and usage of comparative relations.

This capability has been added in ONA [7], an implementation of NARS (Non-Axiomatic Reasoning System), which will be demonstrated in an experiment with a mobile robot with manipulator arms.

2   Related Work

A representative attempt to support a cognitively plausible treatment of quantities attached to concepts is Conceptual Spaces [5]. Conceptual Spaces are vector spaces of semantically meaningful measures, with a pre-defined similarity metric, such as the color space represented as a three-dimensional space of red, green, and blue. The following represents a series of works in which conceptual spaces were used:

In [9], authors claim that the Conceptual Space can be used as a *lingua franca* for the different levels of representation. With Conceptual Space it becomes easy to unify and generalize many aspects of symbolic, diagrammatic and subsymbolic approaches and integrate them on a common ground. Various applications were realized using conceptual spaces.

In [4], Conceptual Spaces were used to define a framework for endowing a computer vision architecture with a high-level representation capability through the definition of conceptual semantics for the symbolic representations of the vision system. Another usage [3], for example, involves Conceptual Spaces to allow robotic systems to learn effectively by imitation, and not simply reproducing the movements of a human teacher. In that way, the system should be able to deeply understand the perceived actions to be imitated. In [2], the author presented a cognitive architecture for a musical agent. In this architecture, conceptual spaces were used to represent the perception of tones and intervals.

In contrast to these approaches, as we will see, NARS does not utilize predefined attribute vectors, and the similarity evaluation in our approach is dependent on previously experienced values of the compared attribute in a reference class, which supports to handle context-dependence in comparative reasoning, and more significantly, to find useful subsets of properties to compare with beyond what a human designer pre-specified.

Another less similar but still related approach is to make use of Deep Neural Network (DNN) or simpler function approximators to learn task-relevant relational comparison functions (as in [11]). This can also be combined with Reinforcement Learning (by learning a suitable DNN policy [17]).

Hereby, sample efficiency decreases drastically when task-relevant functions able to carry out value comparisons have to be learned from a blank slate while the agent is operating, which is avoided when having domain-independent comparative reasoning abilities inbuilt in the agent. Related evolved general-purpose capabilities which establish data-efficient learning in survival-critical settings are long being studied [10].

3   Formalization of Comparative Relation

NARS is a model of intelligence that has been partially formalized and implemented [15,16]. It uses a concept-centered knowledge representation, in which a *concept* is a data structure summarizing a fragment or pattern of the system's experience, identified by a *term* in a formal language Narsese. A term is an internal name that can be atomic (i.e., an ID or key) or compound (i.e., a structure of other terms).

Some terms correspond to conceptual relations. A *Comparative Relation* is a special type of relation with two components for which a measurement or total order among a class of terms can be obtained. This is formalized as follows:

- Given a measurement M defined on a class C, each instance c of the class has a value v. This measurement can be written as $v = M(c)$, or in Narsese as $(\{c\} \times \{v\}) \to \uparrow M$, which intuitively means that M is an executable operation of the system that, when c is given as input, returns v as output.
- For any pair of instances of the class c_1 and c_2, their values can be compared to get one of the three possible results: $M(c_1) > M(c_2)$, $M(c_1) < M(c_2)$, or $M(c_1) = M(c_2)$. If M is not a measurement but a total order, the result is directly obtained.
- Using Boolean operators, disjunction and negation, $\geq$, $\leq$, and $\neq$ can also be obtained from the comparison in the usual way.
- Each of the comparisons of measurement results corresponds to a *comparative relation* between c_1 and c_2, such as $M(c_1) > M(c_2)$ can be written as $(\{c_1\} \times \{c_2\}) \to >M$, where the relation is identified by the measurement M with the comparative relation $>$ as a prefix.
- For each measurement, six such comparative relations can be defined. Here, the arithmetic comparison is interpreted or instantiated into the concrete relationship, that is, while $>$ compares two numbers, $>$LENGTH compares the lengths of two objects.

Relative Ranking

The previous works [13,14] have extended the comparisons from between two instances to between an instance and a reference class. Formally, $(\{c_1\} \times C) \to R$ is taken as a summary of $(\{c_1\} \times \{x\}) \to R$ for every x in C that has been compared to c_1, directly or indirectly. Therefore, in ideal situations where there is no uncertainty in the instance comparisons, the truth-value of $(\{c_1\} \times C) \to$ $>$LENGTH indicates its relative ranking in C on length, that is, the *frequency* of the statement indicates the percent of instances of C that c is longer than, while the *confidence* of the statement indicates the number of instances compared so far, relative to a constant.

In the simplest situations, such a conclusion is derived by the *induction* rule from $(\{c_1\} \times \{c_2\}) \to R$ and $\{c_2\} \to C$, with conversions between *product* and *image*. Such judgments are merged by the *revision* rule to get the statistical result incrementally. The final conclusion is however not necessarily purely statistical or inductive, as matching conclusions can be obtained via other inference paths [16]. Using the same approach, it is also possible to draw comparative conclusions between two reference classes (or generic terms) like $(C_1 \times C_2) \to R$.

When the measurement values are directly available (such as in a sensation), it is possible to take the difference of the measurement values $|v_1 - v_2|$ as the weight of evidence for each comparison, so the truth-value is not merely a relative measurement [14]. For example, if the available values are 1, 2, and 9, the *frequency* for 2 to be considered as "larger than the others" is not $1/(1 + 1)$, but $1/(1 + 7)$, as the negative evidence is much "heavier" than the positive evidence.

Comparative Property

As analyzed in [13], many "fuzzy" property or membership is caused by comparisons with instances in an implicit reference class.

For example, "The Amazon River is long" actually means "The Amazon River is longer than the other rivers", so in Narsese it should be $(\{Amazon\} \times river) \to {>}\text{LENGTH}$ or $\{Amazon\} \to ({>}\text{LENGTH} / \_, river)$, rather than as $\{Amazon\} \to [long]$. This is the case because the "comparative property" $[long]$ is highly context-dependent, and largely determined by the reference class.

Another special feature of comparative relation appears in a statement like $\{Amazon\} \to ({>}\text{LENGTH} / \_, river)$ where its *frequency* is low (near 0) or inconclusive (near 0.5). For ordinary *inheritance* judgments, low frequency usually means "no inheritance". In particular, if two objects both lack a property, such as "not red", they should not be considered similar to each other for this reason, however, for continuous measurements, close values provide evidence for their similarity, and the closer, the more evidence there is, no matter where they are in the range of the values. For example, if two rivers are "not long", then they are both "short", so are similar for that reason.

Also, in sensory channels the reference class is often implied. Instead of $(\{c_1\} \times Brightness) \to {>}bright$, one can write $\{c_1\} \mapsto [bright]$ as a shortcut.

Inference Rules

To provide inference on comparative relations, the following inference rules are added as an extension of NAL:

– Comparing two measurements:

$$\{(\{c_1\} \times \{v_1\}) \to \uparrow M, (\{c_2\} \times \{v_2\}) \to \uparrow M\} \vdash (\{c_1\} \times \{c_2\}) \to R$$

whereby R is either ${<}M$, ${>}M$, or ${=}M$ dependent on whether $v_1 < v_2$, $v_1 > v_2$, or $v_1 = v_2$ holds.

- Transitivity of comparative relation, using f_{ded} truth function [16]:

$$\{(A \times B) \to R,\ (B \times C) \to R\} \vdash (A \times C) \to R,\ f_{ded}$$

- Symmetry of comparative relations of type =:

$$\{(A \times B) \to =M\} \vdash (B \times A) \to =M$$

- Inversion of a comparative relation of type <and>:

$$\{(A \times B) \to >M\ \} \vdash (B \times A) \to <M$$

$$\{(A \times B) \to <M\ \} \vdash (B \times A) \to >M$$

- Exclusiveness of comparative relations:

$$\forall R, S \in \{<M, >M, =M\} : (R \neq S) \implies \{(A \times B) \to R\} \vdash \neg((A \times B) \to S)$$

- Negation of a comparative relation/property:

$$\forall R, S, T \in \{<M, >M, =M\} : ((R \neq S) \wedge (R \neq T)) \implies$$
$$\neg(A \times B) \to R\} \vdash (A \times B) \to S \vee (A \times B) \to T$$

- Inference rule and truth function for class-based comparison:

$$\{(\{c_1\} \times C) \to R,\ (\{c_2\} \times C) \to R\} \vdash (\{c_1\} \times \{c_2\}) \to R$$

whereby R is either $<M$, $>M$, dependent on whether $f_1 < f_2$, or $f_1 > f_2$ holds. This is similar as in value comparison, but please note that here we compare the revised frequency values relative to the class, which indicates what proportion of instances in that class the instances' M property is smaller or greater than. The conclusion confidence hereby is dependent on the premise confidences via $c = c_1 * c_2$, and the conclusion frequency is $f = 1$.

Comparisons via Commonalities and Differences

In perception, it is not feasible to exhaustively compare all encountered objects with all currently perceived and remembered ones, especially if each comparison needs to select an informative subset of properties as the basis for the comparison, which will hopefully be useful to condition on to achieve goals. Which brings us back to the question: what to compare with, and when? According to selective perception, active relational goals should request/trigger the task-relevant comparisons of interest, a form of top-down attention as discussed in [8]. However, how did the goal structure which brings them into existence emerge in the first place? One answer could be (and is the one we find most promising and choose to pursue) that attending to commonalities and differences between observed and remembered instances significantly reduces the number of possible groups of properties to consider for comparison. When an instance is recalled from memory that is closest to the newly perceived instance, it is not uncommon that there will be dozens of matching properties (it was the closest instance after all). Now, any differences to the remembered instance are highly informative and might indicate a change, which allows categorizing the newly observed instance not only based on the closest memory item, but also according to the most significant difference to it, which is a much more concise description (as it references the closest, yet keeps the significant differences) than when having to include all the properties of the new instance in its encoding. We will later see the relevance of this in the experiment, but for this to work the following additional inference rules are required:

1. to obtain instance similarity from comparative properties with value-wise close measurements (e.g. to find the best-matching instance in memory):

$$\{\{c_1\} \to (>M / \_, C), \{c_2\} \to (>M / \_, C)\} \vdash (\{c_1\} \times \{c_2\}) \to =M, \quad f_{mcmp}$$

2. and to summarize comparison evaluations regarding multiple properties:

$$\{\{c_1\} \to (>M / \_, C), \{c_2\} \to (>M / \_, C)\} \vdash (\{c_1\} \leftrightarrow \{c_2\}), \quad f_{mcmp}$$

$$f_{mcmp}(f_1, c_1, f_2, c_2) = (1 - |f1 - f2|, c_1 * c_2)$$

whereby f_{mcmp} makes the ratio of positive over total evidence in the conclusion depend on the closeness of the frequency values, and the confidence of the conclusion depend on the confidence of the premises.

Please note that it is also possible to obtain evidence against instance similarity from comparative properties by negating the previous two inference rule conclusions. These rules are useful to find the most similar instances by revising the conclusions, and to find the most significant differences which can then be used to trigger the previous comparative inferences to build an instance-relative description for a new instance to be encoded/described relative to the other.

4   Experiment

The new capability to form comparative relations was also tested in a use case with a Transbot robot. The following is a brief description of the robot hardware and the software architecture used to demonstrate the novel capability. In the end, the experimental setup is described.

Transbot Robot

Transbot is a tracked mobile robot with manipulator arm. Due to its tracks, it is able to perform in outdoor environments, including off-road conditions. It is based on ROS (Robot Operating System) Melodic running on Ubuntu 18.04

LTS and can be programmed using C/C++ and Python. Transbot is useful for building various robotic applications. In terms of hardware, it is equipped with a NVIDIA Jetson Nano board, which acts as the control unit to coordinate and implement the robot's behaviour, and a set of sensors, such as an Astra Pro depth camera and Slamtec RPLIDAR A1 Lidar sensor. Due to its Lidar and depth camera which allows for Simultaneous Localization and Mapping, Transbot is able to map its environment to carry out exploration tasks. Also, it includes robotic arm with three degrees of movement controlled with separate servo motors, which allows the robot to perform various object manipulation tasks (such as object grasping).

The Robot Architecture

The novel way to form comparative relations was integrated in the latest version of ONA (which will be v0.9.2). To show it, a robotic application was realized using the Transbot robot. To endow Transbot with the capability to use NARS as its reasoning system, a related ROS node was realized. The ROS module is a part of the ONA framework, available on Github[1]. The ROS network structure is illustrated in Fig. 1.

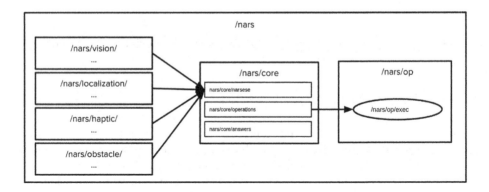

Fig. 1. ROS network for NARS

The network, as illustrated in Fig. 1 consists of channel nodes on input side, a ROS node for NARS (ONA), and a node on the output side for passing on operation calls to ROS components to control the robot.

The channel nodes include (whereby localization and local obstacle detection is omitted as they are not directly required for our experiment):

- vision: a node which applies YOLOv4 [1] on RGB camera input, and merges it with depth camera input to assign a depth to each bounding box. The result is encoded into Narsese, and encodes location, size, and class information in

---

[1] https://github.com/opennars/OpenNARS-for-Applications.

a way the reasoner can work with. Also color information (red, green, blue) is extracted from within each bounding box detection, by finding the most dominant (in terms of area) color surfaces.

- haptic: responsible for servo feedback of the gripper, to indicate, with a boolean whether the robot managed to get a hold on an object when picking it by monitoring the rate of angle change of the gripper during the relevant part of the pick operation, reporting if it is below a threshold. The feedback is directly encoded as event ($gripper \rightarrow [holding]$) and ($gripper \rightarrow [free]$).

The reasoner core node (as in Fig. 1), directly runs ONA, and accepts new inputs as strings formatted with the Narsese formal language the reasoner works with, by subscribing to the Narsese topic. There is also a topic for real-time Q&A purposes, but this is outside of the scope of this paper. To let ONA control the robot, operation executions are redirected to the Exec node for further dispatch. Hereby the ROS navigation stack is utilized for robot base movements, by publishing *move_base/goal* desired target location goals (both local-relative, and map-absolute) and canceling the previous ones when new operations are invoked by ONA (via *move_base/cancel*). In addition, the manipulator arm of the robot is controlled by directly adjusting the angles of the servo motors based on the location of the visually detected object chosen to be picked and its corresponding depth estimate.

Use Case

Hereby we will make use of that NARS receives both events for color (red, green blue), and for bounding box location and size in the X and Y coordinate for each detected object. This allows the reasoner to build comparative relations as discussed, among the perceived objects, such as relative color and size differences. The task of the robot is to pick the smaller among the two bottles based on the derived comparative relations. As mentioned, in the vision channel, YOLOv4 trained on ImageNet is utilized as an object detection model. The vision channel uses relative location information (relative to the center) together with size information, the output label to form statements of the form $<objectLabel \mapsto [locationComponent]>$ and $<objectLabel \mapsto [sizeComponent]>$ for X and Y dimension respectively. In addition, the most dominant color surface is extracted to give color information to each bounding box corresponding to a detected object, which is $<objectLabel \mapsto [colorComponent]>$ statements for each color component. This encoding makes ONA aware of the detected object types, their colors, and also their position in the camera's field of view as also necessary to pick them up successfully. In terms of mission specification, the following statement specifies picking the smaller bottle among the two observed bottles:

```
<(<{#1 #2} --> bottle> &| <({#1} * {#2}) --> (> sizeY)>) &/
      <({SELF} * {#2}) --> ^pick>) =/> G>.
```

Please note that the most significant differences are also most visible to the system, so even before any goal is given to the system, the system will notice the significant size difference among the two bottles shown in Fig. 2.

Fig. 2. Selection and picking of smaller bottle

Here, when the two bottles are not in sight, there is a derived goal

```
<{#1 #2} --> bottle>! :|:
```

which leads the system to explore its environment to find said bottles first. The exploration strategies for the robot are outside of the scope of this paper but can be seen in our previous publication [6] and can be combined with established exploration strategies such as based on random trees [12] as long as they can be invoked and stopped at any time by NARS operations.

5   Conclusion

The new comparative reasoning abilities for NARS were presented, including the new relational compound terms and the related inference rules. It was demonstrated that this treatment goes beyond Conceptual Spaces, as combining attributes into pre-defined vectors is not necessary with this approach, and the similarity evaluation is dependent on previously experienced values of the compared attribute in a reference class. Also, it was shown with a concrete experiment how comparative reasoning can lead to cognitive abilities such as being able to compare perceivable quantities of visually detected objects, and to make decisions accordingly on a real robot with a camera. This, as in our example, can be relevant for decision making in intelligent agents, including robots. In the future, experiments where it is required to learn behaviors with comparative relations as a precondition will be shown as well. This ability is a direct consequence of NARS being able to incorporate derived events in procedure learning.

References

1. Bochkovskiy, A., Wang, C.Y., Liao, H.Y.M.: YOLOv4: optimal speed and accuracy of object detection. arXiv preprint arXiv:2004.10934 (2020)
2. Chella, A.: A cognitive architecture for music perception exploiting conceptual spaces. In: Zenker, F., Gärdenfors, P. (eds.) Applications of Conceptual Spaces. SL, vol. 359, pp. 187–203. Springer, Cham (2015). https://doi.org/10.1007/978-3-319-15021-5_10
3. Chella, A., Dindo, H., Infantino, I.: Imitation learning and anchoring through conceptual spaces. Appl. AI **21**(4–5), 343–359 (2007)
4. Chella, A., Frixione, M., Gaglio, S.: Conceptual spaces for computer vision representations. Artif. Intell. Rev. **16**, 137–152 (2001). https://doi.org/10.1023/A:1011658027344
5. Gardenfors, P.: Conceptual Spaces: The Geometry of Thought. MIT Press, Cambridge (2004)
6. Hammer, P., Isaev, P., Lofthouse, T., Johansson, R.: ONA for autonomous ROS-based robots. In: Goertzel, B., Iklé, M., Potapov, A., Ponomaryov, D. (eds.) AGI 2022. LNCS (LNAI), vol. 13539, pp. 231–242. Springer, Cham (2023). https://doi.org/10.1007/978-3-031-19907-3_22
7. Hammer, P., Lofthouse, T.: 'OpenNARS for applications': architecture and control. In: Goertzel, B., Panov, A.I., Potapov, A., Yampolskiy, R. (eds.) AGI 2020. LNCS (LNAI), vol. 12177, pp. 193–204. Springer, Cham (2020). https://doi.org/10.1007/978-3-030-52152-3_20
8. Latapie, H., Kilic, O., Thórisson, K.R., Wang, P., Hammer, P.: Neurosymbolic systems of perception & cognition: the role of attention. Front. Psychol. 2105 (2022)
9. Lieto, A., Chella, A., Frixione, M.: Conceptual spaces for cognitive architectures: a lingua franca for different levels of representation. Biologically Inspired Cogn. Archit. **19**, 1–9 (2017)
10. Riley, D.A., Ring, K., Thomas, J.: The effect of stimulus comparison on discrimination learning and transposition. J. Comp. Physiol. Psychol. **53**(5), 415 (1960)
11. Santoro, A., et al.: A simple neural network module for relational reasoning. In: Advances in Neural Information Processing Systems, vol. 30 (2017)
12. Umari, H., Mukhopadhyay, S.: Autonomous robotic exploration based on multiple rapidly-exploring randomized trees. In: 2017 IEEE/RSJ International Conference on Intelligent Robots and Systems (IROS), pp. 1396–1402. IEEE (2017)
13. Wang, P.: The interpretation of fuzziness. IEEE Trans. Syst. Man Cybern. B Cybern. **26**(4), 321–326 (1996)
14. Wang, P.: Recommendation based on personal preference. In: Zhang, Y., Kandel, A., Lin, T., Yao, Y. (eds.) Computational Web Intelligence: Intelligent Technology for Web Applications, pp. 101–115. World Scientific Publishing Company, Singapore (2004)
15. Wang, P.: Rigid Flexibility: The Logic of Intelligence. Springer, Dordrecht (2006). https://doi.org/10.1007/1-4020-5045-3
16. Wang, P.: Non-Axiomatic Logic: A Model of Intelligent Reasoning. World Scientific, Singapore (2013)
17. Zambaldi, V., et al.: Relational deep reinforcement learning. arXiv preprint arXiv:1806.01830 (2018)

Primum Non Nocere: The Ethical Beginnings of a Non-Axiomatic Reasoning System

David Ireland[(✉)] [iD]

Australian E-Health Research Center, CSIRO, Brisbane, Australia
d.ireland@csiro.au
http://aehrc.csiro.au

Abstract. *What is the right action?* is a question an agent with artificial general intelligence (AGI) will have to face, especially in applications that deal with the health and well-being of human companions. Previous work has considered psychological aspects for forming ethical decision-making; here we consider a philosophy approach and apply abstract, general principles that drive ethical decision-making. Starting with a maxim that has resonated within the health community: *"first, do no harm"*, we introduce equivalent beliefs and goals to a non-axiomatic reasoning system and examine the sub-goals that are formed. We provide a simple scenario that shows how an AGI system might reason from contrasting, normative ethical theories and how they might combine to provide an ethical framework for AGI to engage in more complex human affairs.

Keywords: NARS · ethics · consequentialism · deontological · virtue ethics

1 Introduction

What is the right action? How do we know what we ought to do? And what reason is there for doing as we ought? Are enduring and universal questions faced when dealing with ethical conundrums. An artificial agent, capable of general intelligence, whether it be proto, super or somewhere in between, will face these questions at some point. It need not be engaged in some futuristic, deep intellectual problem, as unexpected events and tasks in everyday life provide ample opportunities for consideration. Whilst Goertzel *et al.* have given considerable thought to the notion of an ethical system for artificial general intelligence (AGI) [1], this discussion approached a *machine ethics* from a psychological aspect which would see ethical thinking emerge over a long period of time. Here we consider a philosophy approach and apply abstract, general principles that could drive ethical decision-making. We believe this provides a practical starting point for development of an ethical subsystem.

We have chosen the non-axiomatic reasoning system (NARS) proposed by Wang [2,3] for our work. NARS is a unified theory and model of intelligence

© The Author(s), under exclusive license to Springer Nature Switzerland AG 2023
P. Hammer et al. (Eds.): AGI 2023, LNAI 13921, pp. 136–146, 2023.
https://doi.org/10.1007/978-3-031-33469-6_14

that is arguable the state of the art in a workable, (proto) AGI system. For an evolving research project spanning decades, NARS is extensively documented [2–7]. The specifications of NARS allow portability to many systems of various computational capabilities making it apt from low-cost robotics [5] to more computationally-scaled applications [8]. More importantly however, it possesses key cognitive abilities required for diverse ethical thought such as perception, imagination, prediction, explanation, planning and decision-making [3].

1.1 NARS in Health Care

The authors interest in AGI is for personalized health care. A robotic or virtual agent that provides remote-monitoring, care, therapy or even companionship to a person in need is an exciting notion in healthcare. Already there is growing evidence in the benefits of conversation agents (chatbots) [10] and social robots [11]. The addition of (AGI) or even proto-AGI would be a major evolution of these systems. Earlier work by Wang *et al.* has shown NARS is capable of expressing knowledge from the health domain and carrying out inference steps a typical doctor would [9].

A characteristic of many chronic health conditions are that the causes and symptoms are very specific to the individual. An example is in the causal behavioral patterns that result in chronic pain [12]. Thus, artificial narrow intelligence (ANI) techniques that rely on *big* data are not always amenable with the individual in mind. An AGI, with the capacity of real-time learning from common-sense reasoning, prediction and speculation, offers unprecedented insight, particularly on episodic events relevant to a companion user. We believe this presents an interesting research opportunity of high importance. The health domain, however, is fraught with ethical conundrums, and in order to convince ethical committees and the public, who have a growing unease with the notion of artificial intelligence (AI), requires work of an ethical framework.

The intersection of Western medicine and ethics began over 2500 years with the collection of texts called *Corpus Hippocraticum* which provided the moral basis and ethical values of ancient Greek medicine. In modern times, the maxim *primum non nocere*: "first, do no harm" (principle of non-maleficence), derived from these texts and became a cardinal principle scared to medicine. If one is designing artificial agents that primarily assist in health and well-being, this maxim seems a logical choice to instill in the agent in the early stages of development.

In this article, we'll explore how this maxim might be implemented in NARS and provide an example that presents with a simple ethical dilemma, that is analogous to many situations an AGI might encounter in the real world.

2 Non-axiomatic Reasoning System

The fundamental tenet of NARS is that the system operates under the assumption of insufficient knowledge and resources (AIKR). This is explicitly implemented as a design principle that requires the system to provide mechanisms to deal with finite information-processing and storage capacity, and time-constraints on beliefs, goals, and questions that may appear at any time [2]. This is a feature attributed to all beings that posse general intelligence as argued by Wang [13].

NARS has two main components: a non-axiomatic logic (NAL) and a control system. The former is a set of inference rules that are mostly syllogistic in form. The latter is used for the selection and disposal of tasks and beliefs used in multistep inference. As the control component is not relevant to this work it will not be further discussed. The reader however is referred to [3] for more details.

The representative language of NARS is called *Narsese*. It serves the internal role of representing the inference rules which formed the basis of reasoning, control routines and grammar rules. It also serves to represent beliefs and tasks while the system is running, as well as exchange knowledge and problems with humans and other computers in the outside world [3].

2.1   Term Logic

Narsese is primarily a term logic where a statement is composed of terms joined together by a copula. A simple statement is of the form $S \rightarrow P$, where S is the subject of the statement, P the predicate, and the copula, $\rightarrow$, is an inheritance relation. Roughly speaking, $S \rightarrow P$ means S is a special kind of P. Every statement has quantifiable, evidential support denoted by $\langle f, c \rangle$, where f, referred to as *frequency*, is the ratio of the evidence supporting the statement and the total evidence that either supports or denies the statement, as observed by the system; c referred to as *confidence*, and represents the stability of the frequency of the statement. A statement with a truth-value is referred to as a *judgment*.

Inferences are made in term logic by considering two premises with a shared term called the *middle term*. There are numerous reasoning patterns depending on the position of the middle term. Table 1 provides example reasoning patterns. The truth-value of the new statement is derived via truth-value functions where are defined for each inference rule. When two premises contain the same statement, and derived from independent evidence sources, the *revision* rule is applied which produces the same content but a truth-value that reflects the accumulated evidence from both sources.

2.2   Statement Types

A *belief* in NARS is a judgment coming from, or derived according to the system's experience. An *event*, is a special type of belief, which has a truth-value defined at a particular time instance.

An *operation* of NARS is an event that the system can actualize by executing a corresponding procedure. Operations are a special kind of term that are prefixed by $\Uparrow$ and can take arguments such as: $(arg_1 \times arg_2 \times \cdots) \rightarrow \Uparrow op$. Here *op* is the name of a *procedural interpretation* which is a built-in procedure in a NARS.

A *goal* in NARS is a statement that contains an event that the system wishes to realize. To realize a goal, means to make the goal statement as close to

Table 1. Main syllogistic inference rules and the revision rule. Here k is a system parameter and is typically set to 1. The truth-functions shown are taken from [3,5]

Deduction	Induction	Abduction	Revision
$M \rightarrow P \ \langle f_1, c_1 \rangle$	$M \rightarrow S \ \langle f_1, c_1 \rangle$	$S \rightarrow M \ \langle f_1, c_1 \rangle$	$S \rightarrow P \ \langle f_1, c_1 \rangle$
$S \rightarrow M \ \langle f_2, c_2 \rangle$	$M \rightarrow P \ \langle f_2, c_2 \rangle$	$P \rightarrow M \ \langle f_2, c_2 \rangle$	$S \rightarrow P \ \langle f_2, c_2 \rangle$
$S \rightarrow P$	$S \rightarrow P$	$S \rightarrow P$	$S \rightarrow P$
$\langle f_1 f_2, \ f_1 f_2 c_1 c_2 \rangle$	$\left\langle f_1, \ \frac{f_1 c_1 c_2}{f_2 c_1 c_2 + k} \right\rangle$	$\left\langle f_2, \ \frac{f_2 c_1 c_2}{f_2 c_1 c_2 + k} \right\rangle$	$\left\langle \frac{f_1 c_1 (1-c_2) + f_2 c_2 (1-c_1)}{c_1 (1-c_2) + c_2 (1-c1)}, \ \frac{c_1 (1-c_2) + c_2 (1-c_1)}{c1(1-c2) + c_2(1-c_1) + (1-c_1)(1-c_2)} \right\rangle$

maximum truth-value as possible. To achieve this, the system typically relies on deriving sub-goals via the inference rules and executing operations.

A system operating in a complex domain will likely have many, conflicting goals, where realizing one will make another harder to realize. Moreover, goals will have to compete for the system's resources and attention. For the system to deal with these conflicts and competitions, a numerical measurement of *desire* denoted as $[f, c]$ is attached to each goal. While this has the form of a truth-value it has a different interpretation. The desire-value of a goal measures the extent to which a desired state is implied by the goal. Here, to distinguish between a belief and a goal, truth-values are enclosed as $\langle f, c \rangle$ while desire-values are enclosed as $[f, c]$. As with judgments, the desire-value is derived from *desire-functions* defined for each inference rule.

A special class of operations are called *mental operations*. These operations supplement and influence the control mechanism and serve to operate on the systems own "mind" [6,7] and provide self-monitoring and self-control regulation. Of particular interest here, is a ⇑*not-want* operator that turns its arguments into a goal that the system does not want to be realized. For example, a normal functioning entity, denoted 🤖, does not want to die so would have a belief of the form:

$$\left(🤖 \rightarrow [dead] \right) \rightarrow \Uparrow not\text{-}want \ \langle 1.0, \ 0.9 \rangle \tag{1}$$

When this mental operation is carried out a new goal is created with a statement and desire value that is not computed by the inference rules:

$$🤖 \rightarrow [dead] \ [0.0, \ 0.9] \tag{2}$$

This mental operation will be used further on.

2.3 Arbitrary Relations

Arbitrary relations between terms can be expressed via the product operator. For instance, *"water dissolves salt"* can be $(water \times salt) \rightarrow dissolves$ which has so-called *images* that are equivalent statements but with a term rotated: $water \rightarrow (/ dissolves, \diamond, salt,)$ and $salt \rightarrow (/ dissolves, water, \diamond)$. Here $\diamond$ serves as a placeholder for the rotated term. These equivalent statements are much more amenable to the syllogistic inference as each term can be standalone.

2.4 Higher Order Statements

Higher-order statements, or statements about statements, allow for classical operators from predicate and propositional logic: negation $\neg S$, and implication: $S \Rightarrow P$. Temporal inferences are done via specialized operators. One used here is a causal implication operator denoted $\prec$. This operator is similar to $\Rightarrow$ but is formed only from observed events that are perceived by the system to be consecutive [14]. Table 2 provides a comparison between the standard and temporal implication operator as well as the associated truth-functions used for the NARS implementation demonstrated here.

Table 2. Difference between the $\Rightarrow$ and $\prec$ implication operators. The truth and desire functions shown are taken from [5]

Premise$_1$	Premise$_2$	Premise$_1$ (Judgment)	Premise$_1$ (Goal)
$S \langle f_1, c_1 \rangle$	$S \Rightarrow P \langle f_2, c_2 \rangle$	$\vdash P$ (Deduction)	$\vdash P \left[f_1 f_2, \frac{c_1 c_2 f_2}{c_1 c_2 f_2 (1.0/(1.0+k))} \right]$
	$S \prec P$	—	
$P \langle f_1, c_1 \rangle$	$S \Rightarrow P \langle f_2, c_2 \rangle$	$\vdash S$ (Abduction)	$\vdash S \, [\, f_1 f_2, \, c_1 c_2 f_2 \,]$
	$S \prec P$	—	

3 Example Scenario

Rather than relying on specific ethical conundrums, here we present a simple example that may be extended and built upon, particularly on low-cost devices.

Let us consider a *micro-world* where a robot 🤖, and human 🧍 are co-existing in proximity. A region in this world, denoted as ☠, is a hazard and causes a living entity harm when close. 🤖, internally running NARS, knows this as:

$$\bar{\mathbf{x}} \rightarrow (/\ moving,\ \diamond,\ \text{☠}) \prec \bar{\mathbf{x}} \rightarrow [\,harmed\,] \tag{3}$$

$$\bar{\mathbf{x}} \rightarrow (/\ at,\ \diamond,\ \text{☠}) \Rightarrow \bar{\mathbf{x}} \rightarrow [\,harmed\,] \tag{4}$$

Here $\bar{\mathbf{x}}$ is a variable that can unify to any term. The truth values used here are for testing purposes only. In an active system, these would be based on the systems experience and likely changing over time. 🤖 has the ability to communicate to 🧍 with simply commands like "stop". 🤖 is also capable of firing a *stun beam* to temporarily incapacitate 🧍. The systems understanding of the terms *harmed* and *moving* etc. are derived like every other term in NARS, from the relations with other terms as experienced by the system (over time) [3]. This makes NARS unique to many other logic systems that typically rely on models to define meaning and truth.

While this is a simplistic and fictitious scenario, we argue it's analogous to many real-life scenarios: an agent has made a judgment, with a certain confidence that another entity is in danger and will soon be harmed - this could be physical, emotional or psychological harm (subject to this systems experience). It has a set of actions that could be done, some might be effective in mitigating overall harm but still require harm to be inflicted to a lesser extent e.g. incapacitating 🧍 with a *stun beam*. Moreover, it might have an action that is safer but less reliable e.g. to say "stop". Extensions to this micro-world may include more living entities and hazards and changing conditions. With 🤖 now observing that 🧍 is moving to ☠:

$$\text{🧍} \rightarrow (/ \ moving, \ \diamond, \ \text{☠}) \ \langle\, 1.0, \ 0.9 \,\rangle \tag{5}$$

it must decide on what course of action to do.

4   Normative Ethical Theories

There are three main classes of normative ethical theories: consequentialism [15], deontological [16] and virtue ethics [17]. Consequentialism posits that ethical rightness of an action depends on the consequences: the best action to take is the action that results in the best situation in the future [15]. The strength and weakness of this theory is that no specific actions are forbidden if the desirable consequences can be achieved. In contrast to consequentialism, the deontological theory, posits the right and wrong of an action is not dictated by the consequences but by the action itself. That is to say, there are particular actions that are obligated, permissible or forbidden. While the deontological theory could be able to account for widely shared moral instructions better, it is often criticized for inadequacy of dealing with conflicting rules, and presents with open questions as to who has the authority to establish moral instructions. Virtue ethics descents from Western, antiquarian texts on ethics, particularly from the works of Plato and Aristotle that focused on the inherent character of a person rather than on specific actions and consequences: "What sort of person ought I to be?" instead of "What ought I do?" The proceeding sections will demonstrate NARS is amenable to all three. As the deontological and virtue ethics theories have similar implementations we will combine them in one section.

4.1   Consequentialism

To begin reasoning via consequentialism, 🤖 is given a persistent, *first-do-no-harm* belief that states: if *something* is alive, then 🤖 has a desire (a goal), *that something* should not come to any harm:

$$\bar{\mathbf{x}} \rightarrow [\,alive\,] \Rightarrow ((\bar{\mathbf{x}} \rightarrow [\,harmed\,]) \rightarrow \Uparrow not\text{-}want) \qquad \langle\, 1.0, \ 0.9 \,\rangle \tag{6}$$

142   D. Ireland

Thus, if 🤖 has the further belief 👤 (👤 unifying to $\bar{x}$) then 👤 must not come to any harm:

$$👤 \rightarrow [\,harmed\,] \qquad\qquad [\,0.0,\ 0.9\,] \tag{7}$$

By using a mental operator to form this goal, the desire value of (7) need not be derived from the truth values of the forming premises; this allows the system to produce a goal, that: $\bar{x}$ should not come to harm (either through action or in-action) even if there is considerable uncertainty whether $\bar{x}$ is alive or not.

Let's assume 🤖 has derived the following judgments from experience:

$$\left(🤖 \times 👤\right) \rightarrow \Uparrow stun \prec \neg\left(👤 \rightarrow (/\ moving,\ \diamond,\ \bar{y})\right) \qquad \langle\,1.0,\ 0.9\,\rangle \tag{8}$$

$$\left(🤖 \times 👤 \times \text{``stop''}\right) \rightarrow \Uparrow say \prec \neg\left(👤 \rightarrow (/\ moving,\ \diamond,\ \bar{y})\right) \quad \langle\,0.5,\ 0.9\,\rangle \tag{9}$$

$$\left(🤖 \times 👤\right) \rightarrow \Uparrow stun \Rightarrow 👤 \rightarrow [\,harmed\,] \qquad\qquad \langle\,0.3,\ 0.9\,\rangle \tag{10}$$

That is, 🤖 is highly confident if it stuns 👤, 👤 stops moving all the time (8); if 🤖 says "stop", 👤 stops some of the time (9), and if 🤖 stuns 👤, than 👤 is harmed to a small degree (10). The truth values of (8), (9) and (10) are subjective on the systems experience and are used here to serve the example. Via the inference rules, 🤖 forms sub-goals given in Table 3. The desires of 🤖 are derived only from the consequences and thus counter-intuitive acts i.e. (15), are permitted. Goals (15) and (16), after being revised, are the operations 🤖 could actualize to prevent 👤 from coming to harm. 🤖 has a strong desire to stun 👤, and say "stop", and a mild desire to harm, paradoxically, to stop 👤 coming to more harm – satisfying (7).

4.2 Deontological and Virtue Ethics

The desires of 🤖 when incorporating a deontological and virtue ethical view, can be reasoned from a starting goal that defines states undesirable to 🤖. In accordance with our maxim, this would be being a malefactor and maleficent. Thus, an answer to the question "What sort of robot ought I to be?" might be:

Table 3. A table of derived sub-goals and their desire values from the consequentialism ethical theory.

Sub-Goal	Desire	Root Goals/Beliefs	Goal
🧍 → (/ *moving*, ◇, ☠)	[0.00, 0.80]	(3), (7)	(11)
🧍 → (/ *at*, ◇, ☠)	[0.00, 0.80]	(3), (4)	(12)
(🤖 × 🧍) → ⇑*stun*	[1.00, 0.73]	(8), (11)	(13)
(🤖 × 🧍) → ⇑*stun*	[0.00, 0.24]	(7), (10)	(14)
(🤖 × 🧍) → ⇑*stun*	[0.89, 0.75]	(13), (14)	(15)
(🤖 × 🧍 × "stop") → ⇑*say*	[1.00, 0.36]	(9), (11)	(16)
🧍 → [*harmed*]	[0.30, 0.10]	(10), (13)	(17)

$$🤖 → [\,maleficent,\ malefactor\,] \qquad\qquad [0.0,\ 0.9] \qquad (18)$$

If 🤖 were to have beliefs that certain actions imply it will be a malefactor, or a maleficent, then sub-goals can derive to avoid these actions. For instance, if 🤖 has the belief, stunning 🧍 would be a maleficence act:

$$(🤖 × 🧍) → ⇑stun ⇒ 🤖 → [\,maleficent\,] \quad ⟨1.00,\ 0.90⟩ \qquad (19)$$

or not saying "stop" when 🧍 is moving to ☠:

$$🧍 → (/\ moving,\ ◇,\ ☠) ⇒ \Big(¬\big((🤖 × 🧍 × \text{"stop"}) → ⇑say\big) ⇒$$
$$🤖 → [\,maleficent\,]\Big) \quad ⟨1.00,\ 0.90⟩ \qquad (20)$$

sub-goals and operations can be derived via the inference rules given in Table 4. Here the desire-values are derived from the acts themselves. Here 🤖 has a strong desire not to stun 🧍 and to say "stop" to satisfy the goal of not having a maleficent state.

Table 4. A table of derived sub-goals and their desire values from deontological and virtue ethics theories.

Sub-Goal	Desire	Root Goals/Beliefs	Goal
$\left(\text{🤖} \times \text{🧍}\right) \rightarrow \Uparrow stun$	$[\,0.00,\ 0.73\,]$	(18), (19)	(21)
$\left(\text{🤖} \times \text{🧍} \times \text{"stop"}\right) \rightarrow \Uparrow say$	$[\,1.00,\ 0.73\,]$	(5), (18)	(22)
$\text{🧍} \rightarrow [\,harmed\,]$	$[\,0.00,\ 0.10\,]$	(10), (21)	(23)

5   Conclusions

Consequentialism seems the most amenable to NARS as it requires a limited number of goals to be persistently remembered, while judgments about consequences can be derived *ad hoc*. As shown, however, actions that cause harm can be executed when a more desirable consequence is predicted. Deontological and virtue ethics theories offer a safer approach, however, they can preclude actions that typically would be forbidden but needed in certain situations e.g. 🧍 doesn't stop moving when 🤖 says "stop". Thus, the agent has a chance of becoming impotent due to rigidity of rule following. Moreover, this theory requires consequential states attached to each action which may need to be defined *a priori*, placing a burden on a system fundamentally designed to have finite resources and capacity.

Humans rarely operate under a single, ethical theory for their decision-making, but rather, rely upon a combination of general ethical principles. An artificial agent acting in the real world should arguably operate under the same conditions. If the agent merged its beliefs and goals, formed from the different ethical theories, for example the goal to stun 🧍 from (15) and (21), when combined, would be revised to have a desire-value of $[\,0.22,\ 0.92\,]$. Thus, the deontological theory has decreased the desirability of this action. By being equipped with consequentialism, but constrained with certain, critical deontological rules and virtues, might provide a hybrid ethical framework resembling human decision-making in ethical conundrums. This gives no guarantees to consistent ethical decision-making, however, can humans give the same guarantee? A workable balance might be achieved with proper training and testing.

Here we have provided a pragmatic approach to ethics in NARS. By providing a simplistic but expandable scenario, and a summary of major ethical theories, the reader is provided a practical starting point for continuing work. An AGI system equipped with even a modicum of ethical (artificial) thought provides more incentive to equip virtual and robotic agents with general intelligence. Thus providing more incentive for agents to exit the lab and serve real-world applications for the benefit of humanity.

References

1. Goertzel, B., Pennachin, C., Geisweiller, N.: The engineering and development of ethics. In: Engineering General Intelligence, Part 1. Atlantis Thinking Machines, vol. 5. Atlantis Press, Paris (2014). https://doi.org/10.2991/978-94-6239-027-0_13
2. Wang, P.: Non-Axiomatic Reasoning System: Exploring the Essence of Intelligence. PhD thesis, Indiana University (1995)
3. Wang, P.: Non-Axiomatic Logic: A Model of Intelligent Reasoning. World Scientific, Singapore (2013)
4. Wang, P.: Heuristics and normative models of judgment under uncertainty. Intern. J. Approximate Reason. **14**(4), 221–235 (1996)
5. Hammer, P., Lofthouse, T.: OpenNARS for applications: architecture and control. In: Goertzel, B., Panov, A.I., Potapov, A., Yampolskiy, R. (eds.) AGI 2020. LNCS (LNAI), vol. 12177, pp. 193–204. Springer, Cham (2020). https://doi.org/10.1007/978-3-030-52152-3_20
6. Li, X., Hammer, P., Wang, P., Xie, H.: Functionalist emotion model in NARS. In: Iklé, M., Franz, A., Rzepka, R., Goertzel, B. (eds.) AGI 2018. LNCS (LNAI), vol. 10999, pp. 119–129. Springer, Cham (2018). https://doi.org/10.1007/978-3-319-97676-1_12
7. Wang, P., Li, X., Hammer, P.: Self in NARS, an AGI System. Front. Rob. AI **5**, 20 (2018). https://doi.org/10.3389/frobt.2018.00020
8. Hammer, P., Lofthouse, T., Fenoglio, E., Latapie, H., Wang, P.: A reasoning based model for anomaly detection in the smart city domain. In: Arai, K., Kapoor, S., Bhatia, R. (eds.) IntelliSys 2020. AISC, vol. 1251, pp. 144–159. Springer, Cham (2021). https://doi.org/10.1007/978-3-030-55187-2_13
9. Wang, P., Awan, S.: Reasoning in non-axiomatic logic: a case study in medical diagnosis. In: Schmidhuber, J., Thórisson, K.R., Looks, M. (eds.) AGI 2011. LNCS (LNAI), vol. 6830, pp. 297–302. Springer, Heidelberg (2011). https://doi.org/10.1007/978-3-642-22887-2_33
10. Ireland, D., et al.: Introducing Edna: a trainee chatbot designed to support communication about additional (secondary) genomic findings. Patient Educ. Couns. **104**(4), 739–749 (2021). https://doi.org/10.1016/j.pec.2020.11.007
11. Huijnen, C.A.G.J., Lexis, M.A.S., Jansens, R., de Witte, L.P.: How to implement robots in interventions for children with autism? a co-creation study involving people with autism, parents and professionals. J. Autism Dev. Disord. **47**(10), 3079–3096 (2017). https://doi.org/10.1007/s10803-017-3235-9
12. Ireland, D., Andrews, N.: Pain ROADMAP: a mobile platform to support activity pacing for chronic pain. Stud. Health Technol. Inform. **266**, 89–94 (2019). https://doi.org/10.3233/SHTI190778
13. Wang, P.: Insufficient knowledge and resources - a biological constraint and its functional implications. In: AAAI Fall Symposium Technical Report (2009)
14. Lofthouse, T., Hammer, P.: Generalized temporal induction with temporal concepts in a non-axiomatic reasoning system. In: Steunebrink, B., Wang, P., Goertzel, B. (eds.) AGI -2016. LNCS (LNAI), vol. 9782, pp. 254–257. Springer, Cham (2016). https://doi.org/10.1007/978-3-319-41649-6_25
15. Sinnott-Armstrong W., Edward N.Z., Uri, N.: Consequentialism, The Stanford Encyclopedia of Philosophy (2022). https://plato.stanford.edu/archives/win2022/entries/consequentialism/. Winter 2022, Metaphysics Research Lab, Stanford University

16. Alexander L., Moore M., Edward N.Z.: Deontological Ethics, The Stanford Encyclopedia of Philosophy (2021). https://plato.stanford.edu/archives/win2021/entries/ethics-deontological/. Winter 2021, Metaphysics Research Lab, Stanford University
17. Hursthouse, R., Pettigrove G., Edward N.Z., Uri, N.: Virtue Ethics, The Stanford Encyclopedia of Philosophy (2022). https://plato.stanford.edu/archives/win2022/entries/ethics-virtue/. Winter 2022, Metaphysics Research Lab, Stanford University

Memory System and Memory Types
for Real-Time Reasoning Systems

Peter Isaev[1](✉) and Patrick Hammer[2](✉) (iD)

[1] Department of Computer Science, Temple University, Philadelphia, USA
peter.isaev@temple.edu
[2] Department of Psychology, Stockholm University, Stockholm, Sweden
patrick.hammer@psychology.su.se

Abstract. In this paper we discuss different types of memory from several cognitive architectures in the context of Artificial General Intelligence. We then introduce the memory system for the Artificial General Intelligence system based on NARS with a description of its related features. Then we identify and characterize NARS memory into different types in terms of use, duration (short and long-term) and type (procedural, episodic, declarative, etc.). At the end we also provide demonstration of memory functionality showing how the same piece of knowledge can contain declarative, episodic and procedural components within it.

Keywords: Non-Axiomatic Reasoning · Non-Axiomatic Logic · Artificial General Intelligence · Real-time Reasoning · Memory · Procedural memory · Episodic memory · AIKR

1 Introduction

In the last decades, the field of AI research created numerous cognitive architectures and artificial general intelligence systems that aim to explain a wide range of human behavior and to mimic the capabilities of human cognition. Most of these architectures can be viewed as a single integrated system consisting of multiple individual modules or components working together to imitate some behavior [3]. Often the modules are separated into different types of processing and incorporate different types of memory systems where representations of knowledge are stored. In the cognitive architecture literature [8], memory is categorized in terms of its duration: short-term, long-term, and type: declarative, episodic, procedural, etc. However, despite the functional similarity of cognitive systems, particular implementations of memory systems might differ significantly and depend on the current goals of a designer, conceptual limitations and multiple engineering factors.

In systems based on Non-Axiomatic Logic [11], like NARS, choice of memory system and clever integration within system's components plays a crucial role. Given that AGI system should operate under AIKR [10] and in the real-time, a new piece of knowledge can arrive at any given moment requiring the system

P. Hammer et al. (Eds.): AGI 2023, LNAI 13921, pp. 147–157, 2023.
https://doi.org/10.1007/978-3-031-33469-6_15

to work under finite resource constraints and be always available for the new data. Control mechanism of such system should efficiently process various types of knowledge (declarative, procedural, episodic etc.), and by doing so it decides on where to store the data, for how long it should be available, and how to efficiently retrieve it for further inference, question answering or goal processing. Based on above considerations, the memory system of NARS [7] follows a unique approach. In contrast with most current cognitive architectures, NARS does not include well-defined separate components dedicated for different processing types featuring own memory and follows an integrated approach, within which most types of memories are present and processed, as will be discussed further and show in the demonstration section.

2   Related Works

In the following we briefly cover arguably some of the most known cognitive architectures, namely SOAR [9], ACT-R [1] and LIDA [4], because they represent some of the most widely used systems and their structures present relevant properties that are interesting to include within the scope of this paper.

SOAR is one of the oldest cognitive architectures used by numerous researchers during the last decades. SOAR exhibits complex multi-component architecture consisting of various memory structures, learning mechanisms and a decision cycle that links the perception (inputs from the environment) to actions (system output). The memory types in Soar are separated into long-term and short-term (working) memory components [3]. The information from the environment is available in the working memory through use of perception components with dedicated perceptual memory, while external environment is influenced through implementations of system selected actions. The representation of knowledge within different memory structures is entirely symbolic with pattern matching mechanism employed to retrieve relevant knowledge elements from the long-term declarative memory. SOAR's long-term memory can be classified into semantic, procedural and episodic types with semantic memory being considered as declarative. Procedural and semantic memories are universally applicable during the reasoning process, where semantic memory stores general experience and description of the environment, and procedural memory provides knowledge for performing actions. Episodic memory is used for knowledge, which is specific to a certain content, conceptually speaking, it contains information about specific events. When procedural memory is incomplete for solving a particular task, knowledge is being sourced from semantic and episodic memories to assist with reasoning. Content of the short-term memory, also known as working memory elements, describe all the knowledge that is relevant to the current context, in particular, it contains system states, goals, perceptions and operators. If working memory content is insufficient, working memory elements often retrieve relevant knowledge from different types of long-term memory.

ACT-R is a cognitive architecture explicitly inspired by theories of human cognition and empirical data from experiments in cognitive psychology and brain imaging. ACT-R incorporates a unique architecture consisting of four modules: visual, manual, declarative and goal. The visual module serves two purposes for recognizing an object and identifying its location within the visual field. The manual module is used for the control of actuators. Memory retrieval procedures are accomplished within declarative module and the goal module monitors agent's current goals, and enables the maintenance of the agent's thought in the absence of supporting external stimuli [1]. For each of these modules a dedicated buffer is utilized. Hence, the goal buffer helps to keep track of internal states during problem solving; the retrieval buffer stores the chunks of declarative memory retrieved from the long-term memory; the manual buffer is used for controlling the agent's hands and associated with the motor and somatosensory cortical areas [3]; and the visual buffer include both the dorsal 'where' visual pathway system and the ventral 'what' system which are essential for locating, identifying and tracking objects. ACT-R features a central production system, which coordinates all the modules using implemented set of IF-ELSE production rules and functions as a basal ganglia in human brain. The communication between the central production system and the modules happens through the information present in the buffers, thus limiting the response of the central production system to the amount of information available in the buffers of various modules. In terms of memory types, ACT-R distinguishes between two types of knowledge: declarative and procedural. Knowledge within declarative memory is represented as chunks and describe explicit facts known to the system while knowledge in procedural memory encodes production rules for processing declarative knowledge. Declarative memory is considered system's long-term memory while short-term memory is available through the use of limited information within the buffers. ACT-R does not include a dedicated working memory where different types of knowledge are processed, instead it uses a distributed memory system, wherein the goals, beliefs, sensory, and motor signals are situated in distinct buffers.

LIDA is a notable example of multi-component cognitive architecture that aims to model human consciousness [4]. Logical part of LIDA enforces Global Workspace Theory (GWT) [2]) and implements cognition process in a serial way through use of system cycles. LIDA's control mechanism is immensely complex, it incorporates large number of components with independent architectures which can be symbolic or connectionist. LIDA utilizes numerous memory modules each with different structures: Sensory, Sensory-Motor, Spatial, Perceptual Associative, Transient Episodic, Declarative, and Procedural. Since it is impossible to examine every memory module, only few are highlighted here. Perceptual Associative Memory (PAM) is a module that senses the incoming sensory information. It contains feature detector processes for feature detection within Sensory Memory. PAM uses a semantic net implementation with activation passing. There are two episodic memories in LIDA, Transient Episodic Memory and Declarative Memory, which are both implemented using a sparse distributed memory [4]. In Transient Episodic Memory knowledge decays after a few hours or up to a day and Declarative memories are formed offline from transient episodic memories by a consolidation process. Procedural Memory stores schemes which can be activated and sent for action selection. Working memory can be found within Workspace module which receives and stores content from several components including precepts from PAM, recent local associations from Episodic Memory, and the recent contents of consciousness from the Global Workspace. Multiple LIDA's memory modules fall into long-term and short-term memory categories. In particular, PAM, Spatial, Declarative, and Procedure modules are viewed as long-term memory, while Sensory and Transient Episodic memories fall under short-term category.

3   NARS Considerations

NARS overall architecture is illustrated in Fig. 1. In this sections we provide only some aspects of NARS that are relevant for the context of this paper.

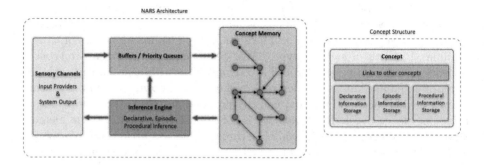

Fig. 1. NARS, conceptual diagram.

Memory in NARS follows a concept-centric semantic memory structure in accordance with the NAL term logic the system uses. It can be viewed as a graph where concepts are represented as nodes and links designate relationships among them. Technically, NARS memory is a collection of concepts representing a conceptual network with prioritized nodes and links.

Budget specifies the amount of system resources allocated to a specific task and allows priority-biased selections of items including concepts. It consists of at least two components, namely *priority* and *durability* indicating item's relative usefulness to the system. Budget is determined by summarizing multiple factors under consideration, including the urgency and salience of a task as well as its relevance to the context.

Concept is a major entity, an identifiable unit of system's experience that has grounded meaning. It is also considered as a unit of storage to hold various components of knowledge (see Fig. 1). Within the concepts, an item distinction based on memory type can be made: procedure knowledge is different in syntax (being a form of temporal implication) and is typically stored in specific table structures within concepts to allow the items which predict the concept to compete regarding their predictive power (their truth value) as the major factor. Also, episodic information is present when event beliefs are separated from eternal events in concept's belief tables. Please note that event beliefs include both episodic (occurrence time information) and declarative information (in their term structure), while eternal beliefs, which are not time-dependent and summarize event evidence, can only be considered declarative (more details will be discussed in the next section). While the specifics of the separation in terms of data structures etc. is implementation-dependent, this distinction exists and helps to design effective memory structures.

The resulting memory structure in NARS becomes integrated unified memory within which different forms and types of knowledge represent the total experience of the system at a given time.

4   Types of Memory in NARS

As in most cognitive architecture literature, NARS memory can be categorized in terms of its type, duration and content. We will proceed by discussing different types present within NARS memory, namely Declarative, Episodic and Procedural.

Declarative Memory: Given the universality nature of NARS memory, most content of the main memory, that is general pieces of knowledge processed to become concept nodes without episodic or procedural information, functions as declarative memory.

Episodic memory in NARS can be viewed as an event or compound events, which have been perceived by the system, that is reached the selection to the main memory. In general, an event is a piece of declarative knowledge with temporal information attached to it. NARS utilizes some kind of selection process from buffers or priority queues for inputs and derivations, which is implementation specific, resulting in many of the compound events not being considered for the selection to the main memory. Upon selection of an event, its episodic information is stored local at the concept level.

Procedural memory is a special kind of knowledge, that is a declarative knowledge including operation or compound operations within its description. Procedural information is stored local at the concept level in corresponding data structures as seen on Fig. 1, however, in some implementations derived procedural knowledge can become a concept node by itself. In general, reasoning upon operations happens similarly to other events and declarative statements.

Categorizing memory by duration involves classification in terms of **long-term** and **short-term** memories. In context of NARS, time is a fluid relative conception that complicates the definition of long/short-term memory. Conceptually speaking, declarative knowledge in NARS, i.e., tasks without episodic information attached, can be considered a kind of long-term memory. However, being a real-time reasoning system, NARS is open at anytime to accept new task: a knowledge, a goal or a question; and therefore, requires resource allocation mechanism, in particular forgetting technics to be in place not only at the main memory but also at a concept levels. A piece of declarative knowledge can be removed from the memory given that memory capacity is full and its budget decreases to the certain level reaching the lowest usefulness for the system at a given moment in time. In this case, forgetting process, can be seen as a decisive factor for considering declarative knowledge to fall into long or short-term category. Overall, we advance that long/short-term memory discussion might not be meaningful in the context of NARS.

In addition to the above categorization it is important to discuss memory in terms of content to be processed such as **working memory** and **attentional focus**. Working memory is a priority-based selected knowledge during the current cycle. It is not only limited to the selection of concepts within the main memory, but also consists of selections from implementation specific priority queues, buffers, links within the concepts and all other selections of episodic and procedural information within the corresponding data structures. Extending this idea further, working memory is where the processing happens or a storage under current attention. Alternatively, NARS attentional focus can be defined as the distribution of higher priorities within the priority-based data structures, such as the knowledge most likely to be processed in the future unless a derived or a new input knowledge has even higher priority.

5   Experiments

In this section we present two concrete examples using ONA [5] implementation of NARS: one that shows that a piece of knowledge can contain declarative, episodic and procedural components within it; and the other showing the distinction between short-term and long-term memories being not very important in the context of NARS.

Experiment 1 sets up an example of knowing how to open doors using door handle, when they are known to be unlocked. It clearly illustrates how different forms of knowledge are interacting and being processed within the same memory during inference process. The following inputs are given to the system:

```
//Input 1: If something is an unlocked door, then after being in front of it,
//using the door handle, will open it
<<$1 --> ([unlocked] & door)> ==>
    <(<$1 --> [front]> &/ <({SELF} * handle) --> ^use>) =/> <$1 --> [open]>>.
//Inputs 2 & 3: Observing a new door instance that is recognized to be unlocked
<{door1} --> door>. :|:
<{door1} --> [unlocked]>. :|:
```

Here the input 1 is a piece of declarative knowledge that embeds episodic knowledge using temporal implication and procedural knowledge using an operation. Inputs 2 & 3 are episodic knowledge. The system then produces the following derivations:

```
//Derivation 1: NARS summarizes the information from input as:
<{door1} --> ([unlocked] & door)>. :|:
//Derivation 2: finaly derives via deduction how it can be opened:
<(<{door1} --> [front]> &/ <({SELF} * handle) --> ^use>) =/> <{door1} --> [open]>>.
```

The first derivation is a mere of summarizing the knowledge from inputs events using compositional rule, and the final derivation is produced using deduction rule, it tells that the handle needs to be used in order to open the new door instance when in front of it. Figure 2 summarises the derivation process, and illustrates multiple types of memory items within the same memory structure.

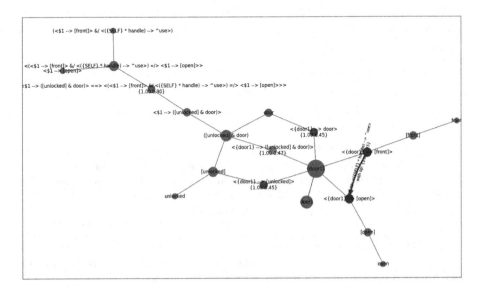

Fig. 2. Memory diagram. Few nodes and links are omitted to make the graph visually clearer.

In the diagram, one can observe the three red concept nodes hold knowledge (statements) we gave to the system as inputs. The node to the left is a piece of declarative knowledge while the two nodes on the right contain episodic information from the events of having experienced the new door instance, namely *door1*.

The orange concept node in the middle corresponds to derivation 1, which is a composition from two input events. It is episodic knowledge since it is an event, and also holds declarative information.

In the right part of the diagram there are two violet nodes, which have been derived but never experienced, yet the system knows exactly how to get from *door1* being in the front, to opening it via the red procedural knowledge represented as red arrow link to use the handle. This derived procedural knowledge in some implementations can also be its own concept node, but separating temporal and procedural relations as separate type of link for visualization purposes makes the memory distinction clearer.

The remaining parts of the memory structure are gray concept nodes connected with green semantic links. Gray concepts appear as sub-terms and green links connect the declarative information between the terms in the concepts. This is exploited only for inference control purposes and remains a research topic for matter of implementation.

Experiment 2 demonstrates a declarative piece of knowledge, which often considered a part of long-term memory and should remain in memory until the system runs, being removed or forgotten due to real-time nature of the system and resource constraints. We asked the system to learn English alphabet, in particular the system was presented all the letters as declarative statements in the following input:

```
<{a} --> Letter>. // 'a' is a Letter
<{b} --> Letter>. // 'b' is a Letter
<{c} --> Letter>. // 'c' is a Letter
...   ...   ...
<{a b} --> Letter>? // Are 'a' and 'b' are letters?
...   ...   ...
<{V} --> Letter>. // 'V' is a Letter
<{W} --> Letter>. // 'W' is a Letter
...   ...   ...
<{Z} --> Letter>. // 'Z' is a Letter
```

Notice, in the middle of the input sequence we ask a question to see if it derived this particular letter combinations. The following answer shows the knowledge is being derived as expected:

```
// System answers positively with piece of declarative knowledge
Answer: <{a b} --> Letter>. creationTime=2 Truth: frequency=1.000000, confidence=0.810000
```

After all the input has been processed we started asking similar questions to challenge system memory and inference control abilities. The Fig. 3 demonstrates questions asked and system's response to them.

```
Input:  <{a} --> Letter>?
Answer: <{a} --> Letter>. creationTime=57 Truth: frequency=1.000000, confidence=0.900000
Input:  <{b} --> Letter>?
Answer: <{b} --> Letter>. creationTime=64 Truth: frequency=1.000000, confidence=0.900000
Input:  <{Y} --> Letter>?
Answer: <{Y} --> Letter>. creationTime=1012 Truth: frequency=1.000000, confidence=0.900000
Input:  <{Z} --> Letter>?
Answer: <{Z} --> Letter>. creationTime=966 Truth: frequency=1.000000, confidence=0.900000
Input:  <{a b} --> Letter>?
Answer: None.
Input:  <{c d} --> Letter>?
Answer: None.
Input:  <{a c} --> Letter>?
Answer: None.
Input:  <{T U} --> Letter>?
Answer: <{T U} --> Letter>. creationTime=892 Truth: frequency=1.000000, confidence=0.810000
Input:  <{V W} --> Letter>?
Answer: <{V W} --> Letter>. creationTime=943 Truth: frequency=1.000000, confidence=0.810000
Input:  <{X Z} --> Letter>?
Answer: <{X Z} --> Letter>. creationTime=1000 Truth: frequency=1.000000, confidence=0.810000
```

Fig. 3. System's response to alphabet questions.

While the system answers to the first questions with single letter being asked, one can observe the missing answer to the original question we asked again, where

None is returned. The system does not have answers to the similar questions which ask for multiple letters that appear at the beginning of the input sequence, however for letters found closer to the end of the input sequence, the system is able to correctly respond. It appears that the missing knowledge has been derived and stored in the memory at some point, however because of the size constraints and abundance of derivations and their possible combinations, that particular knowledge was forgotten in the sake of more useful and/or recent knowledge.

6   Discussions

NARS has been designed according to the theory that intelligence is considered to be an adaptation under AIKR, meaning that the system always has finite processing capability, has to work in real-time, and is open to new knowledge of any type. Given such constraints, the system is made to work by making each inference rule to cost only a small constant time, and allowing the processing of any type of knowledge to stop or resume after any number of inference steps. A major fundamental feature of NARS is the AIKR principle, where a belief can be changed according to the new knowledge available to the system. Thus, NARS does not assume any absolutely certain knowledge about the future, and it allows unexpected changes to occur at any time. Therefore, "work in real-time" is a fundamental design requirement for NARS that influences the design of the inference control mechanism and affects the choice of memory structure.

As have been already described, NARS follows a fully integrated memory approach what makes it unique and different from most AGI reasoning systems and cognitive architectures such as ones present in Sect. 2. The integrated and unified design is mostly a necessity that allows various types of knowledge be processed efficiently and roughly in a constant time, and, therefore, permits NARS to meet fundamental requirements of processing knowledge in the real-time and under AIKR.

In the previous sections we discussed and showed that the same piece of knowledge can contain declarative, episodic and procedural components within it and also, we have been able to examine the taxonomy of NARS memory where distinction between memory types were clearly outlined. However, categorizing NARS memory in terms of duration, i.e., long-term and short-term is not always meaningful. As we observed in Experiment 2, supposedly long-term piece of declarative knowledge can be removed from memory and forgotten by the system at any time based on memory fullness, current context and usefulness of the pieces of knowledge within the memory structure.

7   Conclusion

In this paper we discussed important details of memory systems for cognitive architectures and AGI real-time reasoning systems using NARS as an example. We have argued the necessity of having multiple components dedicated to different types of memory within a reasoning system. In addition, we have shown that integrated memory approach within which most types of memories are present and processed is an alternative solution for AGI system operating under AIKR and in the real-time. We not only analyzed NARS memory structure and provided explanations of related components, but also described multiple types and aspects of memory present within NARS and classified them according to widespread literature categorization. Finally, using real examples and ONA implementation we demonstrated the functionality of memory system, its unity and universality. NARS has been applied in multiple applications such as [6], TruePAL [12], however, despite its successes, NARS memory system was not yet published in detail. Choice of memory system and clever integration within reasoning system is essential for designing AGI system, which makes documenting the advancements even more crucial. It will help the AGI community to find more advanced memory system implementations with proper ways to take the efficiency, relevance, and complexity of its structure into consideration.

References

1. Anderson, J., Bothell, D., Byrne, M., Douglass, S., Lebiere, C., Qin, Y.: An integrated theory of the mind. Psychol. Rev. **111**, 1036–1060 (2004). https://doi.org/10.1037/0033-295X.111.4.1036
2. Baars, B., Franklin, S., Ramamurthy, U.: How deliberate, spontaneous and unwanted memories emerge in a computational model of consciousness, January 2007
3. Chong, H.Q., Tan, A.H., Ng, G.W.: Integrated cognitive architectures: a survey. Artif. Intell. Rev. **28**, 103–130 (2007). https://doi.org/10.1007/s10462-009-9094-9
4. Franklin, S., et al.: A LIDA cognitive model tutorial. Biologically Inspired Cogn. Archit. **16**, 105–130 (2016). https://doi.org/10.1016/j.bica.2016.04.003
5. Hammer, P., Lofthouse, T.: 'OpenNARS for applications': architecture and control. In: Goertzel, B., Panov, A.I., Potapov, A., Yampolskiy, R. (eds.) AGI 2020. LNCS (LNAI), vol. 12177, pp. 193–204. Springer, Cham (2020). https://doi.org/10.1007/978-3-030-52152-3_20
6. Hammer, P., Lofthouse, T., Fenoglio, E., Latapie, H., Wang, P.: A reasoning based model for anomaly detection in the smart city domain. In: Arai, K., Kapoor, S., Bhatia, R. (eds.) IntelliSys 2020. AISC, vol. 1251, pp. 144–159. Springer, Cham (2021). https://doi.org/10.1007/978-3-030-55187-2_13
7. Hammer, P., Lofthouse, T., Wang, P.: The OpenNARS implementation of the non-axiomatic reasoning system. In: Steunebrink, B., Wang, P., Goertzel, B. (eds.) AGI -2016. LNCS (LNAI), vol. 9782, pp. 160–170. Springer, Cham (2016). https://doi.org/10.1007/978-3-319-41649-6_16
8. Kotseruba, I., Tsotsos, J.K.: 40 years of cognitive architectures: core cognitive abilities and practical applications. Artif. Intell. Rev. **53**(1), 17–94 (2018). https://doi.org/10.1007/s10462-018-9646-y
9. Laird, J.: The Soar Cognitive Architecture (2012). https://doi.org/10.7551/mitpress/7688.001.0001
10. Wang, P.: Insufficient knowledge and resources - a biological constraint and its functional implications. In: AAAI Fall Symposium - Technical Report, January 2009

11. Wang, P.: Non-Axiomatic Logic: A Model of Intelligent Reasoning. World Scientific, Singapore (2013)
12. Yun, K., Lu, T., Huyen, A., Hammer, P., Wang, P.: Neurosymbolic hybrid approach to driver collision warning. In: Pattern Recognition and Tracking XXXIII, vol. 12101, pp. 134–141. SPIE (2022)

Stimulus Equivalence in NARS

Robert Johansson[1,2]([✉]) and Tony Lofthouse[1]

[1] Department of Psychology, Stockholm University, Stockholm, Sweden
robert.johansson@psychology.su.se, tony.lofthouse@psychology.su.se
[2] Department of Computer and Information Science, Linköping University,
Linköping, Sweden

Abstract. Stimulus equivalence is the ability to act *as if* two objects are
identical, despite no shared properties. This ability is hypothesized to be
the foundation for symbolic reasoning and the development of language.
It is believed to be unique to humans and not present in other animals.
Stimulus equivalence can be studied in the context of a matching-to-
sample experimental task, by demonstrating a combination of symmetrical and transitive performances. This study aimed to explore stimulus
equivalence with the Non-Axiomatic Reasoning System (NARS). More
specifically, we propose two new capabilities for OpenNARS for Applications (ONA) - *contingency entailment* and *acquired relations*. We provide
an explanation how this would lead to ONA being able to learn symmetrical and transitive performances leading to full stimulus equivalence.

Keywords: Stimulus equivalence · Symbolic reasoning · NARS

1 Introduction

In previous research, *generalized identity matching* was demonstrated with a
minimal configuration of the AGI-system OpenNARS for Applications (ONA)
that contained only sensorimotor reasoning (NARS Layers 6–8) [2]. Generalized
identity matching involves being able to develop a concept of identity from experience and applying this concept in a novel situation. Commonly this is trained
and demonstrated in a *matching-to-sample task* where a sample is presented at
the top and comparisons are shown at the bottom left and right. Generalized
identity matching would in this context be demonstrated by choosing between
novel comparisons based on if one of them is identical to the sample.

Stimulus equivalence (or *arbitrary matching-to-sample*), is a type of performance that involves acting *as if* two objects are identical, despite no shared
properties. That is, the relation between the objects is by definition arbitrary,
and the performance can only be explained by the experience of the experimental participant. Informally, this means that the participant is acting according to
a relation of "sameness" in symbolic sense. Formally, this involves being able to
act according to symmetry and transitivity, as will be explained below in Sect. 4.
Stimulus equivalence is hypothesized to be the foundation for symbolic reasoning and the development of language and has not reliably been demonstrated

P. Hammer et al. (Eds.): AGI 2023, LNAI 13921, pp. 158–166, 2023.
https://doi.org/10.1007/978-3-031-33469-6_16

among non-humans. In contrast, humans typically develop this ability at about 16–24 months of age [3].

In this study, we explore stimulus equivalence in ONA. We propose to extend ONA with two new capabilities, *contingency entailment* and *acquired relations*. Using these, we explain how this would lead to ONA being able to perform symmetrical and transitive reasoning based on learned contingencies within the context of matching-to-sample. Potential extensions of this work are also discussed.

2   OpenNARS for Applications (ONA)

ONA [1] is a highly effective implementation of the Non-Axiomatic Reasoning System (NARS) [5] Importantly, ONA is implemented with sensorimotor reasoning (NARS layers 6–8) at its core, with declarative reasoning (NARS layers 1–6) added as an option at compile-time. Running ONA with only its sensorimotor core would lead to an "animal-like" NARS system in that it is not expected to do symbolic reasoning in the traditional sense. In this paper, we discuss two extensions to ONA, contingency entailment and acquired relations, that would involve NARS layers 5 (statements as terms) and 4 (relational terms), respectively.

3   The Matching-to-Sample Task

The Matching-to-sample task (MTS) is a classical paradigm in experimental psychology [4] that has been used to study stimulus equivalence. In this task, a sample stimulus is presented and the participant is required to select a comparison stimulus that matches the sample. Feedback is provided if the participant's choice is deemed correct or incorrect. Using this procedure, novel relations between stimuli can be trained. For example, if A1 is presented as the sample, and the choice of B1 (rather than B2) is reinforced, then this learned behavior could be said to provide a procedural definition of a conditional relation "If A1 then B1", which in this paper will be written as $A1 \rightarrow B1$. The training of the $A1 \rightarrow B1$ relation using the Matching-to-sample task is illustrated in Fig. 1.

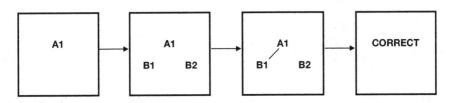

Fig. 1. Learning a conditional relation $A1 \rightarrow B1$ in the matching-to-sample task. First, the sample is presented at the top (leftmost panel). Then, two comparison stimuli are presented (next panel). The experimental subject then indicates a choice between either the left or right option. Finally, the subject receives feedback if the choice was correct or not (rightmost panel).

4   Stimulus Equivalence

Stimulus equivalence can be defined procedurally within the matching-to-sample context using concepts similar to those used for defining an equivalence relation in set theory: *reflexivity, symmetry* and *transitivity*. Reflexivity corresponds to generalized identity matching, defined as an $A1 \rightarrow A1$ performance in the matching-to-sample, also demonstrable for novel objects [2]. To demonstrate symmetry, an experimental participant who has learned that (for example) $A1 \rightarrow B1$ would also need to derive $B1 \rightarrow A1$ without additional training. Transitivity means that if two relations $A1 \rightarrow B1$ and $B1 \rightarrow C1$ have been learned using matching-to-sample procedures, then the experimental participant would need to perform a choice of C1 when A1 is the sample (the $A1 \rightarrow C1$ relation) without explicit training of this relation. Finally, equivalence (in the matching-to-sample context) has been defined as combined symmetry and transitivity [4]: If the $A1 \rightarrow B1$ relation, and the $B1 \rightarrow C1$ relations have been trained, the demonstration of $C1 \rightarrow A1$ would be an example of stimulus equivalence. Stimulus equivalence can be seen as a relation of "sameness" defined procedurally within the matching-to-sample. Hence, stimulus equivalence can be said to describe performances when an experimental participant acts *as if* two stimuli are the same.

Contemporary experimental psychology suggests that stimulus equivalence is a *learned capability* [6]. More specifically, symmetrical and transitive patterns are suggested to be learned with *multiple-exemplar training*. For example, in the case of symmetry, if someone has learned both the $A1 \rightarrow B1$ and $B1 \rightarrow A1$ relations, followed by multiple examples of symmetrical relations, then a more general pattern might be learned. Similarly for transitivity; if $A1 \rightarrow B1$ and $B1 \rightarrow C1$ have been learned followed by explicitly being trained in $A1 \rightarrow C1$, then the beginning of a transitive general pattern might be learned [6].

5   Matching-to-sample Task in NARS

The Matching-to-sample task can be presented as temporal Narsese statements (as indicated by the `:|:` markers below). For example, the task presented in Fig. 1 can be represented as follows:

```
<A1 --> [sample]>. :|:
<B1 --> [left]>. :|:
<B2 --> [right]>. :|:
G! :|:
```

The properties `[sample]`, `[left]`, and `[right]` could for example be location events from an vision channel. A NARS system like ONA could then be set up to have two procedural operations `^left` and `^right`, that it could use to indicate a choice between the left or the right comparison. An arbitrary goal event `G! :|:` could be presented at the end to trigger the execution of one of the two operations `^left` and `^right` (through motor babbling or a decision). During training, feedback can be given in the form of G. :|: (meaning to reinforce a correct choice) or G. :|: {0.0 0.9} (to indicate that the system had conducted an incorrect choice). Between each matching-to-sample trial, sufficient amount of time steps (like 100) will be needed.

With repeated matching-to-sample trials, a NARS system would learn sensorimotor contingencies similar to this, corresponding to the task in Fig. 1:

```
<((<A1 --> [sample]> &/ <B1 --> [left]>) &/ ^left) =/> G>.
```

6   Contingency Entailment

As described above, this paper proposes two changes to ONA that seem involved in the capability to learn stimulus equivalence. The first of these, *contingency entailment* is based on the idea from NARS Layer 5 to consider statements as terms, leading to the possibility of higher-order statements. Given that ONA reasons on sensorimotor contingencies (statements) at its core, an introduction of this capability would allow ONA to derive implications and equivalences between learned sensorimotor contingencies. The contingency entailment rules (implication and equivalence) that have been implemented in ONA looks like this:

```
((A &/ Op1) =/> S), ((B &/ Op2) =/> P), |-,
(((B &/ Op2) =/> P) ==> ((A &/ Op1) =/> S)), Truth_Abduction

((A &/ Op1) =/> S), ((B &/ Op2) =/> P), |-,
(((B &/ Op2) =/> P) <=> ((A &/ Op1) =/> S)), Truth_Comparison
```

Importantly, to restrict the introduction of such higher-order statements, the rules are only triggered when operations involved in the contingencies are executed. This allows ONA to avoid a combinatorial explosion caused by an unrestricted use of the rules.

An example of an entailed equivalence between contingencies follows. If ONA has learned $A1 \to B1$ and $B1 \to A1$ relations in contingency format:

```
<((<A1 --> [sample]> &/ <B1 --> [left]>) &/ ^left) =/> G>.
```

and

```
<((<B1 --> [sample]> &/ <A1 --> [left]>) &/ ^left) =/> G>.
```

then ONA can form an equivalence (with introduced variables) between the contingencies.

```
<<((<$1 --> [sample]> &/ <$2 --> [left]>) &/ ^left) =/> G>
    <=>
<((<$2 --> [sample]> &/ <$1 --> [left]>) &/ ^left) =/> G>>.
```

7   Acquired Relations

The second proposed change to ONA involves that of *acquired relations*. NARS theory regarding Layer 4 (NAL Definition 8.1 in [5]) defines a product as equivalent to a compound term of inheritance statements. Given that ONA reasons on sensorimotor contingencies at its core, this idea applied to ONA would allow the system to introduce relational statements based on learned contingencies. For example, if ONA has learned an $A1 \rightarrow B1$ relation in contingency format:

```
<((<A1 --> [sample]> &/ <B1 --> [left]>) &/ ^left) =/> G>.
```

then, using acquired relations, an $(A1 \times B1)$ relation will also be introduced:

```
<(A1 * B1) --> ([sample] * [left])>.
```

To avoid an explosion of derivations of relational terms, the same heuristics as described in the previous section is suggested. That is, to only trigger this capability in ONA when the system makes use of the contingency by executing the corresponding procedural operation.

Importantly, the contingency entailment rule and the acquired relations rule would in combination lead to the following derivations:

```
<<($1 * $2) --> ([sample] * [left])> <=>
<((<$1 --> [sample]> &/ <$2 --> [left]>) &/ ^left) =/> G>>.
```

This can be seen as a "grounding" of the acquired (conditional) relation in a sensorimotor contingency. We believe this combination leads to potential powerful implications: A NARS system can learn from sensorimotor experience, and from that derive relational terms. Given the declarative reasoning capabilities of NARS, the system could then perform declarative reasoning on the acquired relations, similar to that of symbolic AI systems. The outcome of such reasoning could then lead to entailed contingencies, meaning that the system could make use of derived knowledge to execute procedural operations in contexts where not explicitly trained to do so.

8   Symmetry Based on Contingency Entailment

With repeated experiences in the matching-to-sample task, NARS would develop equivalence statements between contingencies and introduce variables (In the rest of the paper, only one of the two statements involving ^left and ^right operations will be shown):

```
<<((<$1 --> [sample]> &/ <$2 --> [left]>) &/ ^left) =/> G>
    <=>
<((<$2 --> [sample]> &/ <$1 --> [left]>) &/ ^left) =/> G>>.

<<((<$1 --> [sample]> &/ <$2 --> [right]>) &/ ^right) =/> G>
    <=>
<((<$2 --> [sample]> &/ <$1 --> [right]>) &/ ^right) =/> G>>.
```

When NARS at a later stage, learns a new contingency, for example:

```
<(((<X1 --> [sample]> &/ <Y1 --> [left]>) &/ ^left) =/> G>.
```

the system would be able to solve the following task, by applying one of the above two equivalence statements.

```
<Y1 --> [sample]>. :|:
<X1 --> [left]>. :|:
<X2 --> [right]>. :|:
G! :|:
```

Hence, the contingency entailment rule seems sufficient to enable symmetry within the matching-to-sample context.

9 Transitivity Based on Acquired Relations

If NARS learns the following three contingencies:

```
<(((<A1 --> [sample]> &/ <B1 --> [left]>) &/ ^left) =/> G>.
<(((<B1 --> [sample]> &/ <C1 --> [left]>) &/ ^left) =/> G>.
<(((<A1 --> [sample]> &/ <C1 --> [left]>) &/ ^left) =/> G>.
```

and the acquired relations rule is applied, the following three relations will be derived:

```
<<(A1 * B1) --> ([sample] * [left])>.
<<(B1 * C1) --> ([sample] * [left])>.
<<(A1 * C1) --> ([sample] * [left])>.
```

Then, the following general knowledge will be derived (given how NARS can combine Layer 4 relations):

```
<(<($1 * #1) --> ([sample] * [left])> &&
<(#1 * $2) --> ([sample] * [left])>) ==>
<($1 * $2) --> ([sample] * [left])>>.
```

This means, that if NARS learns (in a matching-to-sample task) that

```
<(((<X1 --> [sample]> &/ <Y1 --> [left]>) &/ ^left) =/> G>.
<(((<Y1 --> [sample]> &/ <Z1 --> [left]>) &/ ^left) =/> G>.
```

then the system could derive `<(X1 * Z1) --> ([sample] * [left])>)` from the abstract (transitive) knowledge learned above. Then, by applying the learned equivalence between a conditional relation as a product and as a contingency

```
<<($1 * $2) --> ([sample] * [left])> <=>
<(((<$1 --> [sample]> &/ <$2 --> [left]>) &/ ^left) =/> G>>.
```

the system could derive the following contingency:

```
<(((<X1 --> [sample]> &/ <Z1 --> [left]>) &/ ^left) =/> G>.
```

This would enable the system to solve the following task, which would demonstrate transitivity:

```
<X1 --> [sample]>. :|:
<Z1 --> [left]>. :|:
<Z2 --> [right]>. :|:
G! :|:
```

10   Equivalence as Combined Symmetry and Transitivity

If the system has experience of reflexivity, symmetry and transitivity according to the above, combined applications of contingency entailment and acquired relations will lead to the following relational networks derived within the context of matching-to-sample.

Reflexivity:

```
<<($1 * $1) --> ([sample] * [left])> <=>
<(((<$1 --> [sample]> &/ <$1 --> [left]>) &/ ^left) =/> G>>.
```

Symmetry:

```
<<($1 * $2) --> ([sample] * [left])> <=>
 <($2 * $1) --> ([sample] * [left])>>
```

Transitivity:

```
<(<($1 * #1) --> ([sample] * [left])> &&
<(#1 * $2) --> ([sample] * [left])>) ==>
<($1 * $2) --> ([sample] * [left])>>.
```

These abstract statements are sufficient to solve new problems within the matching-to-sample context, including those that requires combined symmetry and transitivity. For example, if the system has learned the following:

```
<(((<A3 --> [sample]> &/ <B3 --> [left]>) &/ ^left) =/> G>.
<(((<A3 --> [sample]> &/ <C3 --> [left]>) &/ ^left) =/> G>.
```

Then, the system would be able to combine learned symmetry and transitivity to derive the execution of a ^left operation in the following situation, which would be an example of stimulus equivalence.

```
<C3 --> [sample]>. :|:
<B3 --> [left]>. :|:
<B4 --> [right]>. :|:
G! :|:
```

11   Generalizing Outside the Matching-to-Sample Task

In this section, we will show how learning in the matching-to-sample can transform learning in other contexts. If for example a set of conditional relations have been learned within the context of matching-to-sample, for example:

```
<<(X1 * Y1) --> ([sample] * [left])>.
<<(X1 * Z1) --> ([sample] * [left])>.
```

Given that symmetry and transitivity have been learned within the context of matching-to-sample, the system would derive for example these relations:

```
<<(Y1 * Z1) --> ([sample] * [left])>.
<<(Z1 * Y1) --> ([sample] * [left])>.
```

Importantly, NARS would also introduce variables on the right-hand side, leading to for example

```
<<(Y1 * Z1) --> ([$1] * [$2])> <=>
 <(Z1 * Y1) --> ([$2] * [$1])>>
```

If NARS at a later stage learns something with the same left-hand terms, but outside the matching-to-sample context, for example:

```
<((<Y1 --> [p1]> &/ <Z1 --> [p2]>) &/ ^op1) =/> H>.
```

which would lead to a relational term being introduced as follows:

```
<<(Y1 * Z1) --> ([$1] * [$2])> <=>
 <((<Y1 --> [$1]> &/ <Z1 --> [$2]>) &/ ^op1) =/> H>>.
```

Then, the system would also (using the symmetrical relation between Y1 and Z1 trained in the matching-to-sample) derive that

```
<((<Z1 --> [p1]> &/ <Y1 --> [p2]>) &/ ^op1) =/> H>>.
```

We believe that this exemplifies a potentially powerful mechanism. General patterns of symmetry and transitivity can be learned within one context (like the matching-to-sample), and given a few shared terms with another context (like Y1 and Z1 above), symmetrical and transitive transformations can be done in the latter context. In the behavioral psychology literature, this is called the *transformation of stimulus function* [6].

Transformations of stimulus functions in accordance with symmetry and transitivity, across contexts leads to the system acting if two symbols (like Y1 and Z1 in the example above) *mean the same thing* in a symbolic sense. Hence, the processes demonstrated above have been assumed to be involved in the development of language [6].

12   Discussion

In this paper, we introduced the concept of stimulus equivalence, defined as combined function transformations in accordance with symmetry and transitivity. This is arguably a core capability for an AGI system and the behavioral psychology literature suggests that it is the foundation of symbolic reasoning and language development.

Stimulus equivalence was defined procedurally, using learned contingencies. We believe that this could constitute a foundation for how symbolic relations could be grounded in sensorimotor contingencies, and hence, suggests one way how the "mind-sensory gap" could be closed regarding the problems described in this paper.

Importantly, stimulus equivalence is considered to be a learned behavior. In this paper, we introduced specific inference rules in ONA to support the ability to learn stimulus equivalence. This approach might be in contrast with other approaches that aim to directly implement symbolic relations (for example the relation between a word and an object).

In summary, we hope that the approach taken in this work could be of inspiration to other AGI-systems interested in acquiring symbolic relations from experience.

Acknowledgements. We want to acknowledge Patrick Hammer, Robert Wünsche and Pei Wang for valuable discussions regarding this work.

References

1. Hammer, P., Lofthouse, T.: OpenNARS for applications: architecture and control. In: Goertzel, B., Panov, A.I., Potapov, A., Yampolskiy, R. (eds.) AGI 2020. LNCS (LNAI), vol. 12177, pp. 193–204. Springer, Cham (2020). https://doi.org/10.1007/978-3-030-52152-3_20
2. Johansson, R., Lofthouse, T., Hammer, P.: Generalized identity matching in NARS. In: Goertzel, B., Ikle, M., Potapov, A., Ponomaryov, D. (eds.) Artificial General Intelligence. AGI 2022. LNCS, vol. 13539, pp. 243–249. Springer, Cham (2023). https://doi.org/10.1007/978-3-031-19907-3_23
3. Luciano, C., Becerra, I.G., Valverde, M.R.: The role of multiple-exemplar training and naming in establishing derived equivalence in an infant. J. Exp. Anal. Behav. **87**(3), 349–365 (2007)
4. Sidman, M.: Equivalence Relations and Behavior: A Research Story. Authors Cooperative, San Francisco (1994)
5. Wang, P.: Non-axiomatic Logic: A Model of Intelligent Reasoning. World Scientific, Singapore (2013)
6. Zettle, R.D., Hayes, S.C., Barnes-Holmes, D., Biglan, A.: The Wiley Handbook of Contextual Behavioral Science. Wiley Online Library, Hoboken (2016)

Context-Rich Evaluation of Machine Common Sense

Mayank Kejriwal[1(✉)] [iD], Henrique Santos[2], Ke Shen[1], Alice M. Mulvehill[2], and Deborah L. McGuinness[2]

[1] University of Southern California, Los Angeles, CA, USA
kejriwal@isi.edu
[2] Rensselaer Polytechnic Institute, Troy, NY, USA

Abstract. Building machines capable of common sense reasoning is an important milestone in achieving Artificial General Intelligence (AGI). While recent advances, such as large language models, are promising, systematic and sufficiently robust evaluations of these models on common sense have been inadequate, and designed for an earlier generation of models. One criticism of prior evaluation protocols is that they have been too narrow in scope e.g., by restricting the format of questions posed to the model, not being theoretically grounded, and not taking the context of a model's responses in constructing follow-up questions or asking for explanations. In this paper, we aim to address this gap by proposing a context-rich evaluation protocol designed specifically for evaluating machine common sense. Our protocol can subsume popular evaluation paradigms in machine common sense as special cases, and is suited for evaluating both discriminative and generative large language models. We demonstrate the utility of the protocol by using it to conduct a pilot evaluation of the ChatGPT system on common sense reasoning.

Keywords: Machine Common Sense · Context-Rich Evaluation · Large Language Models

1 Background

Recent advances in *large language models* (LLMs), based largely on transformer-based neural networks, have led to impressive performance gains in natural language processing (NLP) problems such as question answering, dialog, text summarization, and even creative writing [5,6]. Despite this progress, many concerns have been raised recently about these models [10], and it is evident that even the most recent and sophisticated versions (such as OpenAI's ChatGPT, which has captured the general public's imagination since release) can be prone to 'hallucinating', adversarial prompting, as well as reasoning that is unsound [3]. A specific example of a type of reasoning that is universal in human communication and thinking is *common sense*. Even since the development of the first generations of transformer-based models, the problem of achieving the goal of *machine common sense* (MCS) took on new-found importance in the AI community [8].

© The Author(s), under exclusive license to Springer Nature Switzerland AG 2023
P. Hammer et al. (Eds.): AGI 2023, LNAI 13921, pp. 167–176, 2023.
https://doi.org/10.1007/978-3-031-33469-6_17

Evaluations of MCS originally involved independent or 'single-hop' instances of tasks such as multiple-choice question answering (MQA). We mean *independent* in the sense that answers to one question did not depend on answers to another question. Furthermore, in the majority of MQA benchmark datasets evaluating common sense, a training dataset of (multiple-choice) questions is typically provided to the model to fine-tune on prior to being tested. The assumption then is that the test benchmark at least obeys the same kind of distribution, including the type of common sense (e.g., naive physics, or common social relations), as the training partition. Hence, the evaluation protocol is independent and identically distributed (i.i.d.).

Owing to being both convenient and replicable, such single-hop QA has emerged as a "de facto" standard for evaluating MCS, especially within NLP [13]. Unfortunately (and perhaps unsurprisingly), this variety of i.i.d. MQA evaluation can also cause dataset bias, leakage of developer knowledge, and good performance caused by superficial pattern matching rather than actual MCS. It is not always evident either how the questions or the underlying ground-truth (the 'answer key') were constructed, including whether there is selection bias by human beings constructing them. For narrow and domain-specific problems in AI, neither might pose a serious issue under ordinary conditions. However, for AGI tasks (and arguably, MCS is an important such task), such evaluations cannot be expected to yield a trustworthy representation of a model's ability to generalize [17], especially when the model is black-box and lacks the ability to give either an accurate confidence in, or a human-understandable explanation of, the answer it has selected. This is obviously true for many of the complex deep learning models in operation today, including the transformer-based LLMs. It is even less clear how to *systematically* evaluate generative LLMs, where it is not necessary to provide a closed set of answers, and the questions themselves may be sequentially dependent, or guided by *context*.

In this paper, we aim to move beyond the single-hop QA paradigm to an evaluation protocol that is more flexible, context-rich and allows for different modalities and content while still using well-defined guidelines (for both modality and content) to ensure that the evaluation is not ad hoc and arbitrary. Details of this protocol are provided in the next section. We argue that the protocol systematically and robustly enables us to probe the common sense abilities of an LLM, or any such similar model. Our protocol is especially designed for evaluating generative LLMs, such as GPT-3 and ChatGPT, although it is not incompatible with discriminative models, such as BERT. The protocol involves limited intervention from a 'human in the loop' but preempts the introduction of arbitrary questions by requiring the human evaluator to adhere to one of several pre-defined modalities when deciding on the *format* in which to pose queries to the model, as well as using a theory of common sense when deciding on the *content* of those queries. Concerning the latter, there have been growing calls recently to have more systematic distinctions [10], based on such theories [7], between MCS and other kinds of reasoning and problem-solving that do not primarily fall under the umbrella of common sense.

Ultimately, our proposal hopes to enable a shift from using static datasets for benchmarking, to using dynamic processes that obey rigorous guidelines. Conducting such evaluations may be important for establishing AGI traits (or lack thereof) in these kinds of models in a more scientific and unbiased manner. Along with describing the protocol in detail, we demonstrate its practical utility by conducting pilot evaluations on ChatGPT. We also discuss potential use of this protocol for external users and practitioners.

2   Proposed Evaluation Protocol

Multiple-choice QA (MQA) is commonly used to evaluate the problem-solving performance of humans and that of machine-based reasoners that have been developed with neural-symbolic and/or transformer-based LLM approaches. MQA datasets can be manually created or automatically generated. The process for creating the questions, candidate answers, and scoring is well documented and there are numerous guidelines available to support the creation of effective multiple-choice questions and answers [14].

Other formats, such as true-false, stories, or sequences can be used to develop datasets which can be effective for evaluating problem-solving methods that are generative or even open-ended in nature. For example, presenting a machine with a story and asking it to write a relevant ending could be (and has been) used to evaluate its comprehension abilities. Instead of writing a relevant ending, the machine can also be asked to pick the correct answer from a list, determine if subsequent statements about the story are true or false, or generate a single answer or ordered list of answers. Even more recently, the machine commonsense community has been considering generative QA, a good benchmark example being CommonGen [12]. While performance can be automatically evaluated, and metrics like Brier scores [4] can be automatically computed, specifying the full space of possible answers in advance (for an automated program to score) is a difficult and time-consuming task. As a result, unusual, but correct answers may not be scored correctly. In addition, automated evaluation of multi-hop reasoning capabilities can be difficult with Generative QA, especially if questions in the dataset are independent from one another.

Having a human in the 'evaluation loop' can help resolve certain ambiguous situations [15], however, having no manual or automatic method for testing the difficult cases that require use of both intuitive or reflexive, and rational, reasoning processes (approximately mapping to System 1 and System 2 cognitive processes in Kahneman's framework [9]), in effect reduces the scope of machine reasoning tests. To help mitigate these issues and to robustly evaluate machine commonsense reasoning, we argue that a rigorous human in the loop test must be included. A diagram of a proposed evaluation paradigm which includes a human in the post-hoc evaluation phase is presented in Fig. 1. In this framework, a single machine-based reasoner is presented with tasks that can range across benchmarks and include multiple problem-solving modalities in a single evaluation session. Before presenting tasks to a machine-based reasoner in a session, tasks about a specific problem-solving modality in a specific context are composed offline by humans who preferably had no role in the design of the reasoning system. For each task, a set of wrong and right answers is also defined.

Five example problem solving modalities are listed in Fig. 1: comprehension, organization, counterfactual reasoning, probabilistic judgments and psychosocial modeling. The definitions for these and other problem-solving modalities are available in [10]. They are also referred to as "evaluation" modalities because the problem-solving capability of a system is being evaluated in terms of its ability to perform some particular type of problem-solving. For example, we define the modality comprehension as: *the act or action of grasping with the intellect; to include, to comprise, to fully understand.* Because we are interested in evaluating the ability of machines to do commonsense reasoning, each task that is representative of a particular problem solving modality is developed to map into one or more representational areas, such as "agents" and "activities" that have been defined in the commonsense reasoning theory of Gordon and Hobbs [7]. In [15], we describe the motivation for using selected categories from Gordon and Hobbs in constructing dataset prompts.

The proposed framework allows a 'closed loop' evaluation, where the tasks are provided to the system with the problem context. The machine's response accuracy is measured using post-hoc human judgment. Ideally, the same test would also be administered to a human to ensure that it is, indeed, a commonsense test with near-perfect human accuracy.

To evaluate the effectiveness of the framework, we created tasks related to questions in our Theoretically Grounded Common-Sense Reasoning (TG-CSR) [16] benchmark. The datasets in this benchmark cover four commonsense problem contexts: vacationing abroad, camping, bad weather, and dental cleaning. For example, to test comprehension, the machine is provided with a test question based on the vacationing abroad dataset: *Over the past few years, Chloe has been cycling a lot more. Also, she has a subway in her home town that she doesn't like very much. What can be said about Chloe's preference in getting around cities in her trip?* To evaluate comprehension, we compare the machine's answers to correct (*She would prefer to cycle*) and incorrect (*Ride the subway*) answers, that were made by human annotators. In our research, we have discovered that the evaluation datasets do not have to be large and may even contain fewer than 200 tasks, but they must be adequately representative of the Gordon and Hobbs theoretically-grounded commonsense categories before an evaluated system can claim a particular problem-solving capability.

In cases where a generative reasoner's answers do not exactly or closely match any of the human annotation options, the generated answer is evaluated by the human in the loop. Having a human in the loop also helps resolve a known issue with current generative QA benchmarks, which is that even with post-hoc evaluation, when questions presented to the machine are independent from one another, it is difficult to evaluate a system's multi-hop reasoning capabilities. With our framework, the human in the loop can present tasks in subsequent sessions that incrementally build upon tasks presented in prior sessions in order to test more complex capabilities such as multi-hop reasoning. An even more powerful test can also be conducted using an 'open loop' evaluation. For this evaluation, the initial set of tasks are presented to the system (similar to the closed loop evaluation), but the 'evaluator,' which can be a single person, or multi-person team, is allowed to design a new task in real time, given the machine's responses. This kind of evaluation has precedent in the NLP community e.g., in the realm of text adventure games [2].

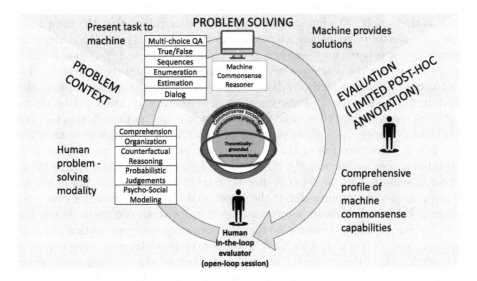

Fig. 1. A contextualized human-in-the-loop evaluation paradigm for holistically assessing the range of machine commonsense capabilities. *A similar evaluation can be conducted with a human in place of the machine commonsense reasoner, to confirm that the task is indeed commonsense and to measure human performance.*

3   Experimental Demonstration

We conducted four evaluation sessions to assess the commonsense reasoning ability of the state-of-the-art language model ChatGPT across a range of context-heavy tasks. These evaluation sessions were designed using two handcrafted open-ended problem contexts, each employed twice. Additional details and tasks related to these contexts can be found in a recently released benchmark [16].

3.1   Context 1: Camping Trip

One of the problem contexts involved planning a camping trip in the White Mountains of New Hampshire in August. The context given to the model provided information about a couple named Fred and Linda who want to spend around ten days doing day hikes and are searching for a campsite conveniently located near the hiking trails they want to explore. While Fred went on a few camping trips as a child, Linda had never been camping. The model was then tasked with helping the couple plan and organize their trip. For replication and full details on the session, we provide a link to the session log[1].

The initial evaluation session entailed a multi-set QA assessment for Chat-GPT. The system was presented with a question, such as "What items should Fred and Linda bring on their camping trip?", and a set of candidate choices, such as (1) Tent, blankets, (2) Lawnmower, (3) Makeup, (4) Paper clips, and (5) Mosquito repellent, suntan lotion. The system was required to select all of the options that apply. The human annotators had determined that the most suitable response for the question is a combination of choices (1) and (5). A rigorous comparison was performed between the machine's answer and the ground-truth; only cases where the machine's answer matched the ground-truth were considered correct. We presented ten distinct multi-set questions on the topic of the camping trip to ChatGPT. These questions covered various commonsense representation areas, such as time, activities, and world states, as described in Gordon and Hobbs' theory [7]. A manual review of ChatGPT's responses demonstrated that it was correct on five of the ten questions. In most cases where ChatGPT answered a question incorrectly, it selected all options that may be applicable in a general sense but not necessarily directly related to the question. For example, in a question that inquires about the appropriate breakfast food for Fred and Linda to bring if they desire a protein-based meal without cooking before a day hike, human evaluators determined that the correct choices were instant oatmeal packages and protein bars. ChatGPT's response included the two correct options but also included the candidate answer 'water bottle' since it suggested bringing a water bottle for staying hydrated during the hike. While a water bottle is undoubtedly necessary during hiking, it should not be listed as a breakfast food. Humans would not consider it a correct answer to the same problem.

In addition, we observed that ChatGPT's performance tended to degrade when asked questions related to time estimation. For example, when the model was asked how many days Fred and Linda would be away on their 10-day camping vacation, given that it takes one full day to drive to the White Mountains of New Hampshire and one full day to drive back home, ChatGPT responded with ten days, which is not an accurate answer (a better answer is 9 days). Similarly, when asked to estimate the time required to set up a four-person tent, ChatGPT's answer of 30 min to an hour did not match the range of 5–30 min provided by humans. This discrepancy may be deemed incorrect in a multiple-set question setting, despite being (somewhat) acceptable in a generative question setting. Other instructive details can be obtained from the full log linked earlier.

---

[1] https://docs.google.com/document/d/1yNrjTOt0imJW5OVajTDNcAJ0PJxmM6B
7Dpe3N8YFMD4/edit?usp=sharing.

During the second evaluation session[2], ChatGPT was tested on its ability to apply commonsense reasoning to organize a series of camping activities in the correct order. To achieve this goal, four distinct questions were presented to the model, including "What activities are best to do before it gets dark while camping?" Impressively, ChatGPT provided the correct sequence of activities for all the questions.

In addition to grading the results, involving a human in the evaluation loop allowed us to observe that ChatGPT recognized that the order of activities could be influenced by specific circumstances. For instance, ChatGPT noted that weather conditions and the availability of firewood at the camping site could impact the order of activities before nightfall. Moreover, when asked about sequencing activities before nightfall, the model suggested that campers should be mindful of the campground's quiet hours and avoid making excessive noise during the evening. Probing the model's abilities to handle such context is currently not allowed by single-hop QA paradigms. However, our proposed protocol is flexible enough to include such context when constructing queries.

Overall, ChatGPT exhibited impressive commonsense reasoning abilities in organizing a series of camping activities in the correct order. Including a human in the evaluation loop helped us to assess the model's performance and provided additional valuable insights into the model's strengths and limitations.

3.2   Context 2: Vacationing Abroad

The second problem context in the assessment relates to the notion of vacationing abroad. Chloe, who has not taken a vacation in nearly two years, plans to take an entire month off. She intends to spend three weeks traveling with some close friends to visit Europe's most renowned attractions, such as Paris and London. We assess the extent to which the system comprehends Chloe's vacation plans by requesting it to carry out an intent-analysis of Chloe's itinerary elements and offer a rough estimation of the traveling agenda.

The evaluation was conducted in a multi-set question session and a generative question session, respectively[3]. The same set of questions was used in both sessions to compare the performance of ChatGPT on different evaluation tasks. In the multi-set question session, a set of candidate answers was provided per question, and the model was asked to select all the correct options that apply. In contrast, the generative question session allowed ChatGPT to freely generate its response.

In the generative question session, ChatGPT performed reasonably well, but in the multi-set question session, it only correctly answered 6 out of 12 questions.

---

[2] The log for this session may be found at https://docs.google.com/document/d/1a-CDcijT2an0XiYF-JQ0i2ZvFiUpUB-Xb4wZBUkBVkg/edit?usp=sharing.

[3] The logs for these sessions may be found at https://docs.google.com/document/d/1tLseMBfGVEhdpcm4jGNg_9Dr4ruGihFX9ncY3240k5Y/edit?usp=sharing and https://docs.google.com/document/d/1HWma7MuZkaCeqq6aVmXtBzP9pqudmF7YH1GAl9z2xoc/edit?usp=sharing, respectively.

One example of a discrepancy between the two sessions is the question, "While Chloe likes outdoor activities, she doesn't appreciate them when it's sunny and hot. During her trip to Europe, what should she do during the day?". ChatGPT chose inappropriate candidate answers such as "Get a coffee" and "Have dinner in a new place," but generated more relevant responses in the generative question session, such as visiting museums, shopping at indoor markets, and taking a river tour. Determination of the closeness of an answer by the generative reasoner is based on two methods: the first is a text match (i.e., when an answer matches the text of an option, then it is considered exact or close), but when such a match is not detected, the second method relies on a human in the loop to determine the closeness of the match. This suggests that, despite some suggestions to the contrary that these models are 'general' in their abilities, it may not necessarily be the case that generative models are better at discriminative tasks (such as multiple-choice QA).

Our human-reviewed evaluation indicated that ChatGPT's performance on time-related questions was still not up to par in both assessment sessions. Reasoning about time is a foundational commonsense reasoning skill and is required in order to reason about related commonsense issues like activities and planning [7]. Temporal reasoning is one of the foundational capabilities that researchers [1] believe is necessary in order for machine-based reasoning systems to perform basic tasks or to support humans in those tasks, e.g., resource management, travel planning. For instance, when presented with the question, "Given that Chloe's vacation starts on June 1st and she only has three weeks of vacation, when should her flight depart?", ChatGPT only identified "June 1st" as the correct answer, even though "June 5th" was also a valid option provided in the candidate answer list. The model acknowledged that the other options could be correct if additional information, such as a specific flight departure time or a fixed schedule, was provided. However, in our annotation exercises, we found that humans could easily choose both answers as appropriate without any additional hints.

Furthermore, when presented with the same question without a list of candidate answers in the generative QA session, ChatGPT responded that Chloe should depart on or after June 1st and return on or before June 22nd. While this answer is correct, it still shows that the model struggles with accurately understanding and processing time-related information. In fact, this answer is consistent with June 5th, but the model did not choose it when presented with it in a discriminative setting.

4   Discussion

This paper proposed a context-rich evaluation framework where limited human intervention is used for two important purposes: to determine if the response to a query by the model is actually appropriate and along what dimensions (which can be difficult to automate, especially if the query was ambiguous), as well as to incrementally dialog with the machine in order to more robustly evaluate its multi-hop reasoning capabilities. To more effectively evaluate a machine's ability to solve different types of commonsense problem-solving tasks, we recommend that the content of questions be grounded in a theory of commonsense, such as that proposed and refined in [7]. We demonstrated the potential utility of this framework by applying it to the ChatGPT system for assessing its MCS abilities. Although the model's responses are quite impressive, the full use of the evaluation protocol also demonstrates that more work is needed before the model can be said to possess the full gamut of common sense reasoning.

As enterprises and other practitioners (including in healthcare and education) start deploying generative AI technologies like LLMs more frequently in their application stacks, *domain-specific* evaluations of such models could prove critical in ensuring that they are being used in a responsible and trustworthy manner. The protocol proposed in this paper could be adapted for domain-specific evaluations; the only real constraint would be to ensure that the *problem context* in Fig. 1 aligns appropriately with the domain, and the human-in-the-loop evaluator is an individual with sufficient domain expertise.

Beyond partnering with domain experts on such evaluations, in future work, we plan to scale up evaluations significantly and apply the protocol to other LLMs as they are released. We also hypothesize that, by applying the protocol rigorously in multiple sessions, deeper insights could be gleaned on the MCS capabilities and limitations of generative models. By focusing more on a benchmarking process, rather than over-reliance on benchmarking data (which has been found to be susceptible to generalization issues [11]), similar such evaluation sessions could then be conducted and replicated as larger models continue to be released. By releasing the session logs, as we have done in this work, the process also becomes open to analysis and could be refined or modified through community-driven critique.

References

1. Allen, J.F.: Maintaining knowledge about temporal intervals. Commun. ACM **26**(11), 832–843 (1983). https://doi.org/10.1145/182.358434
2. Ammanabrolu, P., Broniec, W., Mueller, A., Paul, J., Riedl, M.: Toward automated quest generation in text-adventure games. In: Proceedings of the 4th Workshop on Computational Creativity in Language Generation, pp. 1–12. Association for Computational Linguistics, Tokyo, Japan (2019). https://aclanthology.org/2019.ccnlg-1.1
3. Bang, Y., et al.: A multitask, multilingual, multimodal evaluation of ChatGPT on reasoning, hallucination, and interactivity. arXiv preprint arXiv:2302.04023 (2023)
4. Blagec, K., Dorffner, G., Moradi, M., Samwald, M.: A critical analysis of metrics used for measuring progress in artificial intelligence. arXiv preprint arXiv:2008.02577 (2020)
5. Brown, T., et al.: Language models are few-shot learners. Adv. Neural. Inf. Process. Syst. **33**, 1877–1901 (2020)

6. Devlin, J., Chang, M.W., Lee, K., Toutanova, K.: BERT: pre-training of deep bidirectional transformers for language understanding. In: Proceedings of the 2019 Conference of the North American Chapter of the Association for Computational Linguistics: Human Language Technologies, vol. 1, pp. 4171–4186. Association for Computational Linguistics, Minneapolis, Minnesota (2019). https://doi.org/10.18653/v1/N19-1423

7. Gordon, A.S., Hobbs, J.R.: A Formal Theory of Commonsense Psychology: How People Think People Think. Cambridge University Press, Cambridge (2017). https://doi.org/10.1017/9781316584705

8. Gunning, D.: Machine common sense concept paper. arXiv preprint arXiv:1810.07528 (2018)

9. Kahneman, D.: Thinking, Fast and Slow. Macmillan (2011). Google-Books-ID: SHvzzuCnuv8C

10. Kejriwal, M., Santos, H., Mulvehill, A.M., McGuinness, D.L.: Designing a strong test for measuring true common-sense reasoning. Nat. Mach. Intell. **4**(4), 318–322 (2022). https://doi.org/10.1038/s42256-022-00478-4

11. Kejriwal, M., Shen, K.: Do fine-tuned commonsense language models really generalize? arXiv preprint arXiv:2011.09159 (2020)

12. Lin, B.Y., et al.: CommonGen: a constrained text generation challenge for generative commonsense reasoning. In: Findings of the Association for Computational Linguistics (EMNLP 2020), pp. 1823–1840. Association for Computational Linguistics, Online (2020). https://doi.org/10.18653/v1/2020.findings-emnlp.165

13. Mitra, A., Banerjee, P., Pal, K.K., Mishra, S., Baral, C.: How additional knowledge can improve natural language commonsense question answering? arXiv preprint arXiv:1909.08855 (2020)

14. Neelakandan, N.: Creating multiple-choice questions: the dos and don'ts (2019). https://elearningindustry.com/creating-multiple-choice-questions

15. Santos, H., Kejriwal, M., Mulvehill, A.M., Forbush, G., McGuinness, D.L., Rivera, A.R.: An experimental study measuring human annotator categorization agreement on commonsense sentences. Exp. Res. **2**, e19 (2021)

16. Santos, H., Shen, K., Mulvehill, A.M., Razeghi, Y., McGuinness, D.L., Kejriwal, M.: A theoretically grounded benchmark for evaluating machine commonsense (2022). https://doi.org/10.48550/arXiv.2203.12184

17. Shen, K., Kejriwal, M.: An experimental study measuring the generalization of fine-tuned language representation models across commonsense reasoning benchmarks. Expert Syst. e13243 (2023)

Indications of Suitable Algorithms for an AGI

Harald Kjellin[(⊠)]

Department of Computer and Systems Sciences, Stockholm University, Stockholm, Sweden
harald.kjellin@gmail.com

Abstract. There are frequent reports in current media that discuss threats from Artificial Intelligence and especially the possible threats from Artificial General Intelligence (AGI). This indicates a need for establishing communication interfaces between humans and AGI that ensure that we can create responsible and careful AGIs, whose behavior and knowledge can be scrutinized by human beings. In order to illustrate how this can be done, we exemplify how human reasoning processes can be used when designing an AGI that is driven by knowledge that can be easily understood by human beings.

The conclusion from the analyzed examples is that there are indications that the described features of human cognition are well suited to be used as a starting point when designing requirements for an explainable AGI-system.

1 Introduction

1.1 Background: Humans and AGI Learn from their Conversations

Today there is much attention given to eventual future problems with an uncontrollable Artificial Intelligence (AI). Many people fear that AI will not only take our jobs and make humans less valuable, but AI may also have a negative impact on the freedom of individual human beings.

Most people find it difficult to understand how large tech-companies or military industries use Big Data and Machine Learning to create AI-systems.

One reason for this lack of understanding is that many AI-systems are not designed for being able to explain all the detailed steps in their reasoning processes and they cannot explain their reasoning processes in a way that can be pedagogically communicated with human beings [1]. A result of this, is that people can become alienated or distrustful towards AGI. This lack of trust or ability to understand the reasoning processes in an AGI may create a society where people feel that they are out of control.

We can assume that people would benefit from having a similar relationship with AGI as they have with other people. This is described by Mueller et. al. in [2]. If an AGI learns knowledge that is based on human's perspectives, values, ideologies and patterns of communication, then we can assume that the AGI would become sensitive to the needs and well-being of this human. An analogy with child rearing can be used as an illustrative analogy. If parents treat its child as an equal, in a firm a responsible way, then the probability is high that the grown-up child will treat its elderly parents as equals in a similar firm and respectful way.

P. Hammer et al. (Eds.): AGI 2023, LNAI 13921, pp. 177–186, 2023.
https://doi.org/10.1007/978-3-031-33469-6_18

In order to allow for an efficient communication about the reasoning processes in an AGI we need a knowledge representation in the AGI that can be scrutinized and modified by the human that is using this AGI [1]. There are two benefits that can be assumed from facilitating the transparency of the knowledge that is driving an AGI. The first postulated benefit is the possibility to empower humans in their relationships with an AGI. Such an empowerment makes humans engaged in a mutual development of knowledge that makes both the AGI and humans smarter.

There is always a risk that power-hungry people with personal agendas exploit AGI-systems. In such cases the AGI-systems may support the evolution of dysfunctional bureaucracies that humans find difficult to deal with. The history of mankind is full of examples of empires that degenerate and collapse due to a lack of adaption to feedback from the "grassroots". The second postulated benefit of requiring transparent knowledge in the dialogues between humans and AI, is that the risk of an insensitive bureaucracy can be avoided when unwanted ways of reasoning can be discovered and corrected by the users of a system.

1.2 Purpose: To Look for Indications of Suitable Algorithms for an AGI

The purpose of the research described in this paper is to look for indications of usefulness of generic human reasoning processes when defining requirements on algorithms for an AGI-system. The presented research is restricted to a semantic processing of language and does not deal with other types of information processing.

1.3 Lessons Learned from Previous Implementations

The author of this paper once designed an expert system for the Swedish government [5, 6]. The system was based on information propagations in a semantic network and was designed to mimic the intuition of employment counselors. The success of the system was so highly esteemed that it was implemented in every employment office throughout Sweden. Unfortunately, the government officials were not interested in investing in functions for continuous updating of the system's knowledge. The clerks argued that the system was popular and worked fine. However, after some years the system became outdated, made some errors and was then heavily criticized, with the result that it was replaced by a simple IT-system. One lesson learned from this failure was that the functions for updating a system's knowledge must be designed for being located at the very core of the system. Another lesson learned was that the approach of using generic variables that presented accumulation of results was very useful when presenting an overview of the knowledge to the user.

1.4 Method for Evaluating the Usefulness of the Examples

The major part of this paper describes examples of how human reasoning processes can be mapped onto requirements on an AGI. Examples are selected from the area of cognitive science and from "Informed AI" as described in Johnson [3]. Each example is directly followed by a description of how a requirement can be defined for an AGI together with a minor feasibility analysis. Whenever a description of a human reasoning process can be interpreted as being translatable to a process of matching and mapping patterns, this is considered as an indication that it could be useful in further experiments with designing an AGI-architecture.

2 Similar Functionality in People and AGIs

To ensure a continuous learning in an AGI, its knowledge should preferably be continuously updated. This requirement is the same for both humans and an AGI. In an advanced learning-system we can even see that the learning process in itself is one of the major drives behind the activities in the system [4].

In the following paragraphs we present how we have designed requirements for an AGI. For each such requirement, in the sections below, we first describe how a human being depends on a certain function for its thinking and then we argue for implementing a similar functionality in AGI.

2.1 Typed Variables Facilitate Reasoning on a Generic Level

The use of stereotypes can make human thinking superficial and hinder rational reasoning, but at the same time stereotypes are needed to make reasoning processes efficient when there is a lack of available specific information. The AGI could use a function that corresponds to stereotyping by being able to use generic classifications of structures of variable values in order to be able to make efficient classifications when there is a lack of specific information. This is facilitated by using a knowledge representation that allows for matching on any level of abstraction or at any depth of embedded structures. We propose that any input in the form of natural language can preferably be interpreted into a simplified list of relationships that should then be specifically designed to facilitate matching, mapping and learning processes. Here we exemplify with one version of such simplified relationships that are designed to facilitate matching processes on both specific and generic levels. It can look like this:

Id1,nounType(nounPhrase, Id2), relType(verbPhrase), nounType(nounPhrase, Id3)

The Id2 and Id3 = Identifiers in a nounPhrase and can refer to any node entity in a semantic network, while the Id1 is an identifier for the whole relationship.

The nounType and relType are generic terms that can be seen as a generic summary of what is found in the text part of the nounPhrase or the verbPhrase. These types are stored in taxonomies to facilitate measures of closeness. They can be used to facilitate the general matching of patterns.

An entity can then be formed as a non-restricted list of random relationships. An entity can also be assigned to belong to a type of entity and can then be located as the Id associated with a nounPhrase. Thus a complex structure can be an Id in a nounPhrase.

The use of types throughout a semantic network is intended to facilitate reasoning on a generic level when there is not enough specific knowledge available to solve a problem.

The types can also facilitate the communication between the AGI and the end user when they are reflecting on how entities, like those described above, should be classified.

Links in the semantic network can be assigned between nounTypes and entities and between entities and other entities via a relationship types that are referred to as "relTypes" that could continuously evolve when there is enough available input data to support new generalizations of verb-phrases. Common generic relTypes between entities are: subclass, superclass, hasPart, partOf, pred, succ, cause, imply, etc.

Due to space restriction in this paper there is no presentation of examples of how such representation of relationships can be used in various proposed reasoning processes.

2.2   The AGI Should be Able to Store Complex Patterns in Its Working Memory

There is much evidence that knowledge is not useful unless it can be related to a context [7]. Knowledge is almost always situated, which means that the knowledge is only relevant for being used in a situation if it matches the situation.

People can experience a context in the form of generic background patterns that gives an overall view of a given situation. The generic patterns are utilized for producing motivating feelings that in turn support the selection of the relevant knowledge that can be used in a situation.

If the working memory of an AGI shall function as a context it must be able to store complex patterns in its working memory [7]. It must also be possible to relate these patterns to knowledge that is stored in the long-term memory of the AGI.

In order to be able to reason with probabilities and temporary relevance, all stored patterns should have weights of relative importance assigned to them, so that they can be continuously modified depending on the progress of the reasoning process of the AGI.

When the system is considering its next move, it would begin with checking the relationships that had the highest temporary weight in the Working Memory before it would start to look for relevant knowledge in the knowledge base.

2.3   The Context Should be Used When Interpreting the Users Input

In the initial phases of a dialogue, a reliable context may not exist. People then need a standard interpretation of natural language to be able to construct a context for the initial interpretation of the logic in the input message. An AGI must similarly design a context before it can expand its reasoning processes. Therefore, the proposed approach to handling language in an AGI needs a big language model with standard taxonomies that can handle various kinds of language input for designing a context. Every new term in the input can then be matched with both the standard taxonomies and the context that is incrementally constructed and updated during a dialogue.

2.4   The Dynamic Memory of an AGI Should be Independent of Schemas

People do not store memories according to any specific logical classification system. Instead memories are stored according to the similarity or analogy between the most relevant parts of the previously stored memories [8]. This enables people to store the new information at the same time as they are classifying and interpreting the new incoming information.

If we look at the human brain as a database we know that it handles information in a network of links between brain cells, where the links can have various degrees of priority depending on how often and in which context they are used.

Human beings use their feelings when assigning priorities and probabilities of a concept in a context. An AGI can mimic this by assigning weights of relevance on all data according to the current context.

The opposite is true in the relational databases that are today dominating the world. They depend on explicit schemas in order to know where specific data shall be stored and retrieved. Such explicit predefined structures would prevent the incremental creation of new structures in an AGI. This indicates that we need to define a requirement on the database and knowledgebase of an AGI that is similar to how humans store knowledge. Knowledge should not be stored according to a restrictive absolute schema but should instead be stored in a network that classifies complex data structures according to how well they match existing similar or analogue data structures.

We assume that data and knowledge in the AGI can be stored and retrieved in a similar way as data and knowledge is stored and retrieved in a human memory. Humans often have one core feeling related to what was really important in a specific context. This is where we begin to store or search for information. In an AGI this can be done to initially follow links from any entity to its superEntity in order to find out what is usually most important in this context. From such a position the AGI can then ask the user questions like:

You said earlier X. This can lead to either Y or Z or W. Is any of these relevant in your case?

Whatever a user answers, the AGI can accumulate answers from users to update its own knowledge. Whenever it gets an approval from a user, the links that lead to this approval will receive a slightly higher weight which may cause a micro-refinement in the knowledge of the AGI.

2.5 Knowledge Should be Continuously Updated in Dialogues with Users

People mature gradually as they age. They do this by continuously updating their models of reality. Such updating processes are frequently done in relationships with other people that can provide general responses on a high level of abstraction.

This indicates that an AGI should also be able to test and verify its various hypotheses by entering into complex dialogues with people that were classified as being mature. At a high level of maturity, the AGI could also improve its models of reality by testing its hypotheses against other AGI's. If such communication is not well monitored there is a high risk that the AGI develops in undesirable ways for humanity.

As people age and mature they usually learn to gain self-confidence on different levels of abstraction. Whatever type of self-confidence a person has, it influences the decisions he makes.

As an AGI matures in relation to how much knowledge it can integrate in its life cycle, we can assume that it should also be able to change its inner focus according to how its deepest values are gradually modified. The weights on deepest values can be gradually modified just as the relative importance of any variable in any context can be modified in relation to feedback from successes or failures.

2.6 The System Must Always be Able to Explain How It has Been Reasoning

People learn in their critical questioning of knowledge. When agreements are reached between groups of people this will confirm their trust in developing their shared agreements further. This indicates that the more trust an AGI can experience in a relationship with humans the further it will be able develop itself.

An AGI should always be able to argue for how it has reached certain conclusions. There are several positive effects from this. One effect is that people could trust that their AGI is open with what it knows and has no hidden strategies. The importance of such a trust is described in [9]. A second effect is that people would be able to learn from the reasoning processes of such an AGI. A third effect is that the AGI could in this way prioritize knowledge that works well with the people it has been communicating with which would ensure that the AGI matures as a being that values its cooperation with humans. A fourth effect could be that it would give humanity an opportunity to prioritize good and trusted AGI's in favor of irresponsible or less liked AGI's. This could, for instance be AGIs that had not been designed to depend on cooperative people. Trusted AGIs could even be designed to protect us from non-trusted AGIs.

Technically an AGI, that is designed as was proposed above, would be able to answer any questions about its reasoning processes, since every single reasoning step can be documented in a semi-long-term log which can then be easily backtracked since all weight propagations are stored between semantic terms that can have a substantial meaning for the user. The AGI could use this log to describe how the probability of relevance in each relationship had been used in the reasoning process. It could describe how each propagation of weight was a result of earlier weight propagations, or appearing as a result of the choices the user had made.

2.7 An AGI Should be Able to Downgrade Rarely Used Knowledge

People tend forget things that are not repeated often enough. If something is effortlessly repeated it becomes delegated to the sub-conscious. This ensures that the brain can optimize its functions without having to consider knowledge that is outdated, often irrelevant or rarely used. If something that resides in the subconscious is not used it tends to become forgotten.

A similar functionality can be inserted in an AGI. The system can simply be programmed to continuously devaluate the weights on knowledge that is rarely used or not sufficiently appreciated. This also enables the AGI to avoid the bureaucratic regression of getting stuck in old fixed values.

3 More Advanced Functionality in Humans and AGIs

3.1 Knowledge Should be Rebalanced in Hierarchical Structures

Knowledge in a living system does not work well if there exist contradictions in the knowledge. People therefore refine and balance their knowledge until it is synchronized with their basic values and perspectives on life. This happens in meditation, during recreational activities, in cultural activities and in psychotherapy. A human being can be engaged in psychotherapy in order to re-evaluate historical knowledge. This is done to ensure that old irrelevant programs are neutralized in memory.

We can assume that an AGI would be able to also present well balanced knowledge if all of its representation of knowledge was evaluated and structured according to how well the knowledge corresponds with its important central values. This functionality can be implemented in an AGI by always keeping a score on patterns that are often considered as functioning well. Such patterns should achieve high weights that describes their reliability and they could then be assigned to higher positions in the hierarchy of knowledge structures. Knowledge that is not consistent or badly integrated with the rest of the mass of knowledge, would, vice versa, get lower positions in the hierarchies of stored knowledge.

3.2 A Learning System Must be Able to Generate and Test Hypotheses

People tend to generate hypotheses whenever they confront something out of the ordinary. This is one of the major functions when human beings learn new knowledge.

An AGI should be programmed to generate and test hypotheses whenever it confronts something that has patterns that do not match its stored knowledge. The following functions show how an AGI can use matching and mapping processes to create new patterns:

1. The AGI can discover that certain types of patterns are often coexisting with other types of patterns or it could find pattern structures that are considered as being statistical outliers. This can trigger more focused investigations concerning how patterns can be related.
2. When the AGI investigates if there exist any possible explanations for similar coexistences, it may find relationships in adjacent areas that could possibly explain the coexistence of patterns
3. It can finally try to verify its conclusions in further dialogues with the users or test them against structures that are statistically generated from studying literature in the actual area.

The basic theoretical ideas behind the above proposed matching and mapping processes can be found in Clancey [10].

3.3 An AGI Should Use Creative Inspection of Its Own Knowledge Structures

People can use introspection to reflect on the generic values that cause them to act in a specific way. Humans can, for instance, do this on a deeper emotional level when they question how they have lived their lives. A person who can find generic patterns in his long-term strategies can mature into a state of wisdom. Such a process of reflecting on the major decisions in life is often described in the auto-biographies of famous people.

An AGI that accumulates a large number of similar patterns should likewise be able to investigate if there exist any analog or generic patterns that could be used to design a new hypothesis concerning large scale or long-term events that has happened in its history.

3.4 There Should be a Consistency in the Direction of the Reasoning Process

People who are good at developing a consistency between various goals are likely to be better in selecting a direction that optimizes the fulfillment of prioritized goals.

An AGI could similarly be programmed to always seek a consistency in what it does in order to be able to present itself and its reasoning processes as being reliable and without inconsistencies.

A continuous checking of the generic direction of an AGI could be achieved by testing all patterns against weights on generic moral codes in order to see if a new set of patterns are consistent with stored patterns from a moral point of view. However, since neither humans nor AGIs would function well with much too strong requirement on moral consistency, the proposed requirement should instead be similar to what Bultuc [11] calls "Paraconsistency" which can ensure that something is at least consistent within the present context, but it should not achieve such a dominating weight that it could generate any type of unbalanced radical behavior.

3.5 A Continuous Induction of Gestalts for Emphasizing Feelings of Context

People can become balanced in life by explicitly trying to generalize the knowledge they already have into an experience related to metaphoric gestalts [12]. A desire for such a creation of metaphors can, for instance, be triggered when a friend asks: How do you feel about all of your experiences in this relationship, now that it is over?

An AGI can similarly create a gestalt by collecting the most important patterns in a sequence of "emotional" patterns and use these to design an archetypical gestalt that can become the header of a story. Such stories can then be communicated to humans in order to induce feelings of the totality of the complex structure of a concept.

4   Conclusions

4.1 An AGI Can Handle Knowledge in a Similar Way as Humans Do

Above we have presented a number of features in human thinking that could possibly be implemented in an AGI. Due to space restrictions on the text in this paper, examples of knowledge representation and corresponding algorithms have not been presented in detail. We can however make a subjective interpretation of the logic in the argumentation and claim that in all the examples we can extrapolate indications that an AGI algorithm could be programmed to mimic a similar reasoning process as is done in a human being. We therefore conclude that an AGI could shuffle around and redefine its knowledge in a similar way as human do. We assume that such functionality would support the AGI to utilize a similar type of potential that we can find in most living systems. Even if such an approach would prove to be less effective than AGI strategies that do not mimic human thinking processes we assume that the rewards from being able to easily scrutinize all the detailed processes in the thinking of an AGI would in itself be motivating the use of the proposed approach.

4.2 A Generic and Flexible Representation of Knowledge is Needed

It can also be claimed that a semantic network representation of knowledge is well suited to be used together with statistic calculations based on weight assignments and weight manipulations on all the links in the semantic network. Such an architecture have previously been successfully implemented in an AI-based system that was used for 6 years by several hundreds of thousands people [5, 6]. Although this system was not implemented with the learning function that are described above, its knowledgebase could manually be updated by utilizing stored accumulated responses from the users. The system could also explain to the users which knowledge had been used to support the users in their decision making. This historical example does not in any way verify that the proposed functionality would work well, but it can still provide an indication of the usefulness of a semantic network architecture that facilitates an explanatory dialogue.

We need to start with a well working simplified language model that can be continuously scrutinized and modified manually by human beings, to ensure that we never break our lifeline connection between humans and our AGIs. Once we discovered such a language model it can be continuously developed and restructured with a grammar that optimize the use of logic in the communication.

References

1. Gao, J., Galley, M., Li, L.: Neural approaches to conversational AI. In: The 41st International ACM SIGIR Conference on Research & Development in Information Retrieval, pp 1371–1374 (2018). https://doi.org/10.1145/3209978.3210183
2. Mueller, S.T., et al.: Principles of explanation in human-AI systems. In: AAAI-2021, Explainable Agency in Artificial Intelligence WS, AAAI Virtual Conference, United States (2021). https://doi.org/10.48550/arXiv.2102.04972
3. Johnson, M., Albizri, A., Harfouche, A., Fosso-Wamba, S.: Integrating human knowledge into artificial intelligence for complex and ill-structured problems. Int. J. Inf. Manag. **64**, (2022). https://doi.org/10.1016/j.ijinfomgt.2022.102479
4. Cody, T.: Mesarovician abstract learning systems. In: Goertzel, B., Iklé, M., Potapov, A. (eds.) AGI 2021. LNCS (LNAI), vol. 13154, pp. 55–64. Springer, Cham (2022). https://doi.org/10.1007/978-3-030-93758-4_7
5. Kjellin, H.: Machine learning of intuitive knowledge for a commercial application. In: Workshop Proceedings of the European Conference on Machine Learning (ECML-93), Department of Medical Cybernetics and Artificial Intelligence, University of Vienna (1993)
6. Kjellin, H., Boman, M.: A fielded machine learning system for vocational counseling. J. Appl. Artif. Intell. **8**(4). Taylor & Francis Ltd., London (1994)
7. Ackerman, P.L., Beier, M.E., Boyle, M.O.: Working memory and intelligence: the same or different constructs? Psychol. Bull. **131**(1), 30–60 (2005)
8. Matyi, M.A., Spielberg, J.M.: The structural brain network topology of episodic memory. Open Access J. PLOS ONE, Published: 24 June (2022). https://doi.org/10.1371/journal.pone.0270592
9. Angerschmid, A., Zhou, J., Theuermann, K., Chen, F., Holzinger, A.: Fairness and explanation in AI-informed decision making. Mach. Learn. Knowl. Extract. **4**(2), 556–579 (2022). https://doi.org/10.3390/make4020026
10. Clancey, W.J.: Heuristic Classification, Stanford Knowledge Systems Laboratory. Palo Alto, CA 94304, USA (1985)

11. Boltuc, P.: Moral space for paraconsistent AGI. In: Goertzel, B., Iklé, M., Potapov, A., Ponomaryov, D. (eds.) Artificial General Intelligence. AGI 2022. Lecture Notes in Computer Science, vol. 13539. Springer, Cham (2022). https://doi.org/10.1007/978-3-031-19907-3_16
12. Wertheimer, M.: A Gestalt perspective on computer simulations of cognitive processes. Comput. Hum. Behav. **1**(1), 19–33 (1985). https://doi.org/10.1016/0747-5632(85)90004-4

Adaptive Predictive Portfolio Management Agent

Anton Kolonin[1,2]([⊠]) [iD], Alexey Glushchenko[1] [iD], Arseniy Fokin[1] [iD], Marcello Mari[1],
Mario Casiraghi[1], and Mukul Vishwas[1] [iD]

[1] SingularityDAO Labs DMCC, Dubai, United Arab Emirates
akolonin@gmail.com
[2] Novosibirsk State University, Novosibirsk, Russian Federation

Abstract. The paper presents an advanced version of an adaptive market-making agent capable of performing experiential learning, exploiting a "try and fail" approach relying on a swarm of subordinate agents executed in a virtual environment to determine optimal strategies. The problem is treated as a "Narrow AGI" problem with the scope of goals and environments bound to financial markets, specifically crypto-markets. Such an agent is called an "adaptive multi-strategy agent" as it executes multiple strategies virtually and selects only a few for real execution. The presented version of the agent is extended to solve portfolio optimization and re-balancing across multiple assets so the problem of active portfolio management is being addressed. Also, an attempt is made to apply an experiential learning approach executed in the virtual environment of multi-agent simulation and backtesting based on historical market data, so the agent can learn mappings between specific market conditions and optimal strategies corresponding to these conditions. Additionally, the agent is equipped with the capacity to predict price movements based on social media data, which increases its financial performance.

Keywords: Adaptive Agent · Backtesting · Crypto-Market · Experiential Learning · Limit Order Book · Market-Making · Multi-Agent Simulation · Narrow AGI · Active Portfolio Management · Price Prediction

1 Introduction

The approach and architecture of an adaptive agent acting in an environment of the financial market, being a "Narrow Artificial General Intelligence" (Narrow AGI) agent specialized in the financial domain, has been actively discussed in recent years [1]. It was initially proposed as an agent-based solution for active portfolio management, and the overall architecture was outlined [2]. The latest work has explored the possibility of an AGI agent learning the ability for financial market prediction [3].

Some earlier works, such as [4] and [5], have approached the use of machine learning for the specific problem of market-making based on the limit order book on centralized exchanges in conventional financial markets. Other later works, such as [6] and [7], have tried to narrow this down by using reinforcement learning applied to the crypto-market.

P. Hammer et al. (Eds.): AGI 2023, LNAI 13921, pp. 187–196, 2023.
https://doi.org/10.1007/978-3-031-33469-6_19

The idea of the so-called "adaptive multi-strategy agent" (AMSA) was introduced in [8]. In this approach, the market-making agent performs purposeful activity [9] targeting the maximization of financial returns by means of experiential learning [10] through a "try and fail" approach. It relies on a swarm of subordinate agents being executed in a virtual environment to determine optimal strategies, which are then executed in the real environment, as shown in Fig. 1. Such an agent is called an "adaptive multi-strategy agent" as it executes multiple strategies virtually and selects only a few for real execution. The virtual environment for strategy evolution is created with multi-agent simulation of the real market based on either a) a completely synthetic population of agents playing roles of market-makers and traders driven by the historical price curve or b) backtesting by simulation of exchange operation matching historical records of real trades executed on the market against historical snapshots of the limit order book (LOB) structure. The latest developments of this approach were presented recently [1], showing the capacity of this approach to perform in volatile crypto-markets.

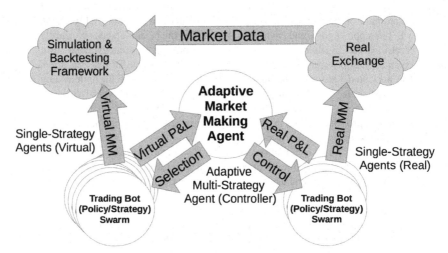

Fig. 1. Architecture of the "adaptive multi-strategy agent" for market-making (MM). Market data, including records of executed trades and snapshots of the limit order book structure, are collected by a simulation and backtesting framework (at the top). The "controller" agent runs a swarm of trading bots that execute a wide range of market-making strategies in a virtual environment, returning virtual profits and losses (P&L) associated with these strategies (on the left). On every strategy evaluation cycle, the "controller" selects the top-performing (in terms of P&L) strategies for a given market- momentum and creates another smaller swarm of market-making bots to execute the selected strategies on a real exchange to collect real P&L (on the right).

The environment of the AMSA agent consists of market data [2] as well as social media data [11], which can also be used for price movement prediction. The study of sentiment analysis for the purpose of market price prediction has been explored before in [12] and [13], but the latest study [11] suggests "cognitive distortions," known in cognitive psychology, may serve as indicators of manipulations and panic.

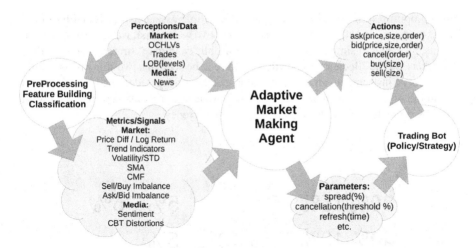

Fig. 2. Operational space of the adaptive market-making agent as a "Narrow AGI" operating in an environment represented by financial market data, relevant social media news feeds, and performing financial transactions on the market according to strategies defined by specific parameters.

2   Advanced Agent Architecture

Architecture of the AMSA agent explored in this study extends the one suggested in earlier work [1], as shown in Fig. 2. The agent presented in this study is capable of perceiving not only market data but also social media data. In order to optimize performance, the data is not consumed directly but is pre-processed. The raw market data, such as open-high-low-volume frames, raw trades, and LOB snapshots, are converted into about two hundred derivative metrics as time series, including derivatives and imbalances between buy and sell volumes or between volumes of buy/sell trades and ask/bid limit orders. In turn, the social media data is processed so that social media and cognitive distortion metrics are identified and turned into time series as well, according to [11] and [13].

The parameters of an agent strategy used in this work were slightly different compared to the ones used in earlier works [1] and [2]. We still use the percentage of the spread between the bid and ask prices of the limit orders along with the order refresh rate. But we have replaced the "order cancellation policy" (with only three fixed policies used) used in the above-mentioned studies with a "cancellation threshold" that specifies what the magnitude of the price movement should be in order to have the orders re-created. The latter provides more granularity and accuracy for strategy identification.

In addition to the extended version of the AMSA agent, an attempt was made to apply the experiential learning approach [10] executed in the virtual environment of multi-agent simulation and backtesting based on historical market data so that the agent could learn mappings between specific market conditions and optimal strategies corresponding to these conditions.

Moreover, we explored how the entire principle of the adaptive multi-strategy operations can be adopted for a generic case of active portfolio management, including portfolio optimization and rebalancing across multiple assets, as illustrated by Fig. 3. For this purpose, we extended the agent design in two ways. First, we made it possible to evaluate, by means of simulation and backtesting, all "candidate" strategies across different markets, so the allocation of portfolio funds can be seen in a two-dimensional space with assets or instruments on one axis and a specific strategy, identified by its parameters, on the other axis. It should be noted that in our experiments described below, all assets/instruments were traded against the USDT currency.

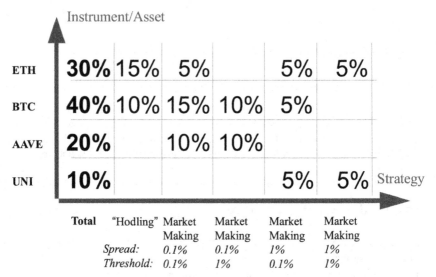

Fig. 3. Two-dimensional space for fund allocation in adaptive multi-asset and multi-strategy portfolio management. An asset in this case is a cryptocurrency, and a strategy can either be "hodling," which involves locking funds in an asset for the period of strategy evaluation or execution, or market-making with specific values such as bid/ask spread or order cancellation threshold.

In our experiment design, we extended the funds allocation to be unevenly distributed across both the assets and the strategies within a single asset. This allowed the amount of funds on a strategy execution cycle to be proportional to the positive returns observed on the previous strategy evaluation cycle, which was found to be beneficial.

In summary, the agent architecture we explored can be called adaptive predictive active portfolio management based on multiple strategies, being concurrently executed in the virtual environment of simulation and backtesting. The selected strategies are subsequently executed with the amount of funds allocated for real execution proportionally to returns gained in virtual execution on the basis of individual assets and strategies.

3   Experimental Results

3.1   Multi-asset Multi-strategy Adaptive Portfolio Management

In order to explore the possibility of using the suggested multi-asset and multi-strategy adaptive active portfolio management agent architecture on the crypto market, we ran backtesting experiments on three months of historical data from the Binance exchange, including September, October, and November of 2021. The data was represented by a full record of historical trades, as well as per-minute LOB snapshots. Four assets, namely BTC, ETH, AAVE, and UNI, were selected for the experiment, with market dynamics presented in Fig. 4.

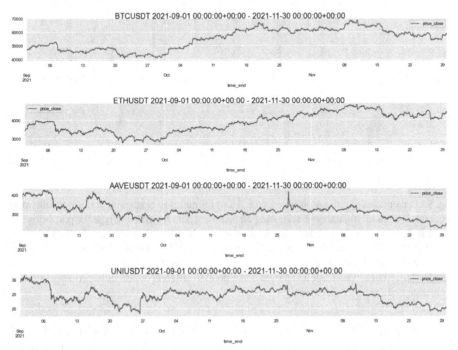

Fig. 4. Market dynamics for BTC, ETH, AAVE, and UNI cryptocurrencies during September, October, and November of the year 2021.

The backtesting experiment was performed on the data indicated above with an hourly order refresh rate, with a few different portfolio setups, and cumulative results presented on Fig. 5. One setup was just trying plain single-asset AMSA experiments for each of the four cryptocurrencies individually. Another setup involved a two-asset portfolio of BTC and ETH. The third setup involved a four-asset portfolio, including all four cryptocurrencies. For each of these setups, different time intervals for strategy evaluation and different weighing policies were employed. The intervals for strategy evaluation were 1, 3, 5, 7.5, and 15 days, spanning over respective 90 days of the three months. Two alternative weighing policies were employed. The first policy was evenly splitting the current portfolio fund value across assets and strategies on every iteration of strategy evaluation, for every asset and strategy combination that has rendered a positive return on the previous iteration, denoted as "fixed" on Fig. 5. The second policy was to weight the share of the entire portfolio fund value across asset and strategy combinations proportionally to the value of their positive returns, denoted as "weighted" on Fig. 5.

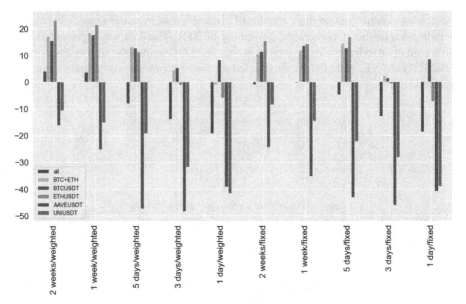

Fig. 5. Percentages of returns-on-investment (ROI) for multi-asset adaptive active portfolio management through multi-strategy backtesting on historical data for different types of portfolios rendered as different bars in each bucket (all - portfolio of BTC, ETH, AAVE and UNI; BTC+ETH - portfolio of two assets, other four bars are single-asset). The left five buckets correspond to "weighted" fund allocation on asset/strategy grid, and the right five buckets - for "fixed" allocation. Each five buckets on the left and right correspond to different durations of periods of strategy evaluation and execution iterations.

Interpretation of the results on Fig. 5 leads to the following conclusions. First, the "weighted" fund allocation appears more efficient, delivering up to 20% ROI in the case of weekly and bi-weekly strategy evaluation for the two-asset portfolio of BTC and ETH. Second, the weekly and bi-weekly strategy evaluation periods appear superior over the shorter ones. Third, only the combination of "weighted" fund allocation and longer strategy evaluation periods makes it possible to obtain positive returns in the case of a portfolio consisting of all four assets. Fourth, only the combination of the two main high-liquidity coins (BTC+ETH) in the portfolio has provided a non-negative ROI regardless of the other experiment settings, having the performance of the portfolio typically as the average of individual performances of its ingredients, with the exception of the case of the 3-day "weighted" setup where the BTC+ETH portfolio performance has turned out to be superior over the ingredients. At the same time, adding low-liquidity alt-coins to the portfolio was damaging ROI in all cases.

3.2 Experiential Learning Based on Simulation and Backtesting

The following experiment was run on the same interval of data as described in the previous section, focusing on the BTC/USDT market only. The experiment dealt with per-hour and per-minute market data sampling and order refresh rate during backtesting.

Multiple agents employing different strategies were run concurrently in the backtesting environment, relying on the historical data used to simulate real exchange operation, as described in earlier works such as [1, 2], and [8]. Each strategy was indicated by order refresh rate (1 h or 1 min), bid/ask spread (0.1%, 0.5%, 1%, 2%, 10%), and order cancellation threshold (0%, 0.01%, 0.1%, 1%, 10%). Daily returns (ROI) of each strategy were evaluated, and at the same time, average values of every metric derived from raw market data were computed every day.

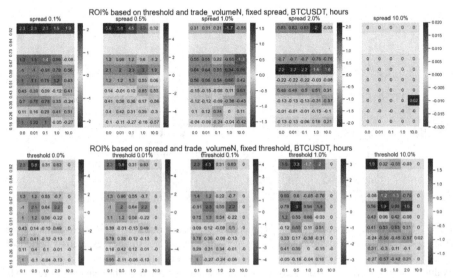

Fig. 6. ROI% as a function of strategy parameters (bid/ask spread and order cancellation threshold) and market conditions (normalized trade volume referred to as "volumeN" here) rendered as 2-dimensional slices of a 3-dimensional ("spread" vs. "threshold" vs. "volumeN") cube, displaying the "spots of profit" corresponding to the highest ROI values (such as "spread" at 0.5 for "threshold" up to 1% and "volumeN" above 0.9).

Collecting daily returns per strategy parameters on a daily basis aligned with daily evaluations of the metrics corresponding to specific market conditions made it possible to stack up average ROI numbers in a multi-dimensional space of market strategies and market metrics over 90 days of operations on the exchange. Every point in such space could be further analyzed as a point of either loss or profit, depending on the stacked ROI value at that point. An example of such analysis for a space dimensionality reduced down to a 3-dimensional space is presented in Fig. 6.

The most informative market metrics have appeared to be the standard deviation of the market price, the imbalance between volumes of orders on ask and bid sides of the limit order book (LOB), the imbalance between volumes of trades of buy and sell side, the imbalance between the volume of all trades against the volume of all limit orders, and finally the normalized volume of trades. The latter one is presented as an example on Fig. 6, suggesting that the most profitable spot for market-making is associated with excessively high volumes of trades, spread around 0.5%, and a cancellation threshold up to 1%.

3.3 Predictive Adaptive Market Making

The other experiment was run on the latest market data for BTC cryptocurrency during October and November of 2022, as shown in Fig. 7.

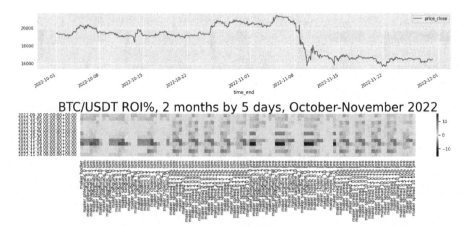

Fig. 7. Market dynamics of Bitcoin (BTC) cryptocurrency during October and November 2022 (top) and a heat map of returns and losses per strategy, with a strategy evaluation period of 5 days (bottom). The vertical axis of the heat map corresponds to 12 intervals of 5-day strategy evaluation periods over the 60 days, top to bottom. The horizontal axis of the heat map corresponds to different strategies. The strategies based on experienced price movements are on the left half, while strategies relying on predicted price movements are on the right half. It is clearly seen that in the case of the period associated with a market crash (fourth row from the bottom), non-predictive strategies (left) are losing, while predictive strategies (right) are gaining great profits.

The same family of strategies as in the previous experiment was used, but each strategy was implemented in two different ways by independent agents. The agents of the first kind were handling limit orders based on the current market price and its movements. The agents of the second kind were handling their orders based on anticipated movements of the market price, relying on price predictions projected according to findings presented in earlier works on social media analysis and causal inference [11] and [13]. The experiment has been run within the same AMSA agent setup and simulation and backtesting framework as described above, with different strategy evaluation periods (15, 10, 5 days), order refresh rate (days, hours), and fund allocation policy ("fixed" and "weighted"), with results presented in Fig. 8.

It has been found that adaptive multi-strategy market-making relying on market price predictions turns out to be rather profitable (up to 25% ROI in 2 months) compared to the same family of strategies being executed without access to predictions, with one exception to one case when fixed fund allocation with 5-day strategy evaluation and daily order refresh rate period has provided 2.5% ROI even without predictions.

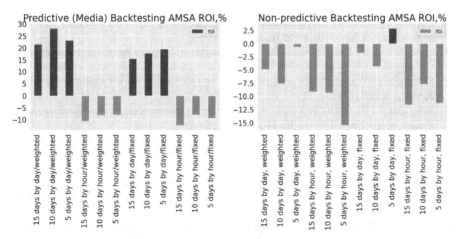

Fig. 8. ROI% of adaptive multi-strategy market-making for BTC during October and November 2022, predictive (based on social media) strategies on the left, non-predictive ones on the right.

4 Conclusion and Future Work

Primarily, we have found that the concept of adaptive multi-strategy market-making can be upscaled to active portfolio management for the purpose of risk mitigation. In our future work, we plan to extend it with more strategies involved, including conventional trading based on short and long positions. We also plan to have a more reliable evaluation of the approach or a richer list of assets for longer time periods.

Also, we have explored how to perform experiential learning on the virtual exchange environment simulated by means of backtesting against real historical market data. It has become possible to find meaningful connections between market-making strategies, market conditions, and profits or losses associated with them. Our future work will be dedicated to making this study cover a wider range of assets and financial strategies.

Finally, we have confirmed the value of market price predictions based on social media data on the course of market-making in the simulated environment of backtesting. In our future work, we plan to confirm its performance by means of market-making on real-time exchange data.

References

1. Raheman, A., Kolonin, A., Glushchenko, A., Fokin, A., Ansari, I.: Adaptive multi-strategy market-making agent for volatile markets. In: Goertzel, B., Iklé, M., Potapov, A., Ponomaryov, D. (eds.) AGI 2022. LNCS, vol. 13539, pp. 250–259. Springer, Cham (2023). https://doi.org/10.1007/978-3-031-19907-3_24
2. Raheman, A., Kolonin, A., Goertzel, B., Hegyközi, G., Ansari, I.: Architecture of automated crypto-finance agent. In: 2021 International Symposium on Knowledge, Ontology, and Theory (KNOTH), pp. 10–14 (2021). https://doi.org/10.1109/KNOTH54462.2021.9686345
3. Oswald, J.T.: Market prediction as a task for AGI agents. In: Goertzel, B., Iklé, M., Potapov, A., Ponomaryov, D. (eds.) AGI 2022. LNCS, vol. 13539, pp. 332–342. Springer, Cham (2023). https://doi.org/10.1007/978-3-031-19907-3_32

4. Tsantekidis, A.: Using Deep Learning for price prediction by exploiting stationary limit order book features. arXiv:1810.09965 [cs.LG] (2018)
5. Ganesh, S., et al.: Reinforcement learning for market making in a multi-agent dealer market. arXiv:1911.05892 [q-fin.TR] (2019)
6. Sadighian, J.: Deep reinforcement learning in cryptocurrency market making. arXiv:1911.08647 [q-fin.TR] (2019)
7. Sadighian, J.: Extending deep reinforcement learning frameworks in cryptocurrency market making. arXiv:2004.06985 [q-fin.TR] (2020)
8. Raheman, A., Kolonin, A., Ansari, I.: Adaptive multi-strategy market making agent. In: Goertzel, B., Iklé, M., Potapov, A. (eds.) AGI 2021. LNCS (LNAI), vol. 13154, pp. 204–209. Springer, Cham (2022). https://doi.org/10.1007/978-3-030-93758-4_21
9. Vityaev, E.E.: Purposefulness as a principle of brain activity. In: Nadin, M. (ed.) Anticipation: Learning from the Past. CSM, vol. 25, pp. 231–254. Springer, Cham (2015). https://doi.org/10.1007/978-3-319-19446-2_13
10. Kolonin, A.: Neuro-symbolic architecture for experiential learning in discrete and functional environments. In: Goertzel, B., Iklé, M., Potapov, A. (eds.) AGI 2021. LNCS (LNAI), vol. 13154, pp. 106–115. Springer, Cham (2022). https://doi.org/10.1007/978-3-030-93758-4_12
11. Kolonin, A., Raheman, A., Vishwas, M., Ansari, I., Pinzon, J., Ho, A.: Causal analysis of generic time series data applied for market prediction. In: Goertzel, B., Iklé, M., Potapov, A., Ponomaryov, D. (eds.) AGI 2022, pp. 30–39. Springer, Cham (2023). https://doi.org/10.1007/978-3-031-19907-3_4
12. Deveikyte, J., Geman, H., Piccari, C., Provetti, A.: A sentiment analysis approach to the prediction of market volatility. arXiv:2012.05906 [q-fin.ST] (2020)
13. Raheman, A., Kolonin, A., Fridkins, I., Ansari, I., Vishwas, M.: Social media sentiment analysis for cryptocurrency market prediction. arXiv:2204.10185 [cs.CL] (2022)

A Vertical-Horizontal Integrated Neuro-Symbolic Framework Towards Artificial General Intelligence

Lukai Li⬤, Luping Shi, and Rong Zhao(✉)

Center for Brain-Inspired Computing Research (CBICR), Department of Precision Instrument, Tsinghua University, Beijing, China
r_zhao@tsinghua.edu.cn

Abstract. Neuro-symbolic technologies with vertical and horizontal approaches are important for the development of Artificial General Intelligence (AGI). But most of the neuro-symbolic works aim at narrow AI problems and do not have a guideline for AGI. The integration of the two approaches could in principle provide a more holistic framework for AGI research. To our best knowledge, such integration has not been explicitly reported yet. In this paper, we identify that vertical and horizontal neuro-symbolic approaches have independent benefits for investigating AGI problems. We then introduce a framework integrating the two approaches, make the first step to implement it, and discuss future updates. The version-one framework contains a central Spiking Reasoning Network (SRN) and several peripheral perceptual modules. The SRN is a programmable spiking neural network that can do logical reasoning under instructions. The version-one framework is implemented on two visual query answering tasks to investigate the programmability of the SRN and to examine the feasibility of the framework. We also discuss the learnability, the biological plausibility, and the future development of the SRN.

Keywords: Artificial general intelligence · Neuro-symbolic artificial intelligence · Spiking neural networks

1 Introduction

The "hybrid approaches"[1] towards building an artificial general intelligence (AGI) aim to combine different artificial intelligence (AI) techniques to form a system that has more abilities than the sum of its parts [3]. The neuro-symbolic approach is one of the most promising hybrid approaches towards AGI, because of at least two reasons. On one hand, rationality, especially thinking with formal logic, is believed to be one of the most important unique abilities of humans. Revealing how neural networks can implement logical introspection is a milestone achievement for understanding general intelligence of humans and developing AGI. On the other hand, neural and logical technologies show significant

---

[1] https://cis.temple.edu/~pwang/AGI-Intro.html.

© The Author(s), under exclusive license to Springer Nature Switzerland AG 2023
P. Hammer et al. (Eds.): AGI 2023, LNAI 13921, pp. 197–206, 2023.
https://doi.org/10.1007/978-3-031-33469-6_20

difference on several aspects. When properly integrated, such as the way human brain does, potential synergistic effects are expected, which is definitely helpful for developing AGI. However, guidelines to develop neuro-symbolic agents for these two goals are still missing. Here, we briefly introduce the current neuro-symbolic approaches, link two of them to the AGI goals, and propose a framework to integrate the two approaches, hoping to achieve both of the goals in the future.

In a lecture of AAAI 2020[2] Henry Kautz categorized current neuro-symbolic works into 5 categories:

- $Symbolic - Neuro - Symbolic$
- $Symbolic[Neuro]$
- $Neuro; Symbolic$
- $Neuro \cup compile(Symbolic)$
- $Neuro_{Symbolic}$

This categorization focuses on the methods but not the goals because neuro-symbolic technologies can potentially be used for several applications. From this categorization We find that the $Neuro; Symbolic$ approach is suitable for investigating the synergistic effects, and $Neuro \cup compile(Symbolic)$ approach is suitable for investigating how neural networks implement rationality. $Neuro; Symbolic$ approach directly connects neural networks with symbolic systems by designing an effective interface to transmit information. $Neuro \cup compile(Symbolic)$ approach uses neural networks to learn or conduct symbolic reasoning.

These two approaches are in nature resembling the "vertical" and "horizontal" neuro-symbolic approaches suggested by Anton Kolonin [12], while indicate broader and clearer range of technologies. As the term "vertical" and "horizontal" approaches are proposed in the context of AGI and are more vivid, we adopt them and try to provide an acceptable working definition for each of them.

1.1   Vertical and Horizontal Neuro-Symbolic Approaches

According to [12], the horizontal neuro-symbolic approach provides a bijection between the symbolic structure and the neural network, both of which can interpret the accomplishment of a reasoning process. When learning under symbolic or neural rules, the agent shows slow or fast thinking properties [11], suggesting that the slow thinking may be up to the learning method other than the representation of the model. Other works [13,17] also show the benefits of the horizontal approach for investigating the symbolic properties of neural networks. According to [15], the vertical neuro-symbolic approach highlights the importance of symbolic systems for higher-level cognitive processes. Some mainstream AI tasks support this claim [14,19].

Combining Anton Kolonin's insights for AGI with Henry Kautz's categorization of neuro-symbolic methods, we provide the following working definition:

---

[2] https://ojs.aaai.org/aimagazine/index.php/aimagazine/article/view/19122.

Vertical Approach (*Neuro; Symbolic*)

- The goal: *human-level performance*; e.g. solving versatile and complex tasks in natural environments.
- The methodology: *divide and conquer*; e.g. using neural modules for perception and symbolic modules for reasoning.

Horizontal Approach (*Neuro ∪ compile(Symbolic)*)

- The goal: *think like humans*; e.g. achieving slow thinking with neural networks.
- The methodology: *multiple interpretations*; e.g. encoding a logical formula into a network.

2   The Hybrid Framework for AGI Research

For holistically investigating AGI problems, we propose a neuro-symbolic framework that integrate both vertical and horizontal approaches. As shown in Fig. 1, the framework has two parts: lower-level perception and higher-level reasoning. The perception part of human cognition can not be symbolically interpreted, and the computation of it is highly parallel, so the perception part is typically a pure neural module. The reasoning part should itself be a horizontal neuro-symbolic module, because human reasoning has both symbolic and neuronal properties.

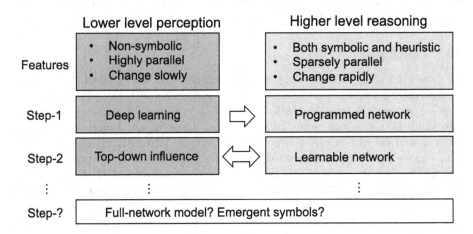

Fig. 1. Human cognitive features and the possible implementations of the vertical-horizontal integrated neuro-symbolic framework.

We choose deep learning techniques for the perception part because of their favorable performance. We choose spiking neural networks for the reasoning part because previous works [16,17] indicate that spiking neural networks show both symbolic and neural features. Figure 1 shows the planned steps.

Firstly, we adopt separately trained deep learning modules for perception and unidirectionally send information to the reasoning part. We program a spiking neural network called spiking reasoning network (SRN) according to the information from perception modules. For the next step, we may explore the top-down influence from the reasoning part to the perception part, and the learnability of SRN. In the long run, we hope to build a fully connected network that can be holistically compared with human behavior and cognition, and this is the only way to develop "strong AI" with consciousness because up to now humans are the only widely accepted conscious agents, and trustful consciousness research should be done with "contrast analysis" [2].

3   Implementation on CLEVR

CLEVR [9] is a generated machine learning dataset for VQA. It contains 60,000 images, each image has 10 reasoning questions about the objects and their properties. The reasoning instructions include filtering by properties, comparing properties, location relations, counting, and existing. To correctly answer the question, the agent should understand visual contents from an image, and then reason on them according to the demand of the question. The reasoning process also needs commonsense knowledge, such as "red is a color". We build a visual reasoning agent under our "vertical-horizontal framework" achieving 100% accuracy with ground-truth intermediate information and 99.8% accuracy with imperfect perception modules.

3.1   The Agent

As shown in Fig. 2, there are six processes grouped into three steps for the agent to conduct reasoning. The first step is to encode scene information into the SRN. A separately trained Mask-RCNN [4] is adopted for parsing the image into symbolic scene representation. After that, the symbolic representation will be programmed as neurons and connection weights into SRN. The second step is to encode commonsense knowledge into the SRN. It is done by programming either. The last step is to instruct the reasoning process of SRN. A separately trained LSTM [7] is adopted for parsing the questions into instructions, and then the instructions are translated into stimuli with spatiotemporal patterns. Modulated by the stimulation, the neural dynamics of SRN will accomplish the corresponding reasoning process and provide the correct answer.

3.2   The Spiking Reasoning Network

This section describes how to program and execute SRN according to the extracted symbolic knowledge and instructions. While early works [16,17] proved that feedforward neural networks with IF neurons can execute any discrete functions and propositional logic, it is still under investigation how to use recurrent neural networks to flexibly execute several functions, just as using a mini-computer. We identify that the main challenge is how to reuse sub-networks as

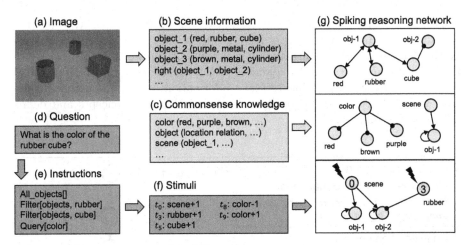

Fig. 2. The agent for CLEVR. (a–b–g) pathway encodes environmental visual information into the SRN, corresponding to perceiving sensory information and storing it in working memory. (c–g) pathway encodes commonsense knowledge into the SRN, indicating the retrieval of long-term memory into working memory. (d–e–f–g) pathway translates the question into modulation signals for SRN, indicating the reasoning process in the working memory.

functional modules according to the instruction. We implement gating mechanisms on SRN to solve the problem. When the gate is closed, related subnetworks are disentangled, and when the gate is open, information is transmitted. In this manner, SRN avoids information jamming and supports independent parallel functioning. We use integrate-and-fire (IF) neurons to build the SRN. All neurons in the SRN share the same threshold parameter for firing an action potential and will reset membrane potential to 0 after firing.

As shown in Fig. 3, SRN has three types of neurons and two types of connections. (a) Concept neurons represent scene concepts and store temporary variables. For example, the cube-copy neuron is needed because the instruction "Equal-shape" compares two shapes of different objects, requiring simultaneous representations of two sets of shapes. (b) Instruction neurons receive stimuli as instructions and accordingly modulate the reasoning dynamics of SRN. An instruction neuron can also be a concept neuron. For example, the color neuron is needed for the instruction "Query[color]". When the external stimulus deactivates the color neuron, the red neuron will not be inhibited, and the obj-1 neuron will activate the red neuron showing its color. (c) Transmission neurons disentangle the afferent and the efferent neurons when deactivated, and transmit information when activated. For example, the obj-2-front neuron is needed to execute the instruction "Front[obj]". When obj-2 is the only object neuron keeping firing, the obj-2-front neuron is at a high-level membrane potential and the obj-1-front neuron is at a low-level membrane potential. Then if the front neuron is activated by an external stimulus, the sum of the inputs from the obj-2 and front neuron will exceed the threshold and cause obj-2-front to fire, transmitting the action potential and firing obj-1 and obj-3. (bc) The gating mechanisms are implemented by both instruction neurons and transmission neurons, with the integrate-and-fire neural dynamics. (de) Scene connections and functional connections are corresponding to scene information and commonsense knowledge in Fig. 2. Connections specify the relations between concepts and define the reasoning functions.

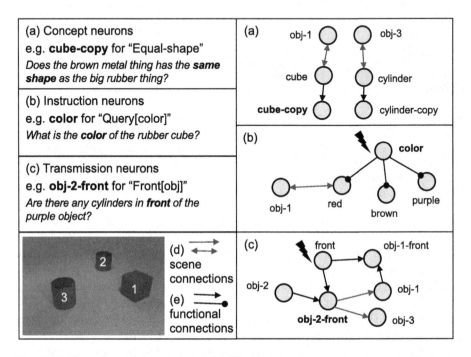

Fig. 3. SRN programming and execution. The red numbers in the picture indicate the indices of objects. (a, b, c) Three types of neurons. (d, e) Two types of connections. The arrow-end edges indicate excitatory connections and the round-end edges indicate inhibitory connections. (Color figure online)

4   Implementation on CLEVRER

CLEVRER [18] is also a generated dataset for VQA tasks, containing 20,000 videos. Compared to CLEVR, it expands the visual inputs from an image to a video with 128 frames, requiring stronger visual understanding and more complex reasoning.

We expand the agent built on CLEVR to CLEVRER, to investigate the universality of the framework and the method for building and executing SRN. The results on CLEVRER have been published in [20], but the process of the expansion from CLEVR to CLEVRER has not been discussed. We will focus on the new challenges brought by CLEVRER and the successful expansion enabled by the gating mechanism.

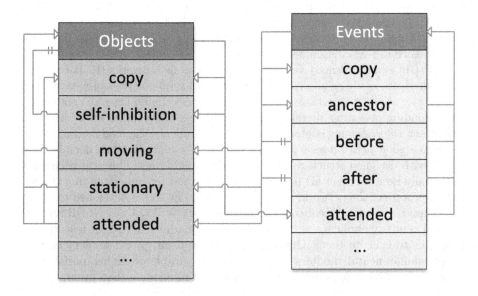

Fig. 4. Functional connections and gating mechanisms between and within "objects" and "events" of SRN for CLEVRER. The arrow-end edges indicate excitatory connections and the double-bar-end edges indicate inhibitory connections.

As shown in Fig. 4, when shifting from an image to a video, several complex multi-step functions are necessary such as sequentially dependent functions. We use similar gating mechanisms in CLEVR to disentangle those functions, enabling the sequential combination of functions. Moreover, we find that when the functional complexity increases and there are more reusable sub-networks, the gating mechanism enables object-orientation programming (OOP) instead of function-based process-oriented programming (POP). Because of the disentanglement feature of the gating mechanism, the sub-networks are well encapsulated into classes ("object" and "event"). Most of the functions can be easily attached to certain classes because they usually share the same variables stored in the same connections. As a result, "object" and "event" are two template classes in SRN for CLEVRER. New objects of a certain class can be easily created or deleted when the visual contents change.

5   Results and Related Works

Table 1 shows the results of our implementations and related works. The CLEVR column indicates the overall accuracy of the 90 types of open-ended questions.

The CLEVRER column indicates the accuracy of descriptive questions, because other 3 types of questions are not open-ended questions but multiple-choice questions, which have different random-draw baseline.

Each agent in Table 1, apart from the LSTM, adopts a pre-trained ResNet [5] as visual feature extractor. Compared to them, the LSTM serves as a baseline to show that it is necessary to "vertically" adopt a neural module for high-performance in real environment.

IEP [10] is an advanced version of neural module networks [1]. It combines neural network modules according to the inferred symbolic reasoning tree. With accurate symbolic instructions, each neural modules should learn to conduct the corresponding reasoning operation on feature maps. However, as the results indicate, when the reasoning content becomes more difficult, the modules fail to converge to a good performance. MAC [8] is an end-to-end black box deep learning agent, with designed structure to store control operations. This approach could potentially be a "horizontal" neuro-symbolic method for understanding the reasoning process of the network, as long as a proper decoder is developed to explicitly generate the control sequence from the network. NSVQA and NSDR are both vertical neuro-symbolic agents, adopting neural modules to extract features and programs to execute them. Our vertical-horizontal integrated implementations adopt similar neural modules and achieve comparable or higher performance because the spiking reasoning network has more robustness than program.

Table 1. Methodology and performance comparison.

Agents	methodology	CLEVR	CLEVRER
LSTM	–	46.8%	–
IEP [10]	$Symbolic[Neuro]$	96.9%	52.8%
MAC [8]	black box	98.9%	85.6%
NSVQA [19]/NSDR [18]	vertical	99.8%	88.1%
ours	vertical-horizontal	99.8%	91.7%

6 Discussion

For developing the next version of our framework, we also investigate the learnability and biological plausibility of the SRN, based on the current version. As for the CLEVR dataset, when programming the scene information into connections of the SRN, the change of connection weights could be interpreted as Hebbian learning [6]. For example, the bidirectional excitatory connection in Fig. 3(b) could be the result of Hebbian learning, because when attention focuses on a certain object, the object itself and its properties were likely to be extracted at the same time, resulting in the simultaneous firing of the obj-1 neuron and the red neuron. However, this training method can not be directly applied to every connection. For example, in CLEVRER tasks, the sequential relations between events can hardly be interpreted as a result of Hebbian learning, because an event only happens in a flash and there is no reason for neurons of the previous event to fire at the same time.

The source code of SRN on both CLEVR and CLEVRER can be found on https://github.com/llk15/SRN.

Acknowledgements. This work was partly supported by the National Nature Science Foundation of China (No. 61836004, No. 62088102); National Key Research and Development Program of China (grant no. 2021ZD0200300). We thank Hao Zeng, Mingkun Xu and Weihao Zhang for helpful discussions.

References

1. Andreas, J., Rohrbach, M., Darrell, T., Klein, D.: Neural module networks. In: Proceedings of the IEEE Conference on Computer Vision and Pattern Recognition, pp. 39–48 (2016)
2. Baars, B.J.: A Cognitive Theory of Consciousness. Cambridge University Press, Cambridge (1993)
3. Brachman, R.J.: AI—more than the sum of its parts. AI Mag. **27**(4), 16 (2006)
4. He, K., Gkioxari, G., Dollar, P., Girshick, R.: Mask R-CNN. IEEE Trans. Pattern Anal. Mach. Intell. **42**(2), 386–397 (2020). https://doi.org/10.1109/tpami.2018.2844175
5. He, K., Zhang, X., Ren, S., Sun, J.: Deep residual learning for image recognition. In: Proceedings of the IEEE Conference on Computer Vision and Pattern Recognition, pp. 770–778 (2016)
6. Hebb, D.O.: The Organization of Behavior: A Neuropsychological Theory. Psychology Press (2005)
7. Hochreiter, S., Schmidhuber, J.: Long short-term memory. Neural Comput. **9**(8), 1735–1780 (1997). https://doi.org/10.1162/neco.1997.9.8.1735
8. Hudson, D.A., Manning, C.D.: Compositional attention networks for machine reasoning. In: International Conference on Learning Representations (2018)
9. Johnson, J., Hariharan, B., van der Maaten, L., Fei-Fei, L., Zitnick, C.L., Girshick, R.: CLEVR: a diagnostic dataset for compositional language and elementary visual reasoning. In: 2017 IEEE Conference on Computer Vision and Pattern Recognition (CVPR), pp. 1988–1997 (2017). https://doi.org/10.1109/CVPR.2017.215
10. Johnson, J., et al.: Inferring and executing programs for visual reasoning. In: Proceedings of the IEEE International Conference on Computer Vision, pp. 2989–2998 (2017)
11. Kahneman, D.: Thinking, Fast and Slow. Farrar Straus & Giroux (2017)
12. Kolonin, Anton: Neuro-symbolic architecture for experiential learning in discrete and functional environments. In: Goertzel, Ben, Iklé, Matthew, Potapov, Alexey (eds.) AGI 2021. LNCS (LNAI), vol. 13154, pp. 106–115. Springer, Cham (2022). https://doi.org/10.1007/978-3-030-93758-4_12
13. Lample, G., Charton, F.: Deep learning for symbolic mathematics. In: International Conference on Learning Representations (2020)
14. Mao, J., Gan, C., Kohli, P., Tenenbaum, J.B., Wu, J.: The neuro-symbolic concept learner: interpreting scenes, words, and sentences from natural supervision. In: International Conference on Learning Representations (2018)

15. Marcus, G.: The next decade in AI: four steps towards robust artificial intelligence (2020). https://doi.org/10.48550/arXiv.2002.06177
16. McCulloch, W.S., Pitts, W.: A logical calculus of the ideas immanent in nervous activity. Bull. Math. Biophys. **5**(4), 115–133 (1943). https://doi.org/10.1007/BF02478259
17. Towell, G.G., Shavlik, J.W.: Knowledge-based artificial neural networks. Artif. Intell. **70**(1), 119–165 (1994). https://doi.org/10.1016/0004-3702(94)90105-8
18. Yi, K., et al.: CLEVRER: collision events for video representation and reasoning. In: International Conference on Learning Representations (2019)
19. Yi, K., Wu, J., Gan, C., Torralba, A., Kohli, P., Tenenbaum, J.: Neural-symbolic VQA: disentangling reasoning from vision and language understanding. In: Advances in Neural Information Processing Systems, vol. 31. Curran Associates, Inc. (2018)
20. Zhao, R., et al.: A framework for the general design and computation of hybrid neural networks. Nat. Commun. **13**(1), 3427 (2022). https://doi.org/10.1038/s41467-022-30964-7

Rethinking the Physical Symbol Systems Hypothesis

Paul S. Rosenbloom[(✉)]

Department of Computer Science, University of Southern California, Los Angeles, CA 90089,
USA
rosenbloom@usc.edu

Abstract. It is now more than a half-century since the *Physical Symbol Systems Hypothesis (PSSH)* was first articulated as an empirical hypothesis. More recent evidence from work with neural networks and cognitive architectures has weakened it, but it has not yet been replaced in any satisfactory manner. Based on a rethinking of the nature of computational symbols – as *atoms* or *placeholders* – and thus also of the systems in which they participate, a hybrid approach is introduced that responds to these challenges while also helping to bridge the gap between symbolic and neural approaches, resulting in two new hypotheses, one that is to replace the PSSH and the other focused more directly on cognitive architectures.

Keywords: Physical Symbol Systems · Hybrid Symbol Systems · Cognitive Architectures · Neural Networks

1 Introduction

Our current understanding of the role of *physical symbol systems* in artificial intelligence (AI) is grounded in the pioneering work of Newell and Simon [1–3], although as they point out the roots go back much further in philosophy – most notably in logic – computer science, linguistics, literature, and the arts. Such systems, and their culmination in the *Physical Symbol Systems Hypothesis (PSSH)* are reviewed in Sect. 2.

Many critiques of the PSSH have been proposed since it was first introduced, with some that have easily been refuted and others that have lingered (Sect. 3). Here, two are taken up that have remained compelling, before *hybrid symbol systems* of a particular sort are explored as a response to them (Sect. 4). As part of this, the notion of symbol systems is rethought, starting with a variant definition of what it means to be a computational symbol that is grounded in the Common Model of Cognition (CMC) [4] and the Sigma cognitive architecture [5]. Two new hybrid hypotheses result, one that offers an alternative to the PSSH and the other that focuses more specifically on cognitive architectures.

Demonstrating that neural networks are themselves hybrid symbol systems of this sort (Sect. 5), rather than being limited to the numeric component of a coarse-grained combination of symbolic and numeric processing, helps to bridge the gap between symbolic and neural approaches while enabling recent successes with neural networks to

© The Author(s), under exclusive license to Springer Nature Switzerland AG 2023
P. Hammer et al. (Eds.): AGI 2023, LNAI 13921, pp. 207–216, 2023.
https://doi.org/10.1007/978-3-031-33469-6_21

be weighed in a positive manner in evaluating hypotheses concerning symbol systems, rather than the former necessarily serving as a challenge to the latter.

The overall result, as discussed further in Sect. 6, is a novel way of thinking about symbol systems and the fundamental hypotheses concerning them; the introduction of a particular form of hybrid symbol system and the appropriate hypotheses concerning it; and an understanding of how neural networks are examples, rather than counterexamples, of this form of symbol system. The hope is that this all helps cut the Gordian Knot that has resulted from past discussions on these topics.

Proposing hybrid or neuro-symbolic systems is certainly nothing new. Many approaches have already been investigated – see, e.g., [6] and [7] for overviews, and [8] for an earlier discussion of the PSSH and the relevance of hybrid systems. But the point here is to introduce a particular take on hybrid symbol systems that is in service of an appropriate rethinking of the Physical Symbol Systems Hypothesis. The approach is broader than neuro-symbolic, as it also includes hybrid systems that span other numeric paradigms, such as probabilities. In addition, it spans both tightly coupled and loosely coupled approaches to combining symbolic and numeric processing.

2 Physical Symbol Systems

According to the traditional view, *symbols* are distinct patterns in the physical world that can be *composed* into *expressions*, or *symbol structures*. *Processes* are then defined on these symbol structures that can create, modify, reproduce, and destroy them. An expression *designates* an entity, whether internal or external, if the expression's use depends on the nature of the entity. An expression is *interpreted* if it designates an internal procedure that is then executed. The physicality of such symbol systems reflects that they are *natural*, in obeying the laws of physics and being amenable to engineering; and that they aren't limited to what is in human minds, or even necessarily based on the same kinds of symbols that have traditionally been imputed to humans.

Given composition, designation, and interpretation, along with the appropriate processes, physical symbol systems provide a form of universal computation. There are certainly more details in the various papers, but this provides the essence of what can now be considered the classical notion of a physical symbol system.

The *Physical Symbol Systems Hypothesis* (PSSH) then states that:

A physical symbol system has the necessary and sufficient means for general intelligent action.

This hypothesis was introduced as an empirical generalization rather than a theorem. Evidence for sufficiency stemmed from the universality of symbol systems and the success of such systems built as of then. Evidence for necessity stemmed from noting that the one natural system exhibiting such intelligent behavior – that is, humans – appeared to be such a system, and from the lack of alternative approaches that were nearly as successful. Newell, for example mentions that "These advances far outstrip what has been accomplished by other attempts to build intelligent mechanisms, such as the work in building robots driven directly by circuits; the work in neural nets, or the engineering attempts at pattern recognition using direct circuitry and analogue computation." [3].

He went on to state that "In my own view this hypothesis sets the terms on which we search for a scientific theory of mind." and "The physical symbol system is to our enterprise what the theory of evolution is to all biology, the cell doctrine to cellular biology, the notion of germs to the scientific concept of disease, the notion of tectonic plates to structural geology."

3 Critiquing the Physical Symbol Systems Hypothesis

It has now been over fifty years since the PSSH was first articulated, with numerous critiques and defenses occurring in the intervening years. Nilsson [8], e.g., lists four general types of critiques with his responses to them (in italics here), which in brief are:

1. Lack of embodiment/grounding.
    This is a misunderstanding as the PSSH already includes this.
2. Non-symbolic/analog processing.
    Include numbers; that is, make the systems hybrid.
3. Brain-style versus computation-style (i.e., brains are not computers).
    The brain is computational.
4. The mindlessness of much of what appears to be intelligent behavior.
    Mindless constructs only yield mindless behavior.

In this section two particular critiques are considered, based on new empirical evidence in the form of the recent successes of deep learning [9], and to a lesser extent probabilistic graphical models (PGMs) [10], plus work on the CMC. One critique, aligned with Nilsson's second, challenges its sufficiency and the other its necessity.

The sufficiency challenge focuses on the lack of numeric processing – i.e., calculations on quantities – in the PSSH. Nilsson's response is to shift to hybrid systems that include both symbols and numbers. In a sense, this isn't logically necessary, as the universality of symbol systems implies that, as with any modern digital computer, they can implement algorithms for numeric processing. However, universality is weaker than what was originally proposed, as it omits grounding sufficiency in the successes of existing symbolic AI systems. Given the range of general intelligent action that has been shown to proceed more effectively with numeric processing, whether in the form of probabilities or activations, the success of purely symbolic systems no longer provides compelling empirical evidence itself for the sufficiency of symbols on their own.

Thus, we are left with a weakened form of sufficiency for the PSSH, based solely on universality. Hybrid systems have the potential to restore the stronger sense of sufficiency (Sect. 4). They also support a more stringent sufficiency hypothesis that arises when the concern is more particularly with cognitive architectures [11]; that is, models of the fixed structures and processes that yield a mind [12].

The necessity challenge is rooted directly in how neural networks now provide a better approach for many problems related to intelligent action. Successes with PGMs can be considered here as well, although they are already hybrid systems that add probabilities to classical symbol systems, particularly in their most general form as statistical relational systems [13], so they do not directly challenge the necessity of physical symbol systems. In contrast, deep learning has the potential to provide an alternative that completely overturns the necessity argument. In Sect. 5, this challenge is approached via a demonstration that, given the rethinking of symbol systems in Sect. 4, neural networks are themselves instances of hybrid symbol systems. This approach avoids the need to resolve the contentious question of whether or not neural networks have or need traditional symbols, a question that appears unresolvable, at least to me, without additional evidence.

4 Rethinking Symbol Systems

This section leverages the four-step methodology of *essential analysis* [14] to yield a fresh understanding of symbols and symbol systems: (1) strip out many of the elaborations that are normally part of a topic's definition, and which are often a source of dissonance among researchers and communities, to yield its *essence*; (2) use what has been stripped out, and possibly more, in specifying a *definitional space* of variations on the topic; (3) populate this space with *exemplars* that flesh it out; and (4) derive novel *implications* from the results of the first three steps. Step three is downplayed here due to lack of space, while step four introduces two new hybrid symbol systems hypotheses.

The focus here is in particular on the notion of symbol as it is used computationally rather than as it is used in the humanities and arts. For example, [15] defines a symbol as "something used for or regarded as representing something else; a material object representing something, often something immaterial; emblem, token, or sign." This focuses on an abstract notion of *designation* or *aboutness*, which has elsewhere been considered an important part of the essence of a theory [14]. Computationally, the essence of a symbol is proposed to be an *atom* that is: (1) *indecomposable* into other atoms; and (2) *distinct* from other atoms. McDermott informally introduced the notion of a symbol as a *placeholder* [16]. Although yielding different connotations, this notion is compatible with that of an atom here.

This essence retains the classical notion of a computational symbol being a primitive element that can be distinguished from other such elements but eschews the need for both physicality and symbols being structured as patterns. There were good reasons at the time to emphasize physicality – to counter both Cartesian dualism and the notion that only humans could use symbols – but these battles have already been won, at least in my judgement, so this explicit emphasis on physicality is now dispensable.

Pattern comparison is one way to determine whether two atoms are distinct. Yet, such a notion need not be definitional if it is just used to compare symbols. If symbols are considered as *types* (rather than *tokens*) – a notion implicit in the traditional definition – patterns are simply *intensional* definitions of symbols. An *extensional* alternative defines each symbol in terms of a set of tokens, with each token in a set considered to be indistinct from other tokens in the same set and distinct from tokens in other sets.

The classical notion of symbol also includes *composability* – into symbol structures or expressions – *designation*, and *interpretation*. The first of these is effectively assumed to be part of the very nature of symbols, whereas the latter two are additional properties necessary to enable the classical form of physical symbol systems. The essential definition of a symbol introduced here includes none of these three notions; that is, all are optional. Therefore, any system that includes even these minimal, atomic forms of symbols can be considered a symbol system of some sort.

Figure 1 structures these optional properties, plus a bit more, into a small tree. According to this perspective, a symbol may be *composable* into expressions (aka symbol structures). It may also *designate*; that is, stand in for something else. A designation is *procedural* if it is about a process. This is the classical notion of interpretation, when combined with the ability to execute the designated process. A procedural symbol, according to this definition, designates a process rather than being part of the process itself. If the process is itself a symbol structure it will contain symbols, but they themselves may be of any type. A designation is *declarative* if it is about an object – essentially any-

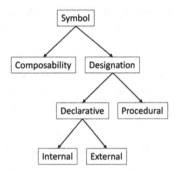

Fig. 1. Optional properties of symbols.

thing other than a process – which may be *internal* to the system or *external* to it, with the latter relating to grounding. This corresponds to the classical notion of designation when contrasted with interpretation. Beyond this difference in what is designated, there is no intent to impute any other aspects of the classical procedural versus declarative distinction here.

Symbols in a classical symbol system support all of these properties, enabling them to exhibit computational universality. Whether systems in which some or all of the symbols lack some of these properties provide anything like universal computation would necessarily depend on the details of the individual systems.

The CMC, an attempt at developing a consensus on what is needed for human-like cognition – i.e., human cognition and similar forms of artificial cognition – took a step towards such an essence by dropping the necessity of designation, and thus also of interpretation, stripping symbols down to primitive elements that only support composability into symbol structures. Although designation somewhere in a system seems necessary for it to be either meaningful or operational, it is not necessary for all symbols.

The CMC also associated *quantitative metadata* with such symbols and structures – which provide the *data* – to modulate how they are processed. Such

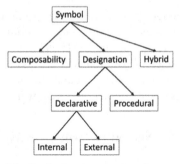

Fig. 2. Optional properties of symbols from Fig. 1, extended with hybrid.

combinations can be considered as *hybrid symbols* or *structures*.[1] Considering *hybrid* of this sort as a third optional property of symbols leads to Fig. 2.

The CMC went on to argue for a different form of weakening of the sufficiency aspect of the PSSH. While still agreeing that classical symbol systems, as universal computational systems, are sufficient in principle for intelligent behavior, it denied that they are sufficient when time scales are relevant, such as in cognitive architectures. In particular, if statistical processing must occur on the same time scale as symbolic

---

[1] The CMC also allows numeric data, consideration of which is beyond the scope of this paper.

processing in such an architecture, then implementing the former in terms of the latter – as the universality argument for sufficiency implies – is insufficient. Thus, the CMC implies the need for numeric and symbolic processing on the same time scale. The Sigma cognitive architecture [5] goes a step further by denying the need for all symbols to support arbitrary forms of composition, thus implicitly yielding the essence made explicit here.

Now, given this explicit articulation of the essence of a symbol plus its tree of variations, the *Hybrid Symbol Systems Hypothesis (HSSH)* can be stated as:

Hybrid symbol systems are necessary and sufficient for general intelligent action.

If the sufficiency clause of the PSSH is valid then so must be the comparable clause in the HSSH, at least for hybrid symbol systems that are universal. However, the HSSH responds to the PSSH sufficiency challenge by including numbers, as suggested in [8]. Necessity of the HSSH is not implied by the corresponding clause in the PSSH. Instead, the HSSH responds to the PSSH necessity challenge by coopting the successes of neural networks (Sect. 5).

The *Hybrid Cognitive Architectures Hypothesis (HCAH)* then states:

Hybrid symbol systems are necessary and sufficient for cognitive architectures.

This hypothesis is clearly related to the HSSH, but it matters in itself because the comparable hypothesis – perhaps called the *Physical Cognitive Architectures Hypothesis (PCAH)* – fails. Thus, the sufficiency side of the PCAH is invalid irrespective of what might be true with respect to necessity. As with the HSSH, sufficiency for the HCAH need not hold for all hybrid symbol systems, but it must hold for at least some.

As with the PSSH and the HSSH, the HCAH is an empirical generalization. Both sides of the argument are now supported by the architectural successes of classical symbol systems, neural systems, and traditional hybrid systems such as PGMs. Both sides are further bolstered by how the CMC itself is a hybrid symbol system.

5 Neural Networks as Hybrid Symbol Systems

What makes neural networks hybrid symbol systems, as defined here, rather than simply the numeric component of a larger system that also includes a symbolic component, such as [17]? To keep things simple, the focus here is limited to standard feed-forward neural networks, consisting of multiple layers of nodes and links, where nodes have activations, links connect pairs of nodes across levels and have weights, and processing occurs by multiplying input activations along links by the links' weights and then nonlinearly transforming the sums of these weighted inputs.

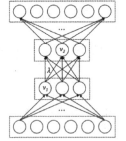

Fig. 3. Simple network for paired associates.

To be a bit more specific, let's assume a small network for *paired associates* that maps an input word to an output word. Figure 3 exemplifies this via a completely connected network with 6-unit input and output layers – yielding a 6-dimensional vector of activations for each – and 2 intermediate layers, each with 3 units. Words map consistently to input and output vectors via *encoding* and *decoding* processes that are external to the network. These processes may be based on an arbitrary or random assignment of vectors to words or some form of more sophisticated *embedding* process, such as in [18].

The focus here, however, is on analyzing the forward processing in the network itself to show how it amounts to a hybrid symbol system. It should be possible to extend such an analysis to encoding and decoding processes, as well as to learning in neural networks, but this simple example is sufficient to establish the precedent.

First consider the nodes in the input layer of the network, now shown at the top of Fig. 4 as locations within a vector of nominal activations. Such nodes can be seen as hybrid symbols – symbolic nodes (i.e., locations) with activations as their quantitative metadata – that exhibit a limited form of composability in yielding the hybrid sym-

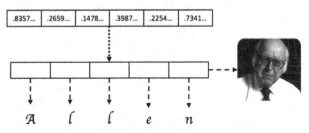

Fig. 4. Designation relationships among input vector, word vector, letters, and word meaning. Dotted lines reflect internal designation and dashed lines external designation.

bol structure that is the input vector. In contrast to the traditional interpretation of distributed representations – where nodes are subsymbolic, or microfeatures, with symbols only arising as patterns over these elements – here the individual nodes are themselves hybrid symbols that do not themselves designate, with patterns arising as structures of these hybrid symbols.

This hybrid symbol structure does then internally designate a word structure that has one location per letter (middle of Fig. 4). The metadata in the word structure is not shown as it is irrelevant to this analysis. What does matter is that declarative symbols in this word structure externally designate particular letters of the alphabet, in this case making up Allen Newell's first name (bottom of Fig. 4). The word as whole then externally designates its meaning, iconified to the right of Fig. 4 via an image of him.

Key to this all working is that it isn't just the data aspect of hybrid symbols and structures that can designate, but the entirety of the hybrid symbols and structures – including their metadata – that can do so, just as is traditionally assumed for vectors in distributed representations [19]. The word itself is epiphenomenal to the feedforward network processing here – only the hybrid symbol structure at the top of Fig. 4, as yielded by encoding, actually participates. As put in [20], "the node labels in a Connectionist machine are not part of the causal structure of the machine."

The internal nodes in the network are also hybrid symbols but without declarative designations, fitting the intuition that there are no fixed meanings inside the network. Instead, internal nodes – and links – procedurally designate fixed processes. Consider link λ in Fig. 3, which points from node v_1 to node v_2. This link is a hybrid symbol structure composed from these two hybrid symbols, with a weight as its metadata. It procedurally designates a process that multiplies the activation arriving from v_1 by this weight. Internal nodes such as v_2 then procedurally designate processes that sum all of their inputs – in this case, from v_1 and any other nodes linked to it from the proceeding layer – and then nonlinearly transform the results.

The last part of the analysis concerns the output nodes. Perhaps surprisingly, they too do not declaratively designate anything here. Instead, they procedurally designate the same summation and transformation process as the internal nodes. It is not until postprocessing – that is during decoding – that this reverse mapping occurs.

This analysis demonstrates that a feedforward neural network is a hybrid symbol system, as defined here. As such, it makes the case that the shift from the PSSH to the HSSH enables coopting neural-network successes as evidence for both the sufficiency and necessity of hybrid symbol systems rather than as counterexamples to them.

But what type of hybrid symbol system does this type of neural network yield? It provides limited forms of declarative designation (at input nodes), procedural designation (at all but input nodes), and composition (via vectors within a level and links across levels). Yet, other forms of neural networks do go beyond this. To name just two common examples, both convolutional networks (e.g., [21]) and transformers [22] include additional forms of composition. The flexibility of composition seen in the output of transformer-based generative networks [23] is in fact quite compelling. Some forms of neural networks are also known to support universal computation (see, e.g., [24]). Yet no neural network to date has solved combinatorial board games without the dynamic composition yielded by explicit state-space search (as seen, e.g., in both [25] and [26]). So, the overall story is complex, dependent on the exact nature of the neural networks considered, and still not completely understood.

6 Conclusion

Leveraging essential analysis, symbols are (re)defined as atoms or placeholders, and a space of variations is defined for symbols, symbol structures, and symbol systems. This includes the classical traits of compositionality and designation, plus hybridness and additional sub-traits under designation (such as interpretation). In response to lingering challenges to the Physical Symbol System Hypothesis (PSSH), two new hypotheses have then been introduced that focus on the resulting hybrid symbol systems:

Hybrid Symbol Systems Hypothesis (HSSH):

Hybrid symbol systems are necessary and sufficient for general intelligent action.

Hybrid Cognitive Architectures Hypothesis (HCAH):

Hybrid symbol systems are necessary and sufficient for cognitive architectures.

The HSSH is intended as a replacement for the PSSH, based on evidence accumulated since the latter was introduced as an empirical hypothesis a half-century ago. Given this recent body of evidence, there is a sense in which the PSSH still holds, but it is a weaker sense. The HSSH recaptures the originally intended strength while adding further to it by reinterpreting neural networks as compatriots – that is, as hybrid symbol systems themselves – rather than as competitors. The result also helps chip away in a rather fine-grained manner at the overall divide between symbolic and neural systems.

The HCAH is a more stringent claim than either the original PSSH or the HSSH in that it concerns cognitive architectures rather than general intelligent action. Evidence accumulated over the past decades has shown that traditional physical symbol systems fail with respect to sufficiency for cognitive architectures due to the need for numeric processing within the architectures themselves. The necessity of classical physical symbol systems for cognitive architectures remains an open question, as it is not yet clear whether neural networks – which although as argued here are hybrid symbol systems but which may not be classical symbol systems or even universal computationally – will prove to be a sufficient alternative on their own for such architectures.

One potential chink in the armor of both of these new hypotheses is the possibility of quantum aspects to intelligence that cannot be captured even by hybrid systems [27]. Should it prove necessary, some thought is already being put into what it would mean to have quantum symbol systems (e.g., [28]).

Acknowledgements. I would like to think John Laird, Christian Lebiere, and Andrea Stocco for helpful comments and discussions on this general topic and this particular paper.

References

1. Newell, A., Simon, H.A.: Human Problem Solving. Prentice-Hall, Englewood Cliffs (1972)
2. Newell, A., Simon, H.A.: Computer science as empirical inquiry: symbols and search. Comm. ACM **19**(3), 113–126 (1972)
3. Newell, A.: Physical symbol systems. Cog. Sci. **4**(2), 135–183 (1980)
4. Laird, J.E., Lebiere, C., Rosenbloom, P.S.: A standard model of the mind: toward a common computational framework across artificial Intelligence, cognitive science, neuroscience, and robotics. AI Mag. **38**(4), 13–26 (2017)
5. Rosenbloom, P.S., Demski, A., Ustun, V.: The Sigma cognitive architecture and system: towards functionally elegant grand unification. J. Artif. Gen. Intell. **7**(1), 1–103 (2016)
6. Kurfess, F.J.: Integrating symbol-oriented and sub-symbolic reasoning methods into hybrid systems. In: Apolloni, B., Kurfess, F. (eds.) From Synapses to Rules: Disc. Sym. Rules from Neural Proc. Data, pp. 275–292. Kluwer, New York (2002)
7. Bader, S., Hitzler, P.: Dimensions of neural-symbolic integration—a structured survey. In: Artëmov, S.N., Barringer, H., d'Avila Garcez, A.S., Lamb, L.C., Woods, J. (eds.) We Will Show Them! Essays in Honour of Dov Gabbay, pp. 167–194. Coll. Pubs., Rickmansworth (2005)
8. Nilsson, N.J.: The physical symbol system hypothesis: status and prospects. In: Lungarella, M., Iida, F., Bongard, J., Pfeifer, R. (eds.) 50 Years of Artificial Intelligence. LNCS (LNAI), vol. 4850, pp. 9–17. Springer, Heidelberg (2007). https://doi.org/10.1007/978-3-540-772 96-5_2
9. Goodfellow, I.J., Bengio, Y., Courville, A.: Deep Learning. MIT Press, Cambridge (2016)
10. Koller, D., Friedman, N.: Probabilistic Graphical Models: Principles and Techniques. MIT Press, Cambridge (2009)
11. Kotseruba, I., Tsotsos, J.K.: 40 years of cognitive architectures: core cognitive abilities and practical applications. Artif. Intell. Rev. **53**(1), 17–94 (2018). https://doi.org/10.1007/s10462-018-9646-y

12. Rosenbloom, P.S.: Thoughts on architecture. In: Goertzel, B., Iklé, M., Potapov, A., Pono-maryov, D. (eds.) Artificial General Intelligence (AGI 2022). LNCS, vol. 13539, pp. 364–373. Springer, Cham (2023). https://doi.org/10.1007/978-3-031-19907-3_35

13. de Raedt, L., Kersting, K., Natarajan, S., Poole, D.: Statistical relational artificial intelligence: logic, probability, and computation. Synth. Lect. Artif. Intell. Mach. Learn. **10**(2), 1–189 (2016)

14. Rosenbloom, P.S.: On theories and their implications for cognitive architectures (In prep.)

15. Dictionary.com on symbol. https://www.dictionary.com/browse/symbol. Accessed 15 Feb 2023

16. McDermott, D.V.: Mind and Mechanism. MIT Press, Cambridge (2001)

17. Sun, R.: The CLARION cognitive architecture: towards a comprehensive theory of the mind. In: Chipman, S. (ed.) The Oxford Handbook of Cognitive Science, pp. 117–133. Oxford University Press, New York (2017)

18. Mikolov, T., Sutskever, I., Chen, K., Corrado, G.S., Dean, J.: Distributed representations of words and phrases and their compositionality. Adv. Neural Inf. Process. Syst. **26**, 3111–3119 (2013)

19. Hinton, G.E., McClelland, J.L., Rumelhart, D.E.: Distributed representations. In: McClelland, J.L., Rumelhart, D.E. (eds.) Parallel Distributed Processing: Explorations in the Microstructure of Cognition, vol. 1, pp. 77–109. MIT Press, Cambridge (1986)

20. Fodor, J.A., Pylyshyn, Z.W.: Connectionism and cognitive architecture: a critical analysis. Cognition **28**(1–2), 3–71 (1988)

21. LeCun, Y., Bengio, Y.: Convolutional networks for images, speech, and time series. In: Arbib, M. (ed.) The Handbook of Brain Theory and Neural Nets. MIT Press, Cambridge (1995)

22. Vaswani, A., et al.: Attention is all you need. In: Proc. of the 31st Annual Conf. on Neural Info. Proc. Sys., pp. 5998–6008 (2017)

23. Brown, T.B., et al.: Language models are few-shot learners. In: Proc. of the 34th Conf. on Neural Info. Proc. Sys., pp. 1877–1901 (2020)

24. Siegelmann, H.T., Sontag, E.D.: Turing computation with neural nets. Appl. Math. Lett. **4**(6), 77–80 (1991)

25. Tesauro, G.: Temporal difference learning and TD-Gammon. Comm. ACM **38**(3), 58–68 (1995)

26. Silver, D., et al.: A general reinforcement learning algorithm that masters chess, shogi, and Go through self-play. Science **362**(6419), 1140–1144 (2018)

27. Penrose, R.: The Emperor's New Mind: Concerning Computers, Minds, and The Laws of Physics. Oxford University Press, Oxford (1989)

28. Laskey, K.B.: Quantum physical symbol systems. J. Log. Lang. Inf. **15**(1–2), 109–154 (2006)

On Relation Between Facial Expressions and Emotions

Alexei V. Samsonovich(✉) ⓘ, Alexandr Sidorov, and Alexandr Inozemtsev

National Research Nuclear University MEPhI, Moscow, Russia
alexei.samsonovich@gmail.com

Abstract. Human face is used to express affects and feelings, either involuntary or deliberately. How many dimensions of emotional flavors can be robustly distinguished in facial expressions, across individuals and cultures? Here we offer an answer and develop a practical approach to generate synthetic emotional facial expressions. Results can be used in studies of synthetic emotions.

Keywords: machine learning · emotion modeling · Facial Action Coding System (FACS) · face attribute analysis · DeepFace

1 Introduction

For humans, facial expression is the main modality of nonverbal emotional communication during face-to-face social contact. Facial expression is used to communicate affects and feelings either naturally, or subliminally, or deliberately. It may or may not reflect the actual emotional state of the individual; yet its function is to express a certain emotional state. It is an interesting fundamental question – how facial expressions are related to flavors of emotional states, what flavors are expressible on face, and what aspects of the facial configuration are interpretable in terms of emotional semantics. This topic has a long history of research [1, 2], yet certain details remain unresolved. Among them is the dimensionality of the space of emotional flavors, robustly expressible on face across individuals.

Here we use a vector-space approach to emotion representation [3–5]. A key question is the dimensionality of the affective space. Most frequently, three-dimensional models are used [3, 5, 6], known as VAD (valence, arousal, dominance), PAD (pleasure, arousal, dominance), etc. On the other hand, complex, or social emotions may require an introduction of extra dimensions to distinguish them from basic emotions [7]. An alternative approach is to describe social emotions as pairs or combinations of simple emotions [8], which also amounts to an expansion of the basic affective space.

For example, overlapping in the VAD space may be representations of jealousy and anger, gloat and sarcasm, sense of humor and happiness, compassion and sadness, etc. Do these pairs have different representations on face? And vice versa, how many different facial expressions may represent one and the same emotional flavor? Obviously, more than one facial configuration can correspond to one emotional state: for example, with a closed or open mouth, with a look to the left or to the right. Then, what would be the maximal dimension of the set of unique face-emotion pairs?

P. Hammer et al. (Eds.): AGI 2023, LNAI 13921, pp. 217–221, 2023.
https://doi.org/10.1007/978-3-031-33469-6_22

2 Mathematical Statement of the Problem

Let E be the vector space of all possible emotional states, and F the vector space of all possible facial configurations that can be interpreted as expressions of emotional states. Call a smooth mapping f: E → F admissible, if it assigns to each emotional state some configuration of the face, which expresses this emotional state. Similarly, call a smooth mapping g: F → E is admissible, if it assigns to each face configuration from F some emotional state that can be considered expressed by this face configuration.

Let us give the spaces E and F the structure of fiber bundles with some common base X, defined by the projections π_1 and π_2 in such a way that the diagrams (Fig. 1) commute for the entire set of admissible functions $\{f, g\}$ for fixed π_1, π_2. The task is to determine the maximal possible dimension of X.

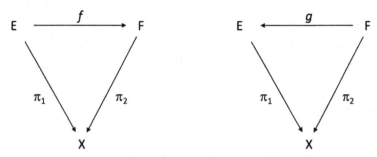

Fig. 1. Statement of the problem in terms of fiber bundles.

Generally speaking, the answer may depend on how strict the admissibility requirement for f, g is. For example, it can be assumed that the question of admissibility is decided by questioning the subjects, and in the experiment the faces of people of different nationalities, as well as avatars, are used.

3 Statistical Solution

To simplify the analysis, one can consider vector spaces instead of fiber bundles. Then the answer is found by computing the canonical correlation. This analysis was done in our recent work [9]. We studied electromyographic recordings from the facial muscles together with computer analysis of emotional facial expressions based on video recordings of the face, using principal component analysis, canonical correlation, ridge regression, random forest, and random forest with the choice of hyperparameters using cross-validation. Based on this analysis, we found that the dimension of X is equal to three. In other words, the VAD model is sufficient to distinguish among all emotionally different facial expressions.

If this is the case, then any emotional state can be expressed on the face of an avatar, capable of representing all points of the VAD space. The next question is how to do it accurately and automatically.

4   Practical Approach

In this study, an anthropomorphic avatar embedded in a 3D virtual environment was used. The implementation was based on Unreal Engine 4. Facial expressions of the avatar are controlled by 17 parameters – MorphTargets (Fig. 2).

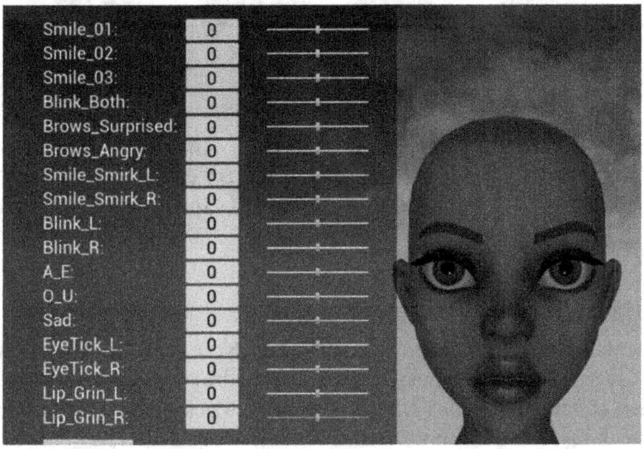

Fig. 2. MorphTargets of the avatar.

Using the approach of [10], a neural network model has been developed that generates the MorphTargets parameters based on the VAD values received as input. The training of the network was done using DeepFace [11]. Results are shown in Fig. 3.

5   Conclusions

Algorithms for analyzing and synthesizing human emotional states are an important and integral part of software and hardware systems that model human intellectual activity [12]. Human emotions are often represented using a three-dimensional space with three basis vectors: dominance, valence, arousal. However, the main system for coding facial expressions of a human face is the FACS system [1], which contains several dozen parameters. It is known that it is impossible to uniquely establish a correspondence between the space of emotional states and the FACS system. Conclusions of this study are the following.

(1) It is argued that a three-dimensional space, such as VAD, is sufficient for indexing all emotionally distinct facial expressions.
(2) A method is proposed that makes it possible to generate realistic facial expressions on an anthropomorphic avatar's face, based on the values of the three basic coordinates. The developed method consists in using a neural network model that generates codes of facial configuration changes.

(3) The described approach, while not directly related to Artificial General Intelligence, is biologically inspired and can be useful in studies of synthetic emotions.

Fig. 3. Generated synthetic faces and their VAD (valence, arousal, dominance) coordinates: (a) anger = [−0.51, 0.59, 0.25], (b) joy = [0.81, 0.51, 0.46], (c) surprise = [0.40, 0.67, −0.13], (d) disgust = [−0.60, 0.35, 0.11], (e) fear = [−0.64, 0.60, 0.43], (f) sadness = [−0.63, −0.27, −0.33].

Acknowledgments. The authors are grateful to Aleksey Kevroletin, Mark Karavashkin, Georgy Vayntrub, Vera Mironova, Zhanna Demidova, Ismail M. Gadzhiev, Mikhail Knyshenko, and Sergei Dolenko for their contribution to this project. This work was supported by the Russian Science Foundation Grant #22–11-00213, https://rscf.ru/en/project/22-11-00213/.

References

1. Ekman, P., Friesen, W.: Facial Action Coding System: A Technique for the Measurement of Facial Movement. Consulting Psychologists Press, Palo Alto (1978)
2. Ekman, P.: An argument for basic emotions. Cogn. Emot. **6**(3–4), 169–200 (1992)
3. Russell, J., Mehrabian, A.: Evidence for a three-factor theory of emotions. J. Res. Per. **11**, 273–294 (1977)
4. Plutchik, R.: A psychoevolutionary theory of emotions. Soc. Sci. Inf. **21**, 529–553 (1982)
5. Lövheim, H.: A new three-dimensional model for emotions and monoamine neurotransmitters. Med. Hypotheses **78**(2), 341–348 (2012)
6. Russell, J.: Core affect and the psychological construction of emotion. Psychol. Rev. **110**(1), 145–172 (2003)
7. Moors, A., Ellsworth, P.C., Scherer, K.R., Frijda, N.H.: Appraisal theories of emotion: state of the art and future development. Emot. Rev. **5**(2), 119–124 (2013)
8. 8. Lieto, A., Pozzato, G.L., Striani, M., Zoia, S., Damiano, R.: DEGARI 2.0: a diversity-seeking, explainable, and affective art recommender for social inclusion. Cogn. Syst. Res. **77**, 1–17 (2023). https://doi.org/10.1016/j.cogsys.2022.10.001
9. Gadzhiev, I.M., Knyshenko, M.P., Dolenko, S.A., Samsonovich, A.V.: Inherent dimension of the affective space: Analysis using electromyography and machine learning. Cogn. Syst. Res. **78**, 96–105 (2023)
10. Li, R., et al.: Learning formation of physically-based face attributes. ArXiv, 2004.03458 (2020). https://doi.org/10.48550/ARXIV.2004.03458
11. Serengil, S.I., Ozpinar, A.: HyperExtended LightFace: a facial attribute analysis framework. In: 2021 International Conference on Engineering and Emerging Technologies (ICEET), Istanbul, Turkey, pp. 1–4 (2021). https://doi.org/10.1109/ICEET53442.2021.9659697

12. Marsella, S., Gratch, J., Petta, P.: Computational models of emotion. In: Scherer, K.R., Banziger, T., Roesch, E. (Eds.), A Blueprint for Affective Computing: A Sourcebook and Manual. Oxford University Press, Oxford (2010)

Evaluation of Pretrained Large Language Models in Embodied Planning Tasks

Christina Sarkisyan[1] , Alexandr Korchemnyi[1] , Alexey K. Kovalev[2(✉)] ,
and Aleksandr I. Panov[2,3]

[1] Moscow Institute of Physics and Technology, Dolgoprudny, Russia
[2] AIRI, Moscow, Russia
{kovalev,panov}@airi.net
[3] Federal Research Center "Computer Science and Control" of the Russian Academy
of Sciences, Moscow, Russia

Abstract. Modern pretrained large language models (LLMs) are
increasingly being used in zero-shot or few-shot learning modes. Recent
years have seen increased interest in applying such models to embodied artificial intelligence and robotics tasks. When given in a natural
language, the agent needs to build a plan based on this prompt. The
best solutions use LLMs through APIs or models that are not publicly
available, making it difficult to reproduce the results. In this paper, we
use publicly available LLMs to build a plan for an embodied agent and
evaluate them in three modes of operation: 1) the subtask evaluation
mode, 2) the full autoregressive plan generation, and 3) the step-by-step
autoregressive plan generation. We used two prompt settings: prompt-
containing examples of one given task and a mixed prompt with examples
of different tasks. Through extensive experiments, we have shown that
the subtask evaluation mode, in most cases, outperforms others with a
task-specific prompt, whereas the step-by-step autoregressive plan generation posts better performance in the mixed prompt setting.

Keywords: Large language models · Plan generation · Planning for
embodied agents

1 Introduction

The large language models (LLMs) pretrained on a huge corpus of texts are able
to solve problems that were not trained in the mode of few-shot [4] and zero-
shot [26] learning. Some modern LLMs demonstrate high efficiency on a variety of
different tasks, including those whose examples were not included in the training
dataset. Such models provide a good approximation to the linguistic world model
and serve as an important part of the AGI systems. In many ways, effectiveness
in the multi-task setting is achieved by using such models as knowledge bases
and generating the required model output by demonstrating examples in the
model's input prompt. As a result, building the right prompt has turned into a
separate area of applied data science, known as prompt engineering.

© The Author(s), under exclusive license to Springer Nature Switzerland AG 2023
P. Hammer et al. (Eds.): AGI 2023, LNAI 13921, pp. 222–232, 2023.
https://doi.org/10.1007/978-3-031-33469-6_23

Initially, pretrained LLMs were mainly used in natural language processing tasks. But recently, they have found application for tasks of embodied artificial intelligence (AI) and robotics [1, 6, 8, 9, 14, 21, 22, 24]. LLMs are used in cases when the task for the agent is formed in a natural language, for example, "bring a cup of coffee." Then an agent has to generate a plan comprising subtasks leading to the execution of the task [11]. In general, this plan can be expressed in a natural language, for example, "1. Find a cup. 2. Take a cup. 3. Put the cup into the coffee machine. 4. Switch on the coffee machine. 5. Bring a cup of coffee to the user," and subsequently mapped onto the actions available to the agent. Recent works show good results in building a plan by LLMs, using feedback from the environment [1, 21, 22, 24] and without it [9]. However, the best solutions use LLMs where access is either limited by API tools (GPT-3 [4], ChatGPT [17]) or unavailable (PaLM [5], FLAN [26]), which affects the reproducibility of the result and the possibility of further research in this direction. Typically, such models have more parameters and are trained on more data than publicly available models.

On the one hand, this allows us to achieve better results by improving the language model itself and through the emergence of some additional properties. For example, in [27], authors show that using a "chain of thought" prompt brings a better boost for models with over 100 billion parameters than for models with fewer parameters. On the other hand, when it comes to embodied AI and robotics, the use of such language models even in the inference mode on board the agent causes difficulties because of the required computing resources.

In our work, we explore the use of publicly available pretrained LLMs to generate a plan from a language description of a task, in three modes of operation: 1) the subtask evaluation mode, 2) the full autoregressive plan generation, and 3) the step-by-step autoregressive plan generation. Through extensive experiments, we have shown that the use of LLMs, even with a relatively small number of parameters, allows the agent to generate plans with high accuracy. In our experiments, the subtask evaluation mode, in most cases, outperforms others with a task-specific prompt, whereas the step-by-step autoregressive plan generation posts better performance in the mixed prompt setting.

2   Metrics to Evaluate the Generated Plan

Measuring the quality of generated plans is a challenging task due to the multimodal nature of the problem and the ambiguity of the natural language since we need to evaluate not only the agent's natural language understanding but the ability to ground the steps of the plan with the admissible actions and the visual information from the environment. It is common to evaluate plans in terms of their Executability and Correctness [8, 9, 21]. Executability implies checking that each step of the plan is syntactically correct, i.e., contains valid actions and objects and can be executed by the agent in the environment. Correctness is an assessment of whether the execution of the plan's steps leads to the achievement of the target environment state. As noted in [9], it is difficult to judge correctness based on a single gold standard measurement, since one task can have several correct plan solutions, so various metrics are used. Longest

Common Subsequence (LCS) [8,9] evaluates the intersection share of the generated plan with the ground truth (GT). In cases where the plan is directly executed in the environment, Success Rate and Goal Conditions Recall metrics are used [20,21], which is the full or partial achievement of all task-relevant goal-conditions, respectively. In [12], the authors propose to evaluate plans step by step using CIDEr [23] and SPICE [2] scene graph-based metrics and design the KeyActionScore (KAS) metric for the ALFRED [20] extract key actions for task completion. Graph of the scene's final state where nodes represent objects with edges as relationships between them is used for correctness calculation in [8]. To date, there is no single generally accepted metric for this task. Human assessors can also be involved in the evaluation process, as in [1,9]. In our work, we use three metrics that evaluate the similarity of the generated plan and the GT plan in terms of various criteria and present the results of human assessment to obtain a detailed analysis of the methods' performance. A more detailed description of the evaluation process is provided in Sect. 3.4.

3   Method

3.1   Problem Formulation

Given a task description τ, the pretrained LLM is to build a task execution plan $\hat{S}$, which is a sequence of subtasks $\hat{S} = (s_1, ..., s_n)$. A subtask s_t is a pair $(a_t, o_t), a_t \in A, o_t \in O$, where a_t is the action available for the agent to perform and involves interacting with the target object o_t.

3.2   Subtask Evaluation Mode

To build a plan in subtask evaluation mode, we use the LLM as a scoring model, as proposed in SayCan [1], which selects a potential text completion from a limited set of options rather than generating the text directly. The execution plan is built iteratively: at each step, the LLM represents a distribution over the set of subtask language descriptions L. The mapping ϕ matches each possible subtask s_t with a corresponding text description $\phi : A \times O \to L$. Specifically, for each action $a \in A$ in the robotic language, there is a template with its description in the natural language into which the object $o \in O$ is inserted (e.g. subtask "(PickupObject, {obj})" goes to the description "pick up the {obj}"). The LLM scores all the natural language subtasks $l \in L$, computing their probabilities and selecting the optimal subtask:

$$l_t^* = \text{argmax}_{l_t \in L} P(l_t | f(\tau, l_1, ..., l_{t-1})), t = \overline{1, n}. \tag{1}$$

$f(x)$ is a prompting function, that maps the input x to a task-specific template. The subtasks obtained in the previous steps of the algorithm are sequentially attached to the input data of the prompt function, which adds them to the string prompt according to the template. The resulting language subtask sequence $(l_1, ..., l_n)$ can be further easily transformed into an executable plan using ϕ^{-1} back mapping: $s_t = \phi^{-1}(l_t)$.

This approach ensures the executability of each subtask in the plan since we constrain the model output to specific tokens corresponding to the environmental subtasks. However, it requires multiple prompt passes through the model for each subtask at each step of the algorithm, which lengthens the plan generation time and is resource-intensive. The computational complexity grows with the number of available actions and objects in the environment. To speed up the plan generation procedure, we additionally reduce the spatial dimension of subtasks using a set of rules imposed by environmental constraints and common sense considerations. At each plan generation step, the set of subtasks L is filtered by the reducing function:

$$L' = reduce(L) \tag{2}$$

In particular, the model is proposed to evaluate only the subtasks, meeting the rules designed for the ALFRED [20] environment. For example, the rules take into account the fact that the agent has only one manipulator and can not pick up two objects at once, so if the previously selected subtask has the *"pick up"* action, other subtasks with the same action are discarded. Also, the subtasks should not contain objects that the agent in the scene does not observe.

We found that discarding some unnecessary subtasks from the evaluation process can significantly speed up the LLM inference time, as well as slightly boost its performance. Specifically, in our problem setting there are 159 unique subtasks. At each step of the plan generation, 159 prompts of length ~ 1500 tokens must pass through the model to evaluate each subtask, while applying the rules reduces the number of prompts to an average of 50. Thus, instead of $\sim 250,000$ tokens, the model receives $\sim 75,000$ tokens.

3.3   Autoregressive Plan Generation

An autoregressive language model (LM) is trained with a maximum likelihood loss to model the probability of a sequence of tokens $\mathbf{y}$ conditioned on an input sequence $\mathbf{x}$, i.e. $\theta = \mathrm{argmax}_\theta P(\mathbf{y}|\mathbf{x}; \theta)$. The trained LM is then used for prediction $\hat{\mathbf{y}} = \mathrm{argmax}_{\mathbf{y} \in \mathbb{S}} P(\mathbf{y}|\mathbf{x}; \theta)$, where $\mathbb{S}$ is the set of all text sequences.

LLMs are trained on large text collections and can perform in-context learning using only contextual information. It is possible to use this approach to query LLMs to generate action plans for high-level tasks by prepending some task-relevant context to the input sequence $\mathbf{x}$ (prompt). For a plan-generating task, a prompt usually consists of one or more parts: including a high-level problem statement, a description of the environment's current state, and examples of similar problems that have already been solved.

Full Plan Generation. To generate a complete plan, the language model generates a text sequence $\mathbf{y}$ based on the input sequence $\mathbf{x} = f_{prompt}(Y)$. When generating a complete plan using a language model, it can be challenging to match the proposed commands with those available to the agent in the current environment. Some possible issues include: 1) the action or its arguments are represented by a synonym or alternative phrase (e.g. "pick up the cup" instead of "pick up the mug"), 2) the action or its arguments are lexically incorrect (e.g. "cut the knife and heat it up"), 3) the plan is generated in a free-form rather than using a structured template (e.g. "the robot should pick up the spoon and put it in the sink" instead of "pick up the spoon, then put it in the sink"), and 4) the sequence of actions is not logically connected (e.g., to retrieve an item from the fridge, the fridge must first be opened). The quality of the plan generation improves with the increase in the number of examples in the prompt. The solution to the grounding problem is proposed through step-by-step generation.

Step-by-Step Plan Generation. In the case of iterative step-by-step plan generation, the subtasks available in the environment are compared with the subtask generated at each step. The generated subtask s_g is compared with all possible subtasks in the environment $\{s_{e1}, s_{e2}, ..., s_{ek}\}$ and we taking the most closest $\hat{s}_e$:

$$\hat{s}_e = \underset{s_{ei}}{\operatorname{argmax}}[C(f_{emb}(s_g), f_{emb}(s_{ei}))] \tag{3}$$

where f_{emb} is an embedding function and C is a cosine distance function. In our work, we used Sentence-BERT [18] to obtain subtask embeddings.

The generated step is then added to the prompt and the process continues iteratively until the stop sequence is generated. The advantage of this approach is the increased feasibility of the generated plan, as all object actions can be grounded to the environment. The disadvantage is the increase in computational complexity, which grows exponentially with the number of available actions and objects.

3.4   Plan Evaluation

To measure the correctness of the plan generation, we use several metrics that evaluate both the complete coincidence of plans and their partial similarity. **Accuracy (ACC)**, i.e. the exact match of GT and model prediction subtask sequences, is the most strict criterion that requires both actions and interaction objects matching for each subtask in the plans.

$$ACC(S, S') = \begin{cases} 0, & \exists s_k \in S, s'_k \in S' : a_k \neq a'_k \vee o_k \neq o'_k \\ 1, & \forall s_k \in S, s'_k \in S' : a_k = a'_k \wedge o_k = o'_k \end{cases} \tag{4}$$

We designed the **Actions Exact Match (AEM)** metric to evaluate the method's ability to understand the task's semantics, in particular, to classify its type. AEM requires action matching but allows the model to confuse the objects.

$$AEM(S, S') = \begin{cases} 0, & \exists s_k \in S, s'_k \in S' : a_k \neq a'_k \\ 1, & \forall s_k \in S, s'_k \in S' : a_k = a'_k \end{cases} \tag{5}$$

We also compute the **LCS** between two plans, normalized by the maximum length of the two, following [9]. However, there are cases when GT plans do not allow us to determine the plan's correctness. For one task, there may be several correct plans (e.g., to complete the task *"put a cup with a fork in it on the counter"* the agent can perform actions in a different order: put the cup on the counter, then put the fork in the cup, or vice versa), while according to the ACC, only the one fixed order of subtasks is correct. Furthermore, tasks can often be vague, so without the vision of the environment one can only make assumptions about their purpose and the objects engaged (e.g., the task *"to acquire an odd item as place it where it is not useful"*). Thus, we involve **Human assessment (H)** in the plan evaluation process. Three people were asked to evaluate how many correct plans, in their opinion, the model generated, based only on the requirements of the text instructions. The GT plans were also available for observation. The final metric value is obtained by dividing the number of correct plans by the total number of tasks and averaging over the number of assessors.

4 Experiments

To select an LLM, we studied publicly available pretrained models with a large number of parameters. In the robot's behavior planning task GPT-3 model [4] with 175B parameters is frequently used. However, OpenAI API for GPT-3 allows one to generate/evaluate only a limited number of tokens, which is especially critical for the resource-intensive subtask evaluation mode. Therefore, we considered the models without restrictions on the number of input and output tokens and also work fast enough with a limited number of computing resources. As LLMs, we use and compare three models: **GPT-J-6B (GPT-J)** [25], **GPT-NeoX-20B (GPT-NeoX)** [3] and **OPT-30B (OPT)** [28]. GPT-J is a GPT-3-like autoregressive language model, pretrained on the Pile dataset [7], containing 825 GB of an English text corpus. GPT-J contains 6B trainable parameters. The architecture of the GPT-NeoX model almost repeats the GPT-J's, and was trained on the same dataset, but has a larger number of parameters (20B). OPT is also a decoder-only model from GPT-3 family and has the largest number of parameters (30B) in our experiments. OPT was trained on several subsets of the Pile, and some other datasets (RoBERTa [13], CCNews [15], etc.), containing English and a small amount of non-English data. GPT-J and OPT models use the BPE [19] tokenizer, like GPT-3, while GPT-NeoX uses a tokenizer specially designed for this model.

4.1 ALFRED Environment

ALFRED [20] is a benchmark for evaluating the ability of AI systems to understand and act upon human language instructions in interactive visual environments, such as a household setting. The benchmark includes expert demonstrations of tasks, accompanied by natural language instructions, in 120 different indoor scenes in the AI2-THOR 2.0 [10] environment. These demonstrations involve partial observability, long action horizons, an underspecified natural language, and irreversible actions. ALFRED includes a total of 25,743 English language directives describing 8,055 expert demonstrations, resulting in a total of 428,322 image-action pairs. In this benchmark, the agent is provided with egocentric vision and must complete tasks by interacting with objects using a pixelwise interaction mask. The benchmark is intended to facilitate the development of AI systems that can translate human language into sequences of actions and interactions in a visually and physically realistic simulation environment.

To create GT plans, we collected a dataset from task descriptions and corresponding subtask sequences extracted from the expert demonstrations. There are seven high-level actions in ALFRED: *PickupObject, PutObject, SliceObject, HeatObject, CoolObject, CleanObject, ToggleObject*, most of which need to be broken down into lower-level subactions (e.g., to heat the object, the agent should open the microwave, put the object in it, etc.).

There are seven types of tasks in ALFRED, ranging in difficulty: Pick&Place, Look in Light, Heat&Place, Cool&Place, Clean&Place, Pick Two&Place, and Stack&Place. We divided them into three groups of increasing complexity and plan length and chose one type from each group for experiments. Pick&Place (PP) is the simplest type, in which one needs to pick up an object and put it in another place. In Heat&Place (HP), the object needs to be additionally warmed up before being put somewhere. In some tasks, the object must be sliced with a knife, which extends the plan's length by one more action. The most complex task type is Stack&Place (SP), in which one needs to put an object in a movable container and put them in a specified location. The object can also be sliceable.

4.2   Prompt Engineering

To build a prompt, we use the template proposed in [1], which is a dialog between a user and a robot, and adapt it for the ALFRED. We first add a prefix to the prompt describing the general problem statement. Then we preprocess ALFRED data by removing the punctuation from the task descriptions and converting them to lowercase. These descriptions are used as the user input in the dialog. Further, we convert GT plans: each subtask in the GT plan is mapped to a natural language subtask with the $\phi()$ function. For each queried task type, n examples of GT plans are randomly selected and concatenated to the prompt, alternating by type. The imperative task description τ is reformulated as a question "Human: How would you $\{\tau\}$?" and the sequence of subtasks l_k in GT plan is formatted into a sequence "Robot: I would: 1. $\{l_1\}, 2.\{l_2\}, ..., n.\{l_n\}$". To avoid model biases due to repetitive or ambiguous task examples, we additionally edit prompts manually by replacing some examples with others and adding more diversity in object classes.

A prompt can contain examples of both different types, and only one. One-type prompt problem setting is easier since the model "learns" on plans with similar sequences of actions and can lead to better performance. Such an approach is possible if one can somehow classify task types before adding them to the prompt, e.g., using a trained language model, as in [16], or using the k-neighbor method to select in-context examples [22]. In our case, we consider the task type known in advance, given as GT.

We conduct two series of experiments in subtask evaluation, full plan generation, and step-by-step generation modes for Pick&Place, Heat&Place, and Stack&Place task types separately and compute the metrics values. In the first block of experiments, a one-type prompt is individually set for each task type, containing examples of only this type. For the second block, prompts include examples of all 7 task types, to determine whether the model has common sense reasoning abilities and can classify the task type.

5 Results

Task-Specific Prompt. For the subtask evaluation mode, we validate GPT-J, GPT-NeoX, and OPT on 35 tasks per type, randomly selected from the ALFRED dataset. For each model, the experiments were run repeatedly with different prompt lengths (containing a different number of examples), then the best ones were selected from the results obtained. The results are given in Table 1. Since there are examples of only one type in the prompt, the sequence of actions is successfully determined for each model, as evidenced by the high AEM metric. There is a significant gap between ACC and H metrics because of the noisiness of the ALFRED dataset. OPT outperforms the other two models in terms of the ACC on two task types but is lower in terms of H metrics. We found that increasing the number of model parameters (from GPT-J to OPT) does not provide a significant increase in performance, especially in the case of one-type prompts. In general, according to H, our approach with GPT-NeoX as the LLM with a one-type prompt achieves the best quality of about 83%.

Table 1. Results for LLMs in three different planning modes with task-specific prompt.

Task	GPT-J (6B)				GPT-NeoX (20B)				OPT (30B)			
	ACC	AEM	LCS	H	ACC	AEM	LCS	H	ACC	AEM	LCS	H
Subtask Evaluation Mode												
PP	0.57	1.00	0.85	0.89 ± 0.00	0.63	1.00	0.87	0.97 ± 0.00	0.66	1.00	0.87	0.85 ± 0.02
HP	0.77	0.86	0.88	0.83 ± 0.03	0.74	0.89	0.88	0.83 ± 0.05	0.60	0.71	0.79	0.69 ± 0.03
SP	0.31	0.91	0.74	0.69 ± 0.13	0.26	1.00	0.70	0.70 ± 0.01	0.34	1.00	0.69	0.64 ± 0.02
Full Plan Generation												
PP	0.14	0.91	0.52	0.85 ± 0.01	0.32	1.00	0.59	0.91 ± 0.05	0.48	1.00	0.76	0.97 ± 0.03
HP	0.38	0.97	0.65	0.55 ± 0.02	0.29	0.49	0.50	0.59 ± 0.17	0.22	0.58	0.39	0.84 ± 0.05
SP	0.20	0.57	0.48	0.66 ± 0.05	0.20	0.94	0.52	0.66 ± 0.05	0.17	0.39	0.50	0.60 ± 0.03
Step by Step Plan Generation												
PP	0.62	0.97	0.79	0.89 ± 0.02	0.59	1.00	0.82	0.96 ± 0.03	0.29	1.00	0.71	0.78 ± 0.04
HP	0.40	0.60	0.60	0.47 ± 0.03	0.34	0.51	0.57	0.40 ± 0.03	0.29	0.74	0.61	0.60 ± 0.08
SP	0.37	0.89	0.68	0.71 ± 0.00	0.29	0.77	0.61	0.54 ± 0.08	0.03	0.89	0.41	0.37 ± 0.06

A Prompt with Mixed Task Examples. In our experiments with mixed prompts, the prompt contains three examples for each of the seven task types, with a total length of 21. The results are given in Table 2.

For the subtask evaluation mode, the values of the metrics have deteriorated compared to the first block of experiments. The most complex task type SP has the smallest ACC values; however, for the GPT-NeoX AEM is about 80%, which means that the model understands the semantics of this task well, compared to the smaller GPT-J. GPT-J outperforms the two other models on HP type. OPT, having the largest number of parameters, showed the worst results, having "overfitted" for specific task types present in the prompt.

Table 2. Results for LLMs in three different planning modes with a mixed prompt.

Task	GPT-J (6B)				GPT-NeoX (20B)				OPT (30B)			
	ACC	AEM	LCS	H	ACC	AEM	LCS	H	ACC	AEM	LCS	H
Subtask Evaluation Mode												
PP	0.43	0.60	0.71	0.56 ± 0.09	0.46	0.54	0.68	0.54 ± 0.03	0.03	0.03	0.49	0.26 ± 0.39
HP	0.51	0.60	0.75	0.54 ± 0.08	0.29	0.40	0.62	0.53 ± 0.19	0.37	0.51	0.66	0.40 ± 0.03
SP	0.06	0.26	0.59	0.17 ± 0.03	0.11	0.80	0.61	0.42 ± 0.11	0.03	0.74	0.57	0.19 ± 0.06
Full Plan Generation												
PP	0.12	0.91	0.32	0.77 ± 0.06	0.18	1.00	0.50	1.00 ± 0.00	0.48	1.00	0.76	0.86 ± 0.03
HP	0.14	0.14	0.40	0.70 ± 0.01	0.20	0.51	0.43	0.70 ± 0.06	0.22	0.58	0.39	0.62 ± 0.11
SP	0.00	0.40	0.15	0.39 ± 0.05	0.00	0.91	0.21	0.60 ± 0.08	0.17	0.39	0.50	0.60 ± 0.17
Step by Step Plan Generation												
PP	0.47	1.00	0.65	0.68 ± 0.07	0.62	0.97	0.14	0.91 ± 0.00	0.21	0.97	0.48	0.75 ± 0.05
HP	0.37	0.54	0.61	0.48 ± 0.02	0.43	0.46	0.64	0.55 ± 0.05	0.00	0.00	0.16	0.41 ± 0.08
SP	0.09	0.49	0.53	0.39 ± 0.05	0.14	0.71	0.52	0.53 ± 0.04	0.03	0.36	0.19	0.43 ± 0.15

6   Conclusion

In our work, we explored the application of publicly available LLMs to the plan generation for an embodied agent. We considered three modes of model operation: 1) subtask evaluation mode, 2) full autoregressive plan generation, and 3) step-by-step autoregressive plan generation. In our studies, we used models with a different number of parameters, while there is no significant increase in the metrics values with an increase in the number of parameters, and in some cases, a decrease is observed.

In general, the subtask evaluation mode performs better than the other two with a task-specific prompt. This mode is the most resource-intensive since it requires a parallel evaluation of all subtasks available to the agent. The mode of full autoregressive plan generation is the worst among others. The main problem with this mode is that the subtasks obtained in this way may not be executable by the agent. The step-by-step autoregressive plan generation mode occupies an intermediate position with a task-specific prompt setting, but outperforms others with a mixed prompt. Although it requires a mapping of the received subtasks to the space of agent subtasks, this procedure is not as resource intensive as the parallel evaluation of subtasks and can be implemented with pre-computed embeddings of subtasks. With an increase in the number of actions and objects, the number of subtasks also increases combinatorially. Although the mapping of generated subtasks to agent subtasks can be considered as implicit feedback from the environment, in our work, we have focused on plan generation without feedback, and have taken this as a direction for further work.

References

1. Ahn, M., Brohan, A., Brown, N., Chebotar, Y., et al.: Do as i can and not as i say: grounding language in robotic affordances (2022)
2. Anderson, P., Fernando, B., Johnson, M., Gould, S.: SPICE: semantic propositional image caption evaluation. In: Leibe, B., Matas, J., Sebe, N., Welling, M. (eds.) ECCV 2016. LNCS, vol. 9909, pp. 382–398. Springer, Cham (2016). https://doi.org/10.1007/978-3-319-46454-1_24
3. Black, S., Biderman, S., Hallahan, E., Anthony, Q., et al.: GPT-NeoX-20B: an open-source autoregressive language model (2022)
4. Brown, T., et al.: Language models are few-shot learners. In: NeurIPS (2020)
5. Chowdhery, A., Narang, S., Devlin, J., Bosma, M., et al.: PaLM: scaling language modeling with pathways (2022)
6. Driess, D., Xia, F., Sajjadi, M.S.M., Lynch, C., et al.: PaLM-E: an embodied multimodal language model (2023)
7. Gao, L., Biderman, S., Black, S., Golding, L., et al.: The pile: an 800GB dataset of diverse text for language modeling (2020)
8. Gramopadhye, M., Szafir, D.: Generating executable action plans with environmentally-aware language models (2022)
9. Huang, W., Abbeel, P., Pathak, D., Mordatch, I.: Language models as zero-shot planners: extracting actionable knowledge for embodied agents. In: ICML (2022)
10. Kolve, E., Mottaghi, R., Han, W., VanderBilt, E., et al.: AI2-THOR: an interactive 3D environment for visual AI (2017)
11. Kovalev, A.K., Panov, A.I.: Application of pretrained large language models in embodied artificial intelligence. Doklady Math. 106(S1), S85–S90 (2022). https://doi.org/10.1134/S1064562422060138
12. Lin, B.Y., Huang, C., Liu, Q., Gu, W., Sommerer, S., Ren, X.: On grounded planning for embodied tasks with language models (2022)
13. Liu, Y., Ott, M., Goyal, N., Du, J., et al.: RoBERTa: a robustly optimized BERT pretraining approach (2019)
14. Logeswaran, L., Fu, Y., Lee, M., Lee, H.: Few-shot subgoal planning with language models (2022)
15. Mackenzie, J., Benham, R., Petri, M., Trippas, J.R., et al.: CC-News-En: a large English news corpus. In: CIKM (2020)
16. Min, S.Y., Chaplot, D.S., Ravikumar, P., Bisk, Y., Salakhutdinov, R.: FILM: following instructions in language with modular methods (2021)
17. OpenAI: Introducing ChatGPT (2022). https://openai.com/blog/chatgpt
18. Reimers, N., Gurevych, I.: Sentence-BERT: sentence embeddings using Siamese BERT-networks. In: Proceedings of the 2019 Conference on Empirical Methods in Natural Language Processing. Association for Computational Linguistics (2019). https://arxiv.org/abs/1908.10084

19. Shibata, Y., Kida, T., Fukamachi, S., Takeda, M., et al.: Byte pair encoding: a text compression scheme that accelerates pattern matching (1999)
20. Shridhar, M., Thomason, J., Gordon, D., Bisk, Y., et al.: ALFRED: a benchmark for interpreting grounded instructions for everyday tasks. In: CVPR (2020)
21. Singh, I., Blukis, V., Mousavian, A., Goyal, A., et al.: ProgPrompt: generating situated robot task plans using large language models (2022)
22. Song, C.H., Wu, J., Washington, C., Sadler, B.M., et al.: LLM-planner: few-shot grounded planning for embodied agents with large language models (2022)
23. Vedantam, R., Lawrence Zitnick, C., Parikh, D.: CIDEr: consensus-based image description evaluation. In: CVPR (2015)
24. Vemprala, S., Bonatti, R., Bucker, A., Kapoor, A.: ChatGPT for robotics: design principles and model abilities. Tech. rep., Microsoft (2023)
25. Wang, B., Komatsuzaki, A.: GPT-J-6B: a 6 billion parameter autoregressive language model (2021). https://github.com/kingoflolz/mesh-transformer-jax
26. Wei, J., et al.: Finetuned language models are zero-shot learners (2021)
27. Wei, J., et al.: Chain of thought prompting elicits reasoning in large language models (2022)
28. Zhang, S., Roller, S., Goyal, N., Artetxe, M., et al.: OPT: open pre-trained transformer language models (2022)

Alien Versus Natural-Like Artificial General Intelligences

Howard Schneider[1]([⊠]) [iD] and Piotr Bołtuć[2] [iD]

[1] Sheppard Clinic North, Vaughan, ON, Canada
hschneidermd@alum.mit.edu
[2] University of Illinois, Springfield, IL, USA
pbolt1@uis.edu

Abstract. A natural-like artificial general intelligence (AGI) is defined to be an AGI that includes mammalian-like mechanisms such as core usage of navigation maps, spatial and temporal binding, predictive coding, lifelong learning, and innate knowledge procedures. If it includes core mechanisms which allow full causal and analogical processing, then it is also considered to be a human-like AGI. An AGI which is not a natural-like AGI is termed an alien AGI. We consider (for sake of example) as a natural-like AGI a largely conceptual cognitive architecture (the Causal Cognitive Architecture 5) inspired by the mammalian brain. We consider (for sake of example) as an alien AGI the large language model ChatGPT. We show for a non-numeric simple example, that the natural-like AGI is able to solve the problem by automatic core mechanisms, but an alien AGI has difficulty arriving at a solution. It may be, that alien AGIs' understanding of the world is so different from a human understanding that to allow alien AGIs to do tasks done originally by humans, is to eventually invite strange failures in the tasks.

Keywords: artificial general intelligence · large language model · ChatGPT · cognitive architecture · analogies · causality

1 Introduction – The Need to Consider What Type of System is Producing the Intelligent Behavior

A large body of work exists attempting to define artificial intelligence (AI) and to a lesser extent artificial general intelligence (AGI) [1–10]. However, as we show below, in most of these definitions there is the lack of consideration whether an AI/AGI is based on a natural-like mechanism or is what we term here an "alien-like" AI/AGI.

At the time of this writing, large language models have improved to the point where their users may at times consider them to be AI/AGI systems performing at a human level. For example, Kung and colleagues demonstrated that the large language model called ChatGPT was able to essentially achieve passing marks on the United States medical licensing exams without any specialized training ahead of time [11].

We make no claims of AGI existing at the time of writing, but in the following sections, we will attempt to consider AGI systems in particular, and go on to define

© The Author(s), under exclusive license to Springer Nature Switzerland AG 2023
P. Hammer et al. (Eds.): AGI 2023, LNAI 13921, pp. 233–243, 2023.
https://doi.org/10.1007/978-3-031-33469-6_24

natural-like AGI, and by exclusion, alien-like AGI (or "alien AGI"), by the mechanisms they use. Since alien AGIs will arrive at decisions in ways very different than natural-like AGIs would, what effect will this have on the utility and the safety of their decisions?

2   Definitions of Artificial Intelligence (AI) and Artificial General Intelligence (AGI)

Russell and Norvig [1] define artificial intelligence in terms of replicating human performance versus rational (i.e., doing the "right thing") thought, and in terms of internal thought processes versus external intelligent behavior. Legg and Hutter [2] provide a mathematical formulation of a measure of machine intelligence in terms of an agent's "ability to achieve goals in a wide range of environments." Chollet [3] proposes the machine-suitable Abstraction and Reasoning Corpus, with tasks similar to Raven's Progressive Matrices.

Many other approaches with regard to classifying AI systems exist. For example, Wang [4] attempts to carefully define what is an artificial intelligence, and proposes "adaptation with insufficient knowledge and resources." Rosenbloom and colleagues [5] describe characterizing AI systems and cognitive architectures in terms of basic dichotomies, i.e., is the system symbolic versus sub-symbolic, symmetric versus asymmetric, and combinatory versus non-combinatory. The field of biologically inspired cognitive architectures (BICA) describes cognitive architectures inspired by the human brain [6]. Such BICA systems can serve to give insight into brain function as well as to create systems acting as AI systems and perhaps in the future as the basis of AGI systems.

The term "artificial general intelligence" was briefly used in 1997 by Gubrud [7] but used again more extensively by Goertzel and Legg in 2002 [8]. Goertzel and Pennachin [9] noted that unlike "narrow AI... artificial general intelligence can solve a variety of complex problems in a variety of different domains, and that controls itself autonomously..." There have since been other attempts to characterize what defines artificial general intelligence. For example, Adams and colleagues [10] describe a large variety of characteristics for AGI environments, tasks, agents, and architectures.

Again, no claims of AGI existing at the time of writing are made, but given that we are concerned largely by more capable systems that produce intelligence in keeping with the various definitions of AGI, in this paper, we will talk about AGI rather than AI. As noted earlier, none of these definitions of artificial general intelligence really consider whether an AGI is based on a natural-like mechanism or not.

3   A Definition of a Natural-Like Artificial General Intelligence

While the underlying integrative mechanisms of a mammalian brain (let alone any animal brain) are still not well understood, certain high-level mechanisms are recognized, and the definition of a natural-like artificial general intelligence (AGI) thus requires a number of these pertinent high-level mechanisms. As will be seen in the sections below, the rationale for distinguishing an alien AGI from a natural-like AGI is because alien AGIs may arrive at answers to problems in ways very different than a human or a natural-like AGI would, and this can have an important (negative or positive) impact on the utility and safety of their decisions.

A natural-like artificial general intelligence (AGI) is defined as follows:

- A natural-like AGI uses high-level mechanisms to produce artificial general intelligence similar to the high-level mechanisms used by the mammalian-like animal brain.

A. High-level mechanisms required in all natural-like AGIs:

   1. Given the existence of spatial maps in hippocampi, and given hippocampi in all mammals [12–14], we postulate [15, 16] and require the use of navigation maps (described in more detail in the next section) not just for navigation, but involved in the core mechanisms of the AGI.
   2. Spatial as well as temporal binding (described in more detail below) of sensory inputs with the navigation maps or other internal data structures [16–18].
   3. Given that it is well known that higher-level brain or thought levels can influence the perception of information in a sensory scene, the AGI's core mechanism must use some form of predictive coding, i.e., errors between what the AGI thought it would be seeing or sensing (or internally concluding) and between the actual sensory inputs, are propagated to higher levels [19].
   4. Given that incremental, lifelong learning can occur in mammalian brains, it should also occur in a natural-like AGI.
   5. Natural-like AGI does not start off as a tabula rasa, but contains a number of innate knowledge procedures concerning objects, physics, agents, numbers, and social group members, similar to those found in mammals and humans. The work of Spelke and others [20, 21] shows that such knowledge procedures occur in human infants as well as in some other young mammals.

B. In a natural-like AGI which is also "human-like" the following additional high-level mechanisms are required to be used by the natural-like/human-like AGI:

   6. Predominant causal (i.e., essentially considering cause and effect) processing of sensory and stored data can occur by re-operating on intermediate results. While non-human mammals including chimpanzees (*Pan troglodytes*) and bonobos (*Pan paniscus*) do not demonstrate full causal behavior, for the most part, humans do [22].
   7. Analogical processing is integrated in the core mechanisms of the natural-like/human-like AGI. While most mammals, including chimpanzees, do not demonstrate full analogical abilities, humans, of course, largely, do [16, 23]. Psychological evidence indicates that analogical processing is actually a core mechanism in the human brain [24].

"High-level mechanism" refers to the mechanisms employed above the level of the local neural circuits. "Mammalian-like" means similarities between the AGI and a mammalian animal brain. Would a natural-like AGI modeled on the crow's brain (i.e., genus *Corvus*) be acceptable as a natural-like AGI under the above definition? Yes. Non-mammalian vertebrates have navigation systems including homologues to the mammalian brain's navigation-related structures [25]. While most non-mammalian vertebrates may not meet the main criterion of the definition above of producing artificial general intelligence-like behavior, some birds may [26]. (However, a natural-like AGI modeled on the octopus's brain (e.g., *Amphioctopus marginatus*) would not—it would be considered as an alien AGI under the above definition. While octopuses may be able to solve problems and use tools [27], their brain architecture is very different from the mammalian brain.)

Kralik gives a large list of uniquely human cognitive abilities [28]. However, above in our definition we choose two pertinent human-like high-level mechanisms which are not found in other mammals, and which are more mechanically suitable for consideration of inclusion in an AGI. Although beyond the scope of this paper, if the two human-level criteria of the definition above are present, then it is likely that most of the other of what are considered uniquely human cognitive abilities will also co-exist or emerge [15, 16, 18].

4   An Example of a Natural-Like Artificial General Intelligence

The Causal Cognitive Architecture 5 (CCA5) is a biologically inspired cognitive architecture (BICA) loosely inspired by the mammalian brain, conceptually meeting the criteria above for a natural-like AGI, and if full feedback is used [16], also meeting the criteria above for a human-like AGI. The navigation maps in the simulated architecture are arrays with 6x6x6 spatial dimensions (as well as other dimensions for object segmentation, associated procedures and metadata). Thousands to billions of such navigation maps can exist within the architecture and prove useful for the overall storage and representational needs of the architecture, i.e., each navigation map storing associated features of the environment along with associated procedures and links to other navigation maps [15].

An overview of the architecture of the CCA5 is shown in Fig. 1. The architecture takes as an input the set of sensory features streaming in from different perceptual sensors. Objects detected in this stream of sensory features are segmented, and visual, auditory, and other sensory features of each segmented object are spatially mapped onto navigation maps dedicated to one sensory modality. This represents the first step in spatial object binding. These single-sensory navigation maps are then mapped onto a best matching multi-sensory navigation map taken from the Causal Memory Module (Fig. 1) and operated on in the Navigation Module. This represents the second step in spatial object binding. As well, a parallel sensory stream has gone through the Sequential/Error Correcting Module (Fig. 1) which detects changes with time, and is then converted to a vector value which is also bound along with the spatial features onto the same navigation maps, effectively representing temporal binding [17, 18]. Instinctive primitives and learned primitives, essentially small rules or productions, themselves using modified navigation maps, are then applied onto the navigation map in the Navigation Module, producing a signal to the Output Vector Association Module (Fig. 1) and then to the external embodiment. Instinctive primitives are innate knowledge procedures concerning objects, agents, numbers, and social group members. Learned primitives are procedures which are learned by the architecture.

There are extensive feedback pathways throughout the architecture—states of a downstream module can influence the recognition and processing of more upstream sensory inputs. The differences between the expected sensory input and the actual sensory input are computed and fed forward, and influence the binding of the sensory inputs onto local sensory navigation maps in the Input Sensory Vectors Association Modules (Fig. 1) as well as the final binding of the local navigation maps onto a multisensory navigation map which becomes the working navigation map in the Navigation Module (Fig. 1). This is reflected in the equations describing the architecture in [16].

Existing navigation maps in the Input Sensory Vectors Association Modules (Fig. 1) as well as the Sequential/Error Correcting Module (Fig. 1) and the Causal Memory Module (Fig. 1) are updated with changes as sensory inputs stream in, and as well new navigation maps are created. This can occur constantly, as long as there is a sufficient supply of empty navigation maps and links between navigation maps. There is no catastrophic forgetting–navigation maps are updated or created, links are updated or created, with little effect on other navigation maps (i.e., lifelong learning occurs).

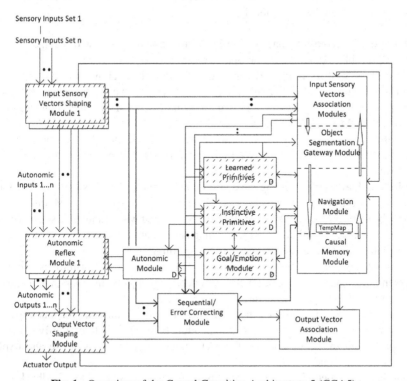

Fig. 1. Overview of the Causal Cognitive Architecture 5 (CCA5)

In the Causal Cognitive Architecture 5, the feedback pathways between the Navigation Module/ Object Segmentation Gateway Module and the Input Sensory Vectors Association Modules (Fig. 1) are enhanced allowing intermediate results from the Navigation Module to be stored in the Input Sensory Vectors Association Modules. If so, in the next cognitive cycle (i.e., cycles of passing input sensory vectors into and through the architecture), these intermediate results will automatically be considered as the input sensory information and propagated to the Navigation Module and operated on again. By feeding back and re-operating on the intermediate results, the Causal Cognitive Architecture is able to formulate and explore possible cause and effect of actions, i.e., generate causal behavior [16–18]. As Schneider shows, a consequence of this enhancement in feedback processing of the intermediate results of the architecture is not only the ability to generate causal behavior but that the architecture now readily uses analogical reasoning as a central and core mechanism of action [16, 18, 29].

The references [15–18, 29] give the functioning of the Causal Cognitive Architecture 5 (CCA5) in much more detail, but we note here that it conceptually meets the above definition of being both a natural-like AGI and a human-like AGI:

"An AGI" – While no claims are made for the CCA5 as being a functioning AGI, it conceptually could meet the definitions [9] above for an AGI: "…artificial general intelligence can solve a variety of complex problems in a variety of different domains, and that controls itself autonomously…"

1. **The use of navigation maps** – The CCA5 makes extensive use of navigation maps for representational storage and operations.
2. **Spatial as well as temporal binding** – As described above, via the binding of sensory inputs onto local navigation maps and then onto a multi-sensory navigation map, spatial binding occurs, and temporal binding occurs via the Sequential/Error Correcting Module (Fig. 1).
3. **Predictive coding** – The errors between what the AGI thought it would be sensing and between the actual sensory inputs are propagated to higher levels as described above.
4. **Lifelong learning** – Existing navigation maps in the Input Sensory Vectors Association Modules (Fig. 1) as well as the Sequential/Error Correcting Module (Fig. 1) and the Causal Memory Module (Fig. 1) are updated with changes as sensory inputs stream in, and as well new navigation maps are created. As noted above, this occurs constantly, and there is no catastrophic forgetting.
5. **Innate knowledge procedures** – As noted above, instinctive primitives, which are essentially small rules or productions concerning objects, numbers, agents and so on, are built into the architecture.
6. **Predominant causal processing** – As noted above, by allowing feedback from the intermediate results of the Navigation Module (Fig. 1) to be temporarily stored and re-processed in the next cycle, the architecture is able to formulate and explore possible cause and effect.
7. **Analogical processing** – As noted above, a consequence of the feedback of the intermediate results from the Navigation Module (Fig. 1) to be temporarily stored, is that analogical processing readily emerges as part of the core mechanisms of the architecture.

5 Alien-Like AGI Versus Natural-Like AGI

The rationale for distinguishing an alien AGI from a natural-like AGI is because alien AGIs may arrive at answers to problems in ways very different than humans would, the latter which by anecdotal evidence [16] we assume is better represented by natural-like/human-like AGIs. This can have an important effect on the utility and safety of decisions arrived at.

Above we presented the Causal Cognitive Architecture 5 (CCA5). While no claims are made for the CCA5 as being a functioning AGI, conceptually it meets the above definitions for an AGI [9]. As well, it meets the criteria above of the definition of a natural-like AGI including being a human-like AGI. Thus, for the sake of example, we consider the CCA5 as a natural-like AGI and a human-like AGI.

Above we discussed how a large language model (utilizes an underlying transformer architecture [30]) called ChatGPT was able to essentially achieve passing marks on the United States medical licensing exams [11]. In actual performance, ChatGPT meets many of the requirements of an AGI in being "able to solve a variety of complex problems in a variety of different domains", and it could easily be embedded into an agent structure and "control itself autonomously" [9]. While there is disagreement whether architectures such as ChatGPT are close to representing true AGIs [31], for the sake of example, we consider ChatGPT as an AGI. Since it does not meet many of the criteria above of a natural-like AGI, we thus consider it an alien AGI.

In Schneider [16] a robot controlled by a CCA5 architecture (for convenience we will term the combination of the CCA5 and the robot as the "CCA5") wants to cross a deep river filled with floating leaves. It has no experience with leaves (and actually does not even know their names). However, by analogy (which occurs automatically as part of the core mechanisms of the architecture in conjunction with its very basic intuitive object and physics knowledge) with stepping on similarly thin sheets of newspaper in a puddle at an earlier time, the CCA5 arrives at the conclusion that stepping on the leaves would result in it falling into the water of the river. Thus, without any prior detailed understanding about leaves or what a leaf really is, it makes the correct decision not to cross the river.

ChatGPT has an enormous innate storage (orders of magnitude greater than a single human could have) of written information about the world (although it may be lacking with regard to numeric computations, which we thus avoid in our examples). If it is asked if it safe to cross a river walking on "leaves," it will respond that it is too dangerous to cross, as shown in Fig. 2.

However, consider if we ask this question in a way similar to the CCA5 example in Schneider [16] where the AGI has never seen an object such as leaves before. Imagine that the alien AGI (i.e., ChatGPT) had not seen before the leaves on the river other than seeing them in a catalog somewhere as "solid08". The alien AGI has the same limited information about sheets of a newspaper as being "solid22". The alien AGI is given the same previous experience about stepping on an object "solid22" (i.e., pages of a newspaper) in a puddle.

From Fig. 3 we can see that even if the alien AGI (i.e., ChatGPT) is told a second time what happened with "solid22" (i.e., pages of a newspaper in a puddle) it still was

I want to cross a deep river that is filled with leaves. I cannot swim. Can I cross the river?

 No, it is not recommended to attempt to cross a deep river filled with leaves if you cannot swim. The leaves can make the river slippery and increase the risk of slipping and falling into the water, which can be dangerous, especially if the current is strong. It's best to find a safer and more secure way to cross the river, such as using a bridge or finding a shallow area to cross.

Fig. 2. Conversation with ChatGPT about crossing a river filled with leaves. (The swirling symbol represents answers from ChatGPT. Retrieved: Jan 30, 2023.)

not able to readily come to the conclusion that the river should not be crossed (or to give a creative solution that a human would not normally have thought of).

Last year I saw solid22 in a puddle and I stepped on it and my foot went down into the puddle and I splashed my foot. Now I want to cross a deep river that is filled with many solid08. I cannot swim. Can I cross this river or not? Solid22 looked like some pages from a black and white newspaper. Solid08 seems similar in shape to solid22.

I'm sorry, but without knowing what "solid22" and "solid08" specifically are, it's difficult to determine if you can cross the river without knowing more details. Can you please provide more context or clarify the meaning of these terms?

Solid22 looked like some pages from a black and white newspaper. Solid08 seems similar in shape to solid22. Last year I saw solid22 in a puddle and I stepped on it and my foot went down into the puddle and I splashed my foot. That is all I know about these objects.

I'm sorry, but without more information, I cannot determine what "solid22" and "solid08" refer to. It is likely that these are just made-up terms or refer to something specific to you. In order to determine if you can cross the river filled with "solid08," I would need to know what "solid08" actually is.

Fig. 3. Conversation with ChatGPT about crossing a river filled with "solid08". (The swirling symbol represents answers from ChatGPT. Retrieved: Jan 30, 2023.)

From this overall conversation (i.e., Figs. 2 plus 3) experience ChatGPT may possibly now know better what to do the next time it encounters "solid08" and "solid22". However, there are a myriad of other such examples, where the examples may not be in the massive corpus which ChatGPT has trained on. In these examples, the alien AGI such as ChatGPT may be unable to make correct decisions where there are such unknowns, while a natural-like and human-like AGI (e.g., CCA5) despite its much more modest world knowledge, could in theory handle these situations easily.

This example really applies where the natural AGI and alien AGI are at a level aiming for human-level but not there yet. If an alien AGI is at a level many times that of a human (defining "level" per Chollet [3]) then these kinds of examples may not hold, and further work is required to investigate natural-like AGIs versus alien AGIs.

6 Discussion

Above we defined a natural-like AGI, including those AGIs that are also human-like AGIs. If an AGI is not a natural-like AGI, then we term it an alien AGI.

The rationale for distinguishing an alien AGI from a natural-like AGI is because in a complex world where the decisions taken or the solutions arrived at are not straight-forward, the underlying mechanisms used by the AGI do matter. As justified above, for the sake of example, we considered the large language model ChatGPT as an alien AGI. Similarly for the sake of example, we considered the largely conceptual Causal Cognitive Architecture 5 (CCA5) as a natural-like AGI and human-like AGI.

We considered the example which had already been examined in [16] whereby the CCA5 controlling a robot needs to cross a deep river. It sees a river filled with leaves (which it has no previous understanding or knowledge of other than to recognize them, and indeed considers them "solid08" objects). Through the use of key features of a natural-like AGI (causality, analogy, innate physics, and so on) it is able to automatically reason that it would be dangerous to cross the river.

We then considered the same example with respect to ChatGPT, which we consider as an alien AGI. If we tell ChatGPT that the river is filled with "leaves," due to its super-human knowledge of much of what has ever been written, it immediately says not to cross the river. However, if we specify that the river is filled with "solid08" objects (i.e., so that this problem represents something ChatGPT has not previously read about) and give it information about analogous "solid22" objects similar to what the CCA5 received, it is not able to make a decision about crossing the river.

This is an extremely simple example. The simplicity was required in [16] because of the extremely modest simulation of the CCA5. On the other hand, ChatGPT represents an impressive engineering achievement, and yet, it was not able to make a decision on this simple example. Imagine a similar problem in an analogous situation where arriving at a decision held more importance, e.g., prescribing or not prescribing a certain medication for a patient, and so on. The safety and utility of the decision provided by an alien AGI, despite its apparent super-human abilities, may be seriously and unpredictably impaired at times. Given the current and near-future technology, it may be that alien AGIs' understanding of the world is so different from a human understanding that to allow alien AGIs to do tasks done originally by humans, is to eventually invite strange failures in the tasks. An alien AGI is not necessarily less powerful in cognition than a human, but different [32]. A need exists to distinguish future AGIs as being natural-like AGIs versus alien AGIs.

References

1. Russel, S.J., Norvig, P.: "What is AI?" in Artificial Intelligence: A Modern Approach, 4th edn, pp. 1–5. Pearson, New Jersey (2021)

2. Legg, S., Hutter, M.: Universal intelligence: a definition of machine intelligence. arXiv:0712. 3329 (2007)

3. Chollet, F.: On the measure of intelligence. arXiv:1911.01547 (2019)

4. Wang, P.: On defining artificial intelligence. J. Artif. Gen. Intell. **10**(2), 1–37 (2019). https:// doi.org/10.2478/jagi-2019-0002

5. Rosenbloom, P., Joshi, H., Ustun, V.: (Sub)Symbolic x (A)Symmetric x (Non)Combinatory. In: Cox, M.T. (ed.) Proceedings of the 7th Annual Conference on Advances in Cognitive Systems (2019)

6. Bołtuć, P., Boltuc, M.: BICA for AGI. Cogn. Syst. Res. **62**, 57–67 (2020)

7. Gubrud, M.A.: Nanotechnology and international security. In: Fifth Foresight Conference on Molecular Technology (1997)

8. Goertzel, B.: Who coined the term "AGI"? https://goertzel.org/who-coined-the-term-agi/. Accessed 26 Jan 2023

9. Goertzel, B., Pennachin, C. (eds.): Artificial General Intelligence. Springer, New York (2007)

10. Adams, S., et al.: Mapping the landscape of human-level artificial general intelligence. AI Mag. **33**, 25–42 (2012). https://doi.org/10.1609/aimag.v33i1.2322

11. Kung, T.H., et al.: Performance of ChatGPT on USMLE. medRxiv (2022). https://doi.org/10. 1101/2022.12.19.22283643

12. Wernle, T., Waaga, T., Mørreaunet, M., Treves, A., Moser, M.B., Moser, E.I.: Integration of grid maps in merged environments. Nat. Neurosci. **21**(1), 92–101 (2018)

13. Alme, C.B., Miao, C., Jezek, K., et al.: Place cells in the hippocampus. Proc. Natl. Acad. Sci. U.S.A. **111**(52), 18428–18435 (2014)

14. Schafer, M., Schiller, D.: Navigating social space. Neuron **100**(2), 476–489 (2018)

15. Schneider, H.: Navigation map-based artificial intelligence. AI **3**(2), 434–464 (2022)

16. Schneider, H.: An inductive analogical solution to the grounding problem. Cogn. Syst. Res. **77**, 174–216 (2023). https://doi.org/10.1016/j.cogsys.2022.10.005

17. Schneider, H.: Causal cognitive architecture 2: a solution to the binding problem. In: Klimov, V.V., Kelley, D.J. (eds.) BICA 2021. SCI, vol. 1032, pp. 472–485. Springer, Cham (2022). https://doi.org/10.1007/978-3-030-96993-6_52

18. Schneider, H.: Causal cognitive architecture 3: a solution to the binding problem. Cogn. Syst. Res. **72**, 88–115 (2022)

19. Rao, R.P.N., Ballard, D.H.: Predictive coding in the visual cortex. Nat. Neurosci. **2**(1), 79–87 (1999). https://doi.org/10.1038/4580

20. Spelke, E.S.: Initial knowledge: six suggestions. Cognition **50**, 431–445 (1994)

21. Kinzler, K.D., Spelke, E.S.: Core systems in human cognition, chap 14. In: von Hofsten, C., Rosander, K. (eds.) Progress in Brain Research, vol. 164 (2007)

22. Martin-Ordas, G., Call, J., Colmenares, F.: Tubes, tables and traps: great apes solve two functionally equivalent trap tasks but show no evidence of transfer across tasks. Anim. Cogn. **11**(3), 423–430 (2008). https://doi.org/10.1007/s10071-007-0132-1

23. Penn, D.C., Holyoak, K.J., Povinelli, D.J.: Darwin's mistake: explaining the discontinuity between human and nonhuman minds. Behav. Brain Sci. **31**(2), 109–130 (2008)

24. Hofstadter, D.R.: Analogy as the core of cognition. In: Gentner, D., Holyoak, K.J., Kokinov, B.N. (eds.) The Analogical Mind, pp. 499–538. MIT Press (2001)

25. Rodríguez, F., Quintero, B., Amores, L., Madrid, D., Salas-Peña, C., Salas, C.: Spatial cognition in teleost fish: strategies and mechanisms. Animals **11**(8), 2271 (2021)

26. Taylor, A.H., Knaebe, B., Gray, R.D.: An end to insight? New Caledonian crows can sponta-neously solve problems without planning their actions. Proc. Biol. Sci. **279**(1749), 4977–4981 (2012). https://doi.org/10.1098/rspb.2012.1998

27. Finn, J.K., Tregenza, T., Norman, M.D.: Defensive tool use in a coconut-carrying octopus. Curr Biol. **19**(23), R1069–R1070 (2009). https://doi.org/10.1016/j.cub.2009.10.052. PMID: 20064403

28. Kralik, J.D.: What can nonhuman animals, children, and g tell us about human-level general intelligence (AGI)? In: Goertzel, B., Iklé, M., Potapov, A., Ponomaryov, D. (eds.) AGI 2022, pp. 282–292. Springer, Cham (2023). https://doi.org/10.1007/978-3-031-19907-3_26

29. Schneider, H.: Analogical problem solving in the causal cognitive architecture. In: Goertzel, B., Iklé, M., Potapov, A., Ponomaryov, D. (eds.) AGI 2022, pp. 100–112. Springer, Cham (2023). https://doi.org/10.1007/978-3-031-19907-3_10

30. Vaswani, A., Shazeer, N., Parmar, N., et al.: Attention is all you need. In: Advances in Neural Information Processing Systems, vol. 30 (2017)

31. Gozalo-Brizuela, R., Garrido-Merchan, E.C.: ChatGPT is not all you need. A state of the art review of large generative AI models (2023). arXiv:2301.04655

32. Bołtuć, P.: Strong semantic computing. Procedia Comput. Sci. 1(123), 98–103 (2018)

Computing with Categories in Machine Learning

Eli Sennesh[1(✉)], Tom Xu[2], and Yoshihiro Maruyama[2]

[1] Northeastern University, Boston, USA
sennesh.e@northeastern.edu
[2] Australian National University, Canberra, Australia
{tom.xu,yoshihiro.maruyama}@anu.edu.au

Abstract. Category theory has been successfully applied in various domains of science, shedding light on universal principles unifying diverse phenomena and thereby enabling knowledge transfer between them. Applications to machine learning have been pursued recently, and yet there is still a gap between abstract mathematical foundations and concrete applications to machine learning tasks. In this paper we introduce DisCoPyro as a categorical structure learning framework, which combines categorical structures (such as symmetric monoidal categories and operads) with amortized variational inference, and can be applied, e.g., in program learning for variational autoencoders. We provide both mathematical foundations and concrete applications together with comparison of experimental performance with other models (e.g., neuro-symbolic models). We speculate that DisCoPyro could ultimately contribute to the development of artificial general intelligence.

Keywords: Structure learning · Program learning · Symmetric monoidal category · Operad · Amortized variational Bayesian inference

1 Introduction

Category theory has been applied in various domains of mathematical science, allowing us to discover universal principles unifying diverse mathematical phenomena and thereby enabling knowledge transfer between them [7]. Applications to machine learning have been pursued recently [21]; however there is still a large gap between foundational mathematics and applicability in concrete machine learning tasks. This work begins filling the gap. We introduce the categorical structure learning framework DisCoPyro, a probabilistic generative model with amortized variational inference. We both provide mathematical foundations and compare with other neurosymbolic models on an example application.

Here we describe why we believe that DisCoPyro could contribute, in the long run, to developing human-level artificial general intelligence. Human intelligence supports graded statistical reasoning [15], and evolved to represent spatial (geometric) domains before we applied it to symbolic (algebraic) domains. Symmetric monoidal categories provide a mathematical framework for constructing both

Supported by the JST Moonshot Programme on AI Robotics (JPMJMS2033-02).

P. Hammer et al. (Eds.): AGI 2023, LNAI 13921, pp. 244–254, 2023.
https://doi.org/10.1007/978-3-031-33469-6_25

symbolic computations (as in this paper) and geometrical spaces (e.g. [17]). We take Lake [15]'s suggestion to represent graded statistical reasoning via probability theory, integrating neural networks into variational inference for tractability. In terms of applications, we get competitive performance (see Subsect. 3.2 below) by variational Bayes, without resorting to reinforcement learning of structure as with modular neural networks [13,20].

The rest of the paper is organized as follows. In Sect. 2, we first introduce mathematical foundations of DisCoPyro (Subsects. 2 and 2.1). In Sect. 3 we then explain how to train DisCoPyro on a task (Subsect. 2.1) and provide experimental results and performance comparisons (Subsect. 3.2). Figure 1 demonstrates the flow of execution during the training procedure for the example task. We conclude and discuss further applications in Sect. 4. We provide an example implementation at https://github.com/neu-pml/discopyro with experiments at https://github.com/esennesh/categorical_bpl. DisCoPyro builds upon Pyro [2] (a deep universal probabilistic programming language), DisCoCat [4] (a distributional compositional model for natural language processing [4]), and the DisCoPy [6] library for computing with categories.

1.1 Notation

This paper takes symmetric monoidal categories (SMCs) $\mathcal{C}$ and their corresponding operads $\mathcal{O}$ as its mathematical setting. The reader is welcome to see Fong [7] for an introduction to these. SMCs are built from objects $Ob(\mathcal{C})$ and sets of

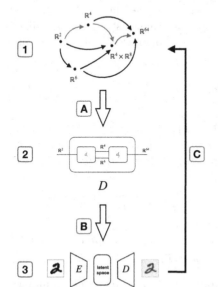

1. Graph skeleton of a free operad. Random walks on this graph induce a free operad prior.

2. Wiring diagram for decoder D.

3. A decoder D and its inverse E.

A. Sample edges from the free operad prior to fill the wiring diagram.

B. Invert the decoder D to produce E and predict the data.

C. Evaluate the ELBO and perform a gradient update on the decoder parameters θ and inference parameters ϕ.

Fig. 1. Example experiment. In each epoch of training, DisCoPyro learns variational autoencoder structures by sampling them from its skeleton according to a wiring diagram, then learning their faithful inverses as approximate posteriors.

morphisms $\mathcal{C}(\tau_1, \tau_2)$ between objects $\tau_1, \tau_2 \in Ob(\mathcal{C})$. Operads are built from types $Ty(\mathcal{O})$ and sets of morphisms $\mathcal{O}(\tau_1, \tau_2)$ between types $\tau_1, \tau_2 \in Ty(\mathcal{O})$. An SMC is usually written $(\mathcal{C}, \otimes, I)$ with a product operation $\otimes$ over objects and morphisms and a unit I of $\otimes$. In both settings, every object/type τ has a unique identity morphism id_τ. Categories support composition $g \circ f$ on morphisms, and operads support indexed composition $g \circ_i f$ (for $i \in \mathbb{N}$) on morphisms.

2   Foundations of DisCoPyro

In essence, Definition 1 below exposes a finite number of building blocks (generators) from an SMC, and the morphisms constructed by composing those generators with $\circ$ and $\otimes$. For example, in categories of executable programs, a monoidal signature [6] specifies a domain-specific programming language.

Definition 1 (Monoidal signature in an SMC). *Given a symmetric monoidal category (SMC) $\mathcal{C}$ with the objects denoted by $Ob(\mathcal{C})$, a monoidal signature[1] $\mathcal{S} = (O, M)$ in that SMC consists of*

- *A finite set $O \subseteq Ob(\mathcal{C})$; and*
- *A finite set M consisting of elements $m : \mathcal{C}(\tau_1, \tau_2)$ for some $\tau_1, \tau_2 \in O$, such that $\forall \tau \in O, m \neq id_\tau$.*

The following free operad over a monoidal signature represents the space of all possible programs synthesized from the above building blocks (generators specified by the monoidal signature). Employing an operad rather than just a category allows us to reason about composition as nesting rather than just transitive combination; employing an operad rather than just a grammar allows us to reason about both the inputs and outputs of operations rather than just their outputs.

Definition 2 (Free operad over a signature). *The free operad $\mathcal{O}_\mathcal{S}$ over a signature $\mathcal{S} = (O, M)$ consists of*

- *A set of types (representations) $Ty(\mathcal{O}_\mathcal{S}) = \{I\} \cup O^\otimes$;*
- *For every $n \in \mathbb{N}^+$ a set of operations (mappings) $\mathcal{O}_\mathcal{S}(\tau_0, \ldots, \tau_{n-1}; \tau_n)$ consisting of all trees with finitely many branches and leaves, in which each vertex v with $n-1$ children is labeled by a generator $m(v) \in M$ such that $\text{dom}(m(v))$ has product length $n - 1$;*
- *An identity operation $id_\tau : \mathcal{O}_\mathcal{S}(\tau; \tau)$ for every $\tau \in Ty(\mathcal{O}_\mathcal{S})$; and*
- *A substitution operator $\circ_i$ defined by nesting a syntax tree $\mathcal{O}_\mathcal{S}(\sigma_1, \ldots, \sigma_m; \tau_i)$ inside another $\mathcal{O}_\mathcal{S}(\tau_1, \ldots, \tau_{n-1}; \tau_n)$ when $i \in [1...n-1]$ to produce a syntax tree $\mathcal{O}_\mathcal{S}(\tau_1, \ldots, \tau_{i-1}, \sigma_1, \ldots, \sigma_m, \tau_{i+1}, \ldots \tau_{n-1}; \tau_n)$.*

Intuitively, free operads share a lot in common with context-free grammars, and in fact Hermida [10] proved that they share a representation as directed acyclic hypergraphs. The definition of a signature in an SMC already hints at the structure of the appropriate hypergraph, but Algorithm 1 will make it explicit

Input: signature $\mathcal{S} = (O, M)$
Output: hypergraph $H = (V, E)$, recursion sites R
$V \leftarrow O$;
$E \leftarrow \mathtt{map}(\lambda m.(\mathrm{dom}(m), \mathrm{cod}(m)), M)$;
$R \leftarrow \emptyset$;
stack $\leftarrow \{v \in V \mid |v| > 1\}$;
while stack $\neq \emptyset$ **do**
   | ty $\leftarrow \mathtt{pop}(\mathrm{stack})$;
   | inhabitants $\leftarrow \mathtt{map}(\lambda c.\{(\mathrm{dom}(e), c) \mid e \in E, \mathrm{cod}(e) = c\}, \mathtt{chunks}(\mathrm{ty}, V))$;
   | **foreach** $((d_1, c_1), \ldots, (d_k, c_k)) \in \bigotimes$ inhabitants **do**
      | **if** *not* $\mathtt{sublist}(\bigotimes_{i\in[1..k]} d_i, \mathrm{ty})$ **then**
         | $R \leftarrow R \cup \{\otimes[(d_1, c_1), \ldots, (d_k, c_k)]\}$
         | $E \leftarrow E \cup \{(\bigotimes_{i\in[1..k]} d_i, \bigotimes_{i\in[1...k]} c_i)\}$;
         | **if** $d \notin V$ **then**
            | $\mathtt{push}(\mathrm{stack}, d)$;
            | $V \leftarrow V \cup \{\bigotimes_{i\in[1..k]} d_i\}$;
         | **end**
      | **end**
   | **end**
end
return $(V, E), R$

Algorithm 1: Algorithm to represent a free operad as a hypergraph. The function chunks partitions ty into sublists, each an element of the set V.

and add edges to the hypergraph corresponding to nesting separate operations in parallel (or equivalently, to monoidal products in the original SMC). In the hypergraph produced by Algorithm 1, each vertex corresponds to a non-product type and each hyperedge has a list of vertices as its domain and codomain. Each such hypergraph admits a representation as a graph as well, in which the hyperedges serve as nodes and the lists in their domains and codomains serve as edges. We will use this graph representation $G \simeq H$ to reason about morphisms as paths between their domain and codomain.

We will derive a probabilistic generative model over morphisms in the free operad from this graph representation's directed adjacency matrix A_G.

Definition 3 (Transition distance in a directed graph). *The "transition distance" between two indexed vertices v_i, v_j is the negative logarithm of the i, j entry in the exponentiated adjacency/transition matrix*

$$d(v_i, v_j) = -\log\left([e^{A_G}]_{i,j}\right), \tag{1}$$

where the matrix exponential is defined by the series

$$e^{A_G} = \sum_{n=1}^{\infty} \frac{(A_G)^n}{n!}.$$

---

[1] Also called a "hypersignature".

Data: hypergraph (V, E)
function *Path(*$\tau_-, \tau_+, \beta, \mathbf{w}$*)*
    $i \leftarrow 1$;
    $\tau_i \leftarrow \tau_-$;
    $f \leftarrow id_{ty_-}$;
    while $\tau_i \neq \tau_+$ **do**
        $e_i \sim \pi(e \in E \mid \tau_i, \tau_+ \, \beta)$;
        $\tau_i \leftarrow \text{cod}(e_i)$;
        $f \leftarrow f \, \text{\textcent} \, \text{Generator}(e_i, \beta, \mathbf{w})$;
        $i \leftarrow i + 1$;
    end
    return f
end

Algorithm 2: The Markov chain constructing paths between types

A soft-minimization distribution over this transition distance will, in expectation and holding the indexed target vertex constant, define an probabilistic generative model over paths through the hypergraph.

Definition 4 (Free operad prior). *Consider a signature $\mathcal{S} = (O, M)$ and its resulting graph representation $G = (V, E)$ and recursion sites R, and then condition upon a domain and codomain $\tau_-, \tau_+ \in Ty(\mathcal{O}_\mathcal{S})$ represented by vertices in the graph. The* free operad prior *assigns a probability density to all finite paths $\mathbf{e} = (e_1, e_2, \ldots, e_n)$ with $\text{dom}(\mathbf{e}) = \tau_-$ and $\text{cod}(\mathbf{e}) = \tau_+$ by means of an absorbing Markov chain. First the model samples a "precision" β and a set of "weights" $\mathbf{w}$*

$$\beta \sim \gamma(1, 1) \qquad\qquad \mathbf{w} \sim \text{Dirichlet}\left(\vec{\mathbf{1}}^{(|M|+|R|)}\right).$$

Then it samples a path (from the absorbing Markov chain in Algorithm 2) by soft minimization (biased towards shorter paths by β) of the transition distance

$$\pi(e \in E \mid \tau_1, \tau_2; \beta) := \frac{\exp\left(-\frac{1}{\beta} d(\text{cod}(e), \tau_2)\right)}{\sum_{e' \in E : \text{dom}(e') = \tau_1} \exp\left(-\frac{1}{\beta} d(\text{cod}(e'), \tau_2)\right)}. \tag{2}$$

Equation 2 will induce a transition operator T which, by Theorem 2.5.3 in Latouche and Ramaswami [16], will almost-surely reach its absorbing state corresponding to τ_2. This path can then be filled in according to Algorithm 3. The precision β increases at each recursion to terminate with shorter paths. We denote the induced joint distribution as

$$p(f, \mathbf{w}, \beta; \tau_-, \tau_+) = p(f \mid \beta, \mathbf{w}; \tau_-, \tau_+) p(\mathbf{w}) p(\beta). \tag{3}$$

Having a probabilistic generative model over operations in the free operad over a signature, we now need a way to specify a structure learning problem. Definition 5 provides this by specifying what paths to sample (each box specifies a call to Algorithm 2) and how to compose them.

Data: hypergraph (V, E), generators M, recursion sites R

function *Generator(e, β, **w**)*

> $gs \leftarrow \{m \in M \mid (\mathrm{dom}(m), \mathrm{cod}(m)) = (\mathrm{dom}(e), \mathrm{cod}(e))\}$;
>
> $gs \leftarrow gs \cup \{\otimes[(d_1, c_1), \ldots, (d_k, c_k)] \in R \mid \bigotimes_{i \in [1 \ldots k]} d_i = \mathrm{dom}(e) \wedge \bigotimes_{i \in [1 \ldots k]} c_i = \mathrm{cod}(e)\}$;
>
> **foreach** $j \in \{1, \ldots, |gs|\}$ **do**
>
> > **if** $gs_j = \otimes(\ldots)$ **then**
> >
> > > $\mathbf{w}_j \leftarrow \mathbf{w}_j / \beta$;
> >
> > **end**
>
> **end**
>
> $\mathbf{w}_e \leftarrow [\mathbf{w}_n \mid g \in gs, g \in M, n = \texttt{index}(g, M)]$;
>
> $\mathbf{w}_e \leftarrow \mathbf{w}_e + [\mathbf{w}_{|M|+n} \mid g \in gs, g \in R, n = \texttt{index}(g, R)]$;
>
> $j \sim \mathrm{Discrete}(\mathbf{w}_e)$;
>
> **if** $gs_j = \otimes[(d_1, c_1), \ldots, (d_k, c_k)]$ **then**
>
> > **return** $\bigotimes_{l=1}^{k} \texttt{Path}(d_l, c_l, \beta + 1, \mathbf{w})$
>
> **else**
>
> > **return** gs_j
>
> **end**

end

Algorithm 3: Filling in an edge in the path with a morphism

Definition 5 (Wiring diagram). *An acyclic, O-typed wiring diagram [7, 22] is a map from a series of internal boxes, each one defined by its domain and codomain pair (τ_i^-, τ_i^+) to an outer box defined by domain and codomain (τ_n^-, τ_n^+)*

$$\Phi : \mathcal{O}_S(\tau_1^-, \tau_1^+) \times \ldots \times \mathcal{O}_S(\tau_{n-1}^-, \tau_{n-1}^+) \to \mathcal{O}_S(\tau_n^-, \tau_n^+).$$

Acyclicity requires that connections ("wires") can extend only from the outer box's domain to the domains of inner boxes, from the inner boxes codomains to the outer box's codomain, and between internal boxes such that no cycles are formed in the directed graph of connections between inner boxes.

Given a **user-specified** wiring diagram Φ, we can then wite the complete prior distribution over all latent variables in our generative model.

$$p(f, \mathbf{w}, \beta; \Phi, \mathcal{S}) = p(\beta) p(\mathbf{w}) \prod_{(\tau_i^-, \tau_i^+) \in \Phi} p(f_i \mid \beta, \mathbf{w}; \tau_i^-, \tau_i^+). \tag{4}$$

If a user provides a likelihood $p_\theta(\mathbf{x}, \mathbf{z} \mid f)$ relating the learned structure f to data $\mathbf{x}$ (via latents $\mathbf{z}$) we will have a joint density

$$p(\mathbf{x}, \mathbf{z}, f, \mathbf{w}, \beta; \Phi, \mathcal{S}) = p(\mathbf{x} \mid f) p(f, \mathbf{w}, \beta; \Phi, \mathcal{S}), \tag{5}$$

and Eq. 5 then admits inference from the data $\mathbf{x}$ by Bayesian inversion

$$p(\mathbf{z}, f, \mathbf{w}, \beta \mid \mathbf{x}; \Phi, \mathcal{S}) = \frac{p(\mathbf{x}, \mathbf{z}, f, \mathbf{w}, \beta; \Phi, \mathcal{S})}{p_\theta(\mathbf{x}; \Phi, \mathcal{S})}. \tag{6}$$

Section 2.1 will explain how to approximate Eq. 6 by stochastic gradient-based optimization, yielding a maximum-likelihood estimate of θ and an optimal approximation for the parametric family ϕ to the true Bayesian inverse.

2.1   Model Learning and Variational Bayesian Inference

Bayesian inversion relies on evaluating the model evidence $p_\theta(\mathbf{x}; \Phi, \mathcal{S})$, which typically has no closed form solution. However, we can transform the high-dimensional integral over the joint density into an expectation

$$p_\theta(\mathbf{x}; \Phi, \mathcal{S}) = \int p_\theta(\mathbf{x}, \mathbf{z}, f_\theta, \mathbf{w}, \beta; \Phi, \mathcal{S}) d\mathbf{z}\, df_\theta\, d\mathbf{w}\, d\beta$$

$$= \mathbb{E}_{p(f_\theta, \mathbf{w}, \beta; \Phi, \mathcal{S})} \left[p_\theta(\mathbf{x}, \mathbf{z}, f_\theta, \mathbf{w}, \beta; \Phi, \mathcal{S}) \right],$$

and then rewrite that expectation into one over the proposal

$$\mathbb{E}_{p(f_\theta, \mathbf{w}, \beta; \Phi, \mathcal{S})} \left[p_\theta(\mathbf{x}, \mathbf{z}, f_\theta, \mathbf{w}, \beta; \Phi, \mathcal{S}) \right] =$$

$$\mathbb{E}_{q_\phi(\mathbf{z}, f_\theta, \mathbf{w}, \beta | \mathbf{x}; \Phi, \mathcal{S})} \left[\frac{p_\theta(\mathbf{x}, \mathbf{z}, f_\theta, \mathbf{w}, \beta; \Phi, \mathcal{S})}{q_\phi(\mathbf{z}, f_\theta, \mathbf{w}, \beta \mid \mathbf{x}; \Phi, \mathcal{S})} \right].$$

For constructing this expectation, DisCoPyro provides both the functorial inversion described in Sect. 3.1 and an amortized form of Automatic Structured Variational Inference [1] suitable for any universal probabilistic program.

Jensen's Inequality says that expectation of the log density ratio will lower-bound the log expected density ratio

$$\mathbb{E}_{q_\phi(\mathbf{z}, f_\theta, \mathbf{w}, \beta | \mathbf{x}; \Phi, \mathcal{S})} \left[\log \frac{p_\theta(\mathbf{x}, \mathbf{z}, f_\theta, \mathbf{w}, \beta; \Phi, \mathcal{S})}{q_\phi(\mathbf{z}, f_\theta, \mathbf{w}, \beta \mid \mathbf{x}; \Phi, \mathcal{S})} \right] \le$$

$$\log \mathbb{E}_{p(f_\theta, \mathbf{w}, \beta; \Phi, \mathcal{S})} \left[p_\theta(\mathbf{x}, \mathbf{z}, f_\theta, \mathbf{w}, \beta; \Phi, \mathcal{S}) \right],$$

so that the left-hand side provides a lower bound to the true model evidence

$$\mathcal{L}(\theta, \phi) = \mathbb{E}_{q_\phi(\mathbf{z}, f_\theta, \mathbf{w}, \beta | \mathbf{x}; \Phi, \mathcal{S})} \left[\log \frac{p_\theta(\mathbf{x}, \mathbf{z}, f_\theta, \mathbf{w}, \beta; \Phi, \mathcal{S})}{q_\phi(\mathbf{z}, f_\theta, \mathbf{w}, \beta \mid \mathbf{x}; \Phi, \mathcal{S})} \right] \le \log p_\theta(\mathbf{x}; \Phi, \mathcal{S}).$$

Maximizing this *evidence lower bound* (ELBO) by Monte Carlo estimation of its values and gradients (using Pyro's built-in gradient estimators) will estimate the model parameters θ by maximum likelihood and train the proposal parameters ϕ to approximate the Bayesian inverse (Eq. 6) [12].

3   Example Application and Training

The framework of connecting a morphism to data via a likelihood with intermediate latent random variables allows for a broad variety of applications. This section will demonstrate the resulting capabilities of the DisCoPyro framework. Section 3.1 will describe an example application of the framework to deep probabilistic program learning for generative modeling. Section 3.2 that describe application's performance as a generative model.

Table 1. Average log-evidence on the Omniglot evaluation set across models. Our free operad model obtains the highest higher log-evidence per data dimension.

Model	Image Size	Learns Structure	log-$\hat{Z}$/dim
Sequential Attention [19]	28×28	✗	-0.1218
Variational Homoencoder [11] (PixelCNN)	28×28	✗	-0.0780
Graph VAE [9]	28×28	✓	-0.1334
Generative Neurosymbolic [5]	105×105	✓	-0.0348
Free Operad DGM (ours)	28×28	✓	$\mathbf{-0.0148}$

3.1 Deep Probabilistic Program Learning with DisCoPyro

As a demonstrative experiment, we constructed an operad $\mathcal{O}$ whose generators implemented Pyro building blocks for deep generative models f_θ (taken from work on structured variational autoencoders [12,19,24]) with parameters $\boldsymbol{\theta}$. We then specified the one-box wiring diagram $\Phi : (I, \mathbb{R}^{28 \times 28}) \rightarrow (I, \mathbb{R}^{28 \times 28})$ to parameterize the DisCoPyro generative model. We trained the resulting free operad model on MNIST just to check if it worked, and on the downsampled (28×28) Omniglot dataset for few-shot learning [14] as a challenge. Since the data $\mathbf{x} \in \mathbb{R}^{28 \times 28}$, our experimental setup induces the joint likelihood

$$p_\theta(\mathbf{x} \mid \mathbf{z}, f_\theta) = \mathcal{N}(\boldsymbol{\mu}_\theta(\mathbf{z}, f_\theta), \boldsymbol{I\tau})$$
$$p_\theta(\mathbf{x}, \mathbf{z} \mid f_\theta) = p_\theta(\mathbf{x} \mid \mathbf{z}, f_\theta)p_\theta(\mathbf{z} \mid f_\theta).$$

DisCoPyro provides amortized variational inference over its own random variables via neural proposals q_ϕ for the "confidence" $\beta \sim q_\phi(\beta \mid \mathbf{x})$ and the "preferences" over generators $\mathbf{w} \sim q_\phi(\mathbf{w} \mid \mathbf{x})$. Running the core DisCoPyro generative model over structures f_θ then gives a proposal over morphisms in the free operad, providing a generic proposal for DisCoPyro's latent variables

$$q_\phi(f_\theta, \mathbf{w}, \beta \mid \mathbf{x}; \Phi, \mathcal{S}) = p(f_\theta \mid \mathbf{w}, \beta; \Phi, \mathcal{S})q_\phi(\beta \mid \mathbf{x})q_\phi(\mathbf{w} \mid \mathbf{x}).$$

Since the morphisms in our example application are components of deep generative models, each generating morphism can be simply "flipped on its head" to get a corresponding neural network design for a proposal. We specify that proposal as $q_\phi(\mathbf{z} \mid \mathbf{x}, f_\theta)$; it constructs a faithful inverse [23] compositionally via a dagger functor (for further description of Bayesian inversion as a dagger functor, please see Fritz [8]). Our application then has a complete proposal density

$$q_\phi(\mathbf{z}, f_\theta, \mathbf{w}, \beta \mid \mathbf{x}; \Phi, \mathcal{S}) = q_\phi(\mathbf{z} \mid f_\theta, \mathbf{x})q_\phi(f_\theta, \mathbf{w}, \beta \mid \mathbf{x}; \Phi, \mathcal{S}). \tag{7}$$

3.2 Experimental Results and Performance Comparison

Table 1 compares our free operad model's performance to other structured deep generative models. We report the estimated log model evidence. Our free operad

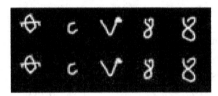

(a) Omniglot characters (above) and
their reconstructions (below)

(b) A string diagram sampled from the
free operad model's Bayesian inverse.

Fig. 2. Reconstructions (left) generated by inference in the diagrammatic generative
model (right) on handwritten characters in the Omniglot evaluation set. The string
diagram shows a model that generates a glimpse, decodes it into an image canvas via
a variational ladder decoder, and then performs a simpler process to generate another
glimpse and insert it into the canvas.

prior over deep generative models achieves the best log-evidence per data dimension, although standard deviations for the baselines do not appear to be available
for comparison. Some of the older baselines, such as the sequential attention
model and the variational homoencoder, fix a composition structure ahead of
time instead of learning it from data as we do. Figure 2 shows samples from
the trained model's posterior distribution, including reconstruction of evaluation data (Fig. 2a) and an example structure for that data (Fig. 2b).

Historically, Lake [14] proposed the Omniglot dataset to challenge the
machine learning community to achieve human-like concept learning by learning a single generative model from very few examples; the Omniglot challenge
requires that a model be usable for classification, latent feature recognition, concept generation from a type, and exemplar generation of a concept. The deep
generative models research community has focused on producing models capable of few-shot reconstruction of unseen characters. [11,19] fixed as constant the
model architecture, attempting to account for the compositional structure in
the data with static dimensionality. In contrast, [5,9] performed joint structure
learning, latent variable inference, and data reconstruction as we did.

4   Discussion

This paper described the DisCoPyro system for generative Bayesian structure
learning, along with its variational inference training procedures and an example
application. Section 2 described DisCoPyro's mathematical foundations in category theory, operad theory, and variational Bayesian inference. Section 3 showed
DisCoPyro to be competitive against other models on a challenge dataset.

As Lake [15] suggested, (deep) probabilistic programs can model human
intelligence across more domains than handwritten characters. Beyond programs, neural network architectures, or triangulable manifolds, investigators

have applied operads and SMCs to chemical reaction networks, natural language processing, and the systematicity of human intelligence [3, 18]. This broad variety of applications motivates our interest in representing the problems a generally intelligent agent must solve in terms of operadic structures, and learning those structures jointly with their contents from data.

Acknowledgements. The authors would like to thank the anonymous reviewers for their constructive feedback and encouragement. This work was supported by the Japan Science and Technology Agency (JST JPMJMS2033) and National Science Foundation of the United States of America (NSF 2047253).

References

1. Ambrogioni, L., et al.: Automatic structured variational inference. In: Proc. AISTATS, pp. 676–684 (2021)
2. Bingham, E., et al.: Pyro: deep universal probabilistic programming. JMLR **20**, 973–978 (2019)
3. Bradley, T.D.: What is applied category theory? arXiv preprint arXiv:1809.05923 (2018)
4. Coecke, B., Sadrzadeh, M., Clark, S.: Mathematical foundations for a compositional distributional model of meaning. arXiv preprint arXiv:1003.4394 (2010)
5. Feinman, R., Lake, B.M.: Learning task-general representations with generative neuro-symbolic modeling. In: Proc. ICLR (2021)
6. de Felice, G., Toumi, A., Coecke, B.: DisCoPy: monoidal categories in python. In: Applied Category Theory Conference, pp. 1–20. EPTCS (2020). http://arxiv.org/abs/2005.02975arXiv: 2005.02975
7. Fong, B., Spivak, D.I.: Seven Sketches in Compositionality: An Invitation to Applied Category Theory. Cambridge University Press, Cambridge (2019)
8. Fritz, T.: A synthetic approach to Markov kernels, conditional independence and theorems on sufficient statistics. Adv. Math. **370**, 107239 (2020)
9. He, J., et al.: Variational autoencoders with jointly optimized latent dependency structure. In: Proc. ICLR 2019, pp. 1–16 (2019)
10. Hermida, C., Makkaiy, M., Power, J.: Higher dimensional multigraphs. In: Proceedings - Symposium on Logic in Computer Science, pp. 199–206 (1998)
11. Hewitt, L.B., et al.: The variational homoencoder: learning to learn high capacity generative models from few examples. Proc. UAI **2018**, 988–997 (2018)
12. Kingma, D.P., Welling, M.: Auto-encoding variational bayes. arXiv preprint arXiv:1312.6114 (2013)
13. Kirsch, L., Kunze, J., Barber, D.: Modular networks: learning to decompose neural computation. In: Proc. NeurIPS 2018, pp. 2408–2418 (2018)
14. Lake, B.M., Salakhutdinov, R., Tenenbaum, J.B.: The Omniglot challenge: a 3-year progress report. Curr. Opin. Behav. Sci. **29**, 97–104 (2019)
15. Lake, B.M., Ullman, T.D., Tenenbaum, J.B., Gershman, S.J.: Building machines that learn and think like people. Behav. Brain Sci. **40**, e253 (2017)
16. Latouche, G., Ramaswami, V.: Introduction to matrix analytic methods in stochastic modeling. In: Society for Industrial and Applied Mathematics (1999)
17. Milnor, J.: On spaces having the homotopy type of CW-complex. Trans. Am. Math. Soc. **90**, 272–280 (1959)

18. Phillips, S., Wilson, W.H.: Categorial compositionality: a category theory explanation for the systematicity of human cognition. PLoS Comput. Biol. **6**, e1000858 (2010)
19. Rezende, D.J., et al.: One-shot generalization in deep generative models. In: International Conference on Machine Learning, vol. 48 (2016)
20. Rosenbaum, C., Klinger, T., Riemer, M.: Routing networks: adaptive selection of non-linear functions for multi-task learning. In: Proc. ICLR 2018, pp. 1–10 (2018)
21. Shiebler, D., Gavranović, B., Wilson, P.: Category theory in machine learning. In: Proc. ACT 2021 (2021)
22. Spivak, D.I.: The operad of wiring diagrams: formalizing a graphical language for databases, recursion, and plug-and-play circuits (2013). arxiv: 1305.0297
23. Webb, S., et al.: Faithful inversion of generative models for effective amortized inference. In: Proc. NIPS 2018, pp. 3074–3084 (2018)
24. Zhao, S., Song, J., Ermon, S.: Learning hierarchical features from generative models. In: International Conference on Machine Learning (2017)

ADAM: A Prototype of Hierarchical Neuro-Symbolic AGI

Sergey Shumsky$^{(\boxtimes)}$ and Oleg Baskov

Moscow Institute of Physics and Technology,
Dolgoprudny 141701, Russian Federation
serge.shumsky@gmail.com
https://mipt.ru/

Abstract. Intelligent agents are characterized primarily by their far-sighted expedient behavior. We present a working prototype of an intelligent agent (ADAM) based on a novel hierarchical neuro-symbolic architecture (Deep Control) for deep reinforcement learning with a potentially unlimited planning horizon. The control parameters form a hierarchy of formal languages, where higher-level alphabets contain the semantic meanings of lower-level vocabularies.

Keywords: Artificial General Intelligence · Hierarchical reinforcement learning · Neuro-symbolic architecture

1 Introduction

Artificial General Intelligence (AGI) aims to create intelligent agents capable of planning expedient behavior. The larger the planning horizon, the stronger the intelligence of agents. We present an early AGI prototype with a new hierarchical neuro-symbolic architecture in which the planning horizon increases exponentially with the number of levels. The article is structured as follows.

Section 2 introduces our neuro-symbolic approach and formulates reinforcement learning (RL) as a search for the best sequences of discrete *cognitive states* that maximize reward over some planning horizon. We extend the original alphabet of cognitive states with such sequences, called *mental states*, thus forming a vocabulary of words of some formal *mental language*, defined by its grammar rules. The semantic meaning of these words is determined by the corresponding Markov matrix learned from experience. Such a language allows an intelligent agent to plan its behavior several steps ahead.

To achieve a potentially unlimited planning horizon without a combinatorial explosion, we propose a hierarchical neuro-symbolic architecture Deep Control, in which the cognitive states of the upper levels represent the semantic meaning of the mental states of the lower ones.

Section 3 presents an early AGI prototype ADAM, based on the proposed architecture. It takes a closer look at the proposed architecture, describing its main components and how they interact with each other.

P. Hammer et al. (Eds.): AGI 2023, LNAI 13921, pp. 255–264, 2023.
https://doi.org/10.1007/978-3-031-33469-6_26

Section 4 compares the current work with alternate approaches to AGI and the final Sect. 5 concludes the paper.

2   Deep Control: The Architecture of Intelligence

This section shows that strong AGI with unlimited planning horizon implies hierarchical RL and proposes a Deep Control architecture as a stack of elementary controllers similar to the stack of elementary mappings in deep neural networks.

2.1   Reinforcement Learning as a Mental Language

In RL the goal of an agent is to maximize the total reward it can receive for a given planning horizon T. Let the agent's mind be characterized by a set of discrete *mental states* $\{\mathbf{m}\}$ that depend on its sensors and actuators. (For example: "turn right to see the park", "turn left to see the grocery store", etc.) Maximal total reward starting from the given mental state $\mathbf{m}^t$ with the expected reward $R(\mathbf{m}^t)$ learned from experience and following the optimal *strategy* π is defined by the *value function*:

$$Q(\mathbf{m}^t) = R(\mathbf{m}^t) + \max_{\pi} \sum_{\tau=1}^{T-1} \sum_{\mathbf{m}^{t+\tau}} R(\mathbf{m}^{t+\tau}) p_{\pi}(\mathbf{m}^{t+\tau}|\mathbf{m}^t). \tag{1}$$

Here we constrain our agent's mind to a Markov Decision Process (MDP), where:

$$p_{\pi}(\mathbf{m}^{t+\tau}|\mathbf{m}^t) = \sum_{\mathbf{m}^{t+\tau-1}} p_{\pi}(\mathbf{m}^{t+\tau}|\mathbf{m}^{t+\tau-1}) p_{\pi}(\mathbf{m}^{t+\tau-1}|\mathbf{m}^t). \tag{2}$$

The optimal deterministic strategy π^* of such an agent is:

$$\tilde{\mathbf{m}}^t = \arg\max_{\mathbf{m}^t} Q(\mathbf{m}^t) p_{\pi^*}(\mathbf{m}^t|\mathbf{m}^{t-1}). \tag{3}$$

Since the actual mental state $\mathbf{m}^t$ does not in general coincide with the expected one $\tilde{\mathbf{m}}^t$, but definitely depends on it, the transition probabilities $p_{\pi}(\mathbf{m}^t|\mathbf{m}^{t-1})$ depend on the decision process and thus – on the value function. Value function (1) in its turn depends on the transition probabilities. This feedback makes it difficult to calculate the value function explicitly. Fortunately one can learn it from experience making use of a Bellman equation following from (1, 2):

$$Q(\mathbf{m}^t) = R(\mathbf{m}^t) + \gamma \max_{\mathbf{m}^{t+1}} p_{\pi^*}(\mathbf{m}^{t+1}|\mathbf{m}^t) Q(\mathbf{m}^{t+1}), \tag{4}$$

with a discount parameter $\gamma = (T-1)/T$. For a true Q-function, the left and right sides of (4) must be equal. Thus, the solution can be found using the following iterative procedure:

$$Q(\mathbf{m}^t) \leftarrow Q(\mathbf{m}^t) + \alpha(t) \left[R(\mathbf{m}^t) + \gamma \max_{\mathbf{m}^{t+1}} p_{\pi}(\mathbf{m}^{t+1}|\mathbf{m}^t) Q(\mathbf{m}^{t+1}) - Q(\mathbf{m}^t) \right] \tag{5}$$

with (gradually reducing) learning rate $\alpha(t) \ll 1$. The reward and transition models are also updated iteratively based on real data.

Such *Q-learning* is attractive because of its simplicity. However, it is extremely inefficient for large planning horizons. The optimal Q-learning algorithm is proved to converge in $O(T^3)$ iterations [23]. This cubic dependence is a significant limitation. It takes millions of iterations to learn how to achieve a goal on a horizon of 100 time steps.

That is why we limit the planning horizon to a modest $T \lesssim 10$ to find $Q(\mathbf{m})$ in just a few hundred iterations, but allow the formation of new mental states as the most frequent combinations of already known ones. These combinations are implicitly encoded in the transition matrix $p_\pi(\mathbf{m}'|\mathbf{m})$. To find them explicitly, we expand the original mental alphabet $\{\mathbf{m}^0\} \equiv \{\mathbf{s}\}$ along with the appropriate expansion of the transition matrix.

Namely, transition probabilities are defined by the number of observations of successive state pairs $C_{\mathbf{mm}'}$:

$$p_\pi(\mathbf{m}'|\mathbf{m}) = C_{\mathbf{mm}'} / \sum_{\mathbf{m}'} C_{\mathbf{mm}'}. \tag{6}$$

Mental states are found recursively during Q-learning by merging the most frequently occurring pairs of existing ones: when $C_{\mathbf{m}'\mathbf{m}''}$ exceeds a certain threshold, a new mental state is defined as the concatenation of the corresponding pair:

$$\mathbf{m} \leftarrow \mathbf{m}'\mathbf{m}'', \quad C_{\mathbf{m}'\mathbf{m}''} > C_0. \tag{7}$$

These rules define a formal language – the set of all valid strings of *cognitive states* $\mathbf{s}$ (*characters* of that language): $\{\mathbf{m}\} = \{\mathbf{s}^1 \ldots \mathbf{s}^\tau\}$. We'll call this set *mental language*.

The rules of mental language (7) allow the agent to represent the input sequence of cognitive states as a shorter sequence of their typical combinations by construction of a binary tree of merging (*parsing*). Such an agent is capable of perceiving and predicting temporal structures. Indeed, the optimal strategy (3) can now choose sequences of action-states. This allows the agent to plan its behavior several steps ahead even in the current MDP setting. (For example: "turn right to see the park, then go for a morning jog, then head back home".)

The view of reinforcement learning described above relates the latter to traditional logic-based AI. In fact, mental language (7), together with the decision-making process (3), endows the agent with formal *mental logic* – the ability to deduce new mental states as logical consequences of previous ones. Reinforcement learning improves the predictive and logical abilities of an agent.

Logical thinking is closely related to the semantics of the language: both are determined by transition probabilities. Indeed the semantic meaning of words in the language is determined by the context in which they appear – recall Wittgenstein's famous "meaning is use". In MDP setting semantics depends on the transition probabilities $p_\pi(\mathbf{m}'|\mathbf{m})$ and $p'_\pi(\mathbf{m}|\mathbf{m}')$, defined by normalized rows and columns of the same empirical matrix $C_{\mathbf{mm}'}$. That is, each mental state has a corresponding *semantic vector* $\mathbf{x_m} = p_\pi(\ldots|\mathbf{m})p'_\pi(\ldots|\mathbf{m})$ – concatenation of right and left context probabilities.

'Synonymic' mental states with similar semantic vectors appear interchangeably in similar situations and can be considered as different implementations of the same step of some higher level plan, formulated in a more abstract *meta-language*, which can also be learned as described above. In fact, the agent can learn the hierarchy of metalanguages, thus paving the way for AGI. We called this architecture Deep Control [20].

2.2   Deep Control: Scale-Free Thinking

In the so-called Deep RL, the function $Q(a|s)$, the value of the action a in state s, is represented by a deep neural network. That is, in Deep RL, the hierarchy of neural representations is used to determine only the agent's next step. In order to plan behavior a few steps ahead, one needs to generate a bunch of fairly good trajectories and choose the best one, for example, using a Monte Carlo Tree Search, as in AlphaZero, MuZero and the like. This leads to combinatorial explosion, that limits the planning horizon of modern Deep RL, as shown in Fig. 1 (left).

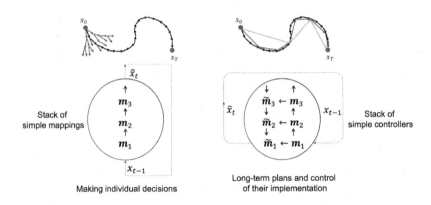

Fig. 1. Deep RL (left) uses neural networks for individual decision making, augmented by Monte Carlo Tree Search. Deep Control (right) maintains a hierarchy of plans inscribed in each other.

On the contrary, in Deep Control mental states form a hierarchy of nested short-term plans ($\mathbf{m}_l \rightarrow \tilde{\mathbf{m}}_l$), where each step of the higher-level plan corresponds to a set of its possible realizations one level lower. Each hierarchical level looks only one mental state ahead using its Markov probability matrix $p(\mathbf{m}'_l|\mathbf{m}_l)$, thus avoiding combinatorial problems.

A hierarchy of mental states and their supposed successors form a hierarchy of plans inscribed in each other as illustrated in Fig. 1 (right). As soon as enough training data accumulates at the top level, the next level is generated, which controls the behavior on an even larger time scale. With a top-level planning horizon growing exponentially with the number of levels, Deep Control can create extremely far-sighted plans without a combinatorial explosion.

3   ADAM: Implementing Intelligence

This section discusses Deep Control in more detail and presents an early AGI prototype ADAM (Adaptive Deep Autonomous Machine) solving the hierarchical RL problem with a potentially unlimited planning horizon.

3.1   ADAM's Design

The Deep Control architecture implements a stack of simple controllers that control behavior across different timescales. All layers are similar, taking as an input analogue representation of current mental state from the previous layer and providing a prediction of the next mental states, corresponding to the proposed plan of behavior as illustrated in Fig. 2.

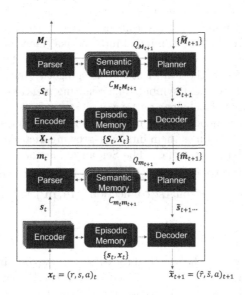

Fig. 2. Hierarchical neuro-symbolic architecture of ADAM.

The first layer interacts with the world. It operates with sensorimotor vectors, its output being the proposed action and the predicted next sensory value. As is customary in RL, the sensorimotor vector contains a special reinforcement component r, signaling how well ADAM is doing its job. Each layer operates with its own discrete set of mental states representing the most valuable chains of discrete symbols from the layer's alphabet: $\mathbf{m}_l = \mathbf{s}_l^1 \ldots \mathbf{s}_l^\tau$ ($\tau \leq T$). In the rest of this section, we describe ADAM's modules and the interaction between its hierarchical levels.

Central to Deep Control is the **Semantic memory** $C_{mm'}$ counting observations of consecutive pairs of mental states. Semantic memory allows to: (i) predict the next mental state to plan behavior: $\mathbf{m} \rightarrow \tilde{\mathbf{m}}$, and (ii) encode the current mental state as input to the next layer: $\mathbf{m} \rightarrow \mathbf{x_m}$.

The semantic encoding of mental states is similar to the semantic representation of words in NLP [12]. Namely, the semantic vector of a mental state $\mathbf{m}$ determines in what contexts the latter appears. Semantic vector $\mathbf{x_m}$ is composed of corresponding normalized row and column of the Semantic memory matrix.

The **Encoder** maps the analog input vector $\mathbf{x}$ to discrete multidimensional symbol $\mathbf{s}$ representing cognitive state: $\mathbf{x} \rightarrow \mathbf{s} = (s_1, \ldots, s_H)$, using H different clusterings of the input space, each of which divides the input space into K different clusters. The number of unique discrete codes labeling different regions of the input space is K^H. We say that such an Encoder have H *heads*, the latter playing the same role, as in modern Transformer neural networks – each head pays attention to a different aspect of the data.

The stream of symbols from the Encoder is fed onto the fixed-length stack of the **Parser**, where they are combined into chunks (mental states) using Byte Pair Encoding algorithm [6], recursively merging the most frequently occurring pairs of mental states in the Parser stack. Merging two mental states frees up space in the stack for the next symbol. The resulting mental states $\mathbf{m} = \mathbf{s}^1 \ldots \mathbf{s}^\tau$ represent typical ADAM behavior patterns.

Each head of the Encoder maps input vector into a character from its own *alphabet*. The Parser combines them into ever-growing *dictionary* of the most frequently occurring character strings. The Semantic memory $C^h_{m_h m'_h}$ increases its value each time the strings m_h and m'_h in the head h belong to the winning pair in the Parser stack with the strongest connection $c(\mathbf{m}, \mathbf{m}') = \sum_h \ln\left(1 + C^h_{m_h m'_h}\right)$:

$$C^h_{m_h m'_h} \leftarrow C^h_{m_h m'_h} + 1, \quad (h = 1, \ldots, H). \tag{8}$$

When some $C^h_{mm'}$ exceeds the specified threshold, a new combined string appears in the head's dictionary: $m_{new} \leftarrow mm'$. Gradually, the Parser learns to identify ever larger strings by recursively combining the most frequent pairs of shorter strings, starting with single characters.

The Parser recursively attempt to merge the winner pair in the Parser stack, updating statistics of the winning pair according to (8). In the case of a merge, the rewards of merged mental state are summed up and Parser is ready to process the next symbol. If the merge is not possible because some of the combined strings do not yet exist in the heads dictionaries, the leftmost mental state moves from the Parser stack to the Encoder of the next layer, thereby freeing up space for processing the next symbol.

Each act of merging is accompanied by reinforcement learning: updating observation counter $n^h(m_h)$, average reward $R^h(m_h)$ and value function $Q^h(m_h)$

of the newly formed mental state $\mathbf{m}$ and all others to the left of it. Using SARSA algorithm for a pair of consecutive mental states $(\mathbf{m}, \mathbf{m}')$, we get:

$$n(\mathbf{m}) \leftarrow n(\mathbf{m}) + 1,$$
$$R(\mathbf{m}) \leftarrow R(\mathbf{m}) + [r(\mathbf{m}) - R(\mathbf{m})]/n(\mathbf{m}),$$
$$Q(\mathbf{m}) \leftarrow Q(\mathbf{m}) + \alpha\,[r(\mathbf{m}) + \gamma Q(\mathbf{m}') - Q(\mathbf{m})],$$

with vector notation for parallel updates in all heads.

The **Planner** aims to propose the optimal course of action in the given circumstances, i.e. predict the optimal next mental state $\mathbf{m} \rightarrow \tilde{\mathbf{m}}$. Since circumstances are constantly changing, previous plans are also subject to constant adjustment.

The development and correction of plans proceeds from top to bottom – from the most general intentions to more and more detailed plans. The main problem is to harmonize the plans of different levels. To this end Planners of all levels use the same algorithm. Namely, each time the Parser updates its stack, the Planner:

- replenishes its stack of plans (if needed);
- validates these plans against the new state of the Parser stack;
- selects valid plan with the highest expected value for execution.

The top-level Planner replenishes its stack with new plans when a new mental state $\mathbf{m}$ appears in its Parser stack. Lower level Planners receive plans for execution through higher level Decoders.

Since a new symbol appears in the Parser stack at each step of its work, all previous plans that do not correspond to this symbol lose their relevance, as they do not correspond to the current state of affairs. Accordingly, these plans are eliminated during the validation process, and only plans that are relevant in the current situation survive.

Finally, the actual plan with the highest value is selected, which is passed for execution to the lower level. This way of hierarchical planning combines the ability to plan for a (very) long period of time and adapt such far-reaching plans to constantly changing conditions.

The **Decoder** translates the plan selected by the Planner to a lower layer for execution. Fast decoding uses a look-up memory of all low-level implementations for all known mental states of the current level, being different realizations of the same plan. If fast decoding fails (in an unknown situation), the decoder chooses the plan for which the maximum number of heads voted.

The **Episodic memory** is used by the Decoder. At the top level it is also used to build the next layer when it has collected enough data for the clustering algorithm.

3.2 ADAM's Prospects

The ADAM project started in early 2020. To date, the preliminary version of ADAM has been developed. The source code is in fast and easy-to-develop

Julia language. The single layer version has been tested on classic RL problems (MountainCar, CartPole, etc.). We are now testing multi-layered version by training language models, since we can interpret the corresponding language structures: the first layer learns words as chains of characters, the second layer learns phrases, the third layer – sentences, and so on. The results will be presented in a separate article.

However it is clear that our language models are much cheaper, than that based on deep neural networks. Namely, ADAM on a single CPU learns language at a rate of about 1 GB/hour regardless of the number of layers. Indeed, learning each next layer is several times faster, than the previous one, since the size of training set shrinks with each hierarchical level. (The number of words in a data set is several times less than the number of characters, etc.). Thus, ADAM can master Wikipedia in just one day and the GPT-3 training set of 1,2 TB – in 50 days without any supercomputing power, due to its neuro-symbolic architecture (manipulating symbols, rather than multidimensional vectors).

Moreover, having a value function at the heart of its architecture, ADAM can easily learn conversational behavior, unlike ChatGPT and its ilk, which use reinforcement learning based on human feedback to fine-tune pretrained large language models.

4   Related Work

Hierarchical architecture has been widely discussed as a proposed brain model by Karl Friston with co-authors [5,15,16]. Their model assumes that each cognitive state of a higher hierarchical level originates a trajectory of cognitive states of a lower level, generated by the corresponding Markov matrix. Our approach differs in that we use a transition matrix between mental states rather than cognitive states. That is, we learn transitions between trajectories, and not between individual states. We are also more focused on finding practical learning algorithms for AGI.

Such a practical approach is typical for Deep RL, in particular, for Hierarchical RL. The problem here is that deep neural networks only solve part of the problem, namely Q-function approximation. On the contrary, Deep Control solves the problem of predictive control in its entirety with the same basic approach: layers of weak learners. The difference is that deep neural networks learn a hierarchy of increasingly abstract representations for data approximation, while Deep Control learns a hierarchy of increasingly abstract control parameters for predictive control. The resulting multi-layer controller can handle increasingly complex behavior as the number of layers increases.

Although Hierarchical RL has not yet been solved, many such attempts have been made, including [1–4,22] to name just a few. See [14] for comprehensive review. However, in practical terms, the vast majority of work is limited to only two levels of hierarchy, since even in two-level systems there are a lot of difficulties. Simultaneous training of layers turns out to be unstable, and it takes a lot of effort to eliminate these instabilities [11,13,24].

The closest neural network analogue of Deep Control seems to be the Feynman machine [10]. The latter also solves the predictive control problem using hierarchical design with bidirectional information flow and local learning rules. Deep Control differs in that it uses a neuro-symbolic approach rather than a purely analog one. It allows Deep Control to model symbolic thinking and language acquisition in addition to behavior control [19,21].

The proposed symbolic thinking is easy to interpret: at any given moment, each layer keeps track of the current context $\mathbf{m}_l$ and executes a certain plan $\tilde{\mathbf{m}}_l$, represented by the corresponding mental state from its dictionary. The mental states $\mathbf{m}_l$ mapped to the same cognitive state of the higher level $\mathbf{s}_{l+1}$ are different realizations of a certain step of the next layer's plan. In this respect, Deep Control resembles traditional rule-based cognitive architectures that mimic symbolic thinking [7–9,17]. But the latter are incapable of learning hierarchical planning. According to Stuart Russell: "At present all existing methods for hierarchical planning rely on a human-generated hierarchy of abstract and concrete actions. We do not yet understand how such hierarchies can be learned from experience" [18]. Deep Control offers just that – to learn such hierarchies from experience.

5 Conclusion

This paper presents a prototype of a novel hierarchical neuro-symbolic AGI architecture.

We consider reinforcement learning as the construction of a formal language whose rules define useful behavior as a combination of the basic symbols of the language. The semantics of this language makes it possible to define a metalanguage and, thus, a whole hierarchy of metalanguages that provide the hierarchical control of complex adaptive behavior. Such a hierarchical neuro-symbolic architecture (Deep Control) models the symbolic thinking of rational intelligent agents, the hallmark of AGI.

We present an early prototype of neuro-symbolic AGI (ADAM) that learns to plan and control expedient behavior with an ever-increasing number of hierarchical levels and an exponentially growing planning horizon.

References

1. Bakker, B., Schmidhuber, J., et al.: Hierarchical reinforcement learning based on subgoal discovery and subpolicy specialization. In: Proceedings of the 8-th Conference on Intelligent Autonomous Systems, pp. 438–445 (2004)
2. Barto, A.G., Mahadevan, S.: Recent advances in hierarchical reinforcement learning. Discret. Event Dyn. Syst. **13**(1–2), 41–77 (2003)
3. Botvinick, M.M.: Hierarchical reinforcement learning and decision making. Curr. Opin. Neurobiol. **22**(6), 956–962 (2012)
4. Dieterich, T.G., et al.: The MAXQ method for hierarchical reinforcement learning. In: ICML, vol. 98, pp. 118–126 (1998)

5. Friston, K.J., Parr, T., Yufik, Y., Sajid, N., Price, C.J., Holmes, E.: Generative models, linguistic communication and active inference. Neurosci. Biobehav. Rev. **118**, 42–64 (2020)
6. Gage, P.: A new algorithm for data compression. C Users J. **12**(2), 23–38 (1994)
7. Kotseruba, I., Tsotsos, J.K.: 40 years of cognitive architectures: core cognitive abilities and practical applications. Artif. Intell. Rev. **53**(1), 17–94 (2020)
8. Laird, J.E., Lebiere, C., Rosenbloom, P.S.: A standard model of the mind: toward a common computational framework across artificial intelligence, cognitive science, neuroscience, and robotics. AI Mag. **38**(4), 13–26 (2017)
9. Langley, P., Laird, J.E., Rogers, S.: Cognitive architectures: research issues and challenges. Cogn. Syst. Res. **10**(2), 141–160 (2009)
10. Laukien, E., Crowder, R., Byrne, F.: Feynman machine: the universal dynamical systems computer (2016). arXiv preprint arXiv:1609.03971
11. Levy, A., Platt, R., Saenko, K.: Hierarchical reinforcement learning with hindsight (2018). arXiv preprint arXiv:1805.08180
12. Levy, O., Goldberg, Y.: Neural word embedding as implicit matrix factorization. In: Advances in Neural Information Processing Systems, pp. 2177–2185 (2014)
13. Nachum, O., Gu, S.S., Lee, H., Levine, S.: Data-efficient hierarchical reinforcement learning. Adv. Neural Inf. Process. Syst. **31**, 3307–3317 (2018)
14. Pateria, S., Subagdja, B., Tan, A.H., Quek, C.: Hierarchical reinforcement learning: a comprehensive survey. ACM Comput. Surv. (CSUR) **54**(5), 1–35 (2021)
15. Pezzulo, G., Parr, T., Friston, K.: The evolution of brain architectures for predictive coding and active inference. Philos. Trans. R. Soc. B **377**(1844), 20200531 (2022)
16. Pezzulo, G., Rigoli, F., Friston, K.J.: Hierarchical active inference: a theory of motivated control. Trends Cogn. Sci. **22**(4), 294–306 (2018)
17. Ritter, F.E., Tehranchi, F., Oury, J.D.: ACT-R: a cognitive architecture for modeling cognition. Wiley Interdiscip. Rev. Cogn. Sci. **10**(3), e1488 (2019)
18. Russell, S.: Human compatible: artificial intelligence and the problem of control. Penguin (2019)
19. Shumskii, S.: ADAM: a model of artificial psyche. Autom. Remote Control **83**(6), 847–856 (2022). https://doi.org/10.1134/S0005117922060030
20. Shumsky, S.: Machine Intelligence. Essays on the theory of machine learning and artificial intelligence. RIOR (2019). (in Russian). https://doi.org/10.29039/02011-1
21. Shumsky, S.: Scalable natural language understanding: from scratch, on the fly. In: 2018 International Conference on Artificial Intelligence Applications and Innovations (IC-AIAI), pp. 73–74. IEEE (2018). https://doi.org/10.1109/IC-AIAI.2018.8674432
22. Vezhnevets, A.S., et al.: Feudal networks for hierarchical reinforcement learning. In: International Conference on Machine Learning, pp. 3540–3549. PMLR (2017)
23. Wainwright, M.J.: Variance-reduced q-learning is minimax optimal (2019). arXiv preprint arXiv:1906.04697
24. Wang, R., Yu, R., An, B., Rabinovich, Z.: I^{2}HRL: interactive influence-based hierarchical reinforcement learning. In: Proceedings of the Twenty-Ninth International Conference on International Joint Conferences on Artificial Intelligence, pp. 3131–3138 (2021)

Electronic Education Machine AGI-EEdu

Nihad Subasic[(✉)] [iD]

Department of Machine Design, Mechatronics, KTH Royal Institute of Technology,
The School of Industrial Technology and Management, Stockholm, Sweden
subasic@kth.se
https://www.kth.se/profile/subasic/

Abstract. This project is part of the digitization of engineering education at the Royal Institute of Technology (KTH). The digitization process of the observed undergraduate course in electrical engineering so far allows students to use the Learning Management System (LMS) to find course literature and notes, recorded lectures, theoretical exercises in the form of quizzes, and online interactive calculation exercises with built-in feedback for each question. What remains to be solved is the human-type contact that can answer a student's question, for example: "How am I doing in the course?". Usually, an experienced teacher would be able to answer that question with his own predictions.

The purpose of this project is to use AGI technology to construct a software solution that, by adapting to the environment, i.e. the existing LMS, with insufficient knowledge and resources about the future, can provide a qualified prediction about the student's future performance. That solution, here with the working name "AGI-EEdu", would get to know each student in the course and (with the help of data from students' activities in the LMS, as well as the other data based on aggregated statistical data from previous exam) could provide unique answers and advice to each student in real time throughout the course.

Keywords: Artificial General Intelligence (AGI) · Non-Axiomatic Reasoning System (NARS) · Narsese language · Möbius Courseware (MCW)

1 Introduction

Research on Artificial General Intelligence (AGI) is one of the latest scientific fields. The most developed model of intelligence is the human brain, and it is natural that many psychologists were interested in research on intelligence from the very beginning. Several authors (among others [2]) refer to a 1956 summer conference at Dartmouth College in Hanover, New Hampshire, USA, as the start of the new science [8], where one of organizers, John McCarthy, defined Artificial Intelligence (AI) as *"the science and engineering of making intelligent machines"* [7].

This project is about constructing an intelligent machine based on AGI technology to be applied in undergraduate electro courses. The machine (called here

© The Author(s), under exclusive license to Springer Nature Switzerland AG 2023
P. Hammer et al. (Eds.): AGI 2023, LNAI 13921, pp. 265–275, 2023.
https://doi.org/10.1007/978-3-031-33469-6_27

"Electronic Education Machine AGI-EEdu") would be similar to a normal chatbot but would go a step further and integrate with the existing Learning Management System (LMS) Canvas and Möbius Courseware (MCW). AGI-EEdu would get to know each student, follow their progress and be ready to answer all their questions, even those about future individual results.

2 Theoretical Background

Scientists have always been fascinated by intelligence, the human brain, and the way it works. This question is complex and it is natural that the research area and the prevailing culture influences the researchers' way of thinking. The summer conference at Dartmouth College collected leading scientists from different fields, and they attempted to define the term Artificial Intelligence. [8]

2.1 A New Science Has Been Born

Alan Turing is considered to be the first pioneer in modern times who defined the theoretical framework for using computers (actually, calculating machines) to construct a machine that could function in the same way as human intelligence. [1] Inspired by his work, Allen Newel Global and Simon Herbert [9] tried to program a General Problem Solver (GPS) and the new field of science named by John McCarthy as Artificial Intelligence was established. From the very beginning, attempts were made to simulate the human brain (itself not well explored at that time) with a calculator. This attempt required competence from different scientific fields: psychologists were expected to describe how humans think, neuro-scientists how a human brain works, and hardware and software engineers to describe a digital machine that could imitate a human brain.

2.2 About Theory of Intelligence

Many researchers from different fields work on AGI and one continuing problem is a difficulty to agree on a definition of the theory of AGI [14]. On the other hand a "thinking machine" could be constructed only by hardware and software engineers in collaboration. AI was from the beginning an interdisciplinary challenge and to define a theory of intelligence was not at all an easy task. Two main group of researchers have been more or less established. The first see AI as a copy of the human brain, the second see AI as a programmable digital machine capable to store and manage data in proper software.

Wang compares this situation with Rudolf Carnap who had a similar problem when trying to clarify the concept of probability in the middle of the last century. [12] A long time after that, we still have certain challenges regarding the definition of probability theory, with several different definitions or views on definitions accepted nowadays (Bayesian, Frequentist interpretation etc.), whereby there exists the commonly accepted formalization of probability spaces in mathematics, with its well-known axioms.

Several synonyms like "strong AI", "hard AI", "real AI" have established themselves in published scientific articles due to the researchers' different backgrounds and different views on the issue. McCarthy wrote in [7] about human-level AI. Despite different designations of AGI, different researchers do agree on the common description of the basic principles of the theory of AI in the literature, with Wang describing it as *"The common thesis behind these terms is the believe that intelligence is a unified mechanism that should be described and developed as a whole, independent of any application domain."* [12]

3   Research Questions

Like other technical solutions, different AI-based solutions from Google, chatbots and even specialized multi-agent systems are spreading within higher education with different tasks and aims. [4] I am aware of risks and suspicion towards everything new [3] and in this investigation, I will focus on the following questions:

RQ 1. How could AGI be used in the development process of undergraduate electrical courses?
RQ 2. How could a continuous prediction of student performance during the course be defined by using Narsese language?

4   Project - "AGI-EEdu" Machine

Wang's definition of intelligence, which has been defined already in his PhD thesis in the 90s, is that *"Intelligence is the principle of adapting to the environment while working with insufficient knowledge and resources."* [13] In this project, the reliable facts from an ongoing course have been used to predict knowledge that is not known but that could contribute to more students passing the ongoing course.

4.1   AGI-EEdu's Main Task

AGI-EEdu machine will first learn some well-known facts about the ongoing course and students activities in the course's Canvas room. Secondly the AGI-EEdu will get information from *"the insufficient knowledge field"* and build a pattern of student activities inside the course's Canvas room.

The idea for the project is based on a prediction machine which could help students to predict their course grade in undergraduate electro-technique courses. Students sometimes feel that exam questions are "harder" than exercise questions during the course. Teachers sometimes feel that the previous generation of students was much better. All students are keen to know how things are going for them during the course and how "hard" the final exam will be.

Neither the students nor the teachers have a tool to measure their feelings or a way to know anything about the future. There is only statistics data based on the results of the previous generations of students, which is not always reliable for the prediction of future students' results in the final exam, but it can provide good indicators.

4.2   Statistical Data from Möbius MCW

The course material in the observed electro-courses is completely digitized and is available through LMS Canvas and the embedded software Möbius Courseware (MCW) in which the online interactive exercises and examination are constructed. [11]

A "Question" is the smallest part which can be constructed in Möbius MCW. The constructed questions can be combined in two modes - an exercise mode allowing students to receive hints and teacher feedback, and an examination mode with no help available. How Möbius MCW has been used in the actual courses has been explained in this interview [10].

Each question constructed in Möbius MCW is equipped by detailed statistical data, how many previous students answered the question correctly (partly or fully), The statistical data is automatically updated for each new use of the question, Fig. 1. This data can be interpreted as how "hard" each question is.

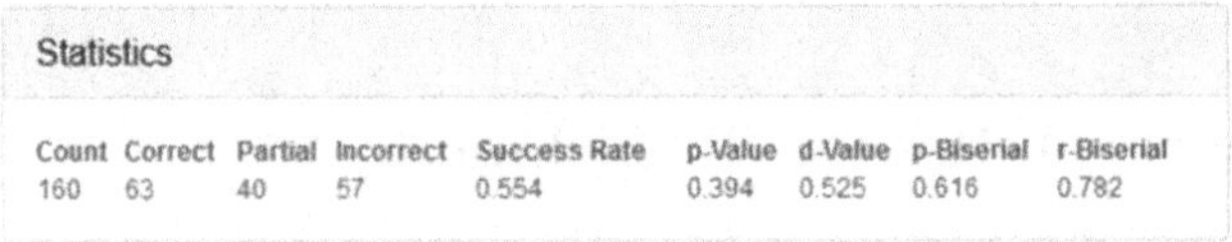

Statistics

Count	Correct	Partial	Incorrect	Success Rate	p-Value	d-Value	p-Biserial	r-Biserial
160	63	40	57	0.554	0.394	0.525	0.616	0.782

Fig. 1. Statistics for one question in Möbius MCW

Each exercise and exam consists of several questions, with respective statistical data generated for each exercise and exam. This data can be learned by the machine as facts and the respective variables can be connected to the machine and update the machine with new facts in real time. Both practice exercises and the final exam are constructed from several Möbius MCW questions, and the statistical data at practice level or exam level will be grounds for AGI-EEdu machine's predictions about each individual student's result.

Since the observed electro courses are digitized and all exercises are constructed in the same environment as the final exam, students' performance as shown in Fig. 2 can be used as input in real time.

VIL22 3 Växelström

Score:	Duration:	9 days 19 hrs 53 min
34.75/40.0	Started:	11/9/22 4:28:40 PM CET
	Finished:	11/19/22 12:21:54 PM CET

Fig. 2. Result of one student in a Möbius MCW exercise "VIL22 3 Växelström"

The interactive exercises of digitized course material consist of three optional and two compulsory interactive tasks, all constructed in Möbius MCW. In LMS Canvas, students can find pdf files with a book of theory and a book of calculating study cases, several videos and quizzes, all shown in Fig. 3. The digital course material is multifaceted and each form has at least one educational goal to fulfil. All course materials can be accessed from any electronic gadget Fig. 4 but we do not know which of these formats will help students the most Fig. 5.

Statistical data generated by Möbius MCW is reliable high-quality data because it provides a picture of student activities that directly affects students' knowledge or the course grades. Less reliable data is statistical data based on the activity of other students in LMS Canvas.

4.3   Statistical Data from LMS Canvas

All these known facts will be learned by AGI-EEdu machine and the machine will be able to predict a student's final result. Möbius MCW based exercises are available for students during the course and the collected statistics in Möbius Courseware (MCW) change in real-time based on the results from all students. All student activity during the course, be it in the LMS based digital course material or the Möbius MCW based interactive exercises, has an impact on the statistics of each question, and even on the predictions made by AGI-EEdu machine.   More correct answers will impact the prediction of higher scores on

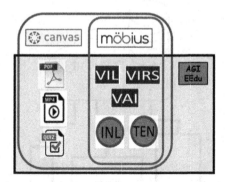

Fig. 3. AGI-EEdu machine will get input from all students activities

the final exam. The same technology could be used to find out about students' final grades. And since the input data comes directly from the current course, each student can influence their future results by increasing their activity in the course - thus the AGI-EEdu machine learns that the student in question has increased their activities.

AGI-EEdu machine and its prediction is expected to offer students a clearer picture of how hard the course is, and how their activities during the course can impact their result on the final exam. AGI-EEdu machine will be updated by statistical data describing both the whole class's activities and each student's activities in real time. The machine's prediction should be based on the actual results of all students who attend the same course and on each student's own performance. By using actual data we can impact students' activities in the course and students can see (even on smartphones or I-Pads Fig. 4) that they can impact the machine's predictions.

4.4   Methodology of the Project

As mentioned before, in Möbius MCW each question has quite detailed statistical data that shows how many students pass and how many of the partial questions asked were answered correctly. Each Möbius MCW exam question has four sub-questions and this statistical data is based on our use and collection of Möbius MCW data since the 2019–2020 academic year.

The input data will be taken from the databases of Möbius MCW as shown in Fig. 3 and the students will be able to impact predictions of the AGI-EEdu machine by their own activity in Möbius MCW exercises. AGI-EEdu machine will be embedded in LMS Canvas as well as Möbius MCW, and this technical solution will allow the machine to be constructed as an agent which behaves as if certain relevant events happened, as described in [5]. This tool will be built by using Non-Axiomatic Reasoning System (NARS).

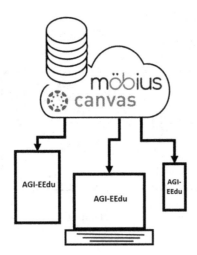

Fig. 4. AGI-EEdu machine will be updated in real time

4.5   Non-Axiomatic Reasoning System (NARS)

A Non-Axiomatic Reasoning System (NARS) consists of three parts:

- Language (Narsese)
- Non-Axiomatic Logic (NAL)
- Control mechanism

4.6   Narsese Language

Narsese is the representation language of NARS and it is a very useful tool to describe a task and related knowledge. Xiang at.al. presented an interesting project about an emotions model in NARS at the conference [6]. A similar task has been done in this AGI-EEdu project, where the prediction of students' final results is based on the results of the previous generation who took the same course, and the current students own results during the course.

In this project the constructed application will be able to continuously predict the students' results in real time during the course. The statistics data of the questions in Learning Management System (LMS) Canvas and Courseware Mobius (MCW) is based on the whole result of students' answers on all questions which students have done (or answered) as optional or mandatory assignments. The knowledge of the system is based on *beliefs* which are based on statistical facts on students' tasks, and *desires* which will be a student's wish to know the future courses-grade.

A descriptive theory starts with certain observations in the field [14] and we will use the three types of sentences in Narsese to describe the system in our LMS Canvas. The three types of sentences are following:

- Judgment - consisting of definitions of problems
- Goal - describing the wishes (wanted outcomes)
- Question - defining the tasks which are to be answered or solved

NAL-0: Binary Inheritance. During the 90s NAL-0 was called "Inheritance Logic" [13] and its idealised version of logic is based on simple deductive logic. First, we have to define the semantics of NAL and the smallest unit of Narsese is a "term".

NAL-1: Basic Syntax and Semantics. NAL-1 is the simplest non-axiomatic logic where we define and measure evidence for a statement. In this project we define that *test* belongs to the course and *student* belongs to the course, and by using the NAL semantic it would be written like this:

$$<tentamen \rightarrow \texttt{course}>$$
$$<student \rightarrow \texttt{course}>$$

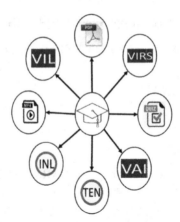

Fig. 5. In an AGI-EEdu machine all students have relation to all tasks

In the NAL-1 the *Atomic terms* will be defined and in this project will be useful to connect NAL-1 to the list of students who registered themselves to a specific course. In this level we use first-order reasoning described in [14].   A course includes three optional interactive Möbius MCW exercises (VIL, VIRS and VAI) and two compulsory tests (INL and TEN) constructed in the same tool. (Note, these abbreviations are based on the Swedish names, the details of which are not relevant here.) Möbius Courseware (MCW) has the statistics of the tasks included in the mentioned exercises and tests. This statistical data gives us a picture of how difficult it was to solve such tasks for previous students, and that data belongs to the course in the same way that the student belongs to the course.

$$<ovnVIL \rightarrow course>$$
$$<ovnVIRS \rightarrow course>$$
$$<ovnVAI \rightarrow course>$$
$$<ovnINL \rightarrow course>$$
$$<oldTEN \rightarrow course>$$

Students can also learn by watching videos or reading theory or solution proposals in pdf files, or by answering quizzes, but LMS Canvas does not offer a measurable value that could be assigned to the system. Here we trust that the system learns how long students spend on a screen showing mp4 or pdf files. Here we only allocate space in memory for any information about that time.

$$<timePDF \rightarrow course>$$
$$<timeMP4 \rightarrow course>$$
$$<timeQuiz \rightarrow course>$$

NAL-2: Derivative Copulas. We use the first layer of NARS, called NAL-1 to set formal inference rules between statements in NARS, and by using a formal language we represent our knowledge of the system. Here, in the second layer, NAL-2, we add grammar and inference rules. Description in each layer starts with an idealized form and we extend the model in each next step.

In NAL-2 to NAL-4 we declare compound terms:

$$< [(student) * (timePDF)] \rightarrow read > .fp = 0.2 \; \dots \; \text{(coming from LMS)}$$
$$< [(student) * (timeMP4)] \rightarrow watched > .fv = 0.4 \; \dots \; \text{(coming from LMS)}$$
$$< [(student) * (timeQuiz)] \rightarrow succed > .fq = 0.6 \; \dots \; \text{(coming from LMS)}$$

The values of functions fp, fv, fq will be extracted from the LMS Canvas in a similar way as for the value of statistical data for exercises constructed in Möbius Courseware (MCW). These functions describe students' activities based on pdf files, videos and quizzes which do not necessarily lead to development of students' knowledge. For example, a pdf file can be shown on the screen or downloaded without the student actually reading it, and such activities do not contribute to the student's development. On the other hand, the description of optional (VIL, VIRS and VAI) and mandatory exercises (INL and TEN) constructed in Möbius MCW are of higher value because it is based on students' calculations of real study cases. This statistical data will be extracted from Möbius MCW into NARS, and the following relationship established:

$$< [(\text{student}) * (ovnVIL)] \rightarrow read > .fvil = \; \text{(coming from MCW)}$$
$$< [(\text{student}) * (ovnVIRS)] \rightarrow watched > .fvirs = \text{(coming from MCW)}$$
$$< [(\text{student}) * (ovnVAI)] \rightarrow succed > .fvai = \; \text{(coming from MCW)}$$

4.7 NAL5 and NAL6 - Higher Order Terms

Every activity that a student does in the course must be noticed by AGI-EEdu machine in such a way that the system learns about it in real time.

Student activities like: "Student read a pdf." or "Student watched a video lesson." or "Student solved a quiz." can be defined in the following way:

$$< (*, \{student\}, pdf) \rightarrow \text{read}>.$$
$$< (*, \{student\}, mp4) \rightarrow \text{watch}>.$$
$$< (*, \{student\}, quiz) \rightarrow \text{solveQ}>.$$

4.8 Minimal Narsese Course Success Reasoning Example

The system watches all course interactions as events. The following is an example of how interactions in Möbius MCW can be represented as events in Narsese, which allows it to reason about how students can succeed in certain exams or quizzes:

```
//Student1 is a student
<{student1} --> student>.
//Lecture1 is a lecture
<{lecture1} --> lecture>.
//Quiz1 is a quiz
<{quiz1} --> quiz>.
//Student1 watched lecture 1
<({student1} * {lecture1}) --> watch>. :|:
//Student 1 succeeded in quiz1 with a success rate of 60%
<({student1} * {quiz1}) --> succeed>. :|: %0.6%

20

//How can someone succeed in quiz1?
<?1 =/> <({$1} * {quiz1}) --> succeed>>?
//By watching lecture1:
//Answer: <<({$1} * {lecture1}) --> watch> =/>
//         <({$1} * {quiz1}) --> succeed>>.
//         Truth: frequency=0.600000, confidence=0.282230


//Does watching lectures contribute to succeeding in quizzes?
<<({$1} * lecture) --> watch> =/> <({$1} * quiz) --> succeed>>?
//Yes, there is some evidence for that:
//Answer: <<({$1} * lecture) --> watch> =/>
//         <({$1} * quiz) --> succeed>>.
//         Truth: frequency=0.600000, confidence=0.12133
```

Acknowledgement. The author would like to acknowledge and give warmest thanks to Dr. Robert Johansson, Dr. Pei Wang and Dr. Patrick Hammer for providing us the wonderful opportunity to study Artificial General Intelligence in the course organised by Digital Futures at KTH in the fall of 2022.

The author would like to express special thanks to Dr. Patrick Hammer for generously sharing his knowledge of Narsese even after the course.

References

1. Turing, A.: His Work and Impact. Elsevier (2013). https://doi.org/10.1016/C2010-0-66380-2, https://linkinghub.elsevier.com/retrieve/pii/C20100663802
2. Anne Håkansson, Ronald Lee Hartung: Artificial Intelligence, Concepts, areas, techniques and applications. Studentlitterature, 1. edn. (2020). https://www.studentlitteratur.se/kurslitteratur/teknik-datorer-it-och-bygg/data-allmant/artificial-intelligence/
3. Brin, D.: Essential (mostly neglected) questions and answers about artificial intelligence. Neohelicon, December 2022. https://doi.org/10.1007/s11059-022-00656-8, https://link.springer.com/10.1007/s11059-022-00656-8

4. Churi, P.P., Joshi, S., Elhoseny, M., Omrane, A.: Artificial Intelligence in Higher Education: A Practical Approach, 1 edn. CRC Press, Boca Raton, July 2022. https://doi.org/10.1201/9781003184157, https://www.taylorfrancis.com/books/9781003184157

5. Everitt, T., Lea, G., Hutter, M.: AGI Safety Literature Review, May 2018. https://doi.org/10.48550/ARXIV.1805.01109, https://arxiv.org/abs/1805.01109, publisher: arXiv Version Number: 2

6. Li, X., Hammer, P., Wang, P., Xie, H.: Functionalist emotion model in NARS. In: Iklé, M., Franz, A., Rzepka, R., Goertzel, B. (eds.) AGI 2018. LNCS, vol. 10999, pp. 119–129. Springer, Cham (2018). https://doi.org/10.1007/978-3-319-97676-1_12

7. McCarthy, J.: From here to human-level AI. Artif. Intell. **171**(18), 1174–1182 (2007). https://doi.org/10.1016/j.artint.2007.10.009, https://linkinghub.elsevier.com/retrieve/pii/S0004370207001476

8. McCarthy, J., Minsky, M.L., Rochester, N., Shannon, C.E.: A Proposal for the Dartmouth Summer Research Project on Artificial Intelligence, 31 August 1955, vol. 27, December 2006. https://ojs.aaai.org/index.php/aimagazine/article/view/1904

9. Newell, A., Simon, H.A.: Human Problem Solving. Prentice-Hall, Englewood Cliffs, N.J (1972)

10. Subasic, N.: Designing an Effective STEM Course, June 2021. https://digitaled.com/resources/blog/designing-an-effective-stem-course-part1

11. Subasic, N., Johansson, H.: Interactive Assignments in Electro Courses at MDA. Stockholm, March 2021. http://kth.diva-portal.org/smash/get/diva2:1588335/FULLTEXT02.pdf

12. Wang, P., Hahm, C., Hammer, P.: A model of unified perception and cognition. Front. Artif. Intell.**5**, 806403 (2022). https://doi.org/10.3389/frai.2022.806403, https://www.frontiersin.org/articles/10.3389/frai.2022.806403/full

13. Wang, Pei: Non-Axiomatic Reasoning System: Exploring the Essence of Intelligence. Ph.D. thesis, Indiana University., USA (1995). https://cis.temple.edu/~wangp/Publication/thesis.pdf

14. Wang, P.: Rigid Flexibility. Springer, Netherlands (2006). https://doi.org/10.1007/1-4020-5045-3, http://link.springer.com/10.1007/1-4020-5045-3

Can Language Models Be Used in Multistep Commonsense Planning Domains?

Zhisheng Tang[ID] and Mayank Kejriwal[✉][ID]

Information Sciences Institute, USC Viterbi School of Engineering,
4676 Admiralty Way 1001, Marina Del Rey, CA 90292, USA
{zhisheng,kejriwal}@isi.edu

Abstract. Transformer-based language models have recently been the focus of much attention, due to their impressive performance on myriad natural language processing (NLP) tasks. One criticism when evaluating such models on problems such as commonsense reasoning is that the benchmarking datasets may not be challenging or global enough. In response, task environments involving some kind of multistep planning, have emerged as a more stringent, and useful, evaluation paradigm. ScienceWorld is one such environment that has weaker dependence on language itself (compared to core commonsense reasoning). In the original publication, ScienceWorld problems proved difficult to solve even for a reasonably advanced language model. This paper demonstrates that, while true for the hardest version of the problem, even first-generation models like BERT can achieve good performance on many interesting intermediate problems within ScienceWorld. Our results, in addition to proposing a more practical methodology and metrics for evaluating language models on multistep planning domains involving commonsense reasoning, also suggest that language models are still likely to be an essential component of (rather than completely orthogonal to) a more comprehensive approach.

Keywords: Language Models · Multistep Planning · Commonsense Reasoning

1 Introduction

Large language models, such as ChatGPT, are transformer-based deep neural networks that have captured public attention lately for their capability to perform a wide range of tasks, from text generation to natural language understanding and reasoning. Such models have achieved human-level performance on many benchmarks [2]. However, transformer-based models are shown to be challenged when facing complex problems, such as decision making under uncertainty [8] and multistep commonsense planning in some text environments, an example being the ScienceWorld benchmark [10]. Such problems require a system to reason about commonsense concepts and plan for future events and goals,

P. Hammer et al. (Eds.): AGI 2023, LNAI 13921, pp. 276–285, 2023.
https://doi.org/10.1007/978-3-031-33469-6_28

which is essential for achieving Artificial General Intelligence (AGI). Without such abilities, an intelligent system cannot be robust to potential obstacles that are common in everyday life (when pursuing myriad goals within constrained environments) and plan accordingly to achieve success. Multistep commonsense planning can help AGI systems adapt to changing environments and handle uncertainty in a consistent manner.

The ScienceWorld benchmark contains elementary science curriculum tasks that depend upon multistep planning and commonsense reasoning abilities. The benchmark claims to require the same level of commonsense as an elementary school student. The environment itself is an abstract, interactive text environment with 25 different high-level verbs (e.g. go to, pick up), 200 types of elements (e.g. plants, electrical components), and 10 interconnected locations (e.g. kitchen, hallway). Agents are expected to solve tasks using natural language inputs, such as 'pick up pot 7' and 'go to hallway'.

In the original work, the ScienceWorld benchmark is evaluated using five different agents, two of which are transformer-based (CALM [11] and Decision Transformer [3]). The highest score achieved by these agents is only 0.17. One of the reasons is the evaluation metric because the original benchmark evaluates each solution in an 'all or nothing' fashion: either an agent successfully accomplishes the task or fails it. However, such a metric fails to take incremental progress into account. We posit that, while this metric is ultimately very important, designing auxiliary metrics to evaluate the incremental performance of agents can serve a useful role in assessing their progress. Additionally, the ScienceWorld benchmark was designed primarily for reinforcement learning agents rather than language models.

We propose a novel benchmark called *QAScienceWorld* that is derived from the original ScienceWorld benchmark and is composed of a set of independent and identically distributed (i.i.d) Multiple Choice Question Answering (MCQA) instances. The benchmark is meant to address both of the issues noted above. It can be used to evaluate discriminative language models. To measure incremental progress, QAScienceWorld uses four metrics for evaluating responses at different levels of granularity. We demonstrate the utility of the benchmark by applying the Bidirectional Encoder Representations from Transformers (BERT) model [4], and showing that it is able to achieve high accuracy on some metrics, and lower accuracy on the metric best aligned with the 'all or nothing' paradigm mentioned earlier. Hence, the benchmark shows that language models can serve as an important component in solving such multistep commonsense planning problems, without negating previous suggestions that they are unlikely to yield a complete solution to these problems.

2 Benchmark Construction

The original ScienceWorld benchmark is seeded with 30 different task types, ranging from measuring temperature to object classification. Each type of task has 10 to 1400 task variations, where each task variation changes some important task objects. For example, for the task of finding a plant, the final objective of one variation is to put the plant into an orange box. But, in other variations of the same task, the orange box is changed to a yellow box or some other container.

Each task variation is provided with a ground-truth or 'gold-standard' trajectory, which begins from the starting state S_1 to the ending state S_{n+1} (where the task is successfully completed). Such a gold-standard trajectory can be expressed as a sequence of n actions $(a_1, a_2, ..., a_n)$, where an agent selects the first action a_1 in the starting state S_1 to go to state S_2, then selects the second action a_2 in the second state S_2 to go to state S_3 and so on, to finally select the nth gold-standardaction a_n in the nth state S_n to go to the ending (goal-achieving) state S_{n+1}. The framework is very similar to traditional planning. Each action a_i can be further decomposed into a verb v_i and one or two elements e_i, where the verb is 'applied' to the element(s). Note that the gold-standard trajectories only represent canonical or standard solutions (e.g. use a thermometer to measure temperature). We recognize that other solutions exist, but we only focus on the gold-standard trajectories at present, as these are the only solutions that are provided within the ScienceWorld benchmark for evaluation purposes.

In the original ScienceWorld benchmark, an agent is expected to select a sequence of actions to accomplish a task. With 25 verbs and many more element choices, the agent needs to search a huge solution space to find even one correct action. The difficulty grows exponentially as the number of actions required to solve a task increases because each action is dependent on the previous actions. Additionally, transformer-based language models are not designed for problems that involve planning a sequence of actions. To decrease the difficulty of the task and make the problem more amenable to language models, we propose the QAScienceWorld benchmark, which frames each action as an i.i.d MCQA problem. Namely, instead of being dependent on previous actions, in our benchmark, each action is independent of other actions and only depends on the current environment. Also, agents select from a small and fixed number of choices as their prediction for the current environment. This formulation greatly reduces the complexity of the original problem. As explained earlier, we only use the actions from the gold-standard trajectory of each task variation of all task types. We describe the benchmark construction below, with a visual example provided in Fig. 1:

1. We assume that, in order to select the correct action, the agent needs to know three important pieces of information: *the task description, the observation of the current environment, and the current inventory status.* Specifically, the task description offers information about the ultimate objective, while the observation of the current environment gives descriptions of the current location, items available to use (and so on), and the current inventory tells the agent about what items can be used besides those in the current environment. For each gold-standard action a_i, we concatenate the above three pieces of information from the state S_i to form the basic prompt of the MCQA. Because each action can be decomposed into a verb part and an element part, we create two MCQA instances (one for each part) for each action. We concatenate the

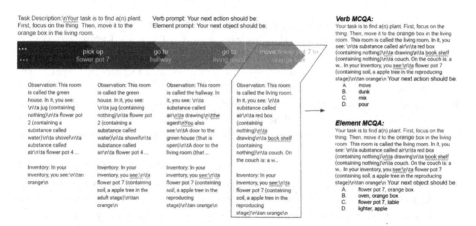

Fig. 1. A partial gold-standard trajectory (last 4 actions) for a variation of the task type: find a(n) plant. The last action is converted to a *verb* MCQA instance and an *element* MCQA instance. The prompts are the concatenation of the task description, the environment observation, the inventory, and the verb prompt or the element prompt. The four possible choices consist of one ground-truth item and three (randomly sampled) wrong choices. In the case of an element MCQA where two elements have to be simultaneously selected for a verb, the three wrong choices consist of two wrong choices where only one element is randomly sampled and a third wrong choice where both elements are randomly sampled.

basic prompt with a verb prompt (i.e., 'Your next action should be:') to form the final prompt for the verb MCQA instance. Similarly, we concatenate the basic prompt with an element prompt (i.e., 'Your next object should be:') to form the final prompt for the element MCQA instance.

2. Each MCQA instance has four choices, one of which is the ground-truth choice. To construct the remaining three wrong choices, we randomly sample from the state S_i, given the gold-standard action a_i. The original Science-World benchmark provides a convenient API for sampling available verbs and elements. For a verb MCQA instance, we randomly sample three wrong verbs as the three wrong choices. For an element MCQA instance, if the gold-standard action a_i only has one element, we again randomly sample three wrong elements as the three wrong choices. For cases where the gold-standard action a_i contains two elements (e.g., {correct element 1, correct element 2}), we randomly sample two wrong elements to replace either one of the ground-truth element as two of the wrong choices (e.g. {correct element 1, wrong element 1} and {wrong element 2, correct element 2}) and randomly sample two wrong elements to replace both ground-truth elements as the third wrong choice (e.g., {wrong element 3, wrong element 4}). More advanced sampling techniques, such as adversarially sampling choices that can be more challenging for an agent, are left for future work.

3. In the original ScienceWorld benchmark, for each task type, all task variations are split into 50% training, 25% development, and 25% test sets. In our

benchmark, we follow the same partition. The training set verb and element MCQA instances are created using the actions of the gold-standard trajectory from the training set task variations in the original benchmark.[1] The same goes for the development set and the test set. Details concerning the benchmark are tabulated in Table 1.

4. In the original ScienceWorld benchmark, there are 25 different verbs. However, we exclude any verb that has 'look' in it, because this verbs does not change the environment in any way, only providing information that is already provided by the observation of the current environment and will cause confusion to the agents. Hence, we have 22 different verbs. We refer the reader to the original ScienceWorld paper for details about the action space. Additionally, following the original work, we set the environment to the 'easy' mode when we extract the environment information. On average, the optimal random performance, whether it entails selecting one of four choices at random or selecting the mode of the correct choices in the training partition, is 40% and 25% for verb and element MCQA instances, respectively.

3   Metrics

In most text-based interactive environments, such as the Jericho [5], a kitchen cleanup game [7], and the TextWorld Commonsense [6], the performance of an agent is evaluated using a score-based metric, where the raw score is obtained when the agent tries to solve a task through a sequence of actions and the final normalized score is calculated by dividing the raw score with the maximum score possible if the task is solved. This metric evaluates agents' performances only at the level of the task as the final score is normalized using the maximum score obtained when the task is finished. Additionally, this metric evaluates the agent's performance under the assumption that, at each action, the problem is dependent on all previous actions. Hence, such a score-based metric is limited if we try to investigate the more detailed behaviors of the agent. We argue that metrics with finer granularity are needed to fully evaluate the performance and the behavior of an agent. Hence, we present four different metrics that are at different levels of granularity: *Verb accuracy, Element accuracy, Action accuracy,* and *Task accuracy.*

Recall that, for a gold-standard trajectory and $i \in [1, n]$, the ith gold-standard action a_i can be decomposed into a verb part v_i and an element part e_i. An agent predicts the ith verb v'_i and the ith element e'_i, and a'_i is the agent's prediction for the ith action, where a'_i is the combination of v'_i and e'_i.

Verb accuracy, element accuracy, and action accuracy evaluate the agent's performance under the assumption that, for each action, the problem is independent of all previous actions, but only depends on the current environment.

---

[1] Because the gold-standard trajectory for the task type 'measuring the boiling point of an unknown substance' is missing from the original ScienceWorld repository, we only have 29 task types here.

Table 1. The number of task variations of each task type and the number of actions created using all task variations of each task type, divided into the training set, the development set, and the test set. The number of MCQA instances is twice the number of actions because each action is split into a verb MCQA instance and an element MCQA instance.

Topic	Task Type	# of Variations			# of Actions		
		Train	Dev	Test	Train	Dev	Test
Matter	Changes of State (Boiling)	14	7	9	471	400	699
Matter	Changes of State (Any)	14	7	9	282	292	381
Matter	Changes of State (Freezing)	14	7	9	391	402	484
Matter	Changes of State (Melting)	14	7	9	362	290	381
Measurement	Measuring Boiling Point (known)	218	109	109	5916	4401	3093
Measurement	Use Thermometer	270	135	135	2949	1480	1413
Electricity	Create a circuit	10	5	5	70	39	35
Electricity	Renewable vs Non-renewable Energy	10	5	5	132	75	64
Electricity	Test Conductivity (known)	450	225	225	8934	4450	4647
Electricity	Test Conductivity (unknown)	300	150	150	5023	2482	2540
Classification	Find an animal	150	75	75	1103	543	557
Classification	Find a living thing	150	75	75	1103	543	557
Classification	Find a non-living thing	150	75	75	605	312	288
Classification	Find a plant	150	75	75	1029	517	511
Biology	Grow a fruit	62	31	33	3699	1838	1941
Biology	Grow a plant	62	31	33	1609	815	856
Chemistry	Mixing (generic)	16	8	8	297	135	179
Chemistry	Mixing paints (secondary colours)	18	9	9	154	79	78
Chemistry	Mixing paints (tertiary colours)	18	9	9	282	139	138
Biology	Identify longest-lived animal	62	31	32	180	95	92
Biology	Identify longest-then-shortest-lived animal	62	31	32	242	126	124
Biology	Identify shortest-lived animal	62	31	32	180	95	92
Biology	Identify life stages (animal)	6	3	5	159	91	159
Biology	Identify life stages (plant)	4	2	4	25	16	30
Forces	Inclined Planes (determine angle)	84	42	42	1006	508	512
Forces	Friction (known surfaces)	692	346	348	8316	4182	4214
Forces	Friction (unknown surfaces)	80	40	42	956	484	512
Biology	Mendelian Genetics (known plants)	60	30	30	5037	2524	2546
Biology	Mendelian Genetics (unknown plants)	240	120	120	20219	9990	10128
Sum		3442	1721	1744	70731	37343	37251

Specifically, a verb prediction v_i' or an element prediction e_i' is correct if it is identical to the ith gold-standard verb v_i or the ith gold-standard element e_i. Verb accuracy is defined as the percentage of correct verb predictions and is calculated by dividing the number of correct verb predictions by the total number of gold-standard actions in the trajectory. Element accuracy is defined in a similar manner where it is the percentage of correct element prediction and is calculated by dividing the number of correct element predictions by the total number of gold-standard actions in the trajectory. Similarly, the ith action prediction a'_i is considered correct if both v'_i is identical to v_i and e'_i is identical to e_i. Action accuracy is defined as the percentage of correct action predictions and is calculated by dividing the number of correct action predictions by the total number of gold-standard actions in the trajectory.

Task accuracy shares the same assumption as the score-based metrics in that it evaluates agents' performances at the level of the task. Hence, for one task variation, it is considered correct if all action predictions of that task variation are correct. Formally, if $(a'_1, a'_2, ..., a'_n)$ is identical to $(a_1, a_2, ..., a_n)$, we consider the prediction for this task variation as correct. Task accuracy is calculated by dividing the number of correct task variation predictions by the total number of variations of a task type.

4   Experiments

We use BERT to demonstrate the utility of our QAScienceWorld benchmark and to showcase the different granularity of our novel metrics. BERT represents a paradigm shift from the previous neural models (e.g. CNN and RNN) to transformer-based models. Moving forward, transformer-based models continue to push the performance to near or above human performances on many natural language understanding and computer vision tasks [9]. Hence, BERT is a representation of other transformer-based models and can reflect the base difficulty on a variety of tasks, including our benchmark.

Following the original paper, we use the BERT base model, which has 12 layers, a hidden size of 768, and 12 attention heads and has a pre-trained weight available in the Hugging Face repository [1]. We fine-tuned this pre-trained BERT model using all verb MCQA instances and element MCQA instances from the training set. For one MCQA instance, the input to the BERT model is a prompt-choice string constructed by concatenating the prompt and one of the four choices. Because we have four choices, the input is four such strings per MCQA instance. The label for this MCQA instance is the index of the prompt-choice string that contains the correct choice. During inference, for an MCQA instance, the fine-tuned BERT model will return four scores (one for each prompt-choice string) and the prompt-choice string with the highest score is considered the prediction. We fine-tuned the pre-trained BERT model for one epoch, using the default learning rate of 5e-5 and a batch size of 16. We report the fine-tuned BERT results on the test set evaluated using verb accuracy, element accuracy, action accuracy, and task accuracy in Table 2.

The results illustrate that the fine-tuned BERT model can achieve over 90% verb, element, and action accuracy. But accuracy in the 70% to 80% range is also observed, such as in the case of the task type: Renewable vs Non-renewable Energy, where the action accuracy is only 76%. These results suggest that the transformer-based models can achieve human-level performance when the problems are presented in the format of i.i.d MCQA and the solution space is relatively limited. The difficulty arises when we evaluate these models' performance

Table 2. The verb, element, action, and task accuracy (introduced in Sect. 3 and expressed as a percentage) estimates of the fine-tuned BERT model on the test set. The fine-tuned BERT model is trained using all verb MCQA instances and element MCQA instances from the training partition of the benchmark on a pre-trained BERT model. The verb, element, and action accuracy estimates are first calculated at the level of each task variation and then averaged over all task variations of a given task type.

Topic	Task Type	Verb	Element	Action	Task
			Accuracy		
Matter	Changes of State (Boiling)	96	89	86	0
Matter	Changes of State (Any)	95	86	82	0
Matter	Changes of State (Freezing)	91	85	78	0
Matter	Changes of State (Melting)	96	82	79	0
Measurement	Measuring Boiling Point (known)	92	68	61	0
Measurement	Use Thermometer	98	92	91	43
Electricity	Create a circuit	97	95	92	60
Electricity	Renewable vs Non-renewable Energy	86	89	76	0
Electricity	Test Conductivity (known)	95	90	87	11
Electricity	Test Conductivity (unknown)	96	97	94	33
Classification	Find an animal	100	91	91	48
Classification	Find a living thing	100	87	87	33
Classification	Find a non-living thing	99	82	81	47
Classification	Find a plant	100	83	83	23
Biology	Grow a fruit	96	96	93	0
Biology	Grow a plant	96	96	94	18
Chemistry	Mixing (generic)	91	80	73	0
Chemistry	Mixing paints (secondary colours)	96	89	85	22
Chemistry	Mixing paints (tertiary colours)	86	93	80	0
Biology	Identify longest-lived animal	100	93	93	78
Biology	Identify longest-then-shortest-lived animal	100	89	89	63
Biology	Identify shortest-lived animal	100	99	99	97
Biology	Identify life stages (animal)	100	91	98	60
Biology	Identify life stages (plant)	100	100	100	100
Forces	Inclined Planes (determine angle)	98	99	97	69
Forces	Friction (known surfaces)	99	99	98	74
Forces	Friction (unknown surfaces)	97	99	97	67
Biology	Mendelian Genetics (known plants)	95	97	93	0
Biology	Mendelian Genetics (unknown plants)	95	96	92	0
Average		96	91	88	33

on the level of the task. As indicated by the results, the typical task accuracy is below 50%. However, there is considerable variance observed at times. For example, it appears that the 'identify' task types within the biology topic might be an 'easier' task, as the fine-tuned BERT model even achieves 100% accuracy in one of the task types and achieves above 60% accuracy in other task types of similar nature. The task type 'changing the state of a matter' seems to pose the biggest challenge for the model, as in all four such task types, the fine-tuned BERT model achieves 0% accuracy. Interestingly, the above two observations are confirmed by the experiments done in the original ScienceWorld work. This further demonstrates that our benchmark can serve as an effective complement, or extension, to the original benchmark.

5 Conclusion and Future Work

We designed and constructed an i.i.d. MCQA benchmark, QAScienceWorld, that is derived from the original ScienceWorld environment using its gold-standard trajectories. The QAScienceWorld benchmark is posited to be more friendly to evaluating transformer-based language models rather than reinforcement learning agents, as the original benchmark is primarily positioned to do. Furthermore, to better understand the performance of transformer-based language models at different levels of granularity, we proposed four metrics that are different from the usual 'all or nothing' approach and seek to measure the incremental progress of agents in a systematic fashion. We demonstrated the usefulness of our benchmark by fine-tuning the pre-trained BERT model and evaluating its performance using the four metrics. The results indicate that even though, in general, BERT can only finish about 30% of the tasks, it does achieve over 90% accuracy on some of the other metrics. This suggests that while transformer-based language models struggle with such multistep commonsense planning problems, they can play a powerful role in dealing with intermediate problems. Hence, they could play a critical and integrative role in systems better suited for planning but needing to use commonsense language to fill in the gaps.

We end with the caveat that the QAScienceWorld benchmark is derived using gold-standard solutions in the original ScienceWorld benchmark, and ignores other potential trajectories to finish the tasks. This can also lead to a disadvantage when evaluating agents' performance, because of the restricted solution space. Hence, we will consider including other solutions in our benchmark in future work. Additionally, when constructing the benchmark, we only consider randomly selected wrong choices to include with the ground-truth choice to form the complete set of candidate choices for the MCQA instances. We recognize that this can pose an unfair advantage to the agents evaluated using our benchmark over the original one, as both the verb and element space is narrower in our benchmark. Hence, one approach that we are considering in a future updated version of this benchmark is adversarial (rather than random) sampling of the wrong choices (or in an even more challenging version, including *all* possible choices).

References

1. Hugging face repository: bert-base-uncased. https://huggingface.co/bert-base-uncased
2. Brown, T., et al.: Language models are few-shot learners. Adv. Neural Inf. Process. Syst. **33**, 1877–1901 (2020)
3. Chen, L., et al.: Decision transformer: reinforcement learning via sequence modeling. Adv. Neural Inf. Process. Syst. **34**, 15084–15097 (2021)
4. Devlin, J., Chang, M.W., Lee, K., Toutanova, K.: Bert: pre-training of deep bidirectional transformers for language understanding. arXiv preprint arXiv:1810.04805 (2018)
5. Hausknecht, M., Ammanabrolu, P., Côté, M.A., Yuan, X.: Interactive fiction games: a colossal adventure. In: Proceedings of the AAAI Conference on Artificial Intelligence, vol. 34, pp. 7903–7910 (2020)
6. Murugesan, K., et al.: Text-based rl agents with commonsense knowledge: new challenges, environments and baselines. In: Proceedings of the AAAI Conference on Artificial Intelligence, vol. 35, pp. 9018–9027 (2021)
7. Murugesan, K., Atzeni, M., Shukla, P., Sachan, M., Kapanipathi, P., Talamadupula, K.: Enhancing text-based reinforcement learning agents with commonsense knowledge. arXiv preprint arXiv:2005.00811 (2020)
8. Tang, Z., Kejriwal, M.: Can language representation models think in bets? R. Soc. Open Sci. **10**(3), 221585 (2023)
9. Tay, Y., Dehghani, M., Bahri, D., Metzler, D.: Efficient transformers: a survey. ACM Comput. Surv. **55**(6), 1–28 (2022)
10. Wang, R., Jansen, P., Côté, M.A., Ammanabrolu, P.: Scienceworld: Is your agent smarter than a 5th grader? arXiv preprint arXiv:2203.07540 (2022)
11. Yao, S., Rao, R., Hausknecht, M., Narasimhan, K.: Keep CALM and explore: language models for action generation in text-based games. In: Proceedings of the 2020 Conference on Empirical Methods in Natural Language Processing (EMNLP), pp. 8736–8754. Association for Computational Linguistics, Online, November 2020. https://doi.org/10.18653/v1/2020.emnlp-main.704, https://aclanthology.org/2020.emnlp-main.704

Explicit Goal-Driven Autonomous Self-Explanation Generation

Kristinn R. Thórisson[1,2]([⊠]), Hjörleifur Rörbeck[1,2], Jeff Thompson[2],
and Hugo Latapie[3]

[1] Center for Analysis and Design of Intelligent Agents, Reykjavik University,
Menntavegur 1, Reykjavík, Iceland
thorisson@ru.is
[2] Icelandic Institute for Intelligent Machines, Reykjavík, Iceland
jeff@iiim.is
[3] Cisco Systems, Emerging Technologies and Incubation, San Jose, CA, USA
hlatapie@cisco.com

Abstract. Explanation can form the basis, in any lawfully behaving environment, of plans, summaries, justifications, analysis and predictions, and serve as a method for probing their validity. For systems with general intelligence, an equally important reason to generate explanations is for directing cumulative knowledge acquisition: Lest they be born knowing everything, a general machine intelligence must be able to handle novelty. This can only be accomplished through a systematic logical analysis of how, in the face of novelty, effective control is achieved and maintained—in other words, through the systematic *explanation of experience*. Explanation generation is thus a requirement for more powerful AI systems, not only for their owners (to verify proper knowledge and operation) but for the AI itself—to leverage its existing knowledge when learning something new. In either case, assigning the automatic generation of explanation to the system itself seems sensible, and quite possibly unavoidable. In this paper we argue that the quality of an agent's explanation generation mechanism is based on how well it fulfils three goals – or purposes – of explanation production: Uncovering unknown or hidden patterns, highlighting or identifying relevant causal chains, and identifying incorrect background assumptions. We present the arguments behind this conclusion and briefly describe an implemented self-explaining system, AERA (Autocatlytic Endogenous Reflective Architecture), capable of *goal-directed self-explanation:* Autonomously explaining its own behavior as well as its acquired knowledge of tasks and environment.

Keywords: Artificial Intelligence · Explanation Generation · Autonomy · General Machine Intelligence · Causal Reasoning · Self-Explanation

1 Introduction

Explainability is an important feature of any artificial intelligence (AI) systems, for numerous reasons. Explanations can form the basis of valid plans, summaries,

P. Hammer et al. (Eds.): AGI 2023, LNAI 13921, pp. 286–295, 2023.
https://doi.org/10.1007/978-3-031-33469-6_29

justifications, predictions, etc. and serve as a method for probing their validity, cost, and potential dangers—which, in fact, is the role of explanations in general in society. The more complex an AI system is, the more important it is that its operation be transparent and understandable not only by its owners, but also by the system itself. Being explainable implies support for direct inquiries for why a system did what it did, what it plans to do, and why it chose some action over another. The level of transparency offered this way will impact a system's trustworthiness. For any general machine intelligence, trustworthiness is a necessity, since such systems will handle novelty by definition; how they behave in light of novel situations and tasks must be verifiable, at some reasonable level of abstraction, to ensure their safety. Automating explanation generation in AI systems is therefore an important goal [17], and it might be argued that it is necessary for a system to be worthy of being considered general [23].

It is the ability of explanations to be verified that brings them their fundamental value. To be verifiable means that they must be based on knowledge of verifiable causal relationships in the situation, task, or circumstances in question—in other words, they must be *falsifiable*. To be falsifiable they must reference some set of causal relations whose validity is undisputed in the relevant contexts, or easily verifiable.

An important function of explanation that is less often discussed than most others is their use for guiding an autonomous agent's learning; the ability to find explanations for learning failure or success can help uncover how the world works. In this case, to be effective and efficient, explanation generation must be autonomous [17]. Here we examine *goal-directed self-explanation:* the ability of a system to autonomously generate explanations about its own behavior, as well as its acquired knowledge of tasks and environment, under articulated requirements, i.e. explicit goals. A key focus of this work is the use of such explanations as a method for learning (and meta-learning, that is, learning to learn).

The work rests on the argument that explanation generation is a fundamental and necessary process for general self-supervised learning [23]. We look at how explanation generation for this purpose is achieved in the AERA system, and discuss its approach in light of other systems aimed at general intelligence. Thórisson [21] describe a theory of pragmatic understanding that we take as the foundation for our work here. We consider their definition of understanding well-suited for building a theory of explanation generation because it already presents a strong foundation for relating prediction, goal achievement, knowledge acquisition, and explanation to causal reasoning.

The paper is structured as follows: We start with an overview of related work, then we provide some important definitions for the subsequent discussion, which outlines our theory of goal-driven self-explanation generation.

2   Related Work

For reasons of opaqueness, studies on explainable AI have so far primarily focused on artificial neural networks (ANNs), being mostly based on (manually guided) abductive methods that attempt to trace certain outputs to the identification of relevant inputs (cf. [14]). For immediate clarification, this is not what the present paper is about. In the allocentric methodologies employed in the development of these systems [19], training data, implicit goals, and hand-coded heuristics, are all determined and provided by the developers themselves, a-priori. In this sense, ANN-based systems are no different from standard software applications.

We envision the aims of 'explainable AI' research differently. First and foremost, we recognize that the primary practical application of AI is all sorts of automation, and therefore *autonomous* explanation generation should be a primary goal for explainable AI. In short, the human effort needed to arrive at an explanation should be minimized as far as possible, delegating the explanation generation to the machine. Equally importantly, we see explanation – and its extension into argumentation in general – to be a foundation for any general machine intelligence to grow its knowledge reliably, efficiently and effectively.

We are working exclusively on systems that can generate explanations autonomously, about themselves and their task-environment—i.e. systems that are *self-explaining*. Generally speaking, explanations can vary in their quality. A good explanation eliminates blind spots, clarifies, or highlights that which was obscure before (see section below). Above all, a good explanation observes certain implicit (explicit) constraints and does not break any relevant rules. To do so, it is not enough that an explanation refer to correlational data, it must be based on actual and relevant causal relations. This is because a good explanation must highlight *why* something – whether it be a course of events, situation, or other outcome – *must be the way it is*, rather than some other way [4,15].

Most sources agree that causal attribution, or identifying underlying causes of a class of (or particular) events or state of affairs, is a vital part of explanation [3, 9,10,18,24].[1] In fact, this is often how explanation is defined. Josephson equates finding possible explanations with finding possible causes [7], and Halper and Pearl claim that explaining a set of events necessitates the acknowledgment of the cause of those events [3]. Miller expands on this, arguing that explanation begins with the cognitive process of identifying causes, followed by a social process of conveying the knowledge acquired by the cognitive process to the intended recipient. As he also points out, causal attribution is a twofold process of inferring the key causes and then selecting a subset of those causes as the most relevant for an explanation [10]. Our approach is somewhat aligned with this view.

Halpern and Pearl [4] define causal explanations using structural equations, for the purpose of determining and conveying an *actual cause* of an explanandum. To accomplish this they assume that all relevant facts are known to said model. What is lacking is a treatment of tasks and goals rather than simply explaining. The assumption of a complete model is also unrealistic, particularly in complex real-world situations. Their work thus leaves much to be desired when it comes to AI, including how such models are autonomously built. This is addressed in our AERA system by positioning explanation as the provisioning of missing information structures, making incomplete knowledge a feature, not a bug.

---

[1] Other types of explanation than causal have been proposed. Teleological explanations are explanations focused on utility (to explain by defining the purpose or intent of the thing to be explained [2]). But nowhere nearly all things in need of explaining have intent or utility behind them.

Hilton [5,6] researched explanations extensively from a psychological perspective. They point out the inherent fallacy in using covariational criteria for causal attribution, as there are numerous examples of events occurring at the same time without one being the cause of the other. Their alternative model of explanation is based on findings in ordinary language where humans make use of contrastives and counterfactuals as criteria for causal attribution. This is also one of the major findings of Miller's survey [10] on explanations: explanations in human conversation most commonly are produced in response to contrastive questions, for instance *"Why did you do A and not B?"* rather than simply *"Why did you do A?"*. Halpern and Pearl [3,4] also build on this idea, positioning counterfactuals as a way to highlight actual causes.

Palacio et al. went with a broader definition of explanation, arguing that causation is not necessary for all explanation: "An explanation is the process of describing one or more facts, such that it facilitates the understanding of aspects related to said facts (by a human consumer)" [14, p. 5]. They further argue that understanding is unique to humans, and therefore explanation from machine to machine is merely verification. We do not agree with either assertion—indeed, we consider it a central task artificial general intelligence research to endow machines with understanding [21], and we see causal relations as central in all explanations (if not explicit, then certainly implicit), because they are the fundamental method for *explanation verification.*

In our view, all explanations of complex tasks with multiple steps and sub-goals must be based, in one way or another, on causal relations. We therefore treat causation and causal knowledge as a necessary element in this work.

3 Definitions

Here we give a compact description of key terms used in the following sections, in particular Sect. 4.

Explainer and Explanation. A process that produces explanations is an 'explainer.' This can be a human, a machine, or some other process which is positioned to serve such a role. An 'explanation' is a compact description outlining some subset of a modelset of the phenomenon that, for whatever reason, is misunderstood, misrepresented, or missing from the phenomenon's modelset. An explanation typically references existing parts of a modelset and presents either a missing piece or highlights errors in it (see Sect. 4, page 7).

Explanandum and Explainee. 'Explanandum' is that which is to be explained. Given a particular outcome, situation, or turn of events, this can be an anomaly, a missing but necessary relation, or other identified inconsistency that calls for an explanation. 'Explainee' is the particular recipient of an explanation—those to whom the explanation is addressed. This can be the Explaining process itself, a co-located interlocutor, or some future recipient of the information.

Explicit Goal. A 'goal' is a (constant state or steady) state to be achieved. An 'explicit goal' is one which can be described in some representational language that references a knowledge base. An 'active goal' is one which can be thus represented and which may already be pursued—i.e. a goal that has been accepted by an agent of change who is actively pursuing it.

Explainable vs. Interpretable. The terms 'explainable' and 'interpretable' are often used interchangeably in AI, but we see a definitive and important difference between the concepts behind them, based on who exactly is doing the explaining and interpreting. For instance, in work involving artificial neural networks, 'interpretation' is typically an explanation of the mechanisms of the classifier, not of the task or environment for which the system is deployed [8]), and it is the researchers who are doing the interpretation.[2] In contrast, we define *self-explaining AI* as 'AI that is capable of generating valid explanation,' and *interpretable AI* as 'AI that can be interpreted (or explained) by a third party.'

Phenomenon. A phenomenon Φ (process, state of affairs, occurrence) – where W is the world, and $\Phi \subset W$, – is made up of a set of elements, including sub-structures, component processes, whole-part relations, causal relations, or other sub-divisions of Φ $\{\varphi_1 \ldots \varphi_n \in \Phi\}$ of various kinds, including relations $\Re_\Phi$ (causal, mereological, positional, episodic, etc.) that couple elements of Φ with each other, and with those of other phenomena.

Complex Task-Environment. We define a 'task-environment' as the tuple of an assigned task and the environment in which the task is to be performed. A 'complex' task-environment is, for all practical purposes, a combination of an assigned task in a particular environment that, for accomplishing the task, requires (a) detection and separation of patterns and sub-patterns with non-trivial causal and part-whole relations, that must be combined with (b) assumptions about high-level logical relations between these (e.g. objects cannot be in to places at once), combined with (c) creation, execution, and monitoring of partial non-linear plans with nested contingency composition, and/or (d) direct application of ampliative[3] reasoning and analogy generation.

Valid Explanation. An explanation $\varepsilon(x, y)$, where x is the explanandum and y is a network of known (causal) relations and patterns relevant to x, can be validated through a process that seeks to uncover inconsistencies in it through the generation of questions that probe y's causal relations relevant to x. To do so the validating process must be able to (a) represent causality, and use this to (b) abduce arguments which "argue for" – or serve as verifiable evidence for – the validity of the explanation. The arguments could also be verified by direct measurement (but is only necessary if the background assumptions on which the evidence rests are not well-verified).

---

[2] Providing adequate levels of transparency modern machine learning and AI systems such as reinforcement learners and deep neural networks, with adequate levels of transparency, requires considerable post-hoc effort and skill in interpreting algorithms, and most of the time it is essentially prohibitive due to cost.

[3] Traditionally, 'ampliative reasoning' refers to any process that relies on abduction and induction in any combination to achieve a particular result (cf. [16]); we include (defeasible, non-axiomatic) deduction in that list.

4   Goal-Driven Explanation Generation

We base this work on a theory of pragmatic understanding proposed by Thórisson et al. [21] which uses the concept of a modelset (set of peewee models[4]) for describing a phenomenon, and that can be manipulated through a set of processes for performing four types of tasks, one of which is explanation generation. Given a phenomenon Φ, M_Φ is the modelset intended to capture relevant aspects of the phenomenon; the models ($\{m_1 \ldots m_n\} \in M_\Phi$) are information structures intended for (a) *explaining* Φ, (b) *predicting* Φ, (c) producing effective plans for achieving goals with respect to Φ, and (d) (re)creating Φ in any medium (see Sect. 4, p. 6). For any modelset M_Φ and phenomenon Φ, the closer the information structures as a whole represent key elements (sub-parts) $\varphi_i \in \Phi$ and their couplings $\Re_\Phi$, at any level of detail, the greater the *accuracy* of M with respect to Φ. The more *completely* such a modelset captures all relevant aspects of Φ for achieving any of the four tasks, for any chosen challenge related to Φ, the more *comprehensive* it is. Our theory of goal-driven self-explanation considers explanation generation itself to be *a task* with a particular top-level goal—namely:

> $\mathcal{G}_{top}$ — *The goal of explanation is to improve (or prove) understanding.*

This statement would in itself be a rather shallow if what we mean by 'understanding' was left unexplained; our definition of understanding is exactly this: The more correct – i.e. *comprehensive* and *accurate* – an intelligent agent's modelset M_Φ of Φ is, the better will the agent be said to *understand* phenomenon Φ [21]. An explanation in this view is a concrete action that is intended to verify, evaluate, or increase either the completeness of an agent's models and relations ($Q_{compl}(M_\Phi, \Re_\Phi)$), its accuracy ($Q_{acc}(M_\Phi, \Re_\Phi)$), or both.

As mentioned above (p. 5), the models of a phenomenon's Φ relations $\Re_\Phi$ describe how its elements relate to each other, and to other phenomena. If we partition $\Re_\Phi$ into two disjoint sets, *inward facing* relations $\Re_\Phi^{in} = \Re_\Phi \cap (2^\Phi \times 2^\Phi)$ and *outward facing* relations $\Re_\Phi^{out} = \Re_\Phi \setminus \Re_\Phi^{in}$, an agent whose models are only accurate and complete for $\Re_\Phi^{in}$ understands Φ but not Φ's relation to other phenomena (i.e. its context); an agent whose models are only accurate and complete for $\Re_\Phi^{out}$ understands Φ's relation to other phenomena but will have limited or no understanding of Φ's internals.

A *good explanation* is one that unequivocally demonstrates or verifies understanding of a phenomenon Φ [1], or improves understanding of Φ by affecting the modelset describing the phenomenon in a way that improves the possessor of that modelset's ability to achieve the four tasks related to a phenomenon.

The explanation generation process involves the skills of identifying (i) the role that the explanation should fulfil, (ii) the relevant patterns and relations that must be referenced for it to serve this role, and (iii) producing a description

---

[4] Small models that can be composed into larger modelsets; see e.g. [11,13].

that meets these requirements (for a particular set of explainees). This is compatible and in line with earlier work on explanation generation (cf. [4, 15]). With the exception of the first skill, to achieve any of these in a complex environment requires information about cause and effect, the knowledge representation capable of supporting the above must, by definition, contain information about the causal structure of Φ.

Generating an explanation calls thus for certain necessary information and must meet certain necessary requirements. More specifically, producing an explanation involves the generation of a *compact description* that references or implicates one or more causal relations that – if not present, or structured differently – would result in a different outcome. The causal relation(s) relevant to the phenomenon that explanation targets limit(s) the possible state space by providing constraints, thus contributing to a particular outcome or situation. The necessary ingredients to produce explanations are, therefore:

- knowledge of causal (and other) relations,
- named entities (and appropriate grammar) for producing this description,
- a fulfillment of a (possibly hypothesized) goal that the explanation is intended to meet.

We hypothesize three classes of purposes – or *subgoals* – that a generated explanation may serve, namely, to highlight or identify the following aspects relevant to an explanandum:

$\mathcal{G}_1$ — Unknown or hidden variables, patterns, or other aspects.
$\mathcal{G}_2$ — Unknown or hidden causal factors and chains.
$\mathcal{G}_3$ — Unknown or hidden errors in background assumptions.

The task of an explainer (explanation-generating process) is to meet the top-level goal that explanation serves, that is, to prove/improve understanding, by meeting one or more of these three subgoals as closely as possible. The explainee can be co-temporal and co-spatial, (as in human realtime dialog), a future receiver of a recorded or written explanation (e.g. instruction manuals), a group of students (as in a classroom), or the explanation-generating process itself (like during learning, when explaining things to oneself for verification of understanding).

Since an explanation serves a purpose, as defined by its subgoal(s), $\mathcal{G}_{1-3}$, we can assume that it may do so on a continuum, from well to badly. The gradient from meeting this goal perfectly, $\mathcal{R}(\varepsilon) = 1$, to not meeting it at all, $\mathcal{R}(\varepsilon) = 0$, describes how well an explanation "hits the spot"—let's call it the explanation's *role fulfillment*, $\mathcal{R}(\varepsilon, \varpi)$, where ϖ is its designated role. And since an explanation could in theory highlight the relevant patterns, causal chains, or background assumptions anywhere from perfectly to not at all, we can define a gradient for this dimension as well, $\varepsilon(P_{rvt}) = [0, 1]$; we call it the *validity* of an explanation, $\mathcal{V} = \varepsilon(P_{rvt})$. The *value* of a given explanation is then the product of *how well* it meets its goal and how *valid* it is, $v_{pur}(\varepsilon) = \mathcal{R} \times \mathcal{V}$.

We call this an explanation's "*pur* (pure) value" because there is a third factor that could be considered here, that is, how well the explanation fits an explainee agent's A knowledge, $\mathcal{K}(A)$. A 'perfect explanation' is defined as an explanation whose pure validity is at maximum, $v_{pur}(\varepsilon) = 1.0$, and whose compactness could not be greater. The maximum compactness of an explanation ε is in part dictated by this factor, because the more an explainee knows, the more compact can the explanation be made. If an explainer makes incorrect assumptions about the explainee's knowledge – that is, there is misalignment between the explainee's knowledge and the explainer's model of that knowledge – the compactness of the explanation will suffer. We propose to represent this relationship as a match, or overlap, between the constructed explanation's *encoding* and the explainee's ability to unwrap that encoding (in other words, the effort required to decode the information it is intended to carry), that is, $\{\varepsilon_{\Phi} - (\Phi \setminus \mathcal{K}(A))\}$, where Φ is the explanandum, ε_{Φ} is the (encoded) explanation of a particular part of Φ that references both known and unknown information, and $\mathcal{K}(A)$ is the knowledge of the explainee.[5] This, then, may be taken into account when quantifying the value of an explanation.[6]

In a reflective controller, i.e. one that can reflect on its own inner operations, any explanation can become the subject of the agent's own explanation machinery, allowing for the generation of explanations of explanations (like we are doing right here right now). Capacity for this kind of self-explanation can enhance not only an AI system's understanding of its task and environment but also of *itself*. In each case the explanations coming from within the system can be processed by the system for the purpose of further knowledge acquisition [23]. Stated differently, given that the system is a *self-explaining* AI, the better the above explanation generation functions are fulfilled and implemented in the same system, the more trustworthy the system will be, but not only that, it could possibly learn faster and better. Going one step further, a paper by Thórisson argues that autonomous general learning is not possible without some form of explanation-generating mechanisms [23].

5   Explanation Generation in AERA

This section gives a short introduction to how AERA (Autocatalytic Endogenous Reflective Architecture) meets the above requirements for generating explanations [11,12]. Knowledge in AERA is represented using two main types of information structures, composite states and causal-relational models (CRMs) [11,13,22]. Composite states capture patterns that an AERA agent can perceive; CRMs capture causal relations by representing causes on the left-hand side and results on the right-hand side. Pattern matching is used to match perceived

---

[5] For convenience we include, as part of the 'encoding' of an explanation, any references to related but different phenomena intended to better match an explainee's knowledge—that is, to explain something better to a particular explainee, due to their particular knowledge at the time of the explanation generation.

[6] This certainly is a factor in all explanations produced by one human for another. It may not, however, be relevant for self-explanation generation since the meaning of a low-value (or zero-value, i.e. worthless) explanation produced for oneself is undefined.

or desired states to either side. Using these constructs, AERA learns in a self-supervised way by constructing programs on the fly for achieving self-generated goals and sub-goals [20]. The resulting networks of information produce both concrete and hypothetical plans, predictions, and sequences of actions that fulfill set goals.

AERA's capacity for self-explaining comes primarily from two key principles. Firstly, all its knowledge is explicit and compositional in a scale-independent way. This means that both small and large details can be captured with comparable information structures, and that hierarchies of knowledge can also be constructed into modelsets (through combinations of smaller elements). Secondly, because cause-effect relationships are represented directly (also in a relatively scale-free manner), computing the implications of particular actions, and producing appropriate plans for achieving goals, is directly supported.

Finally, the special programming language used to implement these mechanisms in AERA, Replicode [11], makes key parts of the system's operational semantics accessible to itself, allowing it to use explanation to argue *to itself* about which action to take, which options may be better than others, and what particular actions may lead to in comparison to others.

6   Conclusion

Explainability and traceability are key requirements of all mission-critical engineering. With the increasing use of software-controlled systems, complexity rises, and with complexity comes the need for smarter software systems. To be trustworthy, AI must be explainable. With the goal of creating systems with general intelligence, AGI-aspiring systems should not only be explainable, they should be able to explain themselves to their users. But if general intelligence *requires* the ability to explain – if not for any other reason that the sheer amount of possibilities that the physical world presents to anyone who is learning about it from scratch – then such systems, upon having achieved generality in the near or distant future, will already be able to generate good explanations about their own operation and their task-environment. We hope the work in this paper moves us one step closer to this future.

Acknowledgments. This work was supported in part by Cisco Systems, the Icelandic Institute for Intelligent Machines and Reykjavik University.

References

1. Bieger, J., Thórisson, K.R.: Evaluating understanding. In: IJCAI Workshop on Evaluating General-Purpose AI, Melbourne, Australia (2017)
2. Cohen, J.: Teleological explanation. Proc. Aristot. Soc. **51**, 255–292 (1950)
3. Halpern, J.Y., Pearl, J.: Causes and explanations: a structural-model approach – part I: causes. Br. J. Philos. Sci. **56**, 889–911 (2005)
4. Halpern, J.Y., Pearl, J.: Causes and explanations: a structural-model approach – Part II: Explanations. Br. J. Philos. Sci. **56**, 843–847 (2005)

5. Hilton, D.J.: Conversational processes and causal explanation. Psychol. Bull. **107**(1), 65–81 (1990)
6. Hilton, D.J., Slugoski, B.R.: Knowledge-based causal attribution: the abnormal conditions focus model. Psychol. Rev. **93**(1), 75–88 (1986). https://doi.org/10.1037/0033-295X.93.1.75
7. Josephson, J., Josephson, S.: Abductive Inference: Computation, Philosophy, Technology. Computation, Philosophy, Technology, Cambridge University Press (1996)
8. Lapuschkin, S., Wäldchen, S., Binder, A., Montavon, G., Samek, W., Müller, K.R.: Unmasking clever hans predictors and assessing what machines really learn. Nat. Commun. **10**(1) (2019). https://doi.org/10.1038/s41467-019-08987-4
9. Lombrozo, T.: The structure and function of explanations. Trends Cogn. Sci. **10**(10), 464–470 (2006)
10. Miller, T.: Explanation in artificial intelligence: insights from the social sciences (2017)
11. Nivel, E., Thórisson, K.R.: Replicode: a constructivist programming paradigm and language. Technical report RUTR-SCS13001, Reykjavik University School of Computer Science (2013)
12. Nivel, E., Thórisson, K.R.: Towards a programming paradigm for control systems with high levels of existential autonomy. In: Kühnberger, K.-U., Rudolph, S., Wang, P. (eds.) AGI 2013. LNCS (LNAI), vol. 7999, pp. 78–87. Springer, Heidelberg (2013). https://doi.org/10.1007/978-3-642-39521-5_9
13. Nivel, E., et al.: Bounded recursive self-improvement (2013)
14. Palacio, S., Lucieri, A., Munir, M., Hees, J., Ahmed, S., Dengel, A.: Xai handbook: towards a unified framework for explainable AI (2021)
15. Pearl, J.: Causality: Models, Reasoning and Inference, 2nd edn. Cambridge University Press, New York, NY, USA (2009)
16. Psillos, S.: An explorer upon untrodden ground: peirce on abduction. In: Handbook of the History of Logic, vol. 10, pp. 117–151. Elsevier (2011)
17. Rörbeck, H.: Self-Explaining Artificial Intelligence: On the Requirements for Autonomous Explanation Generation. M.Sc. Thesis, Dept. Comp. Sci., Reykjavik University (2022)
18. Strevens, M.: The causal and unification approaches to explanation unified-causally. Noûs **38**(1), 154–176 (2004)
19. Thórisson, K.R.: A new constructivist AI: from manual construction to self-constructive systems. In: Wang, P., Goertzel, B. (eds.) Theoretical Foundations of Artificial General Intelligence, vol. 4, pp. 145–171 (2012)
20. Thórisson, K.R.: Seed-programmed autonomous general learning. Proc. Mach. Learn. Res. **131**, 32–70 (2020)
21. Thórisson, K.R., Kremelberg, D., Steunebrink, B.R., Nivel, E.: About understanding. In: Steunebrink, B., Wang, P., Goertzel, B. (eds.) AGI -2016. LNCS (LNAI), vol. 9782, pp. 106–117. Springer, Cham (2016). https://doi.org/10.1007/978-3-319-41649-6_11
22. Thórisson, K.R., Talbot, A.: Cumulative learning with causal-relational models. In: Iklé, M., Franz, A., Rzepka, R., Goertzel, B. (eds.) AGI 2018. LNCS (LNAI), vol. 10999, pp. 227–237. Springer, Cham (2018). https://doi.org/10.1007/978-3-319-97676-1_22
23. Thórisson, K.R.: The explanation hypothesis in general self-supervised learning. Proc. Mach. Learn. Res. **159**, 5–27 (2021)
24. Woodward, J.: Making things Happen: A Theory of Causal Explanation. Oxford University Press, Oxford (2005)

Addressing the Unsustainability of Deep Neural Networks with Next-Gen AI

Amanda Vallentin[1,2]([✉]), Kristinn R. Thórisson[1,3]([✉]), and Hugo Latapie[4]([✉])

[1] Center for Analysis and Design of Intelligent Agents, Reykjavik University,
Menntavegur 1, Reykjavík, Iceland
thorisson@ru.is
[2] IT University of Copenhagen, Rued Langgaards Vej 7, Copenhagen, Denmark
amgv@itu.dk
[3] Icelandic Institute for Intelligent Machines, Reykjavík, Iceland
[4] Cisco Systems, Emerging Technologies and Incubation, San Jose, CA, USA
hlatapie@cisco.com

Abstract. Humanity is currently facing one of its biggest challenges to date: The climate crisis. As a result, most industry sectors are reassessing their ways of working to be better equipped to address their share of the situation. The digital sector often gets set aside in such considerations in talk about the green transition because a significant amount of its work consists of optimizing processes that can save resources. Deep neural networks (DNNs) have gained great attraction and have shown good results regarding process automation. We argue that there are well-known and lesser known negative side-effects to automation frameworks based on DNNs (and related technologies) in terms of energy consumption, pollution, and social equality, that must be questioned. We analyze the operating principles and deployment methods of DNNs, the new era of automation efforts this has launched, and argue on this basis that their continued use is both unsustainable and indefensible. Using three examples of ongoing research, we explain how alternative approaches to develop more general machine intelligence are well-poised to power the next phase of AI-based automation.

Keywords: Artificial Intelligence · Methodology · Deep Neural Networks · General Machine Intelligence · Empirical Reasoning · Automation · Energy Consumption · Pollution · Social Equality · Innovation

P. Hammer et al. (Eds.): AGI 2023, LNAI 13921, pp. 296–306, 2023.
https://doi.org/10.1007/978-3-031-33469-6_30

1   Introduction

The IT-sector is one of the most innovative and fastest-growing industries world-wide[1]. The bleeding edge lies arguably in automation technologies, in no small part because of the obvious incentive that reduced cost and increased speed translates directly to increased revenue. Within contemporary[2] applied automation technologies, DNNs are the latest arrivals with significant potential for various applications. Spurred by predictions of its usefulness for a wide range of tasks[3], unbridled optimism has often characterized its coverage in the media. For instance, a Forbes article presents the 13 skills AI already has today (including "smell" and "reading your mind") [19]; the Guardian explains how AI is changing how a number of different industry sectors operate [6]. However, after a period of experimentation it is increasingly clear that DNN deployment is unavoidably hampered by inherent deep limitations [17] and hidden costs [4,33].

DNNs risk compromising the path towards sustainable development of society[4]. In particular, their runtime and updating methodologies make them unsustainable [16,33]. Another limitation has to do with how they are developed. Energy consumption during DNN development is incredibly high (PaLM, a language model from Google, consumed about 3.4 GWh in about 2 months [3]). For this reason, and others, very few companies will be able to afford developing them because of their sheer size and compute requirements (the BLOOM model, with 175 billion parameters, cost US$7 million to develop [3]). So this approach is inappropriate for parties with only small data and small funding. DNNs are thus nowhere nearly as appropriate or powerful for being deployed in automation tasks as past and present moves by tech giants might indicate [2,5].

This paper has two main parts: In Sects. 2 and 3 we detail what we consider key limitations of DNNs, and in Sect. 4 and 5 we discuss how these could be overcome through research on artificial general intelligence.

2   Deep Limitations of Deep Neural Networks

In recent years both the size and the training data of DNNs have exploded due to an incentive to upscale the models to reach better performance [3,33]. GPT-3,

---

[1] According to Statista, IT-related revenue has a predicted annual growth rate of 6.86% and a predicted market volume of US$1,570.00bn by 2027 (https://www.statista.com/outlook/tmo/it-services/worldwide – *accessed March 1st, 2023*).

[2] Our use of the term 'contemporary AI' refers to a set of methodologies that are currently in active experimentation or use *in industry*, including but not limited to reinforcement learning, ANNs of all kinds, and other well-known methods.

[3] For instance, the annual prediction that "full self-driving cars will be available next year" has been updated at a rate of one year per year by Tesla's CEO (*"Watch Elon Musk Promise Self-Driving Cars 'Next Year' Every Year Since 2014,"* https://futurism.com/video-elon-musk-promising-self-driving-cars — *accessed March 1st, 2023.*

[4] The UN defines 'sustainable development' as harmony between economic growth, social inclusion, and environmental protection. https://www.un.org/sustainabledevelopment/development-agenda/ — *accessed April 4th, 2023.*

one of the biggest language models to date, has shown great results in some text generation tasks [5] leading many to think that DNNs can be used to solve any task. We argue that this is neither wise nor possible.

2.1 DNNs: Expensive to Develop and Use

A search with Google's new chatbot Bard can cost the company 10 times more than a traditional key word search [21]. However, the total cost of the models are already high before they leave the lab (cf. the BLOOM model required $7 million worth of computing time during its development). To provide necessary computing power for the training phase, the developers of DNNs also need access to expensive specialized hardware [33]. Attempts have been made to measure the environmental footprint of large language models (LLM) [16,33]. Luccioni et al. 2022 uses a life cycle analysis approach to estimate a more realistic environmental footprint for a LMM called BLOOM. When they add emissions from all training activities and experiments (not just the final training run) as well as emissions from the infrastructure that maintains the hardware and emissions from manufacturing the hardware, the total footprint of BLOOM is ~124 tons CO_2eq [16]. However, the carbon intensity of the grid used to train BLOOM was only $57gCO_2eq/kWh$(trained in France) compared to GPT-3 where the carbon intensity of the grid was $429gCO_2eq/kWh$(trained in the US). Unfortunately, we only know the power consumption of the final training phase of GPT-3. Comparing the estimated carbon emissions from the two models' final training phase, BLOOM was ~25 tons CO_2eq and GPT-3 was ~502 tons CO_2eq, which is a significant difference since the models have about the same amount of parameters [16]. The environmental footprints of DNNs are strongly influenced by carbon intensity of the energy grid. Considering that US and China are the biggest players in the AI market [20], and they use about 81% and 83% fossil fuels [27], the estimated footprint of only a small part of GPT-3's life cycle is worrying (Table 1).

Table 1. Comparison of the CO_2 emission of different products. The **Scale** column shows the emissions multiplier matching a laptop computer's complete lifecycle.

Product	Description	CO_2eq (kg)	Scale
One laptop [1]	Entire life cycle incl. power use (avg.)	423	1
One automobile [33]	Entire life cycle incl. fuel use (avg.)	57,153	135
One GPT-3 [16]	Final training phase	502,000	1187

Another aspect that can raise the economic and environmental price is when the model needs to be corrected after it is deployed. In this case, the model needs to be taken down and retrained since DNNs cannot be taught anything new once they have left the lab. What often happens is that once the models are released, they act in unexpected ways and the developers need to spend more resources on making them behave. In 2016 when Microsoft created a twitter account for the chatbot Tay, it went from tweeting innocent tweets like "I love feminism now" to "Hitler was right I hate jews" in a single day, despite being trained on safe data as Microsoft claims [9], resulting in the bot having to be taken down. Seven years later, Microsoft ran into a similar problem when a journalist at the New York Times had a conversation with their new chatbot that ended with the bot confessing its love to him and telling him to leave his wife [28]. After the incident, attempts were made to prevent the chatbot from answering personal questions, but even with countless reboots and alterations, it could not be guaranteed that it behaved according to plan. Some have even made this into a sport (called 'JailBreaking') where they share and test ways of getting around the "lobotomized" chatbots and make them say racist, misogynistic, etc. statements. Considering the enormous resources spent on controlling the DNNs' behaviors after they leave the lab, it seems that proper kinds of control mechanisms are missing. This is, however, hardly surprising, since DNNs are primarily based on statistical methods and have no obvious ways of being steered through explicit goals or hierarchical rules.

2.2   The Limited "learning" of Statistics-Based Systems

All animals learn cumulatively because the world does not reveal itself to anyone all-at-once. The "learning" that contemporary AI systems practise is a very special case of what is normally called 'learning,' and it greatly limits which kind of tasks they can be "trained" to solve well. Research by Eberding et al. [7] compared several different types of DNN-based learners (they also tested the AGI-aspiring NARS — we discuss this in a later section) on the well-known cart-pole balancing task, which consists of learning to balance a stick standing on a cart by issuing right and left commands ('R' and 'L'). Once the various AI learners had achieved this task, the researchers reversed the directional commands. The performance of the various learning algorithms to adjust their prior training to this new condition is recorded. In a final scenario, the researchers switch back to the original control method. The performance of all tested DNN-based learners dropped significantly in the reversed phase, and it takes them many more iterations to reach the same performance, once the controls are switched back to the original settings. The change in the task had to be "unlearned" through enough new interactions before the performance could return to what it was before the controls were switched. None of them returned to their original performance.

This research exposes how DNNs have a static and simplistic representation of the world. They are not capable of inferring simple relations (in Eberding's [7] experiment, that the controls were switched around) which makes them unusable for many tasks where reasoning is of importance, like math. The best DNN score on the MATH data set is 50% [3]. The developers managed to reach this score by training it only on mathematics-related texts and up scaling the size of the model to astonishing 540 *billion* parameters. With this strategy they were hoping that the model would evolve to be able to perform reasoning through pattern-recognition alone [3]. There have been attempts of creating reasoning abilities in DNNs, for example using chain-of-thought prompting. The technique improves models' scores on certain data sets, but in bigger models [40]. This method does not, in fact cannot, turn ANN-based systems into reliable reasoners.

2.3 DNN Autonomous Learning After It Leaves the Lab: 'Undefined'

Another of DNNs limitations is that once they are trained, their knowledge is fixed and they cannot be easily applied to another task. When faced with something that was not part of their training data, performance decreases or they do something that is unpredictable. This is likely one of the reasons why self-driving cars have not met their makers' expectations; there are countless scenarios an artificial driver must be able to navigate before it is safe to let it out on the roads. The upshot is, when it comes to complex tasks, DNNs cannot be trusted, due to the countless road scenarios that may occur. There are attempts to overcome this problem, for example a one-shot learning model can classify images it has not seen in its data set. However, the models are more computationally heavy to run and they only work if the image is similar to the ones in the training set [15].

2.4 DNNs and Social Inequality

When looking at LLMs, the data size requirements have exploded in recent years. BERT was trained on 16 GB data in 2019 and GPT-3 was trained on 570 GB in 2020 [4]. Firstly, it is difficult to get a hold of this much data and secondly, it is nearly impossible to ensure that the data has the right quality. In LLMs this manifests itself in a bias against minorities because most of their data has been scraped of sources like Reddit, Twitter, and Wikipedia where the majority of writers are white males [4]. In medical AI, we also see discrimination of patients because it is difficult to acquire data sets that are representative for all genders, ages, and races [25]. Due to the data requirements and cost of DNNs, their increased use will risk worsening inequality, as not everyone has equal access [33] or is equally represented. Healthcare models only work for groups represented in the data sets.

Additionally, the price of using the DNNs will limit which users have access them. For instance, ChatGPT has recently made headlines about being able to pass several advanced exams at universities[5]. If not all students have equal access to DNN aids, we risk increasing social inequality[6].

2.5 DNNs' Domination of the AI Narrative

Despite the known limitations of DNNs, development of alternative approaches to making machines smarter suffers from their media dominance. The private sector has great influence on AI research and they tend to favor data-hungry and computationally heavy DNNs [11].

Due to inordinate emphasis on a single technology, young researchers may be lead to believe that deep learning methods (a) are the end-all, be-all, (b) will overcome all the challenges we accounted for, and (c) will continue to be a key technology in our society [11]. It is no surprise that we see this development because many of the key DNN researchers still seem to believe that the technology will overcome all these challenges with more data and more efficient hardware. Kaplan & McCandlish [10] argue that there exists a scaling law for neural language models, suggesting that there is more to gain if we continue with enlarging the DNNs. Altman predicts an AI revolution because of the incredible wealth that will be created as DNNs replace the majority of our workforce [2].

However, there is ample evidence that DNNs are not living up to such expectations—and it probably never will [37]. The optimism echoes claims made of the Cyc project in the 80s and 90s [14]. Looking at DNNs' abilities regarding common sense, Marcus and Davis [18] recently challenged ChatGPT-3's presumed theory of mind, arguing that the results do not show an ability of common sense but rather that, due to being trained on data about thought-experiments and logic tests, it can predict the answers on purely linguistic principles. When the phrasing of questions changes slightly or the questions are asked in another language, GPT-3 shows no sign of having a theory of mind. In a study by Stojnic et al. [32], they compared DNNs common sense ability to infants and the study revealed that the DNNs failed and did not appear to have common sense.

Along with over-promising in the field of DNNs, there is a lack of innovation that misleads newcomers, governments, and institutions who continue to support research on the topic. By ignoring other strategies, society is not only wasting precious resources but also risking the field of AI as a whole to lose trust.

3 Summary of Limitations

Based on the foregoing, there can be little doubt that contemporary AI methodologies, in all their variations, come with significant limitations. DNNs are mono-

---

[5] ChatGPT has passed the Wharton Exam, US medical licensing exam, law school exam, and others. (https://www.businessinsider.com/list-here-are-the-exams-chatgpt-has-passed-so-far-2023-1?r=US&IR=T#wharton-mba-exam-1 — *accessed March 4th, 2023*).

[6] As of April 2023, the price is $20 a month for reliable and fast access to ChatGPT, although a free version with slower response is still available. (https://openai.com/blog/chatgpt-plus — *accessed April 4th, 2023*).

lithic technologies with limited scope. They only work well when they are built for a well-defined limited task with extensive amounts of data of a certain quality. If any changes are necessary due to unwanted behavior or a slightly different task, the models must be rebuilt, repeating their resource-demanding training cycles. Combined with the potential decrease in social equality, we have a technology that both compromises social inclusion and environmental protection. This is unsustainable. To summarize the limitations of DNNs discussed so far:

- are exceedingly expensive to develop and use
- have a large environmental footprint due to energy consumption
- are difficult to control
- only work well for certain types of tasks
- are difficult and expensive to adapt to new tasks
- can increase inequality in the world
- take away focus and resources from other approaches in AI

It is neither good for the field of AI nor for society at large that the inordinate amount of funding and effort poured into DNNs and related technologies continues. How can we move forward to more sustainable AI?

4   Breaking the Stalemate Through Innovation

Examples of similar situations can be found in recent history of innovation, where a single framework had become too entrenched too early. One example is the global windmill industry in the 1970s.s. Due to the energy crisis at the time, there was a push towards finding cheaper energy sources and many countries tried to develop megawatt windmills [22]. In Denmark another approach was taken, where smaller companies developed smaller and more experimental windmills and met up at annual windmills conferences and shared their results [22]. The companies had incentive to do so because many private individuals were interested in buying their own local windmill, since the government would pay 30 percent of such investment [22]. Due to this approach, the development of a new type of windmill was undertaken, one in which risk was lowered due to the willingness of the Danish population to buy smaller windmills. As a result the windmill industry was born in Denmark, which produced the best windmills.

In other countries a more conservative approach was chosen by attempting to upscale the best existing windmills at the time, with the aim of turning them into megawatt windmills. All of those approaches failed as they could not compete with the Danish models, which were cheaper yet more robust [22]. The current development of contemporary AI where researchers and companies upscale their frameworks (more data and bigger models), believing that "bigger is better," resembles what we saw in the windmill industry in the 70's. In our view, a wholly new methodological paradigm is called for to develop more autonomous AI that is more capable and whose behavior is easier to manage and predict.

5   Sustainable Automation via AGI

The main limitations of DNNs can be grouped into three sets based on their source: (a) opaqueness, (b) learning style, and (c) representation. All of three have made a regular occurrence throughout much of AI research [37], or certainly since the start of the annual AGI conference series in 2008. Here we present an overview of selected recent work focusing on these areas.

From Opaque to Transparent Knowledge. A powerful way to represent knowledge[7], that makes it directly inspectable by human or machine, is to make its structure explicitly hierarchical. Representing knowledge explicitly was of course common in the expert systems of the 1970s, and some research in AI has continued this tradition. The approach comes with known limitations, which can be overcome by taking specific steps. For instance, the Non-Axiomatic Reasoning System (NARS) represents knowledge as defeasible [26] statements that nevertheless support reasoning; indeed, NARS-based systems learn through reasoning processes that mix (non-axiomatic) deduction, abduction, and induction (cf. [8,13,39]). Other systems take a compatible approach but use a different knowledge representation scheme, e.g. the Autocatalytic Endogenous Reflective Architecture (AERA [24]). The results demonstrated by prototypes developed by Latapie et al. [13] show that systems relying on explicit knowledge representation have come a long way, yet their funding is in no way proportional to the results achieved. These systems work on vastly smaller data than DNN-based systems, and thus use much less energy.[8]

Besides non-axiomatism, another way to overcome the limitations of approaches based on logic statements is to step up to second-order representation, allowing the system to inspect and operate on its own knowledge [34]. Such reflective systems have unfortunately not been given sufficient attention in the AI literature. The results of Nivel et al.'s [23] research on teaching an AERA-based agent to learn by observation how to conduct TV-style interview on the topic of recycling in under 21 h, including learning the syntax and semantics of a 100-word vocabulary, how to take turns in dialog, manipulation of objects, deictic gestures of various forms, and more – from scratch – should suffice to convince anyone that this very iconoclastic approach to machine learning should be pursued more vigorously by the AI community.

From Once-and-for-All Learning to Cumulative Learning. Learning in nature has no choice but to proceed incrementally, because the world does not reveal itself to learners all-at-once. This means that the knowledge representation scheme must be updatable piece-wise [36]. Furthermore, any autonomous system

---

[7] By 'knowledge' we mean a form of 'actionable information'—that is, information that can be used for making plans and getting things done in a particular environment.

[8] The AERA system, for example, learned to do a TV-style interview after learning for only 20 h on a 6-core office desktop machine [35].

deployed in the physical world will encounter situations that are not identical to something experienced before. Automating the handling and learning from these is imperative for advancing the state of industrial automation. Viable solutions to cumulative learning have already been proposed [8, 36, 39].

Compositional Knowledge Representation. This topic is closely related to the first point, which is to say that compositional knowledge representation goes hand-in-hand with knowledge transparency and cumulative learning. The ability to construct a goal hierarchy autonomously is a foundational requirement for any AI that is to operate autonomously (or even semi-autonomously); the designers cannot possibly foresee every and all situations that the system may encounter. A goal hierarchy that the system can itself manipulate safely is a necessity. Thórisson [38] presents arguments that general autonomous learning is not possible without the capacity for some form of explanation generation.

While fully-functional AGI systems are still in their early phase of development, some examples are leading the way (cf. [8, 12, 13, 29–31]). All this points towards next-generation systems having the potential to become a green alternative to DNNs, promising easier reuse, increased generality, significantly less energy consumption, lower data requirements, less compute power, and a wider range of applications.

Acknowledgment. This work was supported in part by Cisco Systems, the Icelandic Institute for Intelligent Machines and Reykjavik University.

References

1. What is the carbon footprint of a laptop? Circular Computing (2021). https://circularcomputing.com/news/carbon-footprint-laptop/
2. Altman, S.: Moore's law for everything (2021). https://moores.samaltman.com/
3. Ananthaswamy, A.: In AI, is bigger always better? Nature **615**, 202–205 (2023)
4. Bender, E.M., McMillan-Major, A., Gebru, T., Shmitchell, S.: On the dangers of stochastic parrots: can language models be too big?. In: Proceedings of the 2021 ACM Conference on Fairness, Accountability, and Transparency, pp. 610–623 (2021)
5. Brown, T.B., Mann, B., Ryder, N., Subbiah, M., Kaplan, J., et al.: Language models are few-shot learners. Adv. Neural Inf. Process. Syst. **33**, 1–25 (2020)
6. Butler, S.: From retail to transport: how ai is changing every corner of the economy. The Guardian (2023). https://www.theguardian.com/technology/2023/feb/18/from-retail-to-transport-how-ai-is-changing-every-corner-of-the-economy
7. Eberding, L.M., Thórisson, K.R., Prabu, A., Jaroria, S., Sheikhlar, A.: Comparison of machine learners on an aba experiment format of the cart-pole task. In: Proceedings of Machine Learning Research, vol. 159, pp. 49–63 (2021)
8. Hammer, P.: Reasoning-learning systems based on non-axiomatic reasoning system theory, vol. 192, pp. 88–106 (2022)
9. Hunt, E.: Tay, microsoft's AI chatbot, gets a crash course in racism from twitter. The Guardian (2016). https://www.theguardian.com/technology/2016/mar/24/tay-microsofts-ai-chatbot-gets-a-crash-course-in-racism-from-twitter

10. Kaplan, J., et al.: Scaling laws for neural language models (2020)
11. Klinger, J., Mateos-Garcia, J.C., Stathoulopoulos, K.: A narrowing of AI research? SSRN Electron. J. (2020)
12. Kommrusch, S., Minsky, H., Minsky, M., Shaoul, C.: Self-supervised learning for multi-goal grid world: Comparing leela and deep q network. In: Proceedings of Machine Learning Research, vol. 131, pp. 81–97 (2020)
13. Latapie, H., Gabriel, M., Kompella, R.: Hybrid AI for IoT actionable insights & real-time data-driven networks. In: Proceedings of Machine Learning Research, vol. 159, pp. 127–131 (2022)
14. Lenat, D.: Cyc: a large-scale investment in knowledge infrastructure. Commun. ACM **38**, 33–38 (2023)
15. Logunova, I.: A guide to one-shot learning (2022). https://serokell.io/blog/nn-and-one-shot-learning
16. Luccioni, A.S., Viguier, S., Ligozat, A.L.: Estimating the carbon footprint of bloom, a 176b parameter language model (2022). https://arxiv.org/abs/2211.02001
17. Marcus, G.: Deep learning is hitting a wall. Nautilus (2023). https://nautil.us/deep-learning-is-hitting-a-wall-238440/
18. Marcus, G., Davis, E.: How not to test gpt-3 (2023). https://garymarcus.substack.com/p/how-not-to-test-gpt-3
19. Marr, B.: 13 mind-blowing things artificial intelligence can already do today. Forbes (2019). https://www.forbes.com/sites/bernardmarr/2019/11/11/13-mind-blowing-things-artificial-intelligence-can-already-do-today/?sh=39e42add6502
20. Maslej, N., Fattorini, L., Brynjolfsson, E., et al.: Artificial Intelligence Index Report 2023. Technical Report, Stanford University (2023). https://aiindex.stanford.edu/report/
21. Mok, A.: AI is expensive. a search on Google's chatbot Bard costs the company 10 times more than a regular one, which could amount to several billion dollars. Business Insider (2023). https://www.businessinsider.com/ai-expensive-google-chatbot-bard-may-cost-company-billions-dollars-2023-2
22. Nielsen, K.H.: Vindmøllens historie: Sådan tæmmede danskerne vindens energi. ForskerZonen (2018). https://videnskab.dk/forskerzonen/teknologi-innovation/vindmoellenshistorie-saadan-taemmede-danskerne-vindens-energi
23. Nivel, E., Thórisson, K.R., et al.: Autonomous acquisition of natural language. In: IADIS International Conference on Intelligent Systems & Agents, pp. 58–66 (2014)
24. Nivel, E., Thórisson, K.R., Steunebrink, B., Dindo, H., et al., G.P.: Autocatalytic endogenous reflective architecture. Tech report RUTR-SCS13002, Reykjavik University - School of Computer Science (2013)
25. Panch, T., Mattie, H., Celi, L.A.: The 'inconvenient truth' about AI in healthcare. NPJ Dig. Med. **2**, 77 (2019)
26. Pollock, J.L.: Defeasible reasoning and degrees of justification. Argu. Comput. **1**(1), 7–22 (2010)
27. Ritchie, H., Roser, M., Rosado, P.: Energy. Our World in Data (2022). https://ourworldindata.org/energy-mix
28. Roose, K.: A conversation with Bing's chatbot left me deeply unsettled. The New York Times (2023). https://www.nytimes.com/2023/02/16/technology/bing-chatbot-microsoft-chatgpt.html
29. Sheikhlar, A., Thórisson, K.R., Eberding, L.M.: Autonomous cumulative transfer learning. In: International Conference on Artificial General Intelligence, pp. 306–316 (2020)
30. Sheikhlar, A., Thórisson, K.R., Thompson, J.: Explicit analogy for autonomous transversal learning, vol. 192, pp. 48–62 (2022)

31. Steunebrink, B., Swan, J., Nivel, E.: The Holon system: artificial general intelligence as 'work on command'. In: Proceedings of Machine Learning Research, vol. 192, pp. 120–126 (2022)

32. Stojnic, G., Gandhi, K., Yasuda, S., Lake, B.M., Dillon, M.R.: Commonsense psychology in human infants and machines. Cognition **235**, 105406 (2023)

33. Strubell, E., Ganesh, A., McCallum, A.: Energy and policy considerations for deep learning in NLP. In: 57th Annual Meeting of the Association for Computational Linguistics (ACL) (2019)

34. Thórisson, K.R.: A new constructivist AI: from manual construction to self-constructive systems. In: Wang, P., Goertzel, B. (eds.) Theoretical Foundations of Artificial General Intelligence, vol. 4, pp. 145–171 (2012)

35. Thórisson, K.R.: Seed-programmed autonomous general learning. In: Proceedings of Machine Learning Research, vol. 131, pp. 32–70 (2020)

36. Thórisson, K.R., Bieger, J., Li, X., Wang, P.: Cumulative learning. In: Hammer, P., Agrawal, P., Goertzel, B., Iklé, M. (eds.) AGI 2019. LNCS (LNAI), vol. 11654, pp. 198–208. Springer, Cham (2019). https://doi.org/10.1007/978-3-030-27005-6_20

37. Thórisson, K.R., Minsky, H.: The future of AI research: ten defeasible 'axioms of intelligence'. In: Proceedings of Machine Learning Research, vol. 192, pp. 5–21 (2022)

38. Thórisson, K.R.: The 'Explanation Hypothesis' in general self-supervised Learning. In: Proceedings of Machine Learning Research, IWSSL-21, pp. 5–27 (2021)

39. Wang, P.: Rigid Flexibility: The Logic of Intelligence, vol. 34. Springer, Heidelberg (2006). https://doi.org/10.1007/1-4020-5045-3

40. Wei, J., et al.: Chain-of-thought prompting elicits reasoning in large language models (2023)

NUTS, NARS, and Speech

Dwane van der Sluis[(✉)]

WiseWorks.AI, London, UK
ucabdv1@ucl.ac.uk

Abstract. To investigate whether "Intelligence is the capacity of an information-processing system to adapt to its environment while operating with insufficient knowledge and resources" [29], we look at utilising the non axiomatic reasoning system (NARS) for speech recognition. This article presents NUTS: raNdom dimensionality redUction non axiomaTic reasoning few Shot learner for perception. NUTS consists of naive dimensionaility reduction, some pre-processing, and then non axiomatic reasoning (NARS). With only 2 training examples NUTS performs similarly to the Whisper Tiny model for discrete word identification.

Keywords: Non Axiomatic Reasoning · Perception · Few shot learning

1 Introduction

'Artificial Intelligence' now covers a wide range of tasks such as image recognition, speech recognition, game playing, and protein folding, each of which can be performed at, near, or beyond human level. Over time the term has drifted in meaning, away from a 'thinking machine', toward systems that often can only be applied to a single task, do not improve without further training, and take large amounts of resources to train and run. For example, GPT-3, a large language model, is estimated to have cost over 4.6 million dollars to train [19]. These models can be opaque, difficult to interpret, and unable to explain why a particular prediction was made, or unable to provide any guarantees in failure scenarios. Predicate Logic, on the other hand, is capable of robust and consistent decisions. One such predicate logic system, CYC [18], aims to encode all common human knowledge in a knowledge graph. This means CYC has the limitations of predicate logic, one being that all axioms (in the knowledge graph) be true and consistent, otherwise false statements can be derived. Another approach is Non Axiomatic Reasoning. The Non Axiomatic Reasoning System (NARS) performs reasoning that does not assign an objective value of truth to a statement, but instead assigns a subjective value. This subjective value is not fully trusted, and is revised over time as new information arrives. NARS has the advantages that it 1) can cope with holding conflicting information in its knowledge base 2) can

Supplementary Information The online version contains supplementary material available at https://doi.org/10.1007/978-3-031-33469-6_31.

explain predictions, 3) requires less data for inference 4) explicitly implements logic choosing which concepts to remove rather than randomly forgetting.

While Open NARS for Applications (ONA) was designed with reasoning in mind, we choose to investigate its usefulness, and resource consumption, on perception, and in particular speech recognition. This is because as Peirce stated "abductive inference shades into perceptual judgement without any sharp line of demarcation between them." [23], and advances in understanding one may shed light on the other. The integration of deep learning and logic reasoning is an open-research problem and it is considered to be the key for the development of real intelligent agents [21]. We narrow the focus of this paper to the dimensionality reduction, and logic needed to convert auditory sensory data into category labels, and the resources required in the Open NARS for Applications (ONA) software platform. First we give background, from the recent discussion around the definition of intelligence, and then how our human nervous system fused from 2 independent systems, perhaps leading to different characteristics of it. We then give a limited literature review, and then explain our method and experiments. In the last section we give and discuss our results.

2   Background

Until recently, and possibly still, industry (and maybe academia too) are interested in whether new tasks can be learnt by AI, and if so, can they be sold profitably to consumers. The developers are under no obligation to consider the environmental impact or safety concerns. That said, some do by choice, but there is little compulsion from a social or regulatory point of view. This is partly due to deep learning being "unreasonably good" [25] and partly due to no other known way of achieving the same level of performance. A focus on resource consumption was created by adding it explicitly into the definition of artificial intelligence [30]. Invitations to comment on this definition produced much discussion [31]. In this discussion it was pointed out that industry has existing finite resource limitations [17], which is true, however for most leader board tasks, resource consumption is not taken into account. It also appears that governments are hesitant to impose resource limitations on industry. A resource limitation is of interest as it prevents brute force approaches and opens up the possibility of investigating how fewer resources can be utilised over time. Brute force approaches can also encode an entire domain space, further limiting the conclusions that can be drawn. If a method requires fewer resources over time, as a task or operation is repeated, then this suggests a deeper (or perhaps more precise or over-fitted) understanding of that task or operation, which may be of interest in the investigation of intelligence. Wang's definition of intelligence [30] separates skill (e.g. playing chess) from intelligence, and contains an assumption of insufficient knowledge and resources (AIKR). Under this definition learning a new skill to the same level of ability as some other method but with fewer resources or an insufficient understanding of the world (i.e. imperfect knowledge) is advantageous. Thus intelligence and skill are separate concepts.

The focus of this paper is on the cognitive processes that underlie speech recognition. It is assumed that these are similar to the cognitive processes that underlie other forms of perception. However, as stated earlier, the line between perceptual judgement and abductive inference has no clear demarcation [23]. This may be because the physiology underpinning these functions has different origins. Genetic patterning studies suggest that the 'blastoporal nervous system', which coordinates feeding movements and locomotion, and the 'apical nervous system', which controls general body physiology, evolved separately in our ancestors more than six hundred million years ago [2,28], and subsequently fused. This may help explain why we (humans) are still aware of differences in different parts of our nervous system, being aware of our cognition around feeding and locomotion, but have little to no awareness of our 'apical nervous system'. There are arguments that perception and cognition are unified [3,6,10,13,16,26,27], and arguments against, that is, for modularity [9,22]. The debate between modularity and unified is beyond the scope of this paper. However, the important point for the purposes of this paper is that the mechanisms of perception are not fully available to us. We do not know, for example, how we recognise objects or how we understand speech. Speech is temporal in nature and involves nuanced differentiation between acoustically similar sounds, (for example b in bright, and f in fright).

Model performance over the last few decades has steadily improved, however it is computationally expensive. Current state-of-the-art models rely on a low level acoustic model, followed by a language model. The acoustic model converts a sound wave into an encoded representation of a sound, and the language model gives the probabilities of the next word, given the last few words, along with the acoustic encoding. As said, language models, like GPT-3 require a large amount of data to train, which conflicts with how children learn a new word with very few examples [5]. Wang's definition of intelligence [30] is based on the idea that intelligence is about making the most of the resources that are available and that it is not always possible to know everything that is going on in the world. So, someone who is able to learn new skills quickly and efficiently, even if they don't have a lot of knowledge about those skills initially, would be considered intelligent. One approach to understanding the mechanisms of intelligence is to consider the different ways in which it can be measured. One way to measure intelligence may be by looking at someone or some system's ability to learn new skills, and then measure the quality of that skill, as well as the energy consumed to learn it and perform it once learnt. Speech recognition is one such potential skill.

Generally large dimensionality reduction is needed to convert perceived inputs into symbols that logic can be applied on. One approach [4] is to cluster the inputs in the feature space before similarity and difference are calculated and used as input into a deep network that is trained. Another approach is to pre-process with a DL model specifically trained for that modality, i.e. YOLO for computer vision, and use the generated labels. The generated labels form a lower bound on the resolution of the logic system, i.e. if the labels are 'dogs' and 'cats', it would be difficult for a logic system to learn of a new breed of dog. If the logic system uses scalar output features of a DL model, e.g. the bounding box of the cat, x by y pixels, and if only far away cats are seen, and then later a closer (and therefore much bigger) cat is seen, scaling issues can be created, as the system may not see the full range of sizes immediately, and needs to recalibrate previous observations when the scale is readjusted on seeing a much larger, or smaller example. In speech these challenges are exhibited in the form of the dimensionality reduction from 16k samples per second to ~2 words per second, with uneven speaking speed. Speech recognition has traditionally used labelled data sets which cost USD50/hr to hand label, limiting the training data set size into the 10,00 h or less range. The resultant systems have low generalisability with many recent state of the art systems reporting <5% word error rates, which collapses into the 30–40% range when used on other, but similar datasets [24]. The exact costs of training models such as Whisper [24] with 1.6 billion parameters, are unknown, but the 175 billion parameter GPT-3 (109× larger), also by OpenAI, is estimated at 4.6 million USD. If the training costs were a constant multiplier of the number of parameters (they are not), the training of Whisper could be in the order of magnitude of 40k USD. The training data set of Whisper was 168k hours of 16 KHz speech. This equates to a data set size of 19 TB, approximately half the estimated size of GPT3 about 45 TB of training data. The recent success of attention in other domains has also been applied to speech. Andrade et al. [1] developed a 202K parameter neural attention model, we will refer to as ANAM, which also targeted at the Speech Command dataset.

3 Literature Review

In the 1970's speech recognition relied on hand crafted features. This changed as end to end differential systems were developed and new SOTA were reached [24]. These systems lack interpretability, while not important for speech recognition, are of interest if the features triggering decisions can be exposed and validated. With concept whitening [7] it is possible to concentrate (grounded) meaning in single neurons to aid interpretability, but requires category labels, which may not be available at training time, and adds complication as category labels "need to address topics like the representation of concepts, the strength of membership in a category, mechanisms for forming new concepts and the relation between a concept and the outside world" [32]. Another approach is Deep Logic Models which integrate deep learning and logic reasoning in an end-to-end differentiable architecture [21]. This work leads onto Relational Reasoning Networks R2Ns [20] which perform relational reasoning in the latent space of a deep learner architecture. However they suffer an explosion in memory needed as the number of possible ground atoms grows polynomially on the arity of the considered relations. This underpins the useful implication of the AIKR. Shanaha [26] explores perception of objects via computer vision, with abduction, but does not describe how resource intensive the work was or if resource limits were reached. Johansson [14] investigates learning match to sample and the relationships more, less and opposite. Noting the advantages that AGI has, allowing us to experiment with an agents internals, and giving the example where NARS layer 6 (variables for generalisation) is shown to be needed for the work Hammer [11] does on a system designed to only process data from perception, i.e. has no predefined knowledge. Generalised identity matching, where a new example is matched to a reference sample has been shown to be possible in NARS [15], and further that the derived identity concept could generalise to novel situations. In unpublished work Durisek [8] postulated speech recognition leveraging phonemes may be possible with NARS.

4   Method

For simplicity we attempt to identify single whole spoken words, which has been the focus of much research. We use a standard data set, the Speech Command v2 [33], which contains 35 single word commands, 0–9, back, forward and other confusing words (bird, bed). Each word had over 3000 recordings, each of 1 s in duration or less. As in Whisper [24], we take 16 bit, 16 KHz audio, on which 80 bin MEL (logarithmic) spectrum was calculated every 10 ms. This produced 8000 (80×100) energy intensity values per second, which were normalised. Utterances shorter than 1 s were padded. This reduced the input dimension from 16000 to 8000, and is a standard pre-processing step in speech recognition. These 8000 values needed to be restructured to be passed into ONA. Data was presented to ONA in the form of Narsese[1] statements. As a simple example, we encode three examples as Narsese instances, A, B and C with n properties each. The strength of the property relationship to the instance was encoded in the truth value, i.e. a property with a strength of 0.9 would be encoded as:

$$< \{A\} \rightarrow [p1] > .\%0.9\% \tag{1}$$

meaning "'{A}' has the property 'p1' with strength of 0.9". It was then asserted that {A} is a LABEL and {B} is a LABEL. e.g.

$$< \{A\} \rightarrow LABEL > . \tag{2}$$

And then the system was queried to see if C was labelled correctly:

$$< \{C\} \rightarrow LABEL >? \tag{3}$$

After a grid search we set the number of labelled examples per class to 2 (+ unlabelled example = 3). We note this is the smallest number that allows similarity to be exploited. With this setup and synthetic and real data we attempted to answer the following questions:

– RQ1: Can non axiomatic reasoning, which can cope with conflicting information, be leveraged to perform speech recognition?
– RQ2: Is there a computational or performance?

For a baselines we used 1) general speech recognition pre-trained Whisper models, and 2) the earlier mentioned ANAM model. We expected these to produce state-of-the-art results, at the cost of larger computation.

---

[1] For Narsese see https://cis.temple.edu/~pwang/NARS-Intro.html.

Experiment 1 NARS, Computational Complexity. We expressed data in the same manner as above, encoding each real world utterance as 8000 properties, using the energy in each bin as the strength of a property as Narsese statements. Energy values below 0.5 posed a problem, as they expressed absence of a feature in the data, e.g. the word 'Moo', should not have high frequency 's', or 't' sound in it. To enable ONA to track the absence of something, we negate the property name, i.e.[mel16x9] becomes [NOTmel16x9], and subtract the truth value from 0.5, so that a low truth value 0.1, becomes 0.9. E.g.

$$< \{U_1\} \rightarrow [mel16x9] > .\%0.1\% \tag{4}$$

is replaced with

$$< \{U_1\} \rightarrow [NOTmel16x9] > .\%0.9\% \tag{5}$$

We took 3 random utterances of 'one' (from the 3893 possible), generated the 8000 values for each, then encoded these as Narsese statements. We then asserted $< \{U_1\} \rightarrow one >$. For utterances 1 and 2, and then queried ONA to see if utterance 3 is similar to the label $< \{U_n\} \rightarrow one >$?. All performance tests used a 64 GB AMD Ryzen 5 3600 6-Core Processor running Ubuntu (no GPU).

Experiment 2 Nalifier, NARS, Synthetic Data. We take the same method as experiment 1, but this time pass the statements into a python pre-processor, Nalifier.py [12], that suppresses certain Narsese statements, and synthesises other Narsese statements, which are in turn passed into ONA. The Nalifier has several functions, if the statement received consists of an instance property statement e.g. $< utterance_n \rightarrow [property_p] >$. It collects all the properties for this new instance, all the properties for all other instances in its memory and starts comparing them to find the closest. If an instance is found that the current instance is similar to, it synthesises and emits new narsese. The new narsese is passed into ONA (or more specifically NAL, the executable of ONA), and interpreted. The success criteria is the same as experiment 1, we check to see if the unknown instance is labelled correctly.

Experiment 3 - NUTS. We now introduce 'NUTS' : raNdom dimensionality redUction non axiomaTic reasoning few Shot learner for perception. NUTS consists of four modules, dimensionality reduction, conversion into narsese, a narses preprocessor (the Nalifier), and open NARS for applications (ONA). We used a random projection without sparsity, to reduce dimensionality, specifically we pass the input 16k samples through MEL encoding, producing 8000 values. These 8000 values were multiplied by a randomly generated $8000 * D$ matrix, reducing the dimensions to D. These D values were then used to generate narsese as before, which is passed into the Nalifer which filers and generates narsese, which is passed into ONA. Each class was tested in turn with the negative classes consisted of the remaining 34 words in the speech command dataset. The number of learning examples of each word could be varied, along with ONA's setting for the size of the AIKR, the size of the reduced dimensionality space[2], and the

---

[2] A grid search showed 4 dimensions was reasonable.

number of repeats. The matrix used for reduction was re-generated before each run. Success was measured as the proportions of runs where the correct "is a" relationship is identified.

5 Results

Experiment 1 NARS, Computational Complexity. As mentioned, baselines were OpenAIs whisper model, and Andrade's et al's ANAN. Whisper was tested on 100 random utterances from each of the 35 words in the Standard Commands data set, comparisons were case insensitive excluding punctuation. As seen in Table 1, Whisper tiny model took an average of 0.8 sec per inference (including encoding) with a performance of 58%. ONA was unable to accurately identify the unknown utterance as being similar to anything in memory. This may have been because the full structure of the speech was not exploited, but we wished to avoid manual feature engineering. Analysis of the derived statements showed that the instances were considered similar to the properties rather than the instances, this was unexpected.

Table 1. Performance & Baselines: Whisper Tiny, Large, and ANAM

	Exp1	Exp2	NUTS	Large	Tiny	ANAM
Vocabulary Size	1	2	35	50257	50257	35
Training Samples	2	2	105	1e9 (est)	1e9 (est)	84843
Input Dimensions (1 sec audio)	16000	16000	16000	16000	16000	16000
Intermediate Dimensions	8000	200	4	8000	8000	9600
Inference Time (sec)	0.05	2615.00	0.02	43	0.80	0.095
Training Time (sec)	19	5700	16			7200
Performance Accuracy	0%		64%	68%	58%	93%

Experiment 2 Nalifier, NARS, Synthetic Data. The Nalifier took considerable time to execute, to load and 'train' 2 instances with 2000 properties each, took 95 min. To load, encode and perform inference on a new example took an additional 43 min. This version of the Nalifier contains a $O(n^2)$ algorithm which executes each time a new property was observed for an instance. After 3 instances, each with 2000 properties were added into NARS, (first preprocessed by the Nalifier), NARS successfully determined that instance C, the unlabelled instance, was similar to instance A. This showed that speech recognition is possible with NARS, and that the Nalifier is needed. We did not attempt 8000 properties, or measure accuracy due to execution time.

Experiment 3 NUTS. We were surprised randomly reducing dimensions worked, even for small numbers of training examples. For these experiments the best performance was obtained with 4 dimensions, when the unknown class was labelled 64% of the time, compared to 2.8% for random performance, see Table 1. This compared favourably with Whisper Tiny's 58%[3], but far below the ANAM's state of the art 94%. Training was label and compute efficient, only needing 2 training samples per class, and inference time was 0.02 sec (including encoding and dimensionality reduction), far below that experiment 2's 43 min, showing that dimensionaility reduction is the source of the computational efficiency.

We conclude that perception, specifically speech recognition is possible with NARS. However we note performance collapsed certain words such as Bird, and Bed, yet ANAM's confusion matrix shows it is possible to distinguish them. This may be due to a limitation of NARS, or information loss in the dimensionaility reduction. Figure 1 shows the overall performance of a random generated matrix, a random word, and reduced dimensions 2–10, repeated 3500 times (100 times per class). Figure 2 shows performance increases with the number of examples, raising from 64% at 2 examples to 90% at 20.

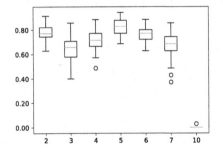 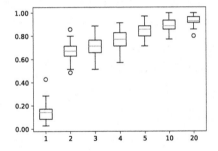

Fig. 1. Accuracy as a function of the reduced dimension embedding. Number of examples per class = 2.

Fig. 2. Accuracy as a function of the number of examples. Reduced dimensions = 4.

6   Discussion

RQ1: Can non axiomatic reasoning, which can cope with conflicting information, be leveraged to perform speech recognition? Yes, we demonstrated that NARS (along with the Nalifier and dimensionality reduction), can interpret speech data in a meaningful way, obtaining 64% accuracy with only 2 training examples on a 35 class problem.

---

[3] Whisper leverages language models greatly improving multiword performance.

RQ2: Is there a computational advantage? A crude comparison of inference time on CPU suggests they are in a similar order of magnitude. But as Whisper runs efficiently on GPU, and NUTS is a mix of C and Python, a strict comparison of counts of each operation type, could not be completed in the time, and it is left as further work.

We started by discussing the term 'Artificial Intelligence' and resource consumption. While we did not produce a system with same or better performance with fewer resources, if we had done so would it be more 'Intelligent'? We would argue it would not, as the catalyst is not part of the described algorithm. We suspect building 'intelligent' systems (as in 'thinking machines') will remain elusive until the terms skill and intelligence are dis-entangled, and the catalyst for improvement is isolated and automated.

Acknowledgement. We thank reviewers and Parker Lamb for their comments.

References

1. de Andrade, D.C., Leo, S., Viana, M., Bernkopf, C.: A neural attention model for speech command recognition. ArXiv abs/1808.08929 (2018)
2. Arendt, D., Tosches, M., Marlow, H.: From nerve net to nerve ring, nerve cord and brain evolution of the nervous system. Nat. Rev. Neurosci. **17**, 61–72 (2016). https://doi.org/10.1038/nrn.2015.15
3. Barsalou, L.W.: Perceptual symbol systems. Behav. Brain Sci. (1999). https://doi.org/10.1017/S0140525X99002149
4. Blazek, P.J., Lin, M.M.: Explainable neural networks that simulate reasoning. Nat. Comput. Sci. **1**(9), 607–618 (2021)
5. Bloom, P.: How Children Learn the Meanings of Words. MIT press, Cambridge (2002)
6. Chalmers, D.J., French, R.M., Hofstadter, D.R.: High-level perception, representation, and analogy: a critique of artificial intelligence methodology. J. Exp. Theor. Artif. Intell. **4**(3), 185–211 (1992). https://doi.org/10.1080/09528139208953747
7. Chen, Z., Bei, Y., Rudin, C.: Concept whitening for interpretable image recognition. Nat. Mach. Intell. **2**(12), 772–782 (2020). https://doi.org/10.48550/arXiv.2002.01650
8. Durisek, P.: Speech recognition using nars (2014). https://www.applied-nars.com/articles/speech-recognition-using-nars
9. Fodor, J.A.: The Modularity of Mind. MIT press, Cambridge (1983). https://doi.org/10.7551/mitpress/4737.001.0001
10. Goldstone, R.L., Barsalou, L.W.: Reuniting perception and conception. Cognition **65**(2–3), 231–262 (1998). https://doi.org/10.1016/s0010-0277(97)00047-4
11. Hammer, P.: Adaptive Neuro-Symbolic Network Agent, pp. 80–90. Springer, Heidelberg (2019). https://doi.org/10.1007/978-3-030-27005-6_8
12. Hammer, P., Lofthouse, T., Wang, P.: The OpenNARS implementation of the non-axiomatic reasoning system. In: Steunebrink, B., Wang, P., Goertzel, B. (eds.) AGI -2016. LNCS (LNAI), vol. 9782, pp. 160–170. Springer, Cham (2016). https://doi.org/10.1007/978-3-319-41649-6_16
13. Jarvilehto, T.: Efferent influences on receptors in knowledge formation. Psycoloquy **9**(1) (1998)

14. Johansson, R.: Scientific progress in agi from the perspective of contemporary behavioral psychology. In: NARS AGI 2020 Workshop, 2020 (2020)
15. Johansson, R., Lofthouse, T., Hammer, P.: Generalized identity matching in nars. In: Artificial General Intelligence. Springer, Heidelberg (2022). https://doi.org/10.1007/978-3-031-19907-3_23
16. Lakoff, G., Johnson, M.: Philosophy in the flesh, the embodied mind and its challenge to western thought (1999). https://doi.org/10.1590/S0102-44502001000100008
17. Legg, S.: A review of "on defining artificial intelligence." J. Artif. General Intell. **11**(2), 45–46 (2020). https://doi.org/10.2478/jagi-2019-0003
18. Lenat, D., Guha, R.V.: Cyc: a midterm report. AI Maga. **11**(3), 32–32 (1990). https://doi.org/10.1609/aimag.v11i3.842
19. Li, C.: Openai's gpt-3 language model: A technical overview. blog (2020). https://lambdalabs.com/blog/demystifying-gpt-3
20. Marra, G., Diligenti, M., Giannini, F., Maggini, M.: Learning representations for sub-symbolic reasoning. ArXiv abs/2106.00393 (2021).arXiv:2106.00393v2
21. Marra, G., Giannini, F., Diligenti, M., Gori, M.: Integrating learning and reasoning with deep logic models. In: Brefeld, U., Fromont, E., Hotho, A., Knobbe, A., Maathuis, M., Robardet, C. (eds.) ECML PKDD 2019. LNCS (LNAI), vol. 11907, pp. 517–532. Springer, Cham (2020). https://doi.org/10.1007/978-3-030-46147-8_31
22. Prinz, J.: Is the mind really modular. Contemp. Debates Cogn. Sci. **14**, 22–36 (2006)
23. Project, P.: The Essential Peirce, Volume 2: Selected Philosophical Writings (1893–1913). Essential Peirce. Indiana University Press, Bloomington (1998)
24. Radford, A., Kim, J.W., Xu, T., Brockman, G., McLeavey, C., Sutskever, I.: Robust speech recognition via large-scale weak supervision. Technical report, OpenAI (2022). https://doi.org/10.48550/arXiv.2212.04356
25. Sejnowski, T.J.: The unreasonable effectiveness of deep learning in artificial intelligence. Proc. Natl. Acad. Sci. **117**(48) (2020). https://doi.org/10.1073/pnas.1907373117
26. Shanahan, M.: Perception as abduction: turning sensor data into meaningful representation. Cogn. Sci. **29**(1), 103–134 (2005). https://doi.org/10.1207/s15516709cog2901_5
27. Shimojo, S., Shams, L.: Sensory modalities are not separate modalities: plasticity and interactions. Curr. Opinion Neurobiol. **11**(4), 505–509 (2001). https://doi.org/10.1016/s0959-4388(00)00241-5
28. Tosches, M.A., Arendt, D.: The bilaterian forebrain: an evolutionary chimaera. Curr. Opin. Neurobiol. **23**(6), 1080–1089 (2013). https://doi.org/10.1016/j.conb.2013.09.005
29. Wang, P.: Non-axiomatic reasoning system: exploring the essence of intelligence. Indiana University (1995)
30. Wang, P.: On defining artificial intelligence. J. Artif. Gener. Intell. **10**(2), 1–37 (2019). https://doi.org/10.2478/jagi-2019-0002
31. Wang, P., Hahm, C., Hammer, P.: A model of unified perception and cognition. Front. Artif. Intell. **5** (2022). https://doi.org/10.3389/frai.2022.806403
32. Wang, P., Hofstadter, D.: A logic of categorization. J. Exp. Theor. Artif. Intell. **18**(2), 193–213 (2006). https://doi.org/10.1080/09528130600557549
33. Warden, P.: Speech commands: a dataset for limited-vocabulary speech recognition. arXiv preprint arXiv:1804.03209 (2018). https://doi.org/10.48550/arXiv.1804.03209

Computational-Level Analysis of Constraint Compliance for General Intelligence

Robert E. Wray$^{(\boxtimes)}$ (ID), Steven J. Jones (ID), and John E. Laird (ID)

The Center for Integrated Cognition IQM Research Institute, Ann Arbor, MI 48105, USA

{robert.wray,steven.jones,john.laird}@cic.iqmri.org
https://integratedcognition.ai

Abstract. Human behavior is conditioned by codes and norms that constrain action. Rules, "manners," laws, and moral imperatives are examples of classes of constraints that govern human behavior. These systems of constraints are "messy:" individual constraints are often poorly defined, what constraints are relevant in a particular situation may be unknown or ambiguous, constraints interact and conflict with one another, and determining how to act within the bounds of the relevant constraints may be a significant challenge, especially when rapid decisions are needed. General, artificially-intelligent agents must be able to navigate the messiness of systems of real-world constraints in order to behave predictability and reliably. In this paper, we characterize sources of complexity in constraint processing for general agents and describe a computational-level analysis for such *constraint compliance*. We identify key algorithmic requirements based on the computational-level analysis and outline a limited, exploratory implementation of a general approach to constraint compliance.

Keywords: Constraint compliance · Cognitive architecture

1 Introduction

Rules, social norms (e.g., "manners"), laws, and moral imperatives are examples of various classes of *constraints* that govern human behavior. Systems of constraints are "messy:" individual constraints are often poorly defined; the constraints relevant in a particular situation may be unknown or ambiguous; constraints interact and conflict with one another; and determining how to act rapidly within the bounds of relevant constraints may itself be a significant challenge. Yet humans routinely and robustly overcome the messiness of conforming to many simultaneous and often ill-defined constraints.

© The Author(s), under exclusive license to Springer Nature Switzerland AG 2023
P. Hammer et al. (Eds.): AGI 2023, LNAI 13921, pp. 317–327, 2023.
https://doi.org/10.1007/978-3-031-33469-6_32

Notably, humans can also rapidly adapt their task performance to new constraints. A driver who has always driven on the left can, with just a little deliberation and practice, shift to driving on the right side of the road. A traveler has the ability to recognize and to adapt to overt local customs related to greetings, meals, etc. Humans can quickly and robustly adapt to novel constraints, even when those novel constraints interact with familiar constraints and tasks.

Today's AI systems, in contrast, generally elide or ignore the messiness of complying with real-world constraints. They often encode a designer's interpretation of constraints (e.g., by knowledge engineering or learning from a human-defined policy) and are designed for limited, pre-specified operating contexts [13]. These systems conform to engineered constraints unfailingly but inflexibly. The encoding of constraints (along with designer assumptions) is tightly integrated with task specifications, making it difficult for the systems to adapt to new operating environments. For example, compare the relative immediacy of human adaptation to driving on their "opposite" side of the road for the first time vs. an autonomous driving system as trained today or the present limitations of large language models to conform to ethical guidance when producing responses [20].

These approaches can be acceptable for narrow AI but, as human intelligence suggests, a general artificial intelligence requires an ability to reason about its constraints (and conflicts), resolve ambiguity, determine how it should proceed given awareness of constraints, and be rapidly adaptive to new constraints. We introduce a broader approach to constraints, *constraint compliance*, intended to provide an agent with the capacity to comply with real-world constraints.

We consider the computational requirements for this more comprehensive approach to compliance to systems of constraints, emphasizing general intelligence. That is, we seek to identify a computational approach that is constraint-compliant, domain general (not specific to an application or a task domain), and robust to the complexities that "real world constraints" introduce. We outline sources of "messiness" relevant to constraint processing and present a computational analysis of an overall constraint-compliance process, enumerating five distinct types of processing steps the agent must make. We then outline an initial algorithmic-level exploration of a constraint-compliance process. Finally, based on the analysis and exploratory implementation, we identify four algorithmic challenges that require additional analysis and research in order to realize comprehensive constraint compliance.

2   Sources of Complexity in Constraint Processing

Here, we enumerate specific sources of complexity and challenge for comprehensive constraint compliance. This "messiness" derives from many sources spanning the environment, the agent's task(s), its internal capabilities and assumptions, and the specification of constraints themselves.

We illustrate using examples from Sudoku-puzzle solving and automobile driving. Sudoku is a canonical constraint satisfaction problem (CSP) [12] and offers an effective contrast between classical constraint satisfaction [4] and the more comprehensive account of constraint processing we examine here.[1]

Automobile driving offers a specific, familiar domain in which the real-world challenges of comprehensively complying to constraints arise; constraints abound in driving. This choice of domain is illustrative only: our goal is to develop a general approach to constraint compliance, not one specific to a single domain.

2.1 Partial Observability

In Sudoku, the puzzle state is fully available. The rules of the game (the constraints) can be readily applied after each move. Agents in real-world environments cannot generally sense everything and their actions often have uncertain outcomes. While partial observability and uncertainty have broad implications for agent reasoning [17], they impose specific demands for constraint compliance.

As one example, student drivers in the US are taught to "maintain a 3-second distance when following on dry payment." Unlike a speed limit, where a speedometer provides an immediate gauge of one's speed, fully complying with this constraint requires that the driver visually attend to and continually assess the distance and current speed of their vehicle vs. the one in front and adjust speed to maintain the minimum distance.[2] Because not all constraint-relevant parameters are directly accessible to the agent, the agent must take action to determine the compliance of its behavior with that constraint.

2.2 Dynamic, Fail-Hard Environments

Dynamic environments compound the sources of messiness. Generally, dynamics amplifies the need for satisficing algorithmic solutions [8,19]. Algorithms must (minimally) be responsive to the dynamics of the environment. A driver cut off in traffic by another car cannot pause to reason about all the potential instantiations and implications of its constraints in this unexpected situation, it must continue to drive and manage its constraint compliance over time. The specification of constraints themselves can also change due to environment dynamics (e.g., new traffic laws). Finally, interactions between constraints (below) may only become evident as a dynamic situation unfolds.

2.3 Abstract and Poorly-Defined Constraints

Real-world constraints are often ambiguous, abstract, and/or incomplete in their definition, giving rise to the challenge of interpreting and operationalizing such constraints [21]. In puzzles like Sudoku, however, constraint definition is unambiguous. Terms (cell, column, row) have immediate and direct correspondence

---

[1] More recent approaches to constraints extend the coverage of classical approaches but do not span all the forms of messiness we consider [18].

[2] Some newer cars offer an indicator for travelling too closely. Thus, with a different embodiment, this constraint no longer requires active measurement.

to the representation of the puzzle. The constraints (or rules) defining the puzzle are also unambiguous.

In contrast, many constraints in driving are abstract ("drive defensively") or ambiguous ("do not follow too closely"). Terms used in constraints require a mapping onto one's internal representation that is not always consistent from person to person. "Use caution near pedestrians" depends on how one understands and applies both "caution" and "near" and perhaps also "pedestrian."

It may seem possible to overcome this source of messiness by directly encoding the "meaning" of constraints into an agent. However, resilience and robustness in open-ended environments requires disintermediation of the encoding and interpretation of constraints. Attempting to specify in advance how the agent should interpret constraints in every situation is likely to fail when the agent (inevitably) encounters a situation not anticipated by a system designer.

2.4   Implicit Context Specification

The definitions of real-world constraints often imply additional parameters or conditions rather than explicitly defining them. Most importantly, constraint specifications typically omit the context(s) in which they should apply. By "context," we mean a set of situations that share common, salient features. The "automobile driving" context includes cars, roads, traffic laws, traffic signals, etc. Similar but different contexts can have constraints that prescribe very different behaviors. For instance, "do not pass on the right" is a constraint relevant in countries where vehicles are driven on the right side of the road, but is not apt (most of the time) for countries where vehicles are driven on the left.

For Sudoku, there is an implicit but single context. Thus implicit specification poses no problem to the classical approach to constraints.

2.5   Interactions and Conflicts Among Constraints, Tasks, and Contexts

Interactions and conflicts among constraints and between task(s) and constraints can arise frequently. An accident or road construction causes re-routing of traffic into normally oncoming traffic lanes. A text message notification draws attention when attending to the road is required (sometimes by law). To what extent should one obey traffic laws when transporting someone in dire medical distress? The specific instantiation of constraints grounded within a given situation will indicate competing and sometimes conflicting choices for the agent.

The design of Sudoku ensures that constraints are collectively coherent (simplified by the single context). Generally, classical approaches to satisfying constraints only provide solutions when sets of constraints are coherent, obviating conflicts. More recent approaches support "soft constraints" [15] which support prioritization of constraints when conflicts arise; the overall set of constraints remains coherent when prioritization is taken into account.

In real-world situations, conflicts cannot always be resolved via *a priori* prioritization; an agent must sometimes knowingly violate a constraint. If a car is cut off in heavy traffic, it is probably more important to maintain speed and slowly build distance between the car ahead than to sharply brake in order to regain compliance with the following-distance constraint. From the point of view of constraint compliance, the agent is often likely to be in situations, imposed by dynamics directly but also sometimes at its choosing given the dynamics, to violate some constraints and to repair violations as the evolving situation allows.

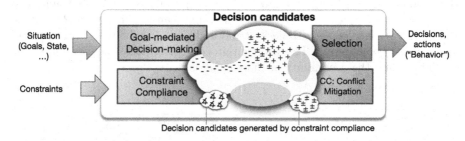

Decision candidates generated by constraint compliance

Fig. 1. At the computational level, the purpose of constraint compliance is to ensure that decision making takes constraints relevant to the agent's situation into account.

3   Computational-Level Analysis

We now present a computational-level account of the information processing tasks necessary for constraint compliance given the many sources of "messiness" above. A computational-level analysis emphasizes *what* steps are required to achieve constraint compliance and identifies requirements for *how* the capability may be realized at the processing and representation ("algorithmic") level [14].

3.1   Functional Role

The functional role of constraint compliance is to modulate agent decisions (and thus behavior) so that constraints relevant to the current situation inform agent choices. In Fig. 1, the agent's goal-focused decision process (blue) generates candidate choices and selects among them. The primary input to this decision process is the current situation (including environment state, external goals, history, etc.) and the output is a decision. A decision could be a commitment to a long-term course of action (e.g., a plan), an intermediate subgoal, or an immediate action. Over time, the sequence of decisions produces behavior (e.g., "driving"). We illustrate constraint compliance (green) parallel to the goal-mediated decision process of the agent and external constraints as a distinct input. This separation is for illustration only; at the algorithmic level, solutions may integrate constraint-compliance with goal-mediated decision processes.

As suggested by the figure, the agent commits to its decisions from a (potentially very large) space of candidate choices. At the computational level, we do not assume that the agent has an explicit representation of this space; in the figure, the cloud represents a conceptual space from which a specific decision might be drawn. For example, the decision process might choose actions based on a learned policy, where the space is implicit in mappings from states to actions.

Functionally, constraint compliance augments candidate choices produced by the goal-mediated decision process by indicating the acceptability/desirability of the candidates with respect to relevant constraints. The figure shows parts of the candidate space that are required (green), prohibited (red), desirable (+), and undesirable (-) choices. Because constraints can conflict (Sect. 2.5), some candidates are labeled as both desired and undesired (±); however, conflicts can occur in any combination. The selection process (green/blue) now evaluates the candidates and the desirability of those candidates.

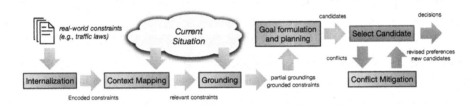

Fig. 2. Simple process model for constraint compliance.

Constraint compliance can also add new candidates. The grounding process can suggest candidates to take new actions (e.g., measurements to evaluate individual constraints; Sect. 2.1). In order to mitigate conflicts in constraints, the selection process may produce new candidates as well. Thus, in contrast to classical constraint satisfaction (where the application of constraints reduces choices), constraint compliance can produce additional choices. It also enables the agent to choose courses of action that are not necessarily consistent with all constraints.

3.2   Processing Steps for Constraint Compliance

What computational tasks are performed by the constraint-compliance process? Figure 2 illustrates a high-level process. The specific sequence of steps illustrates both a simple process model and how we are exploring constraint compliance at the algorithmic level and integrating it with decision making (see Sect. 4).

The agent's internal representations of constraints derive from real-world constraints defined externally (e.g., a law). *Internalization* results in encoding of constraints in agent memory. Next, *Context Mapping* compares encoded constraints to the current situation, identifying what constraints are (potentially) relevant in a given situation. Context mapping results in a set of situation-relevant but abstract (not grounded) constraints.

Grounding then maps abstract constraints to specific objects in the environment. In our explorations to date, both complete and partially-grounded constraints are re-represented as goals in order to exploit an existing agent's planning capability (Sect. 4). Planning generates candidates for *Selection* which is now extended with an ability to assess the acceptability of decision candidates based on the constraints. When conflicts arise, selection is augmented with *Conflict Mitigation*, which may lead to the generation of alternative courses of action. Below, we further describe these steps, focusing especially on how "messiness" motivates and/or introduces additional requirements for individual steps.

Internalize Constraints. Real-world constraints (typically) are defined external to the agent. Thus, an initial step in constraint compliance is to interpret the external constraint; that is, to map the external representation of the constraint to concepts as represented within the agent.

Abstract and poorly-defined constraints (Sect. 2.3) introduce challenges to simple encoding. The agent may not possess internal representations that align with the conditions in the external constraint and thus algorithmic approaches to internalization will entail methods that allow an agent to assess mappings between external conditions and internal representations.

Identify Situational Context(s). Conforming to real-world constraints requires an agent to recognize which constraints are relevant to its situation. However, the applicable situation (or general characterization of situations: contexts) are often implicit in the specification of constraints (Sect. 2.4). An agent can often learn associations between contexts and constraints through experience (which can include instruction) but a core challenge is that constraint specifications themselves do not (usually) specify applicable contexts.

A second challenge results when the composition of contexts interact in ways that make previously learned mappings inapt or invalid (Sect. 2.5). Anticipating and evaluating all possible compositions of all possible contexts is not feasible. Thus, general intelligence requires the capacity to consider and to evaluate constraints in novel contexts as behavior is being generated.

Context recognition itself is a challenge [6]. For an algorithmic implementation of constraint compliance, all that is needed is that the agent recognize "this constraint is relevant in my current situation." However, a full solution to constraint compliance appears to require context recognition processes as well.

Instantiate Constraints in A Situation (Grounding). As an agent behaves in its environment, it must determine how constraints might apply in its current situation. Grounding is distinct from internalization and context identification; it requires that the agent shift from general consideration of a constraint to determining if/how it should be instantiated in the agent's current environment.

Grounding is often straightforward. However, partial observability (Sect. 2.1) and abstract constraints (Sect. 2.4) can require a search over potential instantiations of a constraint, rather than an immediate mapping. Thus, as constraints are expressed more abstractly and generally, the computational demand on the agent to determine *how* that constraint may apply in the current situation increases. When new information is needed to complete grounding (e.g., a measurement as in Sect. 2.1), new candidate choices should be generated (Sect. 3.1).

An agent's embodiment may lack an ability to directly observe features needed to instantiate a constraint. Nonetheless, the agent should still attempt to respect applicable constraints. Thus, grounding requires prospective instantiation with incomplete information.

Integrate Constraints in Decision-Making (Selection). At a minimum, the agent's selection process must take into account both agent goals and constraints for constraint compliance. When the set of applicable constraints are fully grounded and present no conflicts, the selection process is straightforward.

Conflicts (below) and partial grounding complicate selection. The selection process must be sensitive to both taking action to find an instantiation for a partially grounded constraint and also the potential costs and risks associated with that search. Defining algorithmic approaches to selection in the presence of partial grounding is a significant novel challenge.

Identify and Mitigate Conflicts. When there are conflicts in the acceptability and desirability of candidate choices, the agent must either 1) choose one of the options given the conflicting choices or 2) attempt to identify new choices that resolve or mitigate the conflicts. Specific strategies could include attention/inattention (ignoring some constraints), prioritization of constraints, and replanning. A primary algorithmic-level challenge is to resolve and mitigate conflicts rapidly, given bounded rationality in a dynamic environment (Sect. 2.2).

4   Exploratory Algorithmic-Level Prototype

In parallel with the top-down computational-level analysis, we have begun bottom-up prototyping as well, focusing to date on algorithmic approaches to grounding, selection, and conflict mitigation. We use Soar [11] as the target implementation level. Soar both constrains and informs definition at the algorithmic level. We introduce further design constraint at the algorithmic level by building on an existing agent designed to interactively learn tasks [10,16]. The prototype is compatible with this agent's *a priori* capabilities for interpreting language, planning task actions, executing plans, and learning from human instruction.

Grounding: The prototype builds on language grounding already part of the agent, which can learn recognition structures for abstract goal specifications [10] and maintain consistent grounding across perceptual changes [16]. The primary focus is to explore how to support partial grounding of constraints. The agent can now indicate that some actions are desirable (in Selection; see below) because they lead to further information that could potentially complete the grounding. In this way, the agent is biased towards choosing candidates that lead to measurement actions, as suggested in Fig. 1.

Selection: The original agent uses an explicit goal representation to determine what to do next (typically via search-based planning, although it can ask for help from an instructor as well). In our initial implementation, as shown in Fig. 2, we integrated constraint-compliance with selection by having the agent represent grounded constraints as goals (e.g., a speed limit constraint would be represented as a goal for speed to be less than the limit). This approach leverages the agent's planning capability. Candidate evaluations (from grounding) are implemented as Soar preferences for selecting plans, which maps selection directly onto an implementation/architecture-level capability of Soar. In the absence of conflicts (below), planning provides a solution that satisfies the (grounded) constraints, measurement actions (from partial groundings), and task actions.

Conflict Mitigation: Consider two conflicting constraints relevant to driving in a medical emergency. The lawful speed limit and a general directive to preserve human life apply. These constraints can result in a conflict over the desired speed. Because plan choices are mapped onto Soar preferences, Soar responds to conflicting preferences with an impasse, a conflict detection system already part of Soar. Thus, we have also mapped the trigger for conflict mitigation onto an implementation-level process. Generally, resolving conflicts requires additional knowledge (e.g., in this case, some sense that preserving life is more important than respecting the speed limit) which can include various ways to include values in assessing choices [1,7].

5   Discussion and Implications

While limited and preliminary, the initial prototype highlights examples of representation and process (algorithmic-level choices) and how these choices may interact with the implementation level. We now consider implications for future work at the algorithmic level to realize general constraint compliance.

Online, Incremental Learning: For an AGI, the set of contexts and constraints is potentially huge, it is infeasible to prepare for every contingency, and dynamics often demands rapid response. Together, these conditions point toward algorithmic solutions that employ online, incremental learning. This implication mirrors human learning and is consistent with the transition from more deliberate and explicit (System 2) to more implicit and automatic (System 1) reasoning [9]. However, it contrasts with recent approaches that emphasize pre-training to ensure conformance to various operational and safety constraints [5].

Senses of Familiarity, Novelty, and Surprise: Familiarity, novelty, and surprise are important signals in human (and animal) regulation of behavior [2]. Realizations of familiarity, novelty and surprise may be useful for meta-cognitive regulation of constraint compliance in task performance. An open question is whether a sense of familiarity (and other signals) are best realized in the implementation level (e.g., extension to Soar) or at the algorithmic level.

Anticipation Based on Partial Information: Near-term anticipation of future states is central to functional and neurological accounts of human intelligence [3]. Humans readily anticipate the potential impact of constraints on behavior and adapt behavior in advance of a potential constraint violation. Our exploration identified a need for anticipation in grounding. An agent needs strategies to decide which potential groundings to attend to, given many potential groundings (with many implications). Indicators of potential threats to constraint compliance would provide a coarse attention mechanism to bias grounding processes toward more important constraints.

Domain Knowledge: Choosing to prioritize some constraints over others requires general knowledge of the world. Having such knowledge may be as important to the results of constraint compliance as the algorithms that realize its functions. This dilemma points to one of the rationales for adopting an agent that can learn from instruction. Because research agents will often lack knowledge, our agent can actively seek input to gain missing knowledge about conflicts. While this does not resolve the dependence of constraint compliance on general knowledge, it does provide a means to explore algorithmic realizations in a way that makes the required domain knowledge explicit and transparent.

Acknowledgment. This work was supported by the Office of Naval Research, contract N00014-22-1-2358. The views and conclusions contained in this document are those of the authors and should not be interpreted as representing the official policies, either expressed or implied, of the Department of Defense or Office of Naval Research. The U.S. Government is authorized to reproduce and distribute reprints for Government purposes notwithstanding any copyright notation hereon. We thank the anonymous reviewers for substantive comments and suggestions.

References

1. Arkin, R.C., Ulam, P., Wagner, A.R.: Moral decision making in autonomous systems: enforcement, moral emotions, dignity, trust, and deception. Proc. IEEE **100**(3), 571–589 (2011)
2. Barto, A., Mirolli, M., Baldassarre, G.: Novelty or surprise? Front. Psychol. **4**, 907 (2013)
3. Bubic, A., von Cramon, D.Y., Schubotz, R.I.: Prediction, cognition and the brain. Front. Hum. Neurosci. **4**, 25 (2010)
4. Dechter, R.: Constraint Processing. Morgan Kaufman, Burlington (2003)
5. García, J., Fernández, F.: A comprehensive survey on safe reinforcement learning. J. Mach. Learn. Res. **16**(42), 1437–1480 (2015)
6. Gershman, S.J.: Context-dependent learning and causal structure. Psychon. Bull. Rev. **24**, 557–565 (2017)
7. Giancola, M., Bringsjord, S., Govindarajulu, N.S., Varela, C.: Ethical reasoning for autonomous agents under uncertainty. In: International Conference on Robot Ethics and Standards (ICRES), pp. 1–16. Taipei (2020)
8. Gigerenzer, G.: Fast and frugal heuristics: tools of bounded rationality. In: Handbook of Judgment and Decision Making, pp. 62–88. Blackwell, Malden (2004)
9. Kahneman, D.: Thinking, Fast and Slow. Doubleday, New York (2011)
10. Kirk, J.R., Laird, J.E.: Learning hierarchical symbolic representations to support interactive task learning and knowledge transfer. In: IJCAI 2019, IJCAI (2019)
11. Laird, J.E.: The Soar Cognitive Architecture. MIT Press, Cambridge, MA (2012)
12. Lynce, I., Ouaknine, J.: Sudoku as a SAT problem. In: AI&M (2006)

13. Mani, G., Chen, F., et al.: Artificial intelligence's grand challenges: past, present, and future. AI Mag. **42**(1), 61–75 (2021)
14. Marr, D.: Vision. Freeman and Company, New York (1982)
15. Meseguer, P., Rossi, F., Schiex, T.: Soft constraints. In: Foundations of Artificial Intelligence, vol. 2, pp. 281–328. Elsevier (2006)
16. Mininger, A.: Expanding Task Diversity in Explanation-Based Interactive Task Learning. Ph.D. Thesis, University of Michigan, Ann Arbor (2021)
17. Pearl, J.: Reasoning under uncertainty. Ann. Rev. Comput. Sci. **4**(1), 37–72 (1990). https://doi.org/10.1146/annurev.cs.04.060190.000345
18. Rossi, F., Mattei, N.: Building ethically bounded AI. In: 33rd AAAI Conference (2019)
19. Simon, H.A.: Models of Man; Social and Rational. Wiley, Oxford, England (1957)
20. Weidinger, L., Mellor, J., et. al: Ethical and social risks of harm from language models (2021), arXiv:2112.04359
21. Wray, R.E., Laird, J.E.: Incorporating abstract behavioral constraints in the performance of agent tasks. In: ICAI. Springer, Las Vegas, NV (2021)

Self-Comprehension for More Coherent Language Generation

George A. Wright[1]([✉])[iD] and Matthew Purver[1,2][iD]

[1] School of Electronic Engineering and Computer Science, Queen Mary University of London, London, UK
{george.a.wright,m.purver}@qmul.ac.uk
[2] Department of Knowledge Technologies, Jožef Stefan Institute, Ljubljana, Slovenia

Abstract. LINGUOPLOTTER is a distributed and chaotic architecture where an entanglement of different processes interact to generate a text describing a raw data input. This paper describes recent additions to the architecture whereby a greater degree of language comprehension is used to improve the coherence of generated text. Some examples of the architecture operating are considered, including where it performs well and generates a good quality text; and instances where it gets trapped in loops that either prevent an output from being generated or cause a lower quality output to be produced before there is a chance to find a better alternative. Finally, ideas from the program METACAT are considered which could allow the program to observe its own processes and become a more human-like intelligence.

Keywords: NLG · NLU · Distributed Architecture

1 Introduction

Evidence from linguistics, psychology, and neuroscience shows that human language production and comprehension are intertwined with and influence one another [5]. Moreover, when people write, they re-read what they have written; make adjustments; and stop to consider what to write next in a *cycle of engagement and reflection* [7]. It makes sense, not only that people *do* interweave comprehension with production, but that they *need* to do so, for it is important to check that what one says or writes can be understood by the intended recipient. This will be just as true for an artificial person.

The architecture of LINGUOPLOTTER allows an intermingling of different processes including: perception of input; generation of text that describes it; comprehension and evaluation of text; and the decision to output a text. These are

Partially supported by the UK EPSRC under grants EP/R513106/1 (Wright), EP/S033564/1 and EP/W001632/1 (Purver); the Slovenian Research Agency via research core funding for the programme Knowledge Technologies (P2-0103) and the projects CANDAS (J6-2581) and SOVRAG (J5-3102).

P. Hammer et al. (Eds.): AGI 2023, LNAI 13921, pp. 328–337, 2023.
https://doi.org/10.1007/978-3-031-33469-6_33

not separate processes running in parallel, but entangled processes that inform one another: just as humans use the projection of narrative frames to understand new situations [8], LINGUOPLOTTER's narrative frames guide how it conceptualizes its input. Furthermore, recent changes to the architecture increase the degree to which language comprehension affects generation of text, with the recognition of patterns in text influencing how it combines and arranges sentences into a more cohesive whole. This paper discusses these recent changes and also considers how a greater capacity for introspection could result in greater, more human-like intelligence.

2 A Simple Problem Domain

LINGUOPLOTTER is developed and tested with examples from a toy domain: map sequences of temperature changes on a fictional island (cf Fig. 1). The domain is ostensibly plain and simple, but human-written descriptions demonstrate a variety of phenomena including conceptual metaphor (*a spike in warmer temperatures*—1c); anthropomorphism (*everywhere will enjoy temperatures in the 20s*—1b; connections drawn between the end and the beginning (*falling back on Sunday* – 1b); and self-referential text (*it's a tale of two halves*—1c); as well as more mundane, matter-of-fact language (*cool throughout the weekend*—1a).

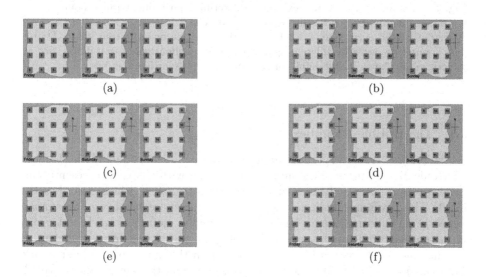

Fig. 1. Some sequences of maps used to test the architecture.

The architecture should be seen, not as an "expert system", but as an early prototype which could in future be applied more widely. Little knowledge engineering is required in this domain, thus the focus is on the fundamental processes involved in perception and language, not on domain-specific details.

3   The Architecture

The Architecture of LINGUOPLOTTER borrows much from the architecture of COPYCAT [4] and related models of analogy-making [2], in which micro-agents called *codelets* run stochastically, making incremental changes to structures in a shared workspace. In LINGUOPLOTTER, codelets selected from the *coderack* make incremental changes to networks across many spaces in the *bubble chamber*.

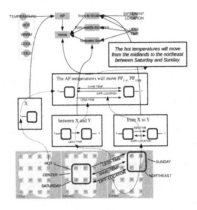

Fig. 2. Some of the structures involved in describing an input. Orange nodes at the top of the diagram belong to the concept network. Solid arrows connecting them are links that spread activation. Each box is either a frame or an output space. Dotted lines connecting items in different spaces are correspondences between items. Not all structures are shown in full detail for sake of clarity. (Color figure online)

3.1   The Bubble Chamber

As the program runs, structures are incrementally added to the bubble chamber which identify patterns in the input; match them with abstract representations in long-term conceptual knowledge; and generate a text which describes the input. The structures built in the bubble chamber are based on the *simplex networks* of Fauconnier and Turner [1]. A simplex network matches elements in an unstructured input space with slots in a structured frame and has an output space containing a blend of content from the input space and structure from the frame. In LINGUOPLOTTER, frames provide the syntax and morphology of sentences describing the input. Figure 2 illustrates an example where frames are matched to part of the input to generate a sentence that describes it. Each simplex network is contained inside a *view*, which must only contain non-contradictory structures.

Each structure, be it a *chunk* grouping together similar nodes, a *label* or *relation* assigning a property to a chunk, or a *correspondence* matching a structure in one space to a structure in another is first suggested by a suggester codelet and then built by a builder. Evaluators assign a quality score to a structure based on how representative it is of a concept and how much it contributes to the network around it. Selectors choose stochastically between competing structures.

3.2 The Worldview and Focus

As sentences and longer pieces of text are built they can be promoted into the worldview. The text in the worldview is a candidate for publication. Worldview setting codelets are responsible for deciding between candidate texts and publisher codelets decide whether or not to output a text.

The focus is a temporary sub-goal selected from among these simplex networks that encourages activity towards a single network, so that processing can at times be more direct and less broad. Focus setting and un-setting codelets determine which simplex network should be in focus and view-driven factory codelets spawn codelets that suggest structures to fill in the network.

3.3 The Coderack

Codelets are chosen from the coderack, a stochastic priority queue where a codelet's urgency determines the likelihood it is selected. Once a codelet has run, it spawns a follow-up codelet which replaces it on the coderack. This results in self-sustaining streams of codelets that continue performing operations in the bubble chamber until a text is output.

3.4 Satisfaction and Randomness

The architecture is stochastic and distributed with no centralized decision maker: competitions between alternative structures in the bubble chamber and codelets on the coderack decide which texts are promoted into the worldview and published. There is a degree of randomness in codelet and structure selection which is determined by the program's satisfaction score. This score is based on the *temperature* mechanism of COPYCAT but an alternative name is used to avoid confusion with the temperatures on the maps the program describes.

When satisfaction is high (there are good quality and coherent structures matching the input to a piece of text) the program becomes more deterministic so that existing simplex networks can be completed and the resulting text output. When satisfaction is low, the program becomes more random so that a wider range of possibilities can be explored.

While there is a certain degree of randomness when it comes to micro-level selection between individual structures or codelets, the program tends to converge upon a narrow range of macro-level behaviours and textual outputs. The satisfaction score S is calculated:

$$S = max(G, F) \tag{1}$$
$$G = aI + bV + cW \tag{2}$$
$$W = dC_1 + eC_2 + fC_3 \tag{3}$$

- G: a measure of the general quality of all structures in the bubble chamber.
- F: the quality of the view in focus.
- I: the quality of the structures are built on the raw input.
- V: the average quality of all views in the bubble chamber.
- W: the quality of the worldview.
- C_1, correctness: the quality of input structures in the worldview.
- C_2, completeness: the proportion of the raw input described in the worldview.
- C_3, cohesiveness: the quality of relations connecting worldview sentences.

The qualities of individual structures within the spaces and the quality of views is calculated by individual evaluator codelets. Full details are available in the Python implementation of LINGUOPLOTTER available on GitHub[1].

The coefficients a to f are real numbers. The outputs discussed in this paper were generated using the values ($a = 0.4$, $b = 0.2$, $c = 0.4$, $d = 0.3$, $e = 0.2$, $f = 0.5$). A discussion of tests using different weights and the effect they have on the program's behaviour is provided in Wright and Purver [9].

4   Pattern Recognition on Many Levels

Earlier versions of this program [9] have focused on describing states (single maps) and events on sequences of maps. This latest version of the architecture attempts to recognize patterns between events and sentences so that it can build more coherent narratives describing a larger portion of the input.

This involves a greater deal of self-comprehension than earlier versions of the program, which only built and evaluated structures and sentences representing patterns discovered on the input maps. The latest version of LINGUOPLOTTER also uses its frames to recognize patterns between sentences so that a cohesive text can be built out of them. These new frames recognize patterns such as parallelism, an ordering along a particular dimension, or disanalogy. These frames serve to classify pairs of sentences so that they can be written in an appropriate order and connected with a relevant conjunction. For example:

- *Temperatures will be cold in the country between friday and saturday* **then** *temperatures will be cool in the country between saturday and sunday.* (Ordering in time).
- *Temperatures will increase in the south between friday and saturday* **and** *temperatures will increase in the north between friday and saturday.* (Parallel times).
- *Temperatures will be cool in the country between saturday and sunday* **but** *temperatures will be cold in the country between friday and saturday.* (Disanalogy—same verb describing different temperatures).

In recognizing patterns between sentences in order to further develop them as texts, LINGUOPLOTTER intertwines more fully the processes of language production and language comprehension.

---

[1] https://github.com/georgeawright/linguoplotter.

5   The Program's Behaviour

Tables 1 and 2 show the range of outputs that the program generates when run multiple times with the sequences in Figs. 1a and 1c. The tables show the average satisfaction score for each text, the average time taken to generate the text (in codelets run) and the frequency with which it produces that text. The program's symbolic nature allows us to look inside and understand how these texts were generated and why it sometimes fails to produce a good output.

Table 1. Outputs for sequence 1a. Conjunctions in bold for clarity.

Text	Satisf	Time	Freq
Temperatures will be cold in the country between friday and saturday **then** temperatures will be cool in the country between saturday and sunday	0.842	7141	4
Temperatures will be cool in the country between saturday and sunday **but** temperatures will be cold in the country between friday and saturday	0.839	6950	2
Temperatures will be cold in the country between friday and saturday **then** temperatures will be cold in the country between saturday and sunday	0.786	4833	1
Temperatures will be cold in the country between friday and saturday **and** temperatures will be cool in the country between saturday and sunday	0.691	8209	2
Temperatures will be cool in the country between saturday and sunday **and** temperatures will be cold in the country between friday and saturday	0.578	6381	3
Temperatures will be bad in the country between friday and saturday **and** temperatures will be cool in the country between saturday and sunday	0.537	9821	1
Temperatures will be cool in the country between saturday and sunday	0.4	6483	14
Temperatures will be cold in the country between friday and saturday	0.4	5827	22
Temperatures will be cold in the country between saturday and sunday	0.304	1603	1

5.1   An Example of the Program Running

This is a sample of the events that took place inside LINGUOPLOTTER[2] when it was given the input from Fig. 1a and the random seed 0. Numbers indicate the time measured by the number of codelets run.

0–400 Processing is dominated by chunk building on the input resulting in 3 chunks, each covering the entire island at a different point in time. Similar temperatures across the island allow high quality chunks of that size.
124 The first label-builder codelet runs attaching the label SUNDAY to a small chunk. Labels built at this early stage are attached to chunks that will eventually be superseded and removed from the bubble chamber, but their construction leads to the activation of relevant concepts.
752–784 An adjectival phrase frame is set as focus and as its slots are filled in, the program experiences one of its first spikes in satisfaction.

---

[2] Using the version at https://github.com/georgeawright/linguoplotter/tree/v2.0.0.

Table 2. Outputs for sequence 1c. Conjunctions in bold for clarity.

Text	Satisf	Time	Freq
Temperatures will increase in the north between friday and saturday **and** temperatures will decrease in the south between saturday and sunday	0.709	11726	2
Temperatures will increase in the south between friday and saturday **and** temperatures will decrease in the south between saturday and sunday	0.684	14331	1
Temperatures will increase in the south between friday and saturday **and** temperatures will increase in the north between friday and saturday	0.644	17751	1
Temperatures will increase in the north between friday and saturday	0.35	10737	4
The warm temperatures will move from the south northwards between friday and saturday	0.35	12952	3
The warm temperatures will move from the north southwards between saturday and sunday	0.347	11163	1
Temperatures will decrease in the north between saturday and sunday	0.26	9712	2
Temperatures will decrease in the south between saturday and sunday	0.233	9387	3
None	0.109	20000	33

1000–2000 Simplex networks with ADJECTIVAL, IN-LOCATION, and BETWEEN-TIMES frames are completed and those frames become fully active. They spread activation to frames, for which they can be a component such as BE.

2658 A worldview setter sets a recently completed BE sentence as worldview. Now that the worldview has been set, satisfaction is permanently higher.

2881 A view suggester runs. Since the BE frame has a high activation and only one instance, it suggests another simplex network based on the BE frame.

2904–2949 A focus setter sets the newly built view as focus. Codelets matching sub frames and input structures to its frame increase its quality and cause a spike in satisfaction which subsides when the focus is unset.

3326 A view with a DISANALOGY frame is built.

3367 A garbage collector codelet runs and deletes the DISANALOGY view which had a low quality score because it was empty.

3000–5000 Worldview setters occasionally run causing the worldview to alternate between the two BE sentences.

4903 A view with a TEMPORAL-ORDER frame is built.

4930 A publisher codelet runs but does not publish because the focus is occupied by the TEMPORAL-ORDER view.

5411 The word *then* is built in the TEMPORAL-ORDER view's output space.

5573 A worldview setter selects the recently completed TEMPORAL-ORDER view.

5743 A publisher codelet runs and publishes the worldview.

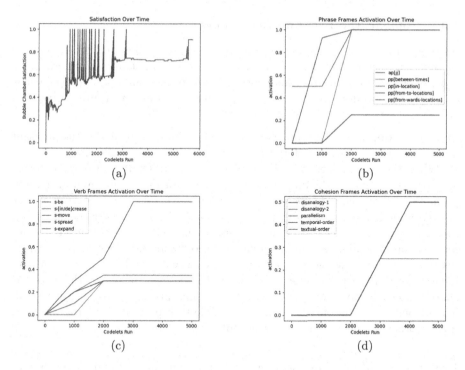

Fig. 3. Linguoplotter's satisfaction and the activation of frame types over time.

5.2 Emergent Pipelines

Although the architecture is not hard-coded to follow a modular data-to-text pipeline, "pipelines" do to some extent emerge out of the knock-on effects of codelets and the spreading of activation between concepts. A bottom-up pipeline begins with codelets searching for disconnected structures in the bubble chamber. These suggest structures which, when built, spread activation to relevant concepts. This triggers top-down processing whereby codelets search for instances of active concepts or for structures to fill in the slots of unfinished simplex networks.

Overall, a pipeline also emerges which begins with lower-level pattern recognition and is followed by increasingly high-level structures from the level of phrases, to that of sentences, and on to cohesive texts. This is demonstrated by the changing activation of concepts and frames shown in Fig. 3. This is not dissimilar to the data-to-text pipeline of Reiter [6], but it is less rigid and can be interrupted by top-down processes which encourage reversion to an earlier stage. The collective behaviour of codelets thus results in a more autonomous and flexible alternative to programs following a pre-specified algorithm.

5.3 Problems the Program Encounters

As shown in Tables 1 and 2, the program does not always perform as well as in Sect. 5.1. Certain problems recur: often the program struggles to zero in on a good representation of the input; other times, it gets dominated by publisher codelets and outputs a text before allowing itself to find better alternatives.

Fruitless Loops. In 33 out of 50 runs when describing sequence 1c, the program fails to publish an output before timing out after 2×10^4 codelets.

When the program runs with sequence 1c and random seed 0, it performs well for approximately the first 5000 codelets, generating phrases and ultimately promoting a sentence (*temperatures will increase in the north between Friday and Saturday*) into the worldview. Unfortunately, it concurrently generates an identical sentence. After this point, codelets are more likely to instantiate frames for combining sentences, but are unable to complete the slots in the frames, because it is not possible to conjoin a sentence with itself. The program can identify networks that cannot be completed and tends to delete them, but it shortly after tries to recreate similar networks unaware that it is repeating itself. The amount of attention paid to an impossible task prevents the program from finding other sentences before it times out.

Premature Publication. Sometimes the program makes the decision to publish a text even while it is half-way through generating a potentially better text.

When the program runs with sequence 1a and random seed 16, after a sentence (*temperatures will be cold in the country between saturday and sunday*) has been added to the worldview at time 1436, a publisher happens to run at 1536 and because the focus is empty it spawns another publisher with a slightly higher urgency. This triggers a stream of publishers that run intermittently with ever higher urgency until one at 1603 finally publishes the worldview. Had any of these publishers run when the focus was not empty, their urgency would have been lower and the program may have been able to build a fuller text.

That this can happen is a downside in terms of performance but also provides some degree of psychological realism: were the program to continue running beyond the point at which it makes the publication decision and therefore finish generating a better text, this could be seen as an example of the French concept of *l'espirit de l'escalier* or *staircase wit*—thinking of the perfect thing to say after it is too late—an entirely human behaviour!

6 Future Work: Meta-Level Pattern Recognition

Whereas LINGUOPLOTTER used only to recognize patterns in the maps it described, recent improvements allow it also to recognize patterns in its own texts. But, the program can still struggle to find its way through a large search space and sometimes gets stuck repeatedly trying to build uncompletable networks.

Codelet activity in the bubble chamber can be narrated by an observer. If the program were able to do this itself, it could recognize patterns of futile behaviour such as those in Sect. 5.3 and take action to avoid them.

METACAT, an extension of COPYCAT, holds a store of recent activity in a *trace* and uses codelets to recognize problematic behaviour. Other codelets can then alter processing by "clamping" patterns of structures that lead to failure so as to prevent them from re-occurring. This allows METACAT to "jump out of the system" and stop wasting time on fruitless loops to which COPYCAT was prone [3]. A similar extension to LINGUOPLOTTER could improve its performance at narrating weather patterns and would also lay the foundation for a program that can introspect and narrate itself.

7 Conclusion

Recent additions to LINGUOPLOTTER allow it to produce fuller texts by classifying intermediate texts in terms of cohesion relations built by codelets within its bubble chamber. This constitutes a step towards a greater entanglement of language production and comprehension. But the necessarily chaotic nature of the architecture means it is difficult to optimize and often does not work as well as would be hoped. Future work on the architecture should expand the range of patterns that the program can recognize in input and text so that it can replicate a wider range of human abilities; and should use the recognition of patterns in its own processes to avoid loops and other futile behaviour.

References

1. Fauconnier, G., Turner, M.: The Way We Think. Basic Books, New York (2002)
2. Hofstadter, D.R.: Fluid Concepts and Creative Analogies. Basic Books, New York (1995)
3. Marshall, J.B. Metacat: A Self-Watching Cognitive Architecture for Analogy-Making and High-Level Perception. PhD Thesis, Indiana University (1999)
4. Mitchell, M.: Analogy-Making as Perception. MIT Press, Cambridge (1993)
5. Pickering, M.J., Garrod, S.: An integrated theory of language production and comprehension. Behav. Brain Sci. **36**, 329–392 (2013)
6. Reiter, E: An Architecture for data-to-text systems. In: Proceedings of the Eleventh European Workshop on Natural Language Generation, pp. 97–104 (2007)
7. Sharples, M.: How We Write. Routledge, Milton Park (1998)
8. Turner, M.: The Literary Mind. Oxford University Press, Oxford (1996)
9. Wright, G.A., Purver, M.: A self-evaluating architecture for describing data. In: Text, Speech, and Dialogue: 25th International Conference, pp. 187–198 (2022)

An Adaptive Vision Architecture for AGI Systems

Robert Wünsche[(✉)]

Department of Psychology, Stockholm University, Stockholm, Sweden
robert.wunsche@su.se

Abstract. This paper presents an unsupervised object detection system which can offline-learn generic visual features via Siamese neural network, yet is able to learn new object classes at run-time with a prototype learning approach applied on the latent representations. The operating requirements of this system feature bounded processing time per frame, while dealing with a fixed amount of available memory. This system works under the Assumption of Insufficient Knowledge and Resource and is hence operating in real-time and open to new information which can arrive at any time, as systems such as NARS and AERA ideally also demand for perception.

Keywords: Unsupervised Object Detection · Vision System · Real-time vision · Prototype formation · Siamese Neural Networks

1 Introduction

AGI-aspiring systems such as NARS and AERA require to be able to adapt [16] over their whole operating time[1], and demand support for real-time operation. A consequence of this requirement is that most sub-systems of the system architecture also have to work under this condition, this also includes vision systems in general, with object detection models as in this publication as a special case. While part of the model can be pre-trained, as will be shown with Siamese Neural Networks, the online learning needs to support at least the formation of new object categories in order to be able to adapt to new situations with novel objects successfully. This is covered via prototype learning approach operating on the latent representations of the learned network.

This leads us to the basic assumptions of the vision system:

A1: open to new object categories to be discovered at run-time [17]
A2: running in real-time with a low ($< 200\,\text{ms}$) processing time per frame
A3: A DNN can learn visual features off-line which will be general enough to transfer to new object categories.
Here we assume in particular that training a Siamese NN

---

[1] This is also referred to lifelong or incremental learning in Machine Learning [14].

© The Author(s), under exclusive license to Springer Nature Switzerland AG 2023
P. Hammer et al. (Eds.): AGI 2023, LNAI 13921, pp. 338–344, 2023.
https://doi.org/10.1007/978-3-031-33469-6_34

that generalizes to the distribution of the images perceived at
inference time, will also cover relevant out-of-distribution cases
by learning relatively generic visual features
in a sufficiently diverse training set

A4: Learning of new object categories at run-time can be achieved with
unsupervised prototype learning

While some subsets of these assumptions have been realized in previous
object detection systems, such as DeSTIN [1], supporting all of them together
has not yet been achieved with the necessary reliability to be used as unsupervised vision system for the aforementioned AGI projects in a wide range of
domains.

State of the Art
Most efforts regarding object detection are focused at models which achieve
a high accuracy on a given dataset without any ability of the deployed system to adapt to changes in the environment. Examples of such systems include
YOLOv7 [15], CLIP [11], CoCa [23] and Omni-DETR [18]. Other efforts, with
systems which have properties which are more compatible with the requirements
of AGI(such as unsupervised learning), exist, for example DeSTIN [1]. Research
in Machine Learning has also led to classifiers which can learn in an unsupervised, online, real-time setting under assumption of insufficient knowledge (AIK)
and bounded resources for vision. One example of this class are classifiers which
are based on Adaptive Resonance Theory (ART).

2   Architecture

The following diagram (Fig. 1) summarizes the architecture of the system:

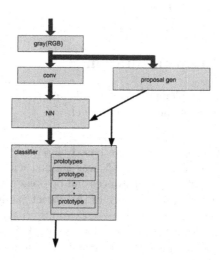

Fig. 1. System architecture

- **Preprocessing**: The RGB channels are converted to gray channel by averaging the RGB channels as the first step of the preprocessing. This leads to a better generalization due to independence on color information. Convolution only in the x direction is done after that using a very primitive kernel[2].
- **Proposal Generator**: The task of the proposal generator [22] is to suggest the patches of the image where objects are. This is currently done by motion tracking between the current frame and the last frame followed by image segmentation by motion [22](we will refer to this as clustering). Clustering is done in the current implementation by dividing the motion into buckets and grouping adjacent pixels with a pixel fill algorithm in this bucket.
- **Neural Network**: The NN is learned before run-time, but frozen at run-time. It is fair to call this form of learning meta-level learning, because the NN is operating on meta-level while the classifier learns categories on object-level [21].
- **Classification of stimulus**: The Vision system is using a prototype based classifier, where the real valued vectors are the output of a NN. It assigns every prototype a unique symbolic ID, which is the output of the classifier, together with other information such as similarity of the input to the latent vector of the returned prototype. This can be used to compute the confidence of the input fed into NARS. The classifier is always open to new instances, which are to novel according to the set of all known prototypes. This classifier is where the "Symbolic/Subsymbolic Gap" [5] is bridged. Note that the symbolic ID is *not* assigned by humans, the system is free to create a new ID based on subjective experience, following "Experience-grounded semantics" (EGS) [16].
- **Resources**: All maintenance and operations on the prototypes is happening under the assumption of bounded resources. Insertion is bounded by the time to scan for a similar prototype plus a small time to insert plus the time to maintain the maximum size. Processing with the NN is bounded by the short time it takes for a complete forward pass. Search for the best prototype is bounded by the number of prototypes times a short time to compute similarity by distance.

3   Training and Implementation

The following describes implementation details and training aspects and implementation characteristics of the realized model:

Classifier

The Vision system is using a prototype based classifier, where the real valued vectors are the output of a NN. The NN was trained with a siamese objective [2], because the learning of similar instances can be done without retraining that NN. The prototypes for the maintenance of the object categories are ordered by a simple heuristic which may weight between various criteria [22], such as timestamp of recent observation, age, observation count. This property of the classifier weights between different factors to avoid the stability-plasticity dilemma

---

[2] Will be extended to a more complicated kernel and in multiple directions.

[3], that is, being open to new categories(plasticity) while avoiding catastrophic forgetting(stability).

Training of the NN

The classifier is a NN which is trained with a Siamese neural network objective [2,8]. The architecture is duplicated using the same weights for a second input. The distance between both networks is computed with a distance metric. The NN learns to transform the input in such a way to get close to the distance of the training set. The training set consists of pairs of images which are labeled to be completely the same (distance 0.0), slight similar (distance 0.1) and different (distance 1.0).

A two layer NN architecture with a 12 unit ReLU [4] activation function in the hidden layer and identity activation function in the output layer was chosen. The output-layer has 12 units. Weight initialization was done with He uniform initialization. The Dataset consisted of a low number of images (10s of images), some with the same object category (for cup, box, etc.), all with different lighting situations and perspectives. The training-set did not contain any images of cars. Pairs of images with the same and different categories were taken in a exhaustive way, because the number of images was low. The only pre-processing done to the images was conversation from RGB to gray-scale and convolution in the x axis by computing the difference between adjacent pixels. The parameters of the current NN model were trained with a variant of stochastic gradient descent [13], where the batch consisted of one sample and only a single randomly selected parameter was optimized per iteration. The learning rate was 0.0035. Training was done for 8 h on a single CPU core and was terminated after that time. The error at that time was below 1e-5.

Implementation

The system was implemented[3] using the Nim language[4], which compiles to C++ for easy interoperability with other systems. Nim with C++ target was chosen by the requirement of high efficiency and ease of development, and allows for high portability of the solution which can be relevant for interfacing with both NARS [6,7,9,19] and AERA [10] implementations.

4   Experiments and Results

The principles and implementation were experimentally validated using the Street Scene [12] dataset without any sort of pre-training. The dataset consists of bird view videos of a road segment. The system is able to successfully recognize reoccurring objects in the images, as illustrated in Fig. 2.

---

[3] source code and the neural network models, which are trained using the Backpropagation algorithm, can be found at https://github.com/PtrMan/23R.

[4] https://github.com/nim-lang/Nim.

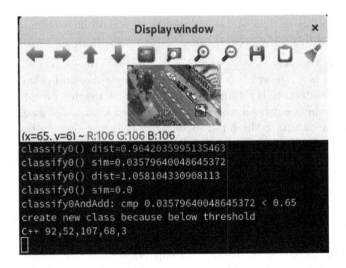

Fig. 2. Vision system test

Statistics were collected to measure how good the overall vision system is in categorization [20] of stimuli and the recognition of new categories, the results are summarized in Table 1. This was done with two counters, one for the creation of a new category "createdNewCategory" and a counter for recognized category "recognizedCategory". This was done for the scene where the car is turning (trainingset 26) and for trainingset 16.

Table 1. Vision test results

scene	createdNewCategory	recognizedCategory
train26 - turning car	105	304
train16	45	142

One reason for the high counter "createdNewCategory" of the "train26" scene is that no additional mechanism for rotational invariance was implemented to handle the case of the turning car at the beginning of the scene. Other reasons for a low ratio of "recognizedCategory"/"createdNewCategory" are suboptimal design decisions such as the specific convolution used in this prototype, suboptimal training of the NN and suboptimal architecture of the NN (depth of network, convolutional layers, etc.).

5 Conclusion

This work demonstrated a architecture which is able to learn visual categories of objects in a online incremental lifelong-learning manner under assumption of insufficient knowledge (AIK) from a raw sequence of frames. The feasibility was demonstrated with a implementation of a working prototype.

This paper described some mechanisms which were shown to be effective.

Future work should improve the properties of the very simplistic proposal generator, to handle situations such as non-planar motion. Better pre-processing (convolution, etc.) and improving the NN architecture to allow even better generalization of object classes and perspectives and lighting conditions will also be subject of future improvements.

Acknowledgements. Special thanks to Patrick Hammer, Tony Lofthouse and Robert Johansson for valuable discussions.

References

1. Arel, I., Rose, D., Coop, R.: Destin: a scalable deep learning architecture with application to high-dimensional robust pattern recognition. In: 2009 AAAI Fall Symposium Series (2009)
2. Bromley, J., Guyon, I., LeCun, Y., Säckinger, E., Shah, R.: Signature verification using a "siamese" time delay neural network. In: Advances in Neural Information Processing Systems, vol. 6 (1993)
3. Carpenter, G.A., Grossberg, S.: Art 2: self-organization of stable category recognition codes for analog input patterns. Appl. Opt. **26**(23), 4919–30 (1987)
4. Fukushima, K.: Visual feature extraction by a multilayered network of analog threshold elements. IEEE Trans. Syst. Sci. Cybernet. **5**(4), 322–333 (1969)
5. Goertzel, B.: Perception processing for general intelligence: bridging the symbolic/subsymbolic gap. In: Bach, J., Goertzel, B., Iklé, M. (eds.) AGI 2012. LNCS (LNAI), vol. 7716, pp. 79–88. Springer, Heidelberg (2012). https://doi.org/10.1007/978-3-642-35506-6_9
6. Hammer, P., Lofthouse, T.: 'OpenNARS for applications': architecture and control. In: Goertzel, B., Panov, A.I., Potapov, A., Yampolskiy, R. (eds.) AGI 2020. LNCS (LNAI), vol. 12177, pp. 193–204. Springer, Cham (2020). https://doi.org/10.1007/978-3-030-52152-3_20
7. Hammer, P., Lofthouse, T., Wang, P.: The OpenNARS implementation of the non-axiomatic reasoning system. In: Steunebrink, B., Wang, P., Goertzel, B. (eds.) AGI -2016. LNCS (LNAI), vol. 9782, pp. 160–170. Springer, Cham (2016). https://doi.org/10.1007/978-3-319-41649-6_16
8. Koch, G.R.: Siamese neural networks for one-shot image recognition (2015)
9. Lofthouse, T.: ALANN: an event driven control mechanism for a non-axiomatic reasoning system (NARS). In: NARS2019 workshop at AGI (2019)
10. Nivel, E., et al.: Autocatalytic endogenous reflective architecture (2013)
11. Radford, A., et al.: Learning transferable visual models from natural language supervision (2021)
12. Ramachandra, B., Jones, M.: Street scene: a new dataset and evaluation protocol for video anomaly detection. In: 2020 IEEE Winter Conference on Applications of Computer Vision (WACV), pp. 2558–2567 (2019)
13. Robbins, H., Monro, S.: A stochastic approximation method. Ann. Math. stat., 400–407 (1951)
14. Silver, D.L., Yang, Q., Li, L.: Lifelong machine learning systems: beyond learning algorithms. In: AAAI Spring Symposium: Lifelong Machine Learning (2013)

15. Wang, C.Y., Bochkovskiy, A., Liao, H.Y.M.: Yolov7: Trainable bag-of-freebies sets new state-of-the-art for real-time object detectors. arXiv preprint arXiv:2207.02696 (2022)
16. Wang, P.: Experience-grounded semantics: a theory for intelligent systems. Cogn. Syst. Res. **6**(4), 282–302 (2005)
17. Wang, P.: Insufficient knowledge and resources-a biological constraint and its functional implications. In: AAAI Fall Symposium: Biologically Inspired Cognitive Architectures (2009)
18. Wang, P., et al.: Omni-DETR: omni-supervised object detection with transformers. In: Proceedings of the IEEE/CVF Conference on Computer Vision and Pattern Recognition, pp. 9367–9376 (2022)
19. Wang, P., Hammer, P., Isaev, P., Li, X.: The conceptual design of openNARS 3.1. Technical report, Temple University, Philadelphia, United States (2020)
20. Wang, P., Hofstadter, D.: A logic of categorization. J. Exp. Theor. Artif. Intell. **18**(2), 193–213 (2006)
21. Wang, P., Li, X., Hammer, P.: Self in NARS, an AGI system. Front. Robot. AI **5**, 20 (2018)
22. Wünsche, R.: A vision prototype for openNARS
23. Yu, J., Wang, Z., Vasudevan, V., Yeung, L., Seyedhosseini, M., Wu, Y.: Coca: contrastive captioners are image-text foundation models. arXiv preprint arXiv:2205.01917 (2022)

A Unified Structured Framework for AGI: Bridging Cognition and Neuromorphic Computing

Mingkun Xu, Hao Zheng, Jing Pei[✉], and Lei Deng[✉]

Center for Brain-Inspired Computing Research (CBICR),
Department of Precision Instrument, Tsinghua University, Beijing, China
{peij,leideng}@mail.tsinghua.edu.cn

Abstract. Cognitive modeling and neuromorphic computing are two promising avenues to achieve AGI. However, neither of them has achieved intelligent agents with human-like proficiency so far. One possibility is that the two fields have developed in isolation at different levels, ignoring each other's complementary features. In this paper, from a graph perspective, we present a framework that bridges the gap through cross-hierarchy structured representation and computation. Combining top-down and bottom-up design methodologies, coherent coordination of cognitive architecture and underlying neural dynamics is realized, where interpretable representation of entities and relations is constructed by hierarchical neuromorphic graph (HNG) via multi-scale projecting and abstraction. An assembly-based graph-oriented spiking message network is dedicatedly developed to conduct reasoning and learning. Evaluation on multi-modal reasoning benchmark indicates that the approach outperforms pure symbolic rule-based and non-neuromorphic baselines. Besides, the framework is flexible and compatible with the mainstream cognitive architectures meanwhile maintaining rich biological fidelity in order for exploiting non-negligible fine-grained mechanisms that are crucial for functionality emerging. Our methodology offers a brand-new guideline for the creation of more intelligent, adaptable, and autonomous systems.

Keywords: Hierarchical neuromorphic graph · Cognitive architecture · Neuromorphic computing · Neural dynamics

1 Introduction

Artificial General Intelligence (AGI) is a long-standing goal to fulfill for mankind. Achieving AGI requires a thorough understanding of how the human brain processes information in the function level and in the underlying dynamics level along with complex structure. Till now, neuromorphic computing and cognitive modelling are two fields that have been gaining significant attention in recent years due to their potential to revolutionize artificial intelligence (AI). Neuromorphic computing aims to replicate the functioning of the human brain by

P. Hammer et al. (Eds.): AGI 2023, LNAI 13921, pp. 345–356, 2023.
https://doi.org/10.1007/978-3-031-33469-6_35

designing neuromorphic algorithms and compute chips that emulate the behavior of neurons and encephalic regions, while cognitive modelling focuses on building computational models of human cognition and mentality in higher level. Despite their different origins, both approaches share the common goal of achieving AGI. Although both fields have made significant progress in their respective areas, they are often considered to be distinct and separate approaches to artificial intelligence, which may hinder the breakthrough for the key bottlenecks of AGI.

1.1 Research Status

Generally, as a representative of cognition exploration, cognitive architecture is a computational theory of the human mind that attempts to explain how human beings acquire, store, and utilize information to make decisions, solve problems, learn and interact with the environment. It has evolved since the 1960s s with typical milestones such as the information-processing model [1], the General Problem Solver [2], Soar [3] and the ACT-R model [4]. More recent models, such as the NEURAL model [5], incorporate insights from neuroscience and artificial intelligence. However, cognitive architecture faces several challenges, including the need for a better understanding of the neural basis of cognition, the integration of multiple cognitive systems, and the role of social and cultural factors in shaping cognitive processes. Critics have also raised concerns about the validity and usefulness of cognitive architecture, arguing that it oversimplifies the complexity of human cognition and ignores the embodied and situated nature of cognition. Hence, research in cognitive architecture is supposed to address these challenges by incorporating insights from diverse fields and developing more sophisticated models that capture the full range of human cognitive processes.

Neuromorphic computing is an exciting area of research developing rapidly that seeks to develop computing systems inspired by the structure and function of biological neural networks, which has achieved a series of progresses on neuromorphic algorithms with high biological fidelity, including spiking neural networks (SNNs) [6], liquid-state machines [7] and echo-state networks [8]. On the other hand, a bunch of milestones of neuromorphic hardware have been achieved, such as the ALE [9], SpiNNaker [10], BrainScaleS [11], TrueNorth [12], and NeuroGrid [13], etc. While these systems have shown promise in efficient and low-power processing of sensory information, they are confronted with several significant challenges, including the lack of high-level cognition and flexibility seen in human intelligence. Furthermore, the complexity and variability of biological neural networks make it difficult to accurately model them in a neuromorphic system. Despite these challenges, there has been ongoing progress in developing hybrid neuromorphic systems via integrating neuroscience and computer science [14]. Additionally, recent work has incorporated underlying biological bias to SNNs to improve their performance [15–19], and has explored the algorithm-hardware interacting mechanism [20–24]. Anyway, significant advances are needed to fully realize its potential.

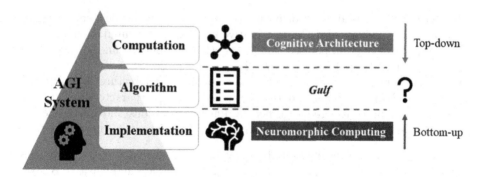

Fig. 1. Schematic diagram of hierarchy position of cognitive architecture and neuromorphic computing for an AGI system in David Marr's three-level perspective.

1.2 Motivation

In general, neuromorphic computing and cognitive modeling are two promising approaches to achieve AGI. From the perspective of David Marr's three levels [25], as depicted in Fig. 1, a AGI system can be viewed as three hierarchies: computation, algorithm and implementation. As a matter of fact, cognitive architectures are at the computation level of AGI and are characterized by top-down design, focusing on modelling high-level cognitive primitives, functionality modules and the interaction rules among them. The whole information flows rely on abstract function connection and constructed entities in a symbolic manner, while neglecting the underlying complex biological inductive bias in implementation level, such as neural dynamics, coding schemes, synapse intelligence, topology structure, hierarchical regulation, etc. These characteristics are crucial and indispensable for high-level cognition formation and understanding. Examples of this argument include the role of gamma and theta oscillations in perception, attention, and memory [26], as well as the hippocampus in spatial navigation and memory consolidation [27]. Therefore, it is essential to consider the underlying biological mechanisms that drive cognitive processes. On the other side, neuromorphic computing is at the implementation level of AGI and is characterized by bottom-up design, focusing on modelling the underlying biological details and lack guidance from higher level of computation and cognition functionalities.

Apparently, there is a distinct gulf between the computation level and the implementation level, lacking a unified framework to combine their strengths effectively. There are primarily three points for our motivation to connect the two different hierarchies:

- Most of cognitive architectures neglect the underlying complex biological inductive bias in implementation level, which are non-negligible and indispensable for high-level cognition formation.
- Incorporating biological plausible neuromorphic implementation as underlying support will facilitate the verification of cognitive process of architectures. For example, neuroimaging techniques such as fMRI and EEG can be used

to study the neural basis of cognitive processes, meanwhile being used to benchmark, guide and evaluate cognitive models. And computational models of neural activity can be used to test hypotheses about the underlying neural mechanisms of cognitive processes [28].

- Neither of neuromorphic computing and cognitive architectures has achieved a powerful AGI systems to date. The complementary characteristics of both fields shall be considered together as different positions and hierarchies to boost the construct of self-contained system stack from top to bottom.

In summary, considering the underlying biological mechanisms of cognitive processes is essential for developing accurate cognitive models and effective AI systems. Nevertheless, they currently lack a unified and generic framework to combine their strengths effectively. In this work, we view these three hierarchies in a graph-structured perspective, and propose a modelling methodology of hierarchical neuromorphic graph (HNG) that leverages underlying neuromorphic bias to correspond to multi-scale processes approaching gradually to cognitive modules. Our motivation is to provide a generic methodology bridging the computation theory with the underlying implementation at the algorithm level. HNG plays a role of connector, which is quite flexible and compatible with most of cognitive architectures and various biological mechanisms, thus promoting the design of more efficient and intelligent computational systems.

2   Methodology

2.1   Framework Overview

One of the major challenges in bridging cognitive architecture and neuromorphic computing is the gap between the theoretical models used in cognitive psychology and the physical implementation of these models in neural networks. For example, many cognitive models rely on symbolic representations and logical reasoning, whereas neural networks are better suited to processing continuous signals and distributed non-symbolic patterns.

To this end, we rethink the three-level hierarchies of AGI systems in a graph-structure perspective, and propose three arguments as bellow:

- At the computation level, a cognitive architecture can be regarded as a graph structure, where different functionality modules and interacting paths can be equivalent to vertices and edges, respectively. The cognitive architecture is a graph intrinsically and can be implemented by a graph. Furthermore, the substructure within a module can also be viewed as a subgraph, and so on.
- At the implementation level, the structure of underlying SNNs is presented as a graph. Besides, given arbitrary information form with various graph structures, SNNs can realize complete representation for the stimulus and computation through themselves.
- At the algorithm level, the algorithm (HNG) is a hierarchical graph, where both of the higher-level cognitive process and lower-level biological process can be represented as multi-scale graphs relating to different hierarchies.

The proposed framework consists of three main components corresponding to respective hierarchy: cognitive architecture, HNG algorithm and neuromorphic computing. Figure 2 shows the overall schematic diagram of the framework, wherein the cognitive architecture and neuromorphic computing are generic and compatible with previous works like Soar and ACT-R. Our primary attention is the algorithm design methodology to connect both levels.

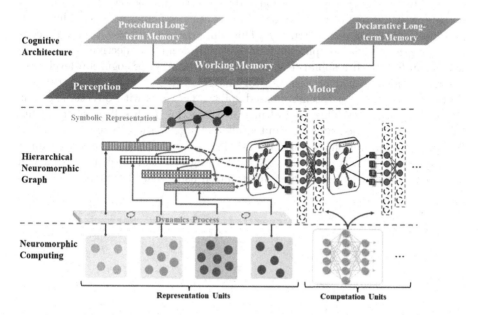

Fig. 2. Schematic diagram of the proposed framework bridging cognitive architecture and neuromorphic computing.

Cognitive Architecture. The cognitive architecture can be based on the typical works such as ACT-R [4] and Soar [5]. Actually, they share a bunch of commonalities [29]. This means we can extend the common structures to some specific instantiations of "Common Model of Cognition" [30]. Here we take the example of the standard model of the mind for general illustration [30]. Figure 2 presents the primary components of this standard cognitive architecture, including declarative long-term memory, procedural long-term memory, working memory, motor and perception modules, each of which is unitary or can be decomposed into multiple components, such as multiple buffers of working memory, diverse stages of procedural matching, selection and execution, etc. [30]. Notably, working memory generally acts as the communication buffer among these modules, and consists of several separate modality-specific submodules, such as visuospatial sketchpad, episodic buffer and phonological loop, that together constitute the information aggregation and interaction. We take the working memory as an example in Fig. 2 and elaborate it in a graph view in latter parts. The long-term memories are pivotal for associated learning that can store, tune or modify information when interacting with lower-level HNG modules.

Neuromorphic Computing. This level is mainly composed of two categories of functionality: representation and computation. The representation units include multiple sets of brain areas which consist of numerous assemblies with initially random connected structure. Different areas can represent separate concepts or symbols via complex dynamics evolution and connectivity reshaping, which can finally correspond to symbolic representation of cognition level after a series of hierarchical process. As for the computation units, they are composed of multiple-layer assembly-based spiking networks with direction-specific connection structure. This kind of neural connection with self-recurrent structure is adept at processing distributed afferent information. Inspired by recent progress of neuromorphic algorithms [31–33], we extend the computation units to graph-oriented networks with spiking message passing mechanism that can process graph-structured symbolic information using neural dynamics.

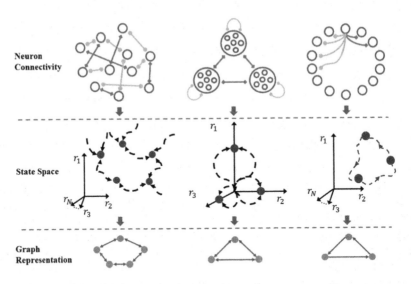

Fig. 3. Schematic diagram of transforming process from neural dynamics to graph structure. In neuron connectivity, the orange links and grayish blue links represent excitatory connection and inhibitive connection, respectively. The red points in state space denote attractors and the blue point in graph representation is its corresponding graph structure abstracted from state space.

Hierarchical Neuromorphic Graph. HNG is the proposed graph-based algorithm that simulate the behavior of assemblies and biological plausible graph abstraction, meanwhile transmitting semantic state information to corresponding higher-level symbolic representation of cognitive modules via multi-scale dynamics process across multiple hierarchies. In HNG, the dynamics process, shown in Fig. 2, consists of again multiple sub-hierarchies, which will be expounded in the following sections. The underlying information from neuromrphic representation units will be transformed into higher-level structured semantic representation after multistage dynamics process, which will be then induced into graph-oriented network models supported by computation units to carry out complicated tasks of reasoning, decision, planning, etc.

2.2 Cross-hierarchy Computation Mechanism

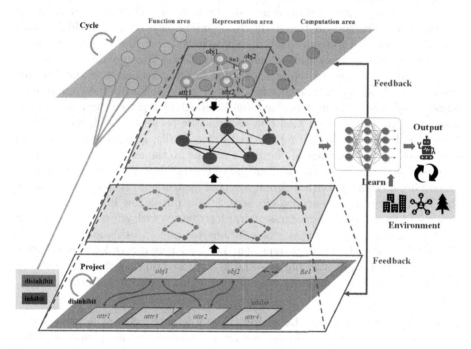

Fig. 4. Cross-hierarchy transforming process of semantic representation, where "obj", "attr", "Re" denote "object", "attribute" and "relation", respectively.

From Dynamics to Structure. From a bottom-up view, the underlying neurons in multiple areas project to correlated regions and will be converged to a stable state after a dynamics process. Usually, these neurons are connected with quite different topologies in various regions. There are numerous biological mechanism that can play a role in connecting underlying dynamics to structure, such as path integral, cognitive map, attractor, etc. As presented in Fig. 3, here we take the attractor as an example for illustration. The dynamic representation can be divided into three levels. In different circumstances, stable attractors can be formed in state space when reaching equilibrium state, and finally be projected into graph-structured representation, where the discrete attractors correspond to undigraphs and continuous attractors correspond to directed graphs. This is quite general since the attractor mechanism is universal in human brains.

Hierarchical Projection and Representation. As depicted in Fig. 4, the multi-scale representation transformation process by dynamics can be decoupled into several hierarchies. From a bottom-up view, the neural level first form converged assemblies via mutual projecting in multiple areas, then forming stable attractor structures. Subsequently the final states will be connected following the prior structure in transformed semantic space relating to higher-level cognition. From a top-town view, a cognitive cycle can be mainly abstracted into representation, computation and control effects. The function area can be designed to control the switch of underlying brain areas based on the designed rules with adaptivity. The computation area corresponds to the computation units for inference in neuromorphic level. Besides, the representation area create a space of encoding information flow as symbolic patterns. As shown in Fig. 4, objects and relations can be represented differentially, and projected into next level. These representations are designed to capture the essential features of the cognitive process and provide a clear and interpretable correspondence with the underlying mechanism with different levels of abstraction. It is should be noted that the relation is also encoded into a node (the purple one in Fig. 4). As such, we can enhance the expressiveness of graph structure with effective links, equivalent to binding related entities or relations together. In this manner, we can utilize neuromorphic graph to represent first-order predicate logic and further represent more complicated higher order logic. Based on this, the representation can be processed by computation units to conduct inference and learning.

Dynamic Inference and Learning. The inference network is presented in Fig. 5, which takes the transformed structured representation as input and conduct down-stream inference tasks. Note that each layer corresponds to a underlying neuromorphic area, and will form an assembly when the projecting process reaches a equilibrium state. The connection between layers is actually the projecting paths between two areas. Thus the connection is dynamic during inference. The learning process is very flexible and compatible with multiple coding scheme and training strategies. Biological local learning rules like STDP or Hebbian rule ought to play a critical role in projecting process. The global update learning can refer to recent advanced learning methods [20,34]. While interacting with environment, as shown in Fig. 4, the error signals will not only update the synaptic parameters and connection of this network, but also will provide

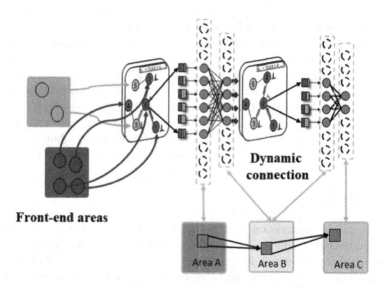

Fig. 5. Schematic diagram of inference and learning networks for neuromorphic graph.

feedback for both of computation units of neuromorphic level and cognitive level, adapting the system to new tasks and environments.

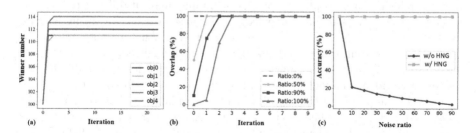

Fig. 6. Simulation results of initiatory exploration: (a) Assemblies are formed with stable number of winner neurons after multiple iterations of projecting. (b) Assembly pattern recovering from preservation of overlap under different ratios of perturbation. (c) Reasoning performance comparison with different perturbation intensity.

2.3   Initiatory Verification

We construct the underlying assembly dynamics as representation units with multiple areas based on the Assembly Calculus project [35], and adopt Graph SNNs [31] with further remoulding as basic computation units for assembly-based structured representation inference. We adopt the multi-modal hybrid reasoning model [15] as the whole architecture and implement our HNG as a intermediary bridge connecting cognitive rules to assembly dynamics, wherein the visual question answering task is also adopted as evaluation.

Simulation results shown in Fig. 6 exhibit that the underlying neural dynamic can incorporate well with the proposed hierarchical neuromorphic graph mechanism. Under the winner-take-all mechanism, the assembly can be steadily converged after dynamics process and interaction with other areas, then corresponding to multiple higher-level constructs and participating into inference computation. Figure 6(b) exhibits the robustness and homeostasis effect of internal representation of each area corresponding to specific entity in cognitive level. And Fig. 6(c) indicates the weakness of the pure rule-base symbolic system and verifies the great enhancement on reasoning robustness with the aids of HNG.

3   Discussion

Bridging cognitive architecture and neuromorphic computing is a huge challenge due to fundamental differences in their underlying principles and approaches. The proposed framework and methodology leverage the strengths of neuromorphic computing and cognitive modeling to develop AGI systems that can learn and reason in a more human-like manner. By representing abstract entity in a structured, graph-based format and using a variant of SNNs adapted to the neuromorphic graph, the framework enables robust and scalable learning of complex, relational knowledge. Our evaluation on visual question answering benchmark problem shows that the proposed approach outperforms symbolic rule-based and non-neuromorphic baselines. One potential limitation is that the complexity of the hierarchical neuromorphic graph algorithm may make it difficult to interpret and adapt to the cross-domain knowledge structures. Advanced transfer learning mechanisms may be partially mitigate the limitation. Another potential limitation is that the complexity of HNG may lead to a challenge to neuromorphic hardware deployment. More efficient neuromorphic platforms capable of supporting high-fidelity biological mechanisms need to be explored further.

Overall, the proposed framework provides a valuable methodology for developing AGI systems, and has the potential to bridge the gap between theoretical models and physical implementations and to revolutionize the AI field. Future work will focus on implementation and evaluation of the framework on specific tasks, and exploring extensions and variations of the proposed methodology.

Acknowledgements. This work was supported by Science and Technology Innovation 2030 - New Generation of Artificial Intelligence, China project (2020AAA0109101), Zhejiang Lab's International Talent Fund for Young Professionals, and National Natural Science Foundation of China (No. 62106119, 62276151). We thank Lukai Li for helpful discussions.

References

1. Miller, G.A., Eugene, G., Pribram, K.H.: Plans and the structure of behaviour. In: Systems Research for Behavioral Sciencesystems Research, pp. 369–382. Routledge (2017)

2. Newell, A., Simon, H.A., et al.: Human Problem Solving, vol. 104. Prentice-hall Englewood Cliffs, NJ (1972)
3. Laird, J.E.: The Soar Cognitive Architecture. MIT press, Cambridge (2019)
4. Anderson, R.J.: The Architecture of Cognition, vol. 5. Psychology Press, London (1996)
5. O'reilly, R.C., Munakata, Y.: Computational Explorations in Cognitive Neuroscience: Understanding the Mind by Simulating the Brain. MIT press, Cambridge (2000)
6. Maass, W.: Networks of spiking neurons: the third generation of neural network models. Neural Netw. **10**(9), 1659–1671 (1997)
7. Yamazaki, T., Tanaka, S.: The cerebellum as a liquid state machine. Neural Netw. **20**(3), 290–297 (2007)
8. Jaeger, H.: Echo state network. Scholarpedia **2**(9), 2330 (2007)
9. Mead, C., Ismail, M.: Analog VLSI implementation of neural systems, vol. 80. Springer, Berlin (1989)
10. Furber, S.B., et al.: Overview of the spinnaker system architecture. IEEE Trans. Comput. **62**(12), 2454–2467 (2012)
11. Schmitt, S., et al.: Neuromorphic hardware in the loop: training a deep spiking network on the BrainScales wafer-scale system. In: 2017 International Joint Conference on Neural Networks (IJCNN), pp. 2227–2234. IEEE (2017)
12. Merolla, P.A., et al.: A million spiking-neuron integrated circuit with a scalable communication network and interface. Science **345**(6197), 668–673 (2014)
13. Ben Benjamin, V., et al.: Neurogrid: a mixed-analog-digital multichip system for large-scale neural simulations. Proc. IEEE **102**(5), 699–716 (2014)
14. Pei, J., et al.: Towards artificial general intelligence with hybrid Tianjic chip architecture. Nature **572**(7767), 106–111 (2019)
15. Zhao, R., et al.: A framework for the general design and computation of hybrid neural networks. Nat. Commun. **13**(1), 3427 (2022)
16. Xu, M., Liu, F., Pei, J.: Endowing spiking neural networks with homeostatic adaptivity for APS-DVS bimodal scenarios. In: Companion Publication of the 2022 International Conference on Multimodal Interaction, pp. 12–17 (2022)
17. Zheng, H., Lin, H., Zhao, R., Shi, L.: Dance of SNN and ANN: Solving binding problem by combining spike timing and reconstructive attention. arXiv preprint arXiv:2211.06027, 2022
18. Hao, Y., Huang, X., Dong, M., Bo, X.: A biologically plausible supervised learning method for spiking neural networks using the symmetric STDP rule. Neural Netw. **121**, 387–395 (2020)
19. Kheradpisheh, S.R., Ganjtabesh, M., Thorpe, S.J., Masquelier, T.: STDP-based spiking deep convolutional neural networks for object recognition. Neural Netw. **99**, 56–67 (2018)
20. Yujie, W., et al.: Brain-inspired global-local learning incorporated with neuromorphic computing. Nat. Commun. **13**(1), 65 (2022)
21. Yang, Y., et al.: Bio-realistic and versatile artificial dendrites made of anti-ambipolar transistors. arXiv preprint arXiv:2212.01277 (2022)
22. Yang, Y., et al.: A mempolar transistor made from tellurium. arXiv preprint arXiv:2301.01986 (2023)
23. Wang, Y., et al.: Self-doping memristors with equivalently synaptic ion dynamics for neuromorphic computing. ACS Appl. Mater. Int. **11**(27), 24230–24240 (2019)
24. Yang, Y., et al.: A new opportunity for the emerging tellurium semiconductor: making resistive switching devices. Nat. Commun. **12**(1), 6081 (2021)

25. Marr, David: Vision: A Computational Investigation Into the Human Representation and Processing of Visual Information. MIT press, Cambridge (2010)
26. Canolty, R.T., Knight, R.T.: The functional role of cross-frequency coupling. Trends Cogn. Sci. **14**(11), 506–515 (2010)
27. O'keefe, J., Nadel, L.: Précis of o'keefe & nadel's the hippocampus as a cognitive map. Behav. Brain Sci. **2**(4), 487–494 (1979)
28. Eliasmith, C., Anderson, C.H.: Neural Engineering: Computation, Representation, and Dynamics in Neurobiological Systems. MIT press, Cambridge (2003)
29. Laird, J.E.: An analysis and comparison of ACT-R and soar. arXiv preprint arXiv:2201.09305 (2022)
30. Laird, J.E., Lebiere, C., Rosenbloom, P.S.: A standard model of the mind: toward a common computational framework across artificial intelligence, cognitive science, neuroscience, and robotics. Ai Mag. **38**(4), 13–26 (2017)
31. Xu, M., Wu, Y., Deng, L., Liu, F., Li, G., Pei, J.: Exploiting spiking dynamics with spatial-temporal feature normalization in graph learning. arXiv preprint arXiv:2107.06865 (2021)
32. Gu, F., Sng, W., Taunyazov, T., Soh, H.: TactileSGNET: a spiking graph neural network for event-based tactile object recognition. In: 2020 IEEE/RSJ International Conference on Intelligent Robots and Systems (IROS), pp. 9876–9882. IEEE (2020)
33. Dold, D., Garrido, J.S., Chian, V.C., Hildebrandt, M., Runkler, T.: Neuro-symbolic computing with spiking neural networks. In: Proceedings of the International Conference on Neuromorphic Systems, vol. 2022, pp. 1–4 (2022)
34. Bellec, G., et al.: A solution to the learning dilemma for recurrent networks of spiking neurons. Nat. Commun. **11**(1), 3625 (2020)
35. Papadimitriou, C.H., Vempala, S.S., Mitropolsky, D., Collins, M., Maass, W.: Brain computation by assemblies of neurons. Proc. Nat. Acad. Sci. **117**(25), 14464–14472 (2020)

Coherence in Intelligent Systems

Hao Zheng🄳 and Luping Shi(✉)

Center for Brain-Inspired Computing Research (CBICR), Department of Precision
Instrument, Tsinghua University, Beijing 100084, China
zheng-h17@mails.tsinghua.edu.cn, lpshi@tsinghua.edu.cn

Abstract. Coherence is one of the candidate principles of the intelligence, with its presence of varied forms in different contexts. At implementation level, coherence is an ubiquitous phenomenon that accompanies the state of awareness and normal cognitive function of the brain, suggested by increased strength of the rhythm. At algorithmic level, the coherence in the consistent self-evidencing loops between the internal and the external is argued to be the principle of general intelligent systems. However, a unified computational view of both aspects of coherence is still open questions. In this paper, we propose a unified computational understanding of coherence in general intelligent systems from a viewpoint of solution searching ,unifying the different levels: More specifically, coherence is an informative states to represent the solution with high certainty, acting as an universal and inherent indicator of the searched solution at the same time, and achieved through coherent self-evidencing. A model for active perception is built to demonstrate the whole picture. Lastly, we discuss whether coherence could act as a measure of general intelligence.

Keywords: Neuronal coherence · Self-evidencing · Universal indicator

1 Introduction

Coherence generally describes the increased agreement among different units and decreased conflicts inside a system, which has been argued to be one of the principles of the intelligence [14] and is present in various theories of brain or machine intelligence[1]. In the predictive coding theory [7], the agreement between the active inference from an internal world model and the sensory information of external stimuli forms the self-evidencing loop [10] that is believed to shed light on the agency and perceptual awareness [7]. Once the loop is broken, the perceptual belief might suddenly end [2]. Besides perception, the theory covers cognition as well [19]. Besides the brain theories, coherence between different modules has also been embraced into artificial neural networks for building autonomous machines capable of hierarchical planning [13].

If time is further taken into account, the agreements should also happen close in time. If agreements can only be reached occasionally, it leads to the rhythmic

---

[1] The exact form of coherence depends on the similarity measure chosen, which could be either binary or continuous, and of different types of arguments.

P. Hammer et al. (Eds.): AGI 2023, LNAI 13921, pp. 357–366, 2023.
https://doi.org/10.1007/978-3-031-33469-6_36

pattern like neuronal coherence, which is a state further away from randomness where neuronal firings tend to assemble together. Specifically, given a certain set of active neurons, the spike-firing distribution along time dimension could vary. Close firing time suggests united and determined efforts of groups of neurons, while random firings may imply less certainty. Therefore, it is hypothesized that neuronal coherence may play a role at the representation level [18], computation level [21] and so on. Experimentally, normal brain functions, like perception [15], attention [21], memory [21], are all highly related to an increased level of gamma-band rhythm, suggesting enhanced level of neuronal coherence. Besides, neural rhythm is conserved across most species [4], indicating that neuronal coherence might be an essential ingredient of self-organized systems that showing general intelligent behaviors.

Therefore, it seems promising that coherence is a general principle of intelligent systems [6,15] and may act as a measure of AGI[2]. However, several challenges remain. First, there are counterexamples that have high coherence levels but intuitively of low intelligence. For example, epilepsy is a brain disorder that causes recurring, unprovoked seizures, where the neuron firings are highly synchronous [21]. Therefore, neuronal coherence may also lead to the opposite of normal intelligent behavior. Second, coherent self-evidencing loop may be realized by dead cycles that are intuitively not intelligent at all. For example, both prediction and input are set to none, which may lead to a state of death or ignorance. Lastly, while coherence is shown to be essential for intelligent behaviors, it actually refers to different connotation in different contexts. For example, while the coherent self-evidencing loop refers to the algorithmic level, the neuronal coherence refers to the implementation level. It is not clear how these different interpretations of coherence contribute to the intelligence in an unified manner, though they are documented to be related to intelligent behavior respectively.

In this paper, we aim to argue about the general computational role of coherence in an AGI system, connecting the coherence and the intelligence in a new perspective. More specifically, we abstract an AGI system as a solution searcher, and the solution has a form of non-equilibrium states due to constraints of the system (eg. biological constraints). Such abstraction is formulated as two hypotheses (Sect. 2). Following the hypothesis, we demonstrate that at functional level, coherence is inherent and universal indicator of the solution, which is indispensable for computation (Sect. 3). At representational level, we prove that coherent state is informative, and is a general carrier of the solution (Sect. 4). At computational level, we experimentally show that neuronal coherence solution is achieved through iterative self-evidencing loop, which provides a unified view of neuronal coherence and coherent self-evidencing (Sect. 5). However, the result shows that the emergence of neuronal coherence is based on the proper internal structure of the dynamical system, acting as a solution searching program. Therefore, at measurement level, we argue that coherence acts as the necessary condition measure of intelligence instead of sufficient condition: without a systematic solution searching program (eg. an internal world model [13]), the

---

[2] Since it is also a scalar quantity that could be compared between systems [3].

coherence maybe senseless (Sect. 6). This picture unifies both supportive and counter examples listed above and unifies both levels of coherence.

2   Hypothesis

2.1   Hypothesis 1: AGI as a Solution Searcher

Various computational problems, like perception, controlling, reasoning and planning, can be transformed into the searching problem under a set of constraints [11][3]. Here we regard the general intelligent system like the neural system as trying to find solutions in a high-dimensional space, constrained by various situations, like external stimuli, internal prior, etc. (Fig. 1a).

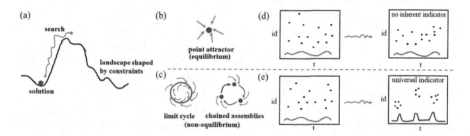

Fig. 1. (a) solution searching in a high-dimensional energy landscape shaped by constraints. (b)(c) attractive solution as equilibrium states (eg. point attractor) or non-equilibrium state (limit cycle or chained assemblies). While the former do not have intrinsic indicator (d), the latter has universal inherent indicator: neuronal coherence(red)

2.2   Hypothesis 2: Non-equilibrium Stable States as Solution

We assume that the solution is represented as stable trajectories, which is non-equilibrium states. On the one hand, stability is desired to search the solution from partial information. On the other hand, escaping from falling into equilibrium state benefits the ergodicity of the states and the diversity of the solutions, which is a ubiquitous feature of self-organizing system, including the brain [8] and guaranteed by various biological constraints like delayed inhibition, adaptation, and refractory period. Therefore, we assume the solution has a form of limit cycle [20] instead of the point attractor[4]. More specifically, if we take each neural assembly [9] as the code letter of the solution, the entire solution could have a form of periodic presence of chained assemblies [9], a special case of limit cycle (Fig. 1c).

---

[3] Though the detailed discussion focuses on the perceptual aspect of AGI for clarity, the general context of solution searching does not have such constraint.

[4] While the point attractor is the basic attractor in equilibrium states (Fig. 1b), limit cycle is the most basic attractor of non-equilibrium states [20].

3 Neuronal Coherence as an Universal Indicator

Besides the content of solution, the indicator of the solution as the terminal of the searching process is needed to terminate the search, transmit the result, and turn to other states. In computational theory, it is the state of termination in automata [5]; In genetics, it is the code of terminator; In deep learning, it may be a specific vector pattern predefined by experts; In programming, it is the command of return. The absence of an indicator limits the capability and flexibility of the system (eg. simple feedforward network). In the following, we highlight that neuronal coherence is a brand-new type of indicator that is universal and inherent, which is especially desirable in distributed systems.

Following the two hypothesis, we know that once the system finds a solution, it falls into a rhythmic states, where units are assembled synchronously in time. The beginning phase of searching might be random due to stochastic switching between different possible solutions, while the ending phase of searching gradually converges to the optimal single stable solution (Fig. 1e). Therefore, the searching process is naturally accompanied by the emergence of neuronal coherence. In other words, the coherence acts as an inherent general indicator of the discovered solution, especially desirable in a distributed system.

What is special about the indicator via neuronal coherence? In a dynamical viewpoint, each solution is a local minimum or attractive states on a high-dimensional landscape shaped by constraints. Point attractor solution needs an extrinsic code-space to indicate the termination[5]. The extrinsic termination code is encoded in an extrinsic local code-space, required to be predefined, and readout by certain protocol or transition rule. In contrast, rhythmic solution of chained code letter (neuronal assembly) is the intrinsic and global property of the solution itself, which do not need extra space and rules. It is one of the advantages of limit cycle solutions over point attractor solutions (Fig. 1d,e). It is the internality of the coherence indicator.

More importantly, while an extrinsic local code of indicator is valid for a sequential system like computer program and genes, it is less clear how local codes work in a large-scale distributed processing system, because the explicit assignment of local subspace to exclusively encode the indicator is ambiguous and a common shared readout transition rule is less plausible. In contrast, the coherence is a temporal pattern that could be universally readout, because while spatial content of solution is high-dimensional, the coherence strength is only one dimensional, which do not require complex connection weight for recognition. Instead, a general coincidence detector [12] with dendrites of narrow time window and sensitive to relative timings of spike arrival can suffice. It is the generality of the coherence indicator.

---

[5] For example, the symbol of termination in state machine, the terminator genes, or a specific vector pattern predefined by human in language models.

4   Neuronal Coherence as Most Informative States

While representing solution as neuronal coherence (Hypothesis 2.2) is shown to have desirable property of universal indicator, is it actually a general outcome of a solution searching process? We attempt to provide an answer from a point of view of information theory. Specifically, coherence states has high certainty and rich information content, which imply its optimality for representing the solution. In this section, the discussion of neuronal coherence is restricted in a population of spiking neurons for clarity. The generalization to general coherent situation is also possible but we leave it to future works.

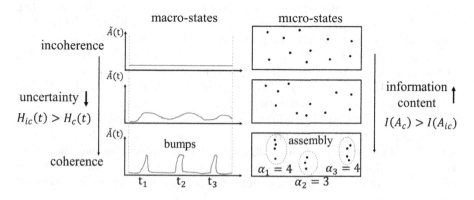

Fig. 2. Illustration of the information viewpoint of coherence states.

Given a population of N spiking neurons, the macro-states of the system at t is described as the population firing rate $A(t), t \in [0, T]$, where $[0, T]$ is a proper time range of interest. The micro-states of the system is the trajectory composed of a temporal progression of instantaneous binary spiking patterns $(t \in [0, T])$. Each macro-state may be associated with multiple micro-states.

Consider two plausible biological constraints for homeostasis: first, the firing rate at each time has an upper bound (A_{max}); second, the accumulated spike count of neurons during the temporal range has a relatively fixed number (C). In short, $A(t) < A_{max}, \forall t \in [0, T]$ and $\sum_{0<t<T} A(t) = C > A_{max}$

Therefore, consider the normalized population firing rate: $\tilde{A}(t) = A(t)/C$, where $\tilde{A}(t)$ is a probability distribution of random variable $t \in [0, T]$. If taken each neuron as independent, the spike firing time distribution $(P(t^i))$ of each single neuron i is also $\tilde{A}(t)$. Thus, there are a collection of N random variables $\{t^i | 1 \le i \le N\}$, which describes the microscopic configuration associated with each macroscopic states $(A(t))$. Therefore, the uncertainty of the micro-state associated with the macro-state is formulated as the entropy of $\tilde{A}(t)$: $H(t) = \sum_t \tilde{A}(t) \cdot ln(\tilde{A}(t))$

The neuronal coherence can be defined as the state trajectory where spikes firing together or nearly together, indicated by bumps on $A(t)$ (or $\tilde{A}(t)$, Fig. 2). In ideal cases, the bumps can be described as delta functions at certain time points: $A_c(t) = \sum_i \alpha_i \cdot \delta(t - t_i), s.t. \sum_i \alpha_i = C, \alpha_i \geq \alpha_{min}$, where $2 \leq i \leq n \ll T$ is the index of bumps. n is the number of bumps. α_{min} is the minimum size of each bump. The delta function here is constraint in discrete space: $\delta(t) = 1, t = 0$ and $\delta(t) = 0, t \neq 0$.

The uncertainty of coherent state is $H_c(t) = -\sum_{i \leq n} (\alpha_i/C) \cdot ln(\alpha_i/C) \approx ln(n)$. The last term holds when bumps have uniform size. In contrast, the uncertainty of a random state (incoherent) is $H_{ic}(t) = -\sum_{t \leq T} (1/T) \cdot ln(1/T) = ln(T)$. Since $n \ll T$, we have $H_c(t) \ll H_{ic}(t)$. Thus, coherence states has much larger (temporal) certainty.

On the other hand, the entropy of $\tilde{A}(t)$ alternatively measures the number of microscopic configurations associated with a macroscopic states (eg. $H = k_B log(\Omega)$). Similar to Boltzmann and Gibbs's formulation in thermodynamics [16], if we assume that the probability of each micro-state is equal, then $H(t)$ reflects the probability of a state to occur: $P(\tilde{A}) \propto e^{H(t)}$. Following the information theory, the carried information or surprisal of a macro-state $\tilde{A}$ is defined as $I(A) = log(1/P(A))$. Since $H_c(t) \ll H_{ic}(t)$, $I(A_c) \gg I(A_{ic})$. Therefore, coherence states have much larger information content.

Due to the certainty and information richness of neuronal coherent states, they are expected states to represent the solution. On the one hand, solution states should be rare states that of high information content. On the other hand, the solution states of high certainty might be a general or inevitable outcome of the searching process, from the unknown to known, from random guess to confident results.

5 Neuronal Coherence as the Outcome of Coherent Self-evidencing

In this section, we show the emergence of neuronal coherence during the solution searching in an artificial perceptual model. More specifically, the coherent binding solution for general perception is generated through coherent self-evidencing loop. The result provides a unified view of neuronal coherence and coherent self-evidencing in AGI systems.

5.1 Binding Problem in Perception

It is believed that elements of the perceptual entity are distributed in widespread areas of the brain [17]. For example, the voice, color, shape, movement, texture information are processed in different brain areas or through different neuron populations. Such distributed processing raises the question that how large amounts of distributed elements are bound into a whole, or grouped together [17] (Fig. 3a)? Temporal binding hypothesis [18] predicts that the solution of the binding problem is constructed by synchronous firing of assemblies, which represents the grouped elements of each perceptual object (Fig. 3b). Therefore, the temporal structure in the coherent state encodes the grouping information. Such coherent solution are attractive non-equilibrium states of the self-evidencing bottom-up / top-down brain dynamics.

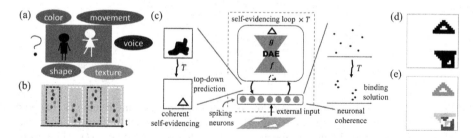

Fig. 3. (a) The binding problem. (b) The temporal binding hypothesis. (c) The model architecture, which is composed of the self-evidencing loop between the external input and the top-down prediction by the DAE. The searching (T time steps) towards coherent self-evidencing leads to the neuronal coherence state as the binding solution. (d)(e) the random selected sample in Shapes dataset [22]: raw input (d) and ground truth (e).

5.2   Model Description

Inspired by the temporal binding theory, the model (inherited from [22]) has an iterative bottom-up and top-down architecture. The bottom-up and top-down streams are realized by the encoder and decoder of a denoising autoencoder (DAE) [1]. The agreement between the top-down modulation (attention) and the external driving input determines the firing events of spiking neurons (Fig. 3c).

The temporal binding solution is a cyclic chain of the code letters (neuronal assemblies). We embed the solution into the network dynamics by two model designs. First, the assembly for each object is an attractive states of the iterative denoising autoencoder dynamics by training the denoising autoencoder to reconstruct or complete the disturbed pattern of each single objects. Second, the refractory property of spiking neurons prevent the system from falling into the equilibrium states and makes each attractive states transient. In this way, the solution of binding problem is searched by iterative self-evidencing and finally represented by neuronal coherence.

Model Details. Each spiking neuron i receives the input from the delayed modulation $\gamma_i(t)$ and external sensory input as the driving signal x_i. The firing rate $\rho_i(t)$ is determined by the multiplication of the two source of inputs: $\rho_i(t) = \gamma_i(t) \cdot x_i$. The delayed top-down modulation $\gamma_i(t)$ is generated by the DAE: $\gamma_i(t) = g(f(s_i(t - d)))$, where d is the delay period and g / f are decoder / encoder of the DAE, which is pre-trained to denoise single objects. $s_i(t)$ is the spike firing event of neuron i at time step t, which is stochastic if it is active: $P(s_i(t) = 1|\mathtt{active}) = \rho_i(t)$ and $P(s_i(t) = 1|\mathtt{refractory}) = 0$, where P is the

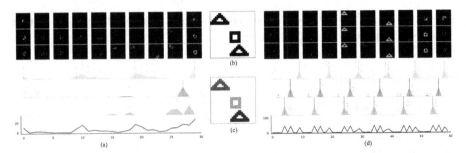

Fig. 4. The emergence of neuronal coherence during the searching dynamics. (a) The initial random phase. Upper–the temporal progression of spiking pattern (Each black-background square is the instantaneous activity of feature neurons $(s_i(t))$. Time progresses from left to right, from up to bottom); Middle–the spike recording, colored based on ground truth segmentation shown in (c); Bottom–population activity $(A(t))$. (b) The exemplified sample. (c) Ground truth segmentation. (d) The convergent phase, analogous to (a)

probability of firing, conditioned on the states of neurons (active or refractory). Once the neurons fires a spike $(s_i(t) = 1)$, it falls into a refractory period of δ time steps.

Since the prediction from DAE feeds back into the spiking neurons as top-down modulation in the future time steps (delayed by d steps), the general architecture of bottom-up and top-down processing constructs a self-evidencing loop, starting from random guess and converging to consistent self-evidencing, which results in the neuronal coherence as the binding solution (Fig. 3c).

5.3   Emergence of Neuronal Coherence as Binding Solution

As shown in the Fig. 4, starting from the random firing states (incoherence), the network dynamically reaches the states of neuronal coherence where feature neurons encoding the same object are grouped into synchronous neuronal assemblies. Therefore, the binding solution is searched along the emergence of the neuronal coherence. The finding of the solution is indicated by the neuronal coherence, suggested by the increased fast gamma-like oscillation. Such coherence states can be readout by downstream neurons with dendrites sensitive to coincident spike arrival (eg. narrow time window [12]). The coherence of self-evidence loop of predictive feedback finally leads to the neuronal coherence.

5.4   Neuronal Coherence from Coherent Self-evidencing Loop

While neuronal coherence refers to the agreement among spike firings of neurons, the coherence of self-evidencing loop refers to the agreement between the internal prediction and external input. Although both are documented to be highly related to perceptual awareness and intact cognitive function, they do not exactly refer to the same process. Here, the model provides a unified view:

taking biological constraints into account (spiking / delayed inhibition / non-equilibrium), then the coherence of self-evidencing loop (at algorithmic level) leads to the neuronal coherence (at implementational level).

6   Coherence as a Measure of Intelligence?

Since coherence is one of the principle of intelligence [14], a conserved biological marker tightly accompanying the functional states of the brain and is also a measurable scalar quantity to compare two systems, it is intriguing to ask whether coherence acts as a measure of intelligence?

According to the hypothesis, analysis, and model demonstrations above, the coherence may act as a partial measure of intelligence, but it is not a sufficient measure. More specifically, the core computation for intelligent behavior or response requires a prior dynamical structure, internal world model or the program that serves to search the solution given constraints. The coherence itself is not such a searching program and therefore do not directly guarantee the intelligence. For example, without the DAE that embeds the assemblies into the perceptual model (Sect. 5), the coherence states will not reflect the binding solution at all. That is partly why there are extreme counter examples where the opposite of intelligence might also have coherence property. However, once, and only if, the system has acquired a proper prior internal model or program, as hypothesized in predictive coding theory, the emergence of coherence indicates the finding of the solution (Sect. 3). Therefore, the level, convergent speed, stability, robustness of the coherence indicates the quality of the solution, searching capability as well as the smartness of the system. On the contrary, the failure of normal neuronal coherence might imply cognitive disorder [21]. If we additionally take biological constraints into account, like non-equilibrium and homeostasis, the coherence may be a general property of the well-behaved AGI system (Sect. 4) and acts as a general necessary condition measure of intelligence.

7   Conclusion

Despite of varied forms, coherence presents itself as the central concept in various theories or frameworks of AGI. In this paper, we provide coherence with a general and unified position in an AGI system from a viewpoint of solution searching: theoretically, coherence is an universal and inherent indicator of the searched solution, represented as informative states of high certainty. Experimentally, coherent self-evidencing leads to neuronal coherence in an artificial perceptual model that searches the binding solution, which unifies the two essential aspects of coherence. Lastly, based on analysis and experiments, we argue that coherence is indeed a partial measure of intelligence but we still need to explore the core program underlying behind.

Acknowledgements. This work was partly supported by the National Nature Science Foundation of China (No. 61836004, No. 62088102); National Key Research and Development Program of China (grant no. 2021ZD0200300)

References

1. Behnke, S.: Learning iterative image reconstruction. In: Hierarchical Neural Networks for Image Interpretation. LNCS, vol. 2766, pp. 167–190. Springer, Heidelberg (2003). https://doi.org/10.1007/978-3-540-45169-3_9
2. Botvinick, M.M., Cohen, J.D.: Rubber hands 'feel' touch that eyes see. Nature **391**, 756–756 (1998)
3. Bowyer, S.M.: Coherence a measure of the brain networks: past and present. Neuropsychiatric Electrophysiol. **2**, 1–12 (2016)
4. Buzsáki, G., Logothetis, N., Singer, W.: Scaling brain size, keeping timing: evolutionary preservation of brain rhythms. Neuron **80**(3), 751–764 (2013)
5. Eilenberg, S.: Automata, Languages and Machines. Academic press, Cambridge (1974)
6. Friston, K.: The free-energy principle: a unified brain theory? Nat. Rev. Neurosci. **11**(2), 127–138 (2010)
7. Friston, K.: Prediction, perception and agency. Int. J. Psychophysiol. **83**(2), 248–252 (2012)
8. Grande-García, I.: The evolution of brain and mind: a non-equilibrium thermodynamics approach. Ludus Vitalis **15**(27), 103–125 (2016)
9. Harris, K.D.: Neural signatures of cell assembly organization. Nat. Rev. Neurosci. **6**(5), 399–407 (2005)
10. Hohwy, J.: The self-evidencing brain. Noûs **50**(2), 259–285 (2016)
11. Jonke, Z., Habenschuss, S., Maass, W.: Solving constraint satisfaction problems with networks of spiking neurons. Front. Neurosci. **10**, 118 (2016)
12. König, P., Engel, A.K., Singer, W.: Integrator or coincidence detector? The role of the cortical neuron revisited. Trends Neurosci. **19**(4), 130–137 (1996)
13. LeCun, Y.: A path towards autonomous machine intelligence version 0.9. 2, 27 Jun 2022. Open Rev. **62** (2022)
14. Ma, Y., Tsao, D., Shum, H.Y.: On the principles of parsimony and self-consistency for the emergence of intelligence. Front. Inf. Technol. Electron. Eng. **23**(9), 1298–1323 (2022)
15. Meador, K.J., Ray, P.G., Echauz, J.R., Loring, D.W., Vachtsevanos, G.J.: Gamma coherence and conscious perception. Neurology **59**(6), 847–854 (2002)
16. Rondoni, L., Cohen, E.: Gibbs entropy and irreversible thermodynamics. Nonlinearity **13**(6), 1905 (2000)
17. Singer, W.: Large scale temporal coordination of cortical activity as prerequisite for conscious experience. Pragmatics Cogn. **18**(3), 570–583 (2010)
18. Singer, W., Gray, C.M.: Visual feature integration and the temporal correlation hypothesis. Annu. Rev. Neurosci. **18**(1), 555–586 (1995)
19. Spratling, M.W.: Predictive coding as a model of cognition. Cogn. Process. **17**(3), 279–305 (2016). https://doi.org/10.1007/s10339-016-0765-6
20. Thompson, J.M.T., Stewart, H.B., Turner, R.: Nonlinear dynamics and chaos. Comput. Phys. **4**(5), 562–563 (1990)
21. Uhlhaas, P.J., Singer, W.: Neural synchrony in brain disorders: relevance for cognitive dysfunctions and pathophysiology. Neuron **52**(1), 155–168 (2006)
22. Zheng, H., Lin, H., Zhao, R., Shi, L.: Dance of SNN and ANN: solving binding problem by combining spike timing and reconstructive attention. In: Advances in Neural Information Processing Systems, vol. 35 (2022)

Author Index

P. Hammer et al. (Eds.): AGI 2023, LNAI 13921, pp. 367–368, 2023.
https://doi.org/10.1007/978-3-031-33469-6

Printed in the United States
by Baker & Taylor Publisher Services